Going All the Way

Going All the Way

Christian Warlords, Israeli Adventurers, and the War in Lebanon

Jonathan C. Randal

Vintage Books
A Division of Random House · New York

Vintage Books Edition, February 1984
Copyright © 1983 by Jonathan Randal

All rights reserved under International and Pan-American Copyright
Conventions. Published in the United States by Random House, Inc., New
York, and simultaneously in Canada by Random House of Canada Limited,
Toronto. Originally published by The Viking Press in 1983. Published by
arrangement with The Viking Press.

Grateful acknowledgment is made for permission to reprint selections from
Moshe Sharett, *Personal Diary* (1953–57), 8 vol. (Hebrew), Maariv Publishing
House, Tel Aviv, 1979, edited by Yaakov Sharett.

Library of Congress Cataloging in Publication Data

Randal, Jonathan C., 1933–
  Going all the way.

  Includes index.
  1. Lebanon—History—Civil War, 1975–1976.
2. Lebanon—History—Israeli intervention, 1982–
3. Randal, Jonathan C., 1933– . 4. Journalists—
United States—Biography. I. Title.
DS87.5.R36 1984   956.92′044   83-21574
ISBN 0-394-72359-7

Manufactured in the United States of America
Cover photograph by
Havakuk Levisom/Woodfin Camp & Associates

For a number of graces, of several ages on various continents, many but not all of them Lebanese, at least one of whom caused me to despair, but all of whom encouraged me to write this book.

Note to the Reader

In this era of truth in packaging, American and other Western readers may be put off by my not having in every instance named names and sources in this book. I will only plead that those many Lebanese, as well as others, who have been kind and courageous enough to help me in my inquiries often did so with the proviso that they keep their anonymity. The "security situation"—as the lack of law and order is known euphemistically in Lebanon—explains their caution in many cases, for they or their families must continue to live there. All I can guarantee the reader is that my essential commitment is to get as near the truth as is possible in a part of the world where, more than in most climes, things appear at best gray rather than black and white.

I can promise that I have indulged in no docudramas, or whatever the current fad is called for sprucing up the facts. Lest anyone feel that I favor one group over another or hold some more responsible for what has happened than others, allow me to insist that I am innocent of special pleading. I will perhaps have disappointed and perhaps enraged many friends and sources who gave generously of their time. As I warned when I first approached them for help, I could promise only that I would be guided by neither personal nor political prejudice. I trust they will credit me with that much.

May I also state the obvious. This book is not meant as a definitive history of what has happened in Lebanon. I do not pretend to cope with all the strands of its tragedy. Nor should I. That is a task that awaits not a Westerner, but a Lebanese, a Palestinian, an Israeli, or a Syrian. I have, however, attempted to look at some of the main regional actors and to understand their behavior.

Preface

A foreign correspondent, which is what I am, more than most travelers, often comes to know cities the wrong way. Take Beirut. For us it used to be the bar at the Hotel St. Georges, the raunchy nightclubs up the street, the waterfront restaurants with their thirty-six *mezzes*—chick-pea paste served on earthenware plates, and salad of crushed wheat, chopped parsley, tomato, and mint. Or maybe some stores in the smart Hamra shopping district or an occasional evening up the coast at the Casino du Liban watching the Saudis and other Gulf Arabs ogle the European girls in the floor show. Especially the blondes. The Gulf Arabs just loved the blondes. And for journalists, information was so readily available that Beirut-based reporters often arrived in countries hundreds, even thousands of miles away better-informed than resident diplomats. Save for the erratic mail, bad telephone service, and epic traffic jams, things worked—for a price, everything and everybody was available without the hassle one encountered elsewhere in the Arab world. Here were professors at the American University of Beirut, knowledgeable Lebanese colleagues from the Arab world's freest and best-informed press, Middle East exiles and revolutionaries of every imaginable ideology in the Hamra cafés, instant visas, currencies for faraway places without red tape. The government presence was unobtrusive, and journalists were left in peace except in rare cases. In short, Beirut was the perfect base, the quintessential public convenience correspondents didn't write about because so many more important things kept happening elsewhere in the Middle East. Or so we thought.

It was easy enough to laugh at Lebanese pretensions and irrepressible ostentation. Despite the visitors from all over, Beirut remained unmistakably provincial. There was something raffish about the place, like Algiers under the French. Maybe the sun and the humidity, the red- or orange-tiled roofs in between the nondescript concrete buildings, the same licorice drink, called pastis at one end of the Mediterranean and arak here, the same steep hills, or the French spoken and Frenchness affected by so many.

Then the war started in April 1975, and something else recalled Algiers—a peculiarly Mediterranean appetite for violence on a scale that I, for one, hadn't experienced since the final spasms of the Algerian war more than a decade earlier. Suddenly, Lebanon's contradictions, complexities, and fragility came into focus—and froze. For right from the start there was an unwillingness to stop and think, a refusal to compromise, a deep-seated delight in striking poses and carrying out acts that could only lead to further murderous adventures.

Nothing brought home so forcefully the destructive impact of the fighting as the changing notions of local geography. Expressway journeys from one side of town to the other, once-carefree five-minute trips, now became hazardous and circuitous adventures through hooded gunmen's roadblocks, which one had to negotiate at reputedly safe times of the day with increasingly dog-eared passes, produced like so many propitiatory talismans. Peripheral neighborhoods were now vital, if dangerous, passageways between the warring sectors of what once had thought of itself as one of the world's more sophisticated cities. The worse the fighting the less the traffic, so that for much of the war, danger was spasmodic in the sense that a reporter could quickly escape from violence. It was a taxi-ride war. The smart people were not taken in. They left—the clever, skilled Lebanese with money, connections, or determination; the Westerners who used Beirut as a base for the Middle East; talented Arabs from other countries who had sought refuge here from earlier turmoil in their native lands and now took their capital and know-how elsewhere. They all abandoned Beirut to the warlords and looters, who stripped away the superimposed veneer of Western civilization as effortlessly as if it were a Band-Aid.

Beirut became synonymous with a new barbarity, its very name becoming shorthand in the world's headlines for chaos, as the Congo had two decades before. Chrome-plated handguns and Russian AK-47 assault rifles gave way to heavier weaponry as local status symbols. Beirutis came to distinguish the sounds of heavy artillery from those of mortars or rocket launchers. What started out as controlled violence gave way to full-fledged conventional warfare by 1982, when the Israelis invaded the country and routinely employed fighter-bombers, heavy artillery, and naval gunfire against residential areas of the capital. Cluster bombs, incapacitating gas, white phosphorus, "smart" bombs were all used. Much of this ordnance was American, and so was much of the responsibility for what happened in Lebanon. But the United States at times seemed interested less in acknowledging that aspect of its aid to Israel than in learning the battlefield effectiveness of its weaponry. Even when the United States ordered a ban on new deliveries of cluster bombs, the shipments kept arriving. What was described as a bureaucratic error in fact reflected Washington's past performance if not necessarily its real feelings. The United States claimed to be investigating whether Israel had violated the guidelines governing use of American weaponry in the Middle East. But the record over the years clearly showed that the U.S. government never found against Israel on that score. For both countries, as for the rest of the world, Lebanon had become a non-place, a killing ground. Undermined by all the modern social viruses, never cured of its atavistic ills, Lebanon probably never had a chance to survive. Lebanon soldiered on, but with each passing month the official optimism became more threadbare. Then, quite abruptly, it was too late—although the Lebanese took a long time to realize what had happened.

"I left for the complicated Orient with simple ideas," General de Gaulle wrote in his World War II memoirs. By the 1970s Lebanon certainly had become too complicated for easy explanation, much less remedy. Out of pure journalistic sixth sense, during a week's visit in

September 1974 I had predicted the coming civil war in print—and was banned from Lebanon until my prophecy came true a half year later. Even I had never imagined that violence could so delight in seemingly endless variations, trapping the forces in Lebanese society and the entire Middle East in shifting alliances. Perhaps because I have a reporter's mind and not a novelist's, lack a mathematical sense for permutations, and knew little about Lebanon or the Arab world, I discovered the limitations of my craft. At the same time, the Lebanese, suffering from similar failings and some others, not entirely unwittingly blew up their country. With a little help from their friends and neighbors. Well before the first year of fighting was over, the Lebanese were no longer calling the shots. All manner of foreigners were. But the Lebanese made it easy. They were hell-bent on going all the way. They still are. And they give no signs yet of having exhausted all the possibilities.

Jonathan C. Randal

Beirut, Lebanon
February 1983

Preface to the Vintage Edition

Perhaps the virtue of second editions is that initial errors have therein been corrected, errors which are all too frequent in books dealing with current events. Even so, I am without illusions about the tentative nature of my carefully hedged thoughts concerning Lebanon in this fall of 1983. If I was not entirely successful in predicting what would happen following the fall of 1982, when the first edition of this book went to press, I now am even less sanguine about the future.

J.C.R.

Paris, France
November 1983

Contents

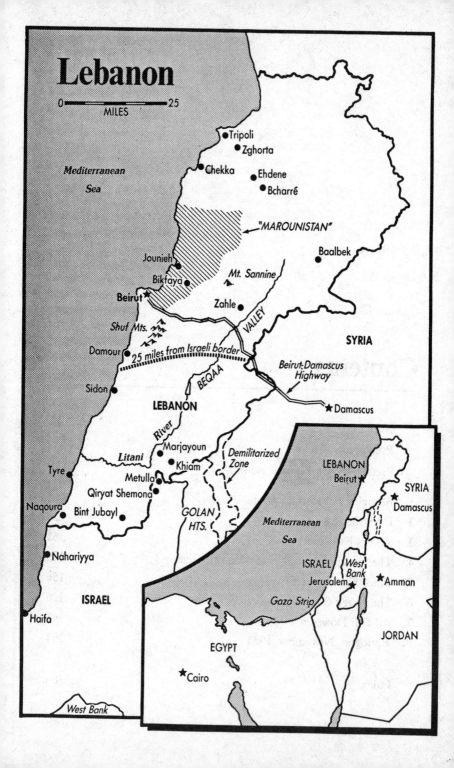

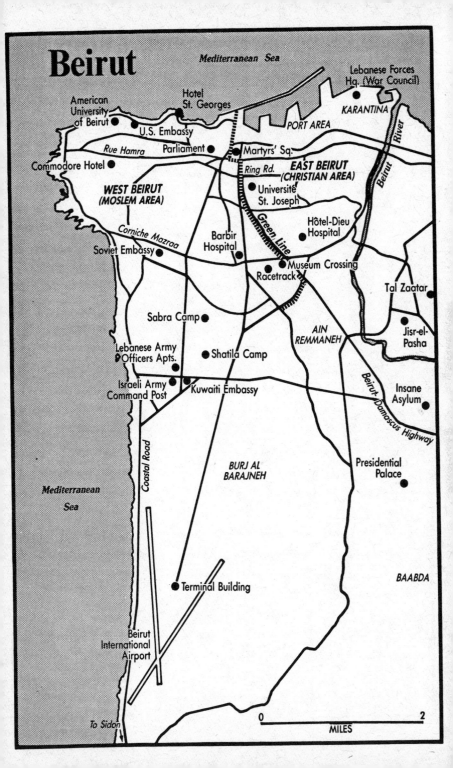

Going
All the Way

1. Miracles
and Hallucinations

When they finally dug him out of the rubble six hours later, what was left of Lebanese President-elect Bashir Gemayel had turned almost blue. The back of his large head was missing, as was most of the back and buttocks. "It's Bashir," said Karim Pakradouni, recognizing the prominent nose, the dimple in the chin, the hexagonal wedding ring, even before extracting a note from the breast pocket of the bloodstained safari jacket. This turned out to be from the nuns of La Croix psychiatric hospital, invoking the Virgin's protection; Gemayel had lunched with them. That clinched the identification for Pakradouni. But one of the six doctors in the emergency room at the Hôtel-Dieu hospital in East Beirut argued with Gemayel's close political adviser. The doctor knew perfectly well that clinically Bashir was dead. But he didn't dare say so, didn't dare have Pakradouni say so. For Pakradouni would have to tell the world the truth. The doctor would have preferred Pakradouni to remain silent, to freeze time. "No, Karim," he said, "you have a grave responsibility."

Pakradouni paid the doctor no mind, but he did discharge his responsibility as he saw fit. He drove his Range Rover, the supreme Lebanese status symbol, back to the windowless concrete bunker headquarters of Gemayel's Lebanese Forces militia near the port. With Fady Frem, the freshly appointed commander of Gemayel's private Christian army, Pakradouni issued orders banning guns on the street and restricting the Christian militiamen to barracks. That was a normal reflex after seven and a half years of violence.

Whoever killed Bashir Gemayel—and there was no dearth of candidates, given the young President-elect's record of murdering his way to the top—would be hoping for an extra dividend in the form of mass reprisals. These regularly occurred in Lebanon after assassinations of political leaders. More than 300 pro-Gemayel Christians had died in retaliation for the 1978 assassination by Bashir's men of Tony Franjieh, elder son of the former President of the Republic, Franjieh's wife and daughter, and thirty-one of his partisans. In 1977 the Druze Moslems slaughtered more than 170 Christians in the Shuf Mountains, south of Beirut, after their leader, Kamal Jumblatt, had been assassinated by Syrian agents. The Lebanese Forces and the Syrians were then nominal allies, but the Syrians had nearly thirty thousand troops in Lebanon, ostensibly keeping peace, and they were too strong for the Druze. In Lebanon you slaughter those you can, not necessarily those you'd like to. Lebanon is not a country where even the most innocent and minor hurt or error is forgiven or forgotten.

But the last thing Pakradouni wanted in the Christian ghetto was militiamen running amok, seeking revenge. More than one hundred thousand Moslem Lebanese who had fled West Beirut during the long Israeli siege were still living in what the Lebanese Forces called their "liberated region"—in contrast with the 85 percent of Lebanon they did not control. Frem and Pakradouni were convinced the Lebanese Forces' elementary precautions were all the more called for since collective hysteria might well follow the mass hallucination that had gripped so many Christian Lebanese that Tuesday, September 14, 1982. The distraught doctor at the Hôtel-Dieu was not the only one who preferred to deny Bashir Gemayel's death. The prospect of Gemayel's impending six years in office solved a variety of problems for a variety of interested parties, domestic and foreign.

Israel had carefully cultivated Bashir Gemayel for years, providing arms and training for his men and invaluable help abroad in his uphill struggle for international respectability. Israel had invaded Lebanon on June 6 for its own reasons, and without the Lebanese Forces' political support and rear-base facilities it is doubtful whether Prime Minister Menachem Begin and Defense Minister Ariel Sharon would have dared launch the operation. But another important Israeli calculation was aimed at electing their protégé to the presidency of Lebanon and ensuring a friendly, Christian-dominated regime there.

The United States was a late convert to Bashir Gemayel's cause. Indeed, the United States came to back him *faute de mieux* and not without second thoughts, as befitted a superpower wary of Gemayel's methods (which included an attempt on the life of an American ambassador) and skeptical of the durability of a man intent on reasserting Christian domination over Lebanon's Moslem majority.

The Lebanese Moslem leaders were resigned to Gemayel, if not volubly enthusiastic about him. Gemayel denounced Lebanon's occupation by Palestinians and Syrians, but the Moslems, not the Christians, had to live with them and their protégés. Along with the now-departed Palestine Liberation Organization, they were the ostensible losers in Israel's summer war of 1982. Their flock was willing to forget its past opposition to Gemayel if he made good on his promise to restore order and get rid of the dozens and dozens of parties, militias, and neighborhood gangs that had reduced life in West Beirut and much of Lebanon to anarchy.

The explosion, which took place at 4:08 p.m., Tuesday, September 14, sent a huge yellow-brown cloud of dust and smoke billowing above the three-story building that housed the main East Beirut branch of the Phalange, the political party founded by Bashir's father, Pierre Gemayel, in 1936. Bits of arms, legs, shoulders, and heads were strewn among the collapsed pillars, concrete rubble, stone, and metal. The street was filled with cries of "Bashir! Bashir! Bashir is inside!" One militiaman pounded the street in frustration. Others took their fury out on the press, confiscating film, beating, even shooting at, photographers. Ambulances and medical teams stood by. Party officials and Bashir's wife, Solange, arrived and waited.

A creature of habit, grown careless in the euphoria of his recent election, Gemayel had refused to call off—or vary the timing of—the meeting at the party headquarters where he had first broken into politics and which he regularly attended every Tuesday afternoon. Even as President he planned to return here often to speak and listen to the taxi drivers, shopgirls, housewives, and old-age pensioners seated on simple wooden chairs drawn up in rows in the ground-floor foyer; it was decorated with photographs chronicling his father's long march to power, now symbolized by his own success. "This is the Levant," he told me in that building, years ago, when I first got to know him. "You have to answer the telephone yourself—no secretary—listen to each conversation, and receive each visitor. That's how you get people to trust you and find out what they are thinking."

Watching the rescue workers, Pakradouni, increasingly worried, asked a doctor how long a man could be expected to live under the rubble. About two hours, he was told, a judgment that soon made the rounds. By six o'clock it was dark. The tension was unbearable. The young rescue workers labored faster and faster under arc lights. Suddenly, a man in a safari jacket was extracted from the wreckage and rushed into an ambulance, which was driven off at breakneck speed. The crowd cheered wildly, shouting, "Bashir! Bashir!" There seemed to be no doubt: the President-elect was safe. What *baraka*! What divinely inspired luck! Even as experienced a correspondent as Lucien George of *Le Monde* was convinced he had "seen" Bashir being helped into the ambulance. A helicopter flew overhead, but was driven off by the random shooting. Friends in the crowd reassured one another that the Israelis had sent the helicopter to take Gemayel to a hospital in Israel. The Voice of Free Lebanon, the pirate radio of the Lebanese Forces, commonly called Radio Bashir, quoted the President-elect as thanking the Good Lord for having spared his life, and reported that he had gone home to change clothes, since his only injury, a bruise on his left leg, did not require hospitalization.

Relieved, Solange and Pakradouni left, and drove down the steep hill to the Hôtel-Dieu. Bashir was not there, they were told. Still confident, they rushed to the Rizk Hospital, where they were greeted by Dr. Assaad Rizk. Bashir was not there, he said.

"Don't play games with me," Pakradouni barked.

"Are you crazy, Karim?" the doctor replied. "Do you think for a second I would dare joke about Bashir?"

It was almost 8:00 p.m. Only then did Solange and Pakradouni realize that Bashir was still under the rubble—and very likely dead.

That was a calculation that various embassies had made hours earlier, when they sent staffers to look at the wreckage. Pakradouni returned to the party building. Rescue workers, still convinced Gemayel was safe and sound, slapped him on the back and joked with him. Pakradouni did not have the heart to tell them the truth. Gemayel's stocky body was one of the last to be removed, just after 10:00 p.m., and finally taken by ambulance to the Hôtel-Dieu.

Prime Minister Shafik Wazzan announced the President-elect's death at midnight. But hours earlier the public had surmised the truth. The evening television news was dispatched in barely three minutes. For the first time since the killing started in Lebanon on April 13, 1975, Beirut Radio interrupted its usual pop fare to play classical music. None of the previous seventy-five thousand victims had warranted such a mark of respect. It broadcast classical music for a week.

The somber music, meant for Gemayel alone, might have been dedicated to others as well. His assassination ushered in a week surpassing everything Lebanon had managed to provide by way of violence, horror, and mindlessness; it further undermined American credibility in the Middle East, sullied Israeli honor, and added yet another unwanted chapter to the liturgy of Palestinian martyrdom.

The music also interrupted many Lebanese Christians' collective hallucination. This temporary suspension of disbelief corresponded to a genuine reluctance to accept Bashir Gemayel's death. By their own peculiar lights who could blame them? Not in their wildest dreams could they have imagined things going so smoothly. Now, logically, they joined the Palestinians and the Lebanese Moslems in the losers' circle they so steadfastly had fought to avoid over the years. For with Gemayel's death they had lost their best chance of reimposing their hegemony on Lebanon's Moslem majority, their undeclared goal during more than seven years of fighting and scheming.

Impenitent gamblers that they are, the militant Christians of Lebanon, especially the many Maronites who form their core, had played and lost time and again, then doubled the stakes; never listening for long to moderate counsel, supping with dangerous foreign allies they privately derided as little better than devils, they never, never abandoned hope. They were the despair of the other Lebanese, including their less extremist co-religionists. The militant Christians had signed the 1969 Cairo accords legitimizing the Palestine Liberation Organization's pretensions to being a state-within-a-state. Then they had moved heaven and earth to bring in the Syrian Army to save them from the Palestinians in 1976. And they had concluded a de facto alliance with Israel—long before Egyptian President Anwar Sadat embarked on his fatal adventure with the Jewish state. King Abdullah of Transjordan in 1951, Sadat in 1981, and now Bashir Gemayel—all the Arab leaders who dared to deal openly with Israel ended up assassinated.

Yet all during the summer of 1982, from the narrow confines of their ghetto outlook, the militant Christians witnessed not just one miracle but a series of miracles.

First Israel unleashed its terrible swift sword at long last, smiting the dreaded Syrians and the hated Palestinians rather than just playing them off against each other and preserving the despised status quo. Lebanon for the Lebanese, the Christian leaders had said all along, and now that it was happening they intended to make sure it would be a Christian-run Lebanon. The best part was that it was not even the Christian militia's war: Israel was doing the fighting, but the Christians stood to share the fruits of victory whether or not they took an active part. The Israelis were openly resentful of their "chocolate soldier" allies for failing to honor their word and join the fighting. But Bashir Gemayel repeatedly denied he had made any such undertaking. Israel, he hinted, should be content with the rear-base facilities it had in the Christian ghetto of Beirut and the alliance with the Lebanese Forces that had served as the intellectual foundation justifying the invasion.

It was the Lebanese Forces' decision not to fight alongside the Israelis that helped win over a suspicious United States government to Gemayel's presidential ambitions. The Americans feared that any Christian militia's participation in the fighting would split Lebanon, perhaps for good, and make reconciliation with the country's Moslem majority all but impossible. Despite the massive Israeli destruction visited upon the mostly Moslem sectors of West Beirut, which left most Christians unmoved and ensured the opposition of the mainstream Moslem leadership to Bashir Gemayel, he won the presidency, traditionally reserved for one of his sect. His was a campaign combining muscle, money, and persuasion so convincingly that no other Maronite Christian dared run against him for the land's highest office.

More miraculous yet, the United States government did nothing to stop the Israelis, either in the first two days of the invasion in south Lebanon, or once the invaders swept north and encircled half a million West Beirutis along with the PLO leadership. For Gemayel the American forbearance marked an extraordinary change of heart. Both during the 1978 Israeli invasion of south Lebanon and again in 1981, during the battle of Zahle and the ensuing missile crisis in the Beqaa valley, the United States had moved forcefully to stop the Israelis. Now, under Secretary of State Alexander M. Haig, Jr., the Reagan administration gave every indication of letting events—Israeli-dictated events—take their course. The Lebanese Christians had doubted this briefly, in late June, when Haig resigned—in part because of the controversy that his Lebanese policy caused. But then the United States dispatched Marines abroad in battle formation to supervise the departure of the PLO leadership. By late August, Marines were in Beirut. Whatever the consequences for the other participants in the conflict, the Lebanese Forces convinced themselves that the Americans had finally come around to their way of seeing things. In the past, the United States had allowed Lebanon to remain a sideshow of the Middle East, a killing ground where all the regional powers vented their aggressions. Now the United States, they kept persuading themselves, was willing to find a separate solution to Lebanon's travail, rather than subordinating its fate to an overall Middle East settlement

Estranged for years from successive American administrations, all of which had mistrusted the muscular Christians' scheming to involve the United States against its will in major policy changes in the Middle East, Gemayel was not that unhappy with the frictions between Washington and Jerusalem provoked by the summer war of 1982. For him, Israel had always been second best, an ersatz Western power and only an alternative when the Christians' traditional Western friends refused to follow them down their path of death and destruction. The world's number-one nation was a more attractive ally than the Middle East's superpower. The United States was immeasurably more acceptable to the Arab world and conveniently separated from it by thousands of miles of ocean. It was not a dangerously meddlesome neighbor. If Israel now opted for a weak Lebanon, partitioned between itself and Syria, in preference to its publicly stated support for a strong central government in Lebanon, then the United States could be counted on to fight the battle for the Christians. Or so the muscular Christians argued, jubilant at what they considered their windfall backing from the United States. They were convinced they could play the Americans off against the Israelis for their own greater glory. Some Gemayel lieutenants even talked of turning their overarmed country into a neutral state, the Switzerland of the Middle East that the tourist brochures had so inaccurately touted before things fell apart in 1975.

But these two miracles paled in comparison with the third.

Only weeks after his election, and nine days before he was due to take office for a six-year term, Gemayel was well on his way to winning over a largely suspicious nation, especially its Moslems. In part this success was due to a newfound willingness to say the politic thing: reunification, reconciliation, turning the page, homage to his old enemies' dead, guaranteeing press freedom—promises dictated not only by common sense but by his insistent American protectors. The tough, ruthless, impulsive warlord, so often depicted as a bloodthirsty, monomaniacal defender of muscular Christianity, the bogeyman with whom many a Moslem mother threatened her disobedient child, was now transmogrified into President of all the Lebanese. And what a task that was—uniting three million members of sixteen officially recognized sects living in a country the size of Connecticut, at times held together only in their paranoid fear and loathing of each other. If the civil servants were any yardstick, he might just succeed. For years either absent or surly, always corrupt and unhelpful, now suddenly they were at their offices all day long, protesting feigned shock at the bribes proferred by the populace as the routine price of doing business. "Sheikh Bashir would hang me by my thumbs," said a frightened repairman when I pulled out money to speed the repair of my telephone, which in the past regularly went on the blink to round out his wages.

Completing Gemayel's new, post-election image was a suggestion of his nascent independence from the Israelis to whom he owed so much. As far as can be ascertained, he did nothing more to shed his quisling clothes than discourage Israel's insistent demands for an immediate peace treaty with Lebanon. A treaty was sure to create even greater Christian-Moslem tensions inside Lebanon and to threaten it with a humbling Arab economic boycott. The endless violence had destroyed so much of Lebanon's economic infrastructure—and discouraged so many Lebanese—that hundreds of thousands had sought security and employment in the conservative oil nations of the Persian Gulf; their remittances kept the Lebanese economy afloat. And Arab oil money could rebuild the damage sustained in the war, much of it caused by the Israeli invaders.

Nonetheless, Menachem Begin adamantly insisted on the treaty, which he saw as a companion accomplishment to the one he had signed with Egypt. For years, he had regularly accompanied often unprovoked Israeli air or land raids against Lebanon by pious proposals that he meet with President Elias Sarkis to sign such a treaty, repeatedly deemed the sovereign cure for bilateral Israeli-Lebanese problems. In the past such gestures had been dismissed in Lebanon as further manifestations of Begin's inability or unwillingness to understand the country's suffering, an Israeli joke in the worst possible taste. Gemayel came to realize the dangers of a peace treaty with Israel—at least before an overall Middle East settlement was achieved—despite that old saw of some thirty years' standing that insisted that Lebanon would be the second Arab state to do so. During the summer of 1982, even the state-owned Israeli Radio acknowledged that Begin was faced with a straight choice: a strong Lebanese central government friendly to Israel or a peace treaty; he could not have both. Gemayel's hesitation to agree to Begin's demands pleased many wary Christians and Moslems in Lebanon. Coming from a man widely suspected of abject fealty to Israel, any show of independence was seized upon as evidence that he was coming to understand the constraints of national office. It bespoke common sense—and Western, especially American, influence, which was judged more evenhanded and disinterested than Israel's.

In any event, Gemayel was caught in the emerging test of wills between the United States and Israel, which flattered his sense of self-importance. He had felt at home enough with the Israelis to have bought three hundred sixty military trucks from Automotiv Industries of Israel, which began delivery just before the war. He dined openly with Ariel Sharon during the Israeli Defense Minister's Beirut visits. And American senators and other officials now started popping up regularly. But on September 1 President Reagan gave a speech advocating a freeze of Israeli settlements in the West Bank and Gaza Strip pending a solution for those Israeli-occupied territories, and the tensions between Washington and Jerusalem immediately increased. Two days later, Israeli troops conspicuously violated their undertakings to the United States and advanced 600 yards into West Beirut to positions overlooking the Palestinian refugee camps of Shatila and Sabra. As so often in the past, Israeli displeasure with American policy first became visible in Lebanon.

But even as President Reagan was speaking in California on September 1, Begin was meeting secretly with Gemayel in northern Israel in yet another of their periodic encounters. Begin left the Carlton Hotel at Nahariyya on the Mediterranean coast at 11:00 p.m. and appeared at an Israeli government guesthouse closer to the Lebanese border, where he had kept Gemayel cooling his heels for two hours. Accompanying Begin were Sharon and Saad Haddad, a cashiered Lebanese army major who commanded a border militia paid, provisioned, and armed by Israel. Begin routinely used Haddad to float Israeli trial balloons, and the tone of Haddad's utterances more and more closely reflected Israel's anguish about Bashir's "ingratitude" for the invasion and Israel's help in his election.

It was not a good meeting. For Begin and Sharon, Topic A was the peace treaty they wanted Lebanon to sign quickly, no later than a month after Gemayel's inauguration on September 23. When Gemayel once again explained his problems with a treaty—and proposed instead a nonaggression pact—Begin cited Haddad's case. Haddad knew how to take orders, knew what was best for both Israel and Lebanon; he was an example to be followed, he said. But even on that score there was confrontation. Bashir had wanted to put Haddad on trial for dereliction of duty and treasonable trafficking with Israel (although aides suggested the major would be let off with only a pro forma condemnation). Yet here was Begin insisting that Haddad serve as Defense Minister or army commander in Bashir's new government. Gemayel and Begin ended up shouting at each other. Sharon said that when he held someone or something in his grasp, he did not give them up. Israel was in the driver's seat, he made clear, and Bashir had better do what was expected of him. Gemayel at one point held out both arms and said, "Put the handcuffs on!" Then he shouted, "I am not your vassal!"

Of course, by many accounting systems, he was. That was what rankled the Lebanese, especially after the Israelis leaked news of what they'd agreed would remain a secret conversation, much to Bashir's fury. His office issued a formal denial that any such encounter had taken place. But in private Gemayel retaliated in kind: back in Beirut, he talked his head off. Clutching his throat with both hands in imitation of Begin's tactics, he told one group after another that he had been treated "like a bellboy." Begin, whom he had once considered a "wise man," had "betrayed and insulted" him. "He did not let me have my dignity," Bashir complained.

Among those he talked to were the Americans, especially visiting Secretary of Defense Caspar Weinberger. Bashir made it clear that he felt Begin's churlish behavior had "set me free" and liberated him from any earlier commitments he might have made with Israel. Five days after the meeting at Nahariyya, Bashir offered the United States military bases, radar facilities in Lebanon's mountains to scan the eastern Mediterranean and the Arab hinterland, and basically "anything you want." Weinberger acted as if he had not heard these remarks and went on to the next item on their agenda. But doubtless Gemayel believed the offer of military facilities fitted into the Reagan administration's fascination with having a rapid deployment force to protect the Gulf oil states. He apparently had not noticed that American interest in this project, once at the center of a now-downgraded theory that the Gulf, rather than the Palestine issue, lay at the heart of a Middle East policy, was waning. Nor could a young man largely untutored in the ways of the world understand that for Weinberger the last thing the United States wanted was to get caught for long in Lebanon's quicksands. The Secretary of Defense in fact was in Beirut to ensure that the Marines left later that week, well before their month-long mandate was due to expire.

Reasonable or not, the offer was yet another example of Gemayel's seemingly infinite capacity to keep moving, to dazzle and to impress. As many Lebanese will volunteer to tell even chance foreign acquaintances, they have few pretensions to profound thought. And indeed, by the yardstick of the rational West, Gemayel's accomplishments were slim. Yet rarely in contemporary history has a man been credited by both friend and foe in his own society, on the basis of so little hard fact, with such a total change of heart—even before assuming power and encountering the eroding demands of office. At thirty-four (a year older than Christ, as his devotees noted with increasing piety), Bashir was instantly on his way to canonization.

"Never in Lebanon's ancient or contemporary history," proclaimed a black-bordered half-page newspaper advertisement the day after Gemayel's assassination, "has a single man given rise to so much hope or prompted so many tears." The Lebanese were watching, indeed actively encouraging, yet another act of mass hallucination. They were blotting out the past in a strange reenactment of *The Picture of Dorian Gray* in reverse. Such was the depth of longing for clear, unequivocal leadership to cut through the encrusted hatreds of Lebanese society and bring order out of nearly a decade's chaos.

Yet there was a telltale clue in that advertisement, a historical arrow that pointed to a nastier past. The advertisement was sponsored by the management and employees of a mattress company called Sleep Comfort. And the main Sleep Comfort factory was the scene of one of the first of Lebanon's major massacres, in January 1976. Christian militiamen had then killed hundreds of mostly unarmed civilian Kurds, Shia Moslem Lebanese, and Palestinians. That was the massacre of Karantina (the Arabic name for the old quarantine area down by the port of Beirut), cheek-by-jowl with the three-story War Council headquarters of the Lebanese Forces. Karantina was the first Lebanese massacre I witnessed. Christian militiamen with outsize wooden crosses around their necks, high on hashish or cocaine, and some wearing Nazi surplus helmets, killed to their heart's content. It was always the same—men, women, and children. Sometimes Christians were butchered by Palestinians, Syrians, and Lebanese Moslems, but in most cases Lebanese Christians killed Palestinians and their Lebanese friends and neighbors. Dbeyeh and Black Saturday had come before. Damour, Ayshiye, Jisr-el-Pasha, Tal Zaatar, Qaa, Khiam, Ehdene, Safra-Marine, Zahle, and others of less import followed. Was Sleep Comfort's eulogy, I wondered idly, an unintended reminder of Bashir Gemayel's past savagery, or was it a portent of things to come? Exhausted by the unending violence, few Lebanese indulged in the luxury of such questions. The Lebanese wanted peace, law, and order. At any price—even including Gemayel's know-it-all sermonizing. He had promised to give Lebanon order and calm, contrasting the no-nonsense surface tranquillity of his policed Christian ghetto with the anarchy rampant in so much of the rest of the country. He always made it sound easier than it was likely to be. He constantly harped on the Moslems' alleged passivity compared with his Christians' militant rejection of Palestinian and Syrian tutelage, conveniently forgetting that neither Palestinians nor Syrians existed in his ghetto. And then Bashir Gemayel was dead.

Now, buried beneath the rubble with Gemayel lay the underpinnings of the great, if fragile, enterprise he had worked so hard to fashion. He had been so anxious for outside approval, longed so touchingly for respectability, especially in the eyes of what he always insisted on calling the "Free World." He had prided himself on being the first leader to build a disciplined, modern organization outside the feudal clan system that since time immemorial had monopolized power in Lebanon. He often boasted that his own person was of no importance, that he could be killed, but that his Lebanese Forces would continue to function, indeed prosper, without him.

The pity is that the Lebanese Forces functioned all too well—if not wisely—when put to the test. Apparently Bashir's military lieutenants did not realize that in the three weeks following his election he had changed and expected his organization to change, too. He no longer deemed the radical methods, the killings, the rough stuff of the years past to be necessary. Soon he would become the state, with all the state's formal legal powers at his disposal to do his bidding. No one who listened to Bashir Gemayel for more than five minutes ever doubted his abiding and visceral hatred not just of the PLO, but of all Palestinians. He made no secret of his intention to drive as many Palestinians as he could from Lebanon, turning the refugee camps into so many tennis courts. But not even his most dedicated enemy could imagine that as President-elect he would have tolerated what his lieutenants began planning after his death.

At 3:30 a.m. on Wednesday, September 15, Bashir's military lieutenants met with Lieutenant General Rafael Eitan, Israeli Chief of Staff, and Major General Amir Drori, in charge of Israel's Northern Command and in effective charge of the entire Lebanese operation. The Israelis were going to invade West Beirut—in defiance of promises to the United States, Lebanon, and the PLO made during the peaceful evacuation of more than eleven thousand Palestinian guerrillas completed just two weeks earlier. Bashir's death simply left too many possibilities for error that could nullify Israel's sacrifices and benefits in the war to date. The Israelis had counted on Gemayel to clean up West Beirut with its armed leftist militias and the two thousand PLO fighters who, the Israelis had convinced themselves, on the basis of erroneous electronic eavesdropping, had been left behind. But with Gemayel dead, Sharon and Begin panicked. They felt they could not risk leaving West Beirut intact now that their own feel for the Lebanese situation had disappeared. An invasion of West Beirut, so long taboo, was going to commence in ninety minutes. (Even before the meeting with the militia leaders, Sharon had ordered troops and matériel flown up from Israel in anticipation of the operation. The first Hercules C-130s began landing at Beirut airport barely two hours after the Ashrafieh explosion.) The Israeli cabinet, when eventually informed, justified the patent violations of the accords negotiated by U.S. special envoy Philip Habib by insisting that Israeli troops "have taken up positions in West Beirut to prevent the danger of violence, bloodshed, and anarchy" after Gemayel's death. In fact, neither the Christians in East Beirut nor the Moslems in West Beirut were guilty of any violence. "Half the country is deep in despair," a prescient Palestinian said within hours of the explosion, "and the other half is petrified with fear." With the PLO fighters gone, and with Lebanon's main roads demined, thanks to diligent French Foreign Legionnaires, and with most of the sand barricades dismantled, an invasion of Beirut involved no great military genius. Nor would Israeli casualties, once a key deterrent, be high.

But for political reasons the Israelis shied away from entering the Palestinian camps in Beirut and winkling out the Palestinian fighters—the "terrorists," as they called them—that their intelligence insisted were there. There was another, less charitable view of Sharon's thinking. He had never masked his desire to get into West Beirut proper, indeed had nibbled his troops' way forward to within spitting distance of the camps. He was obsessed by the PLO's success in winning world opinion to its cause during his siege of West Beirut. He would destroy West Beirut's camps—and the PLO myth—and use the Christians to do the job. If Sharon really believed the camps were manned by two thousand armed Palestinians, why did he commit only two hundred men? Israel had its own men inside the Lebanese Forces, and from Frem on down, the organization was shaken by the assassination and only too willing to listen to the Israelis' insistent argument that the Palestinians in the camps had killed Bashir and should pay. If that wasn't enough, a leading Phalangist said months later, the Israelis pressured their Lebanese Forces friends by claiming that Saad Haddad's men were ready to go into the camps without them. "Entry into the camps was mentioned" at that early Wednesday meeting, Sharon conceded the following week in the Israeli parliament. By Thursday, after another meeting with Frem, his own intelligence chief, Elie Hobeika, and others, Drori telephoned Sharon.

"Our friends are moving into the camps. I coordinated their entrance with their top men," he reported.

"Congratulations," Sharon replied, "the friends' operation is authorized."

The operation served both Israeli and Lebanese Forces' purposes. As the Israeli Army monthly *Skira Hodechith* was to note blandly by way of confirmation, the Lebanese Forces hoped to provoke "the general exodus of the Palestinian population, first from Beirut, then from all over Lebanon. The Christians," the monthly added, "wanted thus to create a new demographic balance in Lebanon." No more than two hundred Lebanese militiamen crossed the lines of Israeli troops surrounding the camps on Thursday after dusk. Virtually without letup, for the next thirty-eight hours they massacred men, women, children—even horses, dogs, and cats—in cold blood. Although Israeli commanders and troops surrounding the camp knew what was going on inside, as Israel's Kahan Commission established in its investigation of the massacre, they did nothing to stop the slaughter. An Israeli lieutenant who witnessed the murder of two unarmed Palestinians was told by his battalion commander, "We know, it is not to our liking, and don't interfere." Almost all the victims were unarmed civilians. Grenades, knives, hatchets, revolvers, and assault rifles as well as occasional artillery were used in the butchery. In some cases, breasts and penises were hacked off, crosses carved into the flesh as a Christian signature, pregnant women's bellies ripped open, and, in one instance, the members of a baby cut off and disposed on an ironing board in a circle around his head. Some of the bodies were booby-trapped, so that burial of them was difficult and dangerous. Before the burial parties stopped counting—in the Levantine sun, bodies became rapidly unidentifiable—the official International Committee of the Red Cross death toll stood at 313. The civil-defense organization counted another 43 dead, and at least 146 further victims were buried by friends and relatives. Mass graves are known to exist but have not been dug up. Months later, some Palestinians remained convinced that as many as 3,000 camp residents were missing and presumed dead. In the absence of any accurate statistics, some serious reckonings suggested that the Palestinians may have accounted for as few as one third of the victims. Indeed, some sources indicated that Lebanese Shia Moslems made up at least a third—perhaps one-half—the death toll, with citizens of Egypt, Syria, and other Arab countries accounting for the remainder. Other sources reported that 991 camp residents remained unaccounted for; as many as a third of these may have been Lebanese. The use of bulldozers, both to trap people inside their cinder-block homes and to hide the evidence, bespoke of both barbarity and a certain confusion born of fear that these misdeeds would come to light.

Months later, one of the killers spoke movingly of his part in the massacre. Taking down his personal diary, he read aloud, "Shoot them against the pink and blue walls, slaughter them in the half-light of evening." Asked how many Palestinians had been killed in the camps, his boss, also present, said, "You'll find out if they ever build a subway in Beirut." He left no doubt there were many, many more victims than listed in the official account.

For anyone with the slightest understanding of Lebanon, the massacre was a foregone conclusion once the Lebanese Forces were authorized to enter the camps. It was just as natural as cats chasing rats. Equally predictable was Israel's desire to put the responsibility for whatever might happen thereafter squarely on the Lebanese Forces. Yet even as experienced an observer as I failed to understand what was happening. I was inside Shatila on Friday afternoon, watching smoke rise from buildings less than a half mile away, talking to militiamen who readily conceded that fighting was in progress. I watched a militiaman twirl the chamber of his revolver, took in the camp I knew so well, whose fate I had worried and written about so often, and yet I did not comprehend that the massacre I long had feared was taking place there and then. In retrospect, my colleagues and I have wondered what might have happened if the world had been told a day earlier about the massacre. Certainly the killing went on through Friday night and early Saturday. I assumed then that the camp residents had fled at the first sight of the militiamen on Thursday evening—fled as they had in June, when Israeli gunboats, artillery, tanks, and aircraft first began attacking the camps as prime targets. I was wrong. Many of them believed the war was over and they had nothing to fear from Israeli troops. The guerrillas, after all, had left in the evacuation. So they stayed, while others who tried to get away were stopped by a blocking force of Israeli and sometimes even Lebanese Army troops.

With just such a massacre in mind, Gemayel had kept his men on the tightest possible leash starting June 5, the eve of the Israeli invasion, when he mobilized the Lebanese Forces. Even so, throughout the summer those forces committed numerous small-scale outrages against Palestinian civilians in south Lebanon, where Gemayel's control of his men was more tenuous. And there was no secret about the Israelis' frustrated desire to involve the Lebanese Forces in the fighting. From Begin on down, they were on record expressing their disappointment with the Christians for holding off. They had, after all, trained the key Lebanese Forces cadres and commanders. They knew perfectly well that the militiamen generally felt that the only good Palestinian was a dead Palestinian and that a good massacre or two would drive the refugees out of Beirut and Lebanon once and for all. (The Israelis had even tried to enlist the Lebanese Army itself in such an operation. After the massacre, a Lebanese officer recalled that during the day on Thursday a senior Israeli officer, presumably General Drori, judging from the Kahan Report, had taken him to the airport, where militiamen were starting to assemble, and pleaded with the army to enter the camps. "If your men won't do it," he quoted the Israeli as saying, "I know someone who will." The Lebanese refused the offer.) The Guardians of the Cedars, a onetime splinter group that Gemayel had incorporated into the Lebanese Forces in 1980, held as an article of faith that Palestinian infants must be killed, since they eventually grew up to be "terrorists." Had not Bashir himself over the years said the Palestinians were "a people too many" in Lebanon, and "We will not rest until every true Lebanese has killed at least one Palestinian"? Old Christian friends of mine of less bellicose disposition complained that the Palestinians had proved their villainy by going back and mutilating the corpses in the camps to make the Lebanese Forces look even worse. Indeed, that visceral hatred of the Palestinians was what had made the Christians attractive allies for Israel since 1976.

In the furor after the massacre at Shatila, the Lebanese Forces leadership publicly denied any involvement there. Their line was that they had conducted their own investigation, knew exactly what had happened, hour by hour, and had turned over all their information to Assaad Germanos, the military prosecutor officially entrusted with investigating the massacre for the government. (The Lebanese Forces knew they ran little risk from that quarter: Germanos had set some kind of record for failing to bring to trial all but a handful of those involved in the tens of thousands of violent crimes perpetrated in

Lebanon since 1975, and before beginning his new investigation he remarked that the massacres were "nothing but lies and exaggerations—there are only two hundred dead.") But in private, Lebanese Forces leaders cryptically refused to say anything after the massacre about their participation in the operation because they were "very, very scared." In the words of Fady Frem, "We said yes because we felt we could not afford a dilemma with Israel." It is difficult to pin down what they were hinting at, or what they hoped those hints would be taken to mean. Did they mean that the Israelis, especially the Mossad intelligence agents, who long had handled the Lebanese Forces, had some deep, dark secret they had threatened to reveal and thus had forced the operation on the unwilling militiamen? That seemed unlikely, since Israeli politicians had more openly conceded the once-secret connection with the Christian forces, much to the anguish of the latter.

Or could they be hinting that the Israelis were tired of the Christians' unwillingness to commit their troops—contemptuously called "chocolate soldiers" because of their inactivity—and now possessed some particularly compromising information that would blackmail the Lebanese Forces into compliance? After all, Bashir either had or hadn't promised to sign a peace treaty with Israel and to commit his troops to the war against the Palestinians. Even if he had, since his election he had come to understand the constraints of office. The Arab world, humiliated by its inability to thwart the Israeli invasion or to blunt its thrust, was in no mood to accept a new peace treaty with Israel, a second breach in its once-uniform ranks. And without natural resources other than its enterprising citizens, Lebanon needed Arab financial aid to rebuild its shattered economy and housing. Thus, as President, Bashir had a perfect pretext to justify changing his mind. He also had a ready answer when the Israelis pressed him to fight alongside them. He had told so many people privately that the Lebanese Forces would not join the war that the only way his promise to "liberate" West Beirut from the PLO could come true rested on the notion that the guerrillas would run for their lives once the Israelis reached the capital's outskirts. In any case his "liberation" talk had been part of his election-campaign strategy, designed to convince the Moslems that he was an irresistible force. In the same vein he had imposed compulsory military service on Christian high-school students in his "liberated" regions, and cajoled arms, uniforms, and training out of the Israelis, who hoped he would commit his men against the PLO.

But instead of fleeing, the Palestinians stood and fought in Beirut for two and a half months, winning sympathy in the world at large. Their stalwart behavior during the Israeli siege temporarily erased the bitter legacy of hatred that their sloppy, often thoughtless behavior in Lebanon had created over the years.

Or did those sibylline words mean that Israel had so infiltrated the Lebanese Forces that it exercised virtual control over key units and commands? In the Kahan Report, General Eitan is quoted as having, during that first fateful meeting early on Wednesday, "ordered the Phalangist commanders to effect a general mobilization of all their forces, impose a general curfew on all the areas under their control, and be ready to take part in the fighting." Ordered, indeed—the same Eitan who, the Sunday after the massacre ended, said, "We don't give the Phalangists orders and are not responsible for them. The Phalangists are Lebanese and Lebanon is theirs, and they do as they see fit." The Report gave no explanation of that stunning thought, in keeping with its preoccupation with obscuring the identity of the Christians involved in the slaughter. "Kiss the hand you cannot bite and implore God to break it" is an old saying much honored in Lebanon, where centuries of foreign occupation have left a legacy of surly deference to the ruler.

Or were the Lebanese Forces commanders just doing what came naturally, tired of enduring the taunts of their Israeli comrades-in-arms, itching to kill Palestinians, suspecting in their heart of hearts that the Palestinians must have been responsible for Bashir Gemayel's death, and now free from his control? His lieutenants without major exception had all trained in Israel and had many Israeli friends. There was always something cynical and contemptuous about Gemayel's view of mankind, and his attitude toward his own militiamen brought out the Mr. Hyde, rather than the Dr. Jekyll, side of his own character. Whatever else might be said of them, his lieutenants were scarcely men of subtlety or discernment.

Or was it all just a clumsy appeal for sympathy and understanding by hinting at dark thoughts, playing the underdog while respecting a Levantine variant of *omertà*, the Mafia's law of silence? Whatever voyage they once thought they were embarking on with the Israelis, the Lebanese Forces—and many other Lebanese—now believed Israel had tricked them. So why not blame Israel?

The Israeli government argued, with some justice, that Lebanon (and the world) was applying a double standard in assigning responsibility for the massacre to its army. To be sure, Sharon conceded that Israeli troops coordinated, planned, and monitored the operation, then did nothing to stop the killing clearly visible around the clock (thanks to flares) and audible from Israeli positions surrounding the camps. (In its only obviously wrongheaded factual error, the Kahan Report insisted Israeli troops couldn't see into the camp's alleyways, even with giant telescopes on the command-post roof. Journalists who climbed the seven-story building had no such difficulty with their own naked eyes.) But the killing itself was done by the Lebanese Christians—even if survivors' testimony, and the chance discovery of an Israeli Army dog tag, placed Sharon's troops at the killing ground. (Some of Haddad's men were also involved. Survivors told of men speaking with a south Lebanese accent and calling each other Ali and Abbas, typical names for Shia Moslems, who made up the bulk of his troops. But these militiamen were evidently free-lancing without orders from their commander. In any case, Haddad was scarcely on good enough terms with the Lebanese Forces to participate formally in such a sensitive operation.) As Begin said, "Why all the commotion about one set of *goyim* killing another and blaming it on the Jews?" Still, such is the Jewish heritage of persecution throughout history—and Israel's reputation as a democratic state set amid military dictatorships, David against the Arab Goliath—that the world judged Israel by the highest standards. In a way this was only fair. Israeli governments over the years had invoked that image to defend their policies vis-à-vis the Arabs, especially in Lebanon. At first Begin stonewalled, refused to authorize the official inquiry his detractors demanded. Thanks to a mammoth demonstration in which 15 percent of the Israeli population participated— and to increasing criticism from within the once unanimously supportive armed forces—the "good" Israel won out, the Israel that the West, and especially the United States, had defended despite years of steadily mounting evidence of aggressively predatory policies toward the Arabs. The system, or at least what the West took to be the system, worked, and the Israeli government, however reluctantly, finally followed Western norms and agreed to the state investigation it initially sought to avoid.

But when it came to the massacre, the Lebanese were not Westerners, no matter how much they tried to ape Western behavior on other occasions. (General Eitan testified that he for one knew perfectly well what Lebanese Christian militiamen were capable of. He told the Kahan Commission that he had felt, "I can read vengeance in their eyes. They are sharpening their knives.") If Begin and Sharon rode out the initial storm, then the Lebanese would do their damnedest to follow suit. In any case, the world had not been so squeamish about other massacres in Lebanon, so why all the fuss this time?

Old Lebanese friends of mine, normally of liberal disposition, railed at foreign correspondents of their acquaintance who insisted on piecing together the story of the massacre in its most minute details. "Don't you understand, we are all sick and tired of your muckraking," my Moslem friend Dina said. "Go away and leave us alone. Don't you understand that finally the Christians have understood that it is impossible to go on fighting, that the war is over, but it is going to be hard to make the peace." Lebanon's unending troubles had all congealed in one unsavory mass. What mattered now was avoiding something worse. Hushing up the massacre became a *raison d'état*, and not just at the laughable level of the Germanos investigation—a procedural farce, reminiscent of Deep South judicial formalities, that frightened survivors of the massacre into swearing that all the killers were Hebrew-speaking Israelis. Rather, denying the evidence became a positive act bordering on patriotism. Lebanese Christian and Moslem leaders, whatever their deep differences, were determined not to let the massacre destroy whatever still held them together.

Each religious group had its own reasons, but both found common ground in blaming Israel. The Christians felt used by the Israelis. They drew no distinction between the Israeli government, which sought to defend them, and an enterprising press, an outraged population, and a revivified opposition that were determined to get at the truth. Nor were they convinced that Israel was innocent of Gemayel's assassination. Even in the Gemayel family seat, the mountain village of Bikfaya, and even among key members of his clan, the episode at Nahariyya was cited as sufficient proof that Israelis preferred a partitioned Lebanon to the prospect of a strong government under Bashir. Succumbing to the prevalent view of an omniscient, omnipotent, ubiquitous Israel, many Lebanese argued that only the Jewish state was clever enough to have killed Gemayel in the party building, that holy of holies.

Moslem leaders in West Beirut, realizing they could do little for the

Palestinians, also chose to deny the evidence and blame the Israelis. Their attitude was dictated in part by indifference to the Palestinians bordering on animosity—a hostility now released after years of chafing under the PLO and especially after the massive destruction of the summer war, which, after all, had been brought on by the guerrillas' presence in West Beirut. But they also felt humiliated and betrayed by the Israelis. No Moslems copied the Christians in welcoming the Israelis to Beirut with rice and flowers. Their dignity was intact.

On Saturday morning, when the first reports of the massacre reached West Beirut (but mentioning only thirty dead), a breathless man arrived at the stately home of Saeb Salam in the heavily populated, Moslem working-class neighborhood of Mousseitbe. Salam was the seventy-seven-year-old, six-time former Prime Minister, who during the summer had reasserted himself as "Mr. Moslem" in Beirut, thanks to his key role as a go-between in the tortuous negotiations between the United States and the PLO.

"Saeb bey," the visitor said, "the Lebanese Forces are loose in West Beirut and are arresting and killing people."

"How do you know it's the Lebanese Forces?" asked a trusted adviser.

"Because it is written on their uniforms, over their chests."

"Since when do you know how to read?" snapped the adviser.

Saeb bey nodded.

The nod in no way signified approval of what had happened. Saeb Salam had warned Bashir Gemayel about the dangers of partition and further violence if the Lebanese Forces ended up fighting alongside the Israelis. All summer long, he had worked tirelessly to save the PLO's honor, to save West Beirut, and to deliver Lebanon from its many demons. No, the nod was one of resignation. Salam was a veteran politician and a Sunni Moslem, a member of that mainstream Moslem sect long accustomed to power. What could such a mandarin, a politician who prided himself on possessing a businessman's pragmatism, do when faced with what he saw as a convergence of Israeli and Christian-militia paranoia?

What madness propelled militiamen and Israelis to those camps, the nearest thing the landless Palestinians ever had to a capital? Had they become some latter-day Carthage, to be seized and sown with salt, to put paid to the PLO's pretensions? What demons played in the minds of Sharon, Begin, Drori, and the rest of the Israeli Army—an army that prided itself on the doctrine of the "purity of the weapon," that one should kill only when absolutely necessary?

A high Israeli official with long experience in dealing with the Lebanese Forces expressed to some newsmen his astonishment that a body of men that seemed so disciplined could have perpetrated such a crime. It never crossed his mind—and he knew the ins and outs of the Lebanese Forces perhaps better than any other Israeli—that they could do what they did precisely because they *were* disciplined. The only sure protection against their running amok, of course, was to assign subalterns—junior officers—in amongst the Lebanese Forces, the way the French and British armies did for centuries with their native troops. But those were the methods of colonialism, the very mention of which made members of the Israeli establishment bridle, despite mounting indications that indeed the Lebanon war of 1982 was Israel's first colonial war, just as its occupation of the West Bank and Gaza Strip was an out-and-out colonial enterprise. It was easier to argue that for the Israelis this was a military operation pure and simple, no politics, to say simply that they were determined to knock out "two thousand terrorists"—who turned out not to be in those camps after all.

As for the Lebanese Forces, even in a part of the world where revenge is a dish best eaten cold, it was hard to understand the timeliness of this further massacre. Back in 1976, when the bloodletting in Lebanon was relatively new, it was difficult to follow the tortured reasoning the Lebanese Christians invoked to justify the series of massacres distinguishing that civil war. Karantina had been said to justify the killings at Damour, the Christian coastal town where the PLO and their Lebanese allies had killed between one hundred fifty and two hundred civilians (not the five thousand more recently claimed by some errant Christian clerics). In turn, the Christian militias had then butchered thousands at the refugee camp of Tal Zaatar. But now, what was one to think about the militiaman who told a Lebanese Army trooper as he entered the camp, "I've been waiting for years to get in here"? When did the killing stop? The young men who joined a special Lebanese Forces unit called the Damour Brigade had sworn an oath to avenge their fallen relatives and stop only when all the Palestinians had been driven from Lebanon. But where were they to go? No other country, Arab or not, was willing to take the Palestinian civilians, but the mindless Lebanese Forces never thought about this. They never reflected on the PLO's—and Philip Habib's—headache in persuading the Arab world to take in the guerrillas evacuated from Beirut.

In this, they shared with the Israelis a contempt for the Palestinians as non-people. Golda Meir when Prime Minister of Israel had contributed to this doctrine of non-peoplehood in a June 1969 interview with *The Sunday Times* of London. Asked about the Palestinians, she had replied, "They do not exist." Now, more than a decade later, the Palestinians still existed nonetheless, but, for Israelis, only as "terrorists." Begin, in June, had described them as "two-legged animals." As such they were not considered worthy by Israel of prisoner-of-war status. Their dead, their wounded—civilian or military—their families were never included in Israeli statistics during the Lebanese war. Now, in late September, their children, women, and old men (males of arms-bearing age were all taken off to Israel and later to a camp at Ansar, in south Lebanon) were allowed to camp out in the ruins of the refugee camps that the Israelis had shelled, bombed, and dynamited before bulldozing them flat. At first the Israelis refused to allow the United Nations Relief and Works Agency, which has cared for the refugees for more than thirty years, even to bring in tents stored in Cyprus. They became more forthcoming, indeed insistent on helping, when the Lebanese authorities began dragging their feet. Yet, various militias in south Lebanon harass the Palestinians freely to this day. Israeli troops intervene only when matters get out of hand: their presence is preferred to that of the various militias they tolerate. But many refugees would like to leave Lebanon.

In this kind of situation it is difficult to know who is fooling whom. But the Lebanese Forces did learn one harsh lesson from the massacre. And that is that the Israelis use other people and cannot be used. The United States could have told them that, had any Maronite bothered to listen to advice over the years. Yet for some Lebanese Forces leaders, the massacre was well worth it, anyway. Consider Dib Anastase, now Lebanese Forces police chief and before 1975 a minor employee of the elite Hotel St. Georges. He told a visitor he had everything figured out; it was all a matter of proportion. Sure, the Palestinians had lost hundreds of martyrs in the camps. But, "We lost Bashir and twenty-five other people inside the party building." There was no question in his mind. His loss was greater.

2. Does the Rooster Know?

By the time I returned to Beirut in the late spring of 1975, during the early stages of what the Lebanese still refused to admit was a civil war, I had spent the better part of twenty years watching Third World countries suffering post-colonial travail. For better or for worse, I had become something of a specialist in upheaval on the outer marches of former empire—from Algeria and the Congo to the Dominican Republic and Vietnam. But never before had I seen an entire society collapse so thoroughly and so quickly. One day, rational discourse was flourishing in one part of the capital; the next, mad jabberings and madder acts had taken its place. Neighborhoods, towns, cities, finally an entire country slipped out of control, never to return to the realm of right reason. Lebanon was possessed and could only await exorcism. Long-suppressed hatreds, resentments, fear, and loathing coursed through the enfeebled body politic like some debilitating scourge from which no remission could be expected.

In the first sixteen months of violence—covering the civil war—a country of three million inhabitants lost at least thirty-five thousand dead, mostly civilians. Proportionately, that is as if the United States had lost, not fifty-five thousand men—and soldiers at that—killed in the eight years of American troop involvement in Vietnam, but two and a half million citizens. Or maybe twice that number, since statistics are suspect in Lebanon, especially casualty figures, which are often exaggerated to wheedle more funds out of overseas backers. The violence never stopped for long. No one ever disarmed willingly. The stopgap remedy was always the same: more troops and more armies for a country saturated by both.

Over the years, the Syrians maintained at least twenty-five thousand troops in Lebanon, under a mandate from the Arab League to keep the peace, although Lebanese of all persuasions increasingly came to resent them as an occupation force. Six countries contributed six thousand troops to serve under the United Nations flag and keep the peace in south Lebanon. Palestinian guerrillas of one description or another kept tens of thousands of men under arms of ever greater sophistication. Private armies ranged from the dozens of militias sometimes controlling no more than a few city blocks to the Lebanese Forces running the Christian ghetto of East Beirut with Israeli arms. The Israelis also pulled the strings of ex-Major Haddad's militia along the Israeli-Lebanese border. A Lebanese army of sorts, which never fully recovered from a split into Christian and Moslem segments in early 1976, also existed, if mostly on paper.

Such was the messy state of play in June 1982, when Israel invaded Lebanon, destroyed the PLO's military strength, and humiliated the Syrians. But as the months dragged on, less appeared to have changed than might have been expected. To this day, part of the Lebanese collective psyche protestingly refuses to believe what has happened, and another declines any responsibility for the deepening chaos, which briefly but deceptively shows signs of subsiding now and again. Self-inflicted wounds are never pleasant to contemplate. Nor is manifest outside interference. Taken together, they sum up much of Lebanon's troubles and nurture that well-known characteristic of political under-development, the perceived prevalence of plots. Such remain the mysteries of the defense mechanism in a part of the world where the past and all its horrors are ever present but its lessons are rarely learned.

Arbitrarily, I decided in 1975–76 to take a closer look at the

Lebanese Christians, more especially at the Maronites, who constitute their numerical and political backbone. Perforce, my inquiry struck many Maronites as unfair, because it supposedly distorts their foibles without providing sufficient understanding of their conviction that they have been left no real alternative action, given the *others'* scheming (real or imagined). I protested that I was not a historian. Had I been, I might have chosen the Shia or the Sunni Moslems, the Druzes, or some or all of these and twelve other officially recognized religious communities who reside in Lebanon, a historical zoo of the Middle East's losers. Or the Palestinians, Israelis, Syrians, Egyptians, Libyans, Iraqis, Iranians, Jordanians, Americans, or Russians. They all have complicated Lebanon's fate by sins of omission and commission. Why the Lebanese Christians? As I found it prudent to explain to the various Maronite warlords before I began poking around in earnest, I wanted to know how the Christians who ran—or thought they ran— Lebanon before 1975 had been reduced to a rump state. What had amounted to the only Christian state in the Middle East since the Crusaders' *Outremer* had been theirs, fruit of a millennium's longing and scheming. This was a feat in some ways no less remarkable than the Zionists' return to the land of Israel after nearly two millennia. Lebanon was the only country in the Middle East where Christians had resisted the trend toward assimilation, although their delight in arms and violence did not necessarily ensure their long-term future.

In my investigations I was treated—not for the first time in my long acquaintance with the Lebanese—to history, massive doses of often carefully pruned and ideologically dictated history that smacked of special pleading. Bashir Gemayel heard me out about my project, scolded me about my past sins in reporting his rise as the Maronites' favorite son, then thrust upon me a photocopy of a French account of the Druzes' massacre of Maronites in 1860. Offered like some auto- graphed baseball or other token of endorsed authority, the tome clearly contained the wisdom of the ages in his eyes, a key to understanding the Maronites so compendious as to answer all my questions once and forever. Various clerics and laymen did not let me off so easily. In his published diary, former President Camille Chamoun quotes at length a nineteenth-century French historian in order to compare the Maro- nites' dilemma to that of the Orthodox Christians of Constantinople who were abandoned by their Western coreligionists to the Moslem onslaught of the Ottoman Turks in 1453. At the time of Chamoun's diary entry, the Maronites were in very serious military straits, but to an outsider their plight scarcely seemed in the same league as the capture of Byzantium. That was my error. To his fellow Maronites, Chamoun was perfectly clear and consistent. He was talking about security, and that is what always has been uppermost in the Maronite mind.

Chamoun was reflecting that widely held Maronite conviction that the West—that is, Western Christians—have no interest in them, ignore their existence, and wish that they would go away. These Eastern Christians sometimes wear their religion with arrogant rigidity, with a militancy so uncompromising that it resembles nothing so much as the underside of an inferiority complex borne by a minority long reduced to second-class citizenship. Thus, a foreigner is lucky if the discussion goes back no further than the Crusades. That is the short version. For many of my interlocutors, Lebanese politics of the day could be understood only if I accepted the premise—doubtful, it seemed to me, on the face of it—that the Lebanese were descended from those masterly traders of antiquity, the Phoenicians. Everything was fashioned to fit snugly into a continuum of myth that sustained the Maronites in times of trouble. I learned to sit through these séances making no more than pro forma grunts. My interlocutors brooked no substantive questioning of the truths they revealed. Long ago I learned to weigh carefully what I said in such circumstances.

At one point in my inquiries I was invited by a European ecclesiastical scholar living in Lebanon to study a crudely carved wooden sculpture hanging on his wall. At first glance I found nothing unusual. A mounted horseman dressed in white was spearing a black devil writhing on the ground. On closer examination, I saw that the horseman was wearing golden earrings in the form of little crosses, and a cross also decorated his lance. I confessed I could make no meaningful sense of it. My host smiled, then launched into an explanation of the problem he felt lay at the heart of the plight of the scattered millions of Eastern Christendom.

"Copy of an original twelfth-century work, found in a Christian village about twenty miles outside Mosul, in northern Iraq," he said, as if reeling off clues to a puzzle. My ignorant silence clearly disappointed him.

"Under the Abbasids, who ran the Caliphate from Baghdad," he continued, "the Moslems tolerated the Christians but, among other things, forbade their owning horses, wearing earrings or white, showing the cross in public, or, of course, bearing arms."

"But the knight is doing all that."

"Wish fulfillment, that's what it was. The Christian sculptor must have been inspired by seeing a Crusader prisoner paraded through Mosul. That would explain the white tunic, and the earrings were probably just dreamed up."

Just what did the devil stand for?

"Islam and all its works. The Christians could only dream of power for themselves, a state of their own. Equality meant nothing for them or for their Moslem masters. You either dominated or were dominated. Christians and Jews were tolerated by the Moslems as 'people of the book'—the Bible—and called *dhimmi*, or protected, and had to pay special taxes. But the Christians hated the notion of being protected, tolerated, accepted on sufferance. The little sculpture demonstrates what Christians meant when they spoke of the triumph of the Church, for in their eyes the Church was triumphing over something—to wit, its enemies."

"And," I asked, "*did* the Eastern Christians triumph?"

His reluctant answer could be summed up—not really, or, rather, not for long. In its initial seventh-century A.D. conquest of the Middle East, Islam was remarkably forbearing and tolerant toward the Christians of the Byzantine Empire and a variety of schismatic churches that sprang up. The conquerors were few in number and at first relied on the local population, which was largely Christian. Conversion to Islam was a constant process. Historians of many persuasions tend to agree that social pressure—the desire to conform, to be assimilated in the mainstream—rather than force, was the chosen instrument.

The two hundred years or less of Crusader presence along the Mediterranean littoral in the twelfth and thirteenth centuries at best proved a mixed blessing for the native Christians, whose liberation from Islam was the newcomers' proclaimed goal. Welcomed at first as fellow Christians, the Crusaders so misbehaved that the Christians of the Orient at times even entered into alliance with the nominal Moslem foe, and Crusaders occasionally mounted punitive raids on local Christians. Thrown out of their always precarious perch on the mainland in the closing years of the thirteenth century, the Crusaders distinguished themselves by sacking Alexandria as they had sacked Constantinople years before—two major centers of trade, learning, and culture, a destruction of Byzantium that opened the door to the Moslem invasion of Europe. The sack of Alexandria and other excesses led the Moslems to end their indulgent tolerance toward Christians in the East and impose the kind of restrictions and other vexatory measures that inspired the anonymous Iraqi sculptor.

In the mid-thirteenth century the Christians of Iraq had allied themselves with the all-conquering Mongols then destroying the Persian and Abbasid empires. In 1258 the Christians of Baghdad alone were spared when troops from Christian Georgia joined the Mongols in slaughtering eighty thousand men, women, and children in the Abbasid capital in forty days. But two years later, the Moslem Mamluks defeated Mongol leader Hulagu's Christian general at Ain Jalut. It was one of history's truly decisive battles: the last chance expired for a viable and vibrant Christianity throughout the East. The Mongols, who thanks to Hulagu's Christian wife had favored the Christians, eventually accepted Islam. The Christians of Iraq, who had idolized the Mongols as instruments of divine vengeance and as deliverers from the "second Babylon," were now worse off than ever. They even had Hulagu and his wife, Doghuz Khatun—complete with Asian features—depicted in a painting as the latter-day Constantine and Helena who had converted the Roman Empire to Christianity nine centuries before.

Right from the start of the Moslem conquest, Christians, better educated than their Moslem masters, served as court physicians, secretaries, pharmacists, and the like. In the century following the conquest, Syria alone gave the world five popes; John of Damascus, a great theologian; and the greatest Christian poet of the period, Akhtal. Thanks to their knowledge of languages, the Christians aided mightily in transmitting Greek civilization by translating works on physics, medicine, geometry, architecture, and other disciplines. The most resolute Christians sought refuge in geography, more often than not in hills and mountains remote from, and inaccessible to, their Moslem temporal rulers. There, they survived, held out, but often stagnated. Whether Maronites of Lebanon, Armenians or Jacobites of Turkey, Nestorians or Chaldeans of Iraq, these Christians hankered after the foreign protector who someday, somehow would deliver them from Islam and help them create their own independent states. Not for them the subservience and resignation of the Copts of Egypt or the Greek Orthodox of Byzantium, who learned to live with their Moslem masters and not challenge them for political rights. The Copts and Orthodox were by far the largest Christian denominations in the Moslem world. But they refused to share the fears or demand the guarantees of the smaller churches. Over the centuries they all shared the benefits reaped when various European powers in the sixteenth century started extracting "capitulations" from the Ottomans amounting to protection for all Christians and even virtual extraterritoriality in some cases. These privileges did little to endear the Christians to the Moslem majority. Nor did the rich Christians' penchant for showing off their wealth. Just as the Christians yearned for European support so as to turn the tables on their Moslem masters, so the Ottomans became suspicious of their restive charges, who came to be seen as potential traitors, a fifth column for increasingly powerful and dangerously threatening Western interests. In the best-known catastrophe (by no means an isolated one) more than a million Armenians were killed or perished through neglect at Ottoman instigation during World War I. A contributing factor in the tragedy was European encouragement provided to the Armenians over the years, which the Ottomans seized on to justify one of history's first instances of government-ordered genocide.

Years before the most recent Lebanese war, during an assignment in Beirut in the 1960s, I was overcome by a sense of hopelessness upon seeing "Free Armenia" painted on the walls of the Lebanese University Law School. What chance was there for the Arabs and Jews to find a solution when the Armenians were still demanding justice in the name of their dead? Some two hundred thousand descendants of the Armenians who had sought refuge in Lebanon from the Ottomans had prospered. But the Lebanese civil war drove at least a tenth of them to less violent, and often American, shores. So, too, did the Maronite militias' brief but bloody efforts to cow the Armenians into submission by force of arms in 1978 and 1979. The Armenians in Lebanon, many of whom lived in the middle of Maronite territory, had refused to take sides in the civil war, and they refused to pay taxes to the militias, which objected to this loss of revenue from so many potential clients.

More recently, the militant example of the Palestinian guerrilla movement had contributed to the formation of an extremely effective Armenian Secret Army dedicated to the slaying of Turkish officials abroad and to regaining an independent Armenian state. Ruminating on what seemed the gradual but unbroken decline in the fortunes of Eastern Christians, brought on at times as much by their own errors as by the Moslem majority, I asked my ecclesiastical host now if he thought there was much hope for their survival. After all, Christians had been leaving Israel and the Occupied Territories for years, and there was a steady exodus from revolutionary Iran as well as less publicized but still sizable departures of Christians from Lebanon, Syria, and Iraq.

"I hope the Christians of the East are not condemned, but the way they're going, I don't see how it is to be avoided," he said.

"How long will it take?" I asked.

"As an effective force, maybe fifty to one hundred or one hundred fifty years," he said, staring at the sculpture on the wall.

"Are you surprised that any Christians remain in the Middle East?"

"You cannot tell when and where the river disappears into the sands of the desert," he replied.

A literal-minded Lebanese Christian almost certainly would take issue with both the thought and the image. It's difficult to say with accuracy what the various Christians—or many of the other Lebanese communities—really are. But one thing they are not is a desert people—at least not now, whatever their various origins may have been. For what makes Lebanon different in the Middle East are its mountains, its relative abundance of water, and its access to the Mediterranean—a combination that has provided refuge for dissidents determined to maintain their separate identity. Lebanon, in its 4,015 square miles (10,452 square kilometers), provides geographical diversity—10,000-foot peaks, sandy beaches, fertile fields—which in more peaceful times delighted the writers of tourist brochures. Lebanon's name is thought by some to be derived from a Semitic word signifying whiteness, but whether because of its limestone or the snow on its mountains is unclear. Less than 135 miles long and never more than 35 miles wide, Lebanon is enclosed by two mountain ranges: the Lebanon, which at times descends to the rocky Mediterranean coast, and the Anti-Lebanon, which forms the eastern border with Syria and is crowned at its southern end, near the Israeli frontier, by snow-covered Mount Hermon. In between the two ranges lies the Beqaa valley, a narrow, fertile strip rarely more than 6 miles wide. Another agricultural plain, the Akkar, is situated in the extreme north, between the port of Tripoli and the Syrian border. Leading back from the very narrow coastal plain, averaging little more than a mile in width, are a series of mountain valleys running east to west. They lead to the heart of Mount Lebanon—the Mountain, as it is called by the Lebanese—which is the historic center of the Maronites.

From these now largely bald limestone and sandstone heights dominating the Mediterranean, for two millennia came the wood that built fleets for the coastal Phoenicians, pharaonic Egypt, and imperial Rome. The best of the forests—the cedars of Lebanon mentioned in the Bible—also provided the oil and resins that the ancient Egyptians required for mummification. "Every time an Egyptian died, the Lebanese made money," a professor of history at the American University of Beirut used to say. Lebanon supplied the cedars and the workmen for King Solomon to build the Temple in Jerusalem.

The first Phoenicians, who lived in coastal city-states with little hinterland, were innocent of great inventions. They added little that changed man's material lot or philosophical development. Although not great creators, they were major transmitters of culture and are generally credited with the first cultural synthesis. Despite Lebanese claims, the Phoenicians did not invent the alphabet. But they spread it across their vast trading empire, which at its zenith stretched from the Lebanese coast to Carthage (in present-day Tunisia), to Spain, and beyond. The Lebanese coast was a multilingual meeting place for people drawn from all over the ancient world, an intellectual center as befitted a great trading society. The Phoenician cities of Byblos, Beirut, Sidon, and Tyre were nexuses of the foreign-trade routes that led west across the Mediterranean and east to the Persian Gulf, India, China, and beyond.

Throughout its history, Lebanon has fulfilled roles similar to those of the Phoenicians. Contemporary Lebanese, like the Phoenicians, have no real sense of the state. Phoenician cities were truly united only when ruled by an outside power. Not far north of Beirut, on the banks of the Dog River, where the Mountain descends to the sea, stand the records carved in a sheer cliff face of some of those who came and conquered: among others, Hittites and Assyrians, Romans and Greeks, French and British. Few conquerors bothered with the mountains. As long as lines of communication and tax revenue were guaranteed, what went on in the mountains was not worth interfering with.

Yet, how could the Maronites, so proud of their mountain independence and implied racial purity, born of centuries of isolation, compare themselves to the Phoenicians of the mongrelized coast? And why did the Maronites insist they were also descended from the Mardaites, a mysterious but fierce people mentioned in the history of the early Islamic period as having been left behind by the beaten Byzantines to harass the Moslem conquerors?

The answer proved simple enough. If the Lebanese Christians could establish ties with the Phoenicians or Mardaites, then they could dissociate themselves from the Arabs and Islam. Starting in the nineteenth century, this became a constant Maronite preoccupation. Anything pointing toward a pre-Islamic existence was grist to the Maronite mill, or rather to that part of the Maronite mind which rejects the Arab world and its culture. Another strand is proud of its Arab roots and contributions to Arab culture and society. But much of Maronite history in the last two centuries has been written by church and other historians determined to prove the non-Arabic case by hook or by crook. Revisionist historians, and even church officials, in recent decades have taken a more jaundiced view toward such efforts, and aside from the scholarly pleasure of unraveling the highly political motives of the early Eastern Church, these works are regarded as fanciful frauds.

But who indeed were the Maronites? Named after a fifth-century hermit and saint named Maron, at their beginnings the Maronites were a Christian sect of obscure origin active in what today is the valley of the Orontes River in northern Syria, around the city of Hama. Some historians have theorized that Maron won his sainthood by stamping out the last traces of paganism in that part of Syria. (At least, other saints were rewarded for fulfilling similar tasks—they were farmers thought to have been at odds with the dominant and more urbanized Orthodox Church of Byzantium, whose temporal rulers held sway throughout much of the Middle East.) The Byzantines looked askance at the Maronites and other schismatic Christian sects that flowered before the Islamic invasion in the seventh century. Where the Maronites originally came from is shrouded in the mist of history, but much of Syria was inhabited by Semitic peoples who had migrated from the same Arabian peninsula that later debouched the all-conquering followers of Mohammed. Maronite historians like to give the impression that the Maronites fled from the Orontes valley to escape Moslem persecution. Yet the evidence suggests that the Moslems initially—and for several centuries—were extremely tolerant toward the dissident Eastern Christians and that their main argument was with the Byzantine rulers in Constantinople. Legend has it that the Maronites danced to welcome the Arabs in the seventh century, so delighted were they to throw off the Byzantine yoke. In any event, at one point a peace was arranged between Byzantines and Moslems, and Constantinople reasserted control over much of the Orontes for the better part of a hundred years. It is for this period that no further documented mention of the Maronites in the Orontes valley can be found. And that has led to the assumption that the Byzantines once again had sought to bring the Maronites to heel. Suffice it to say that Abbot Yohanna Maron, who took the saint's name around the turn of the eighth century, is credited with having led the Maronites south to northern Lebanon, where they settled along the coast at Batroun and Byblos (Jubail). The Maronites were the only Christian sect to emerge after the Moslem conquest and the only one to use Arabic for church records from the very start. They appear to have had no serious problems with Islam until their collaboration with the Crusaders cast suspicions on their loyalty. The Maronites joined the Crusaders, it is sometimes advanced, because the latter were as opposed to the Byzantines as they were to the Moslems.

It was well into the fifteenth century when Mamluk persecution drove the Maronites from the lower hills along the coast to the inaccessible recesses of the Qadisha (holy) valley. To this day, the Qadisha remains their spiritual center. But Yohanna Maron, noting that the Byzantine see of Antioch was vacant, declared himself Patriarch of "Antioch and all the East." The assumption of the grandiloquent title was symptomatic of the Maronites' abiding high opinion of themselves and a tendency, shared with other Lebanese, to megalomania. "God is great, but who can compare with Saint Maron?"

Their historians over the centuries spun the Maronites a special role in Christendom. At one time or another, for example, they claimed that the Maronite Patriarch (who has in fact never exercised patriarchal power in Antioch or, for that matter, in "all the East") was the only legitimate successor of Saint Peter, founder of the Church of Antioch. This claim was advanced to buttress Maronite assertions of "perpetual orthodoxy" and seniority over Rome. (In fact, the Maronites were glossing over their belief in the Monothelete heresy, which holds that Christ has two natures so suffused as to produce one energy and one will—one of many doctrines condemned by either Rome or Byzantium in the early centuries of Christianity.) But in an act that set the pattern of Maronite policy lasting to modern times, within a year of the First Crusade's success in 1099 in seizing Jerusalem, the Maronite Patriarch dispatched a message of congratulation to the Pope. Thus began the Maronites' long relationship with the West, unequaled in the annals of other Eastern Christians. To this day, such major northern Maronite families as the Franjiehs and their rivals the Douaihis claim descent from Crusaders, pointing out that their names stand for the Franks, in the first case, and the French city of Douai, which contributed knights, in the second. A close friend of mine, a Maronite, remembers as a child studying a family tree that, her mother insisted, traced the family's lineage back to Godfrey of Bouillon, a Crusader leader.

The Maronites at first supplied the Crusaders with a unit of archers, who fought alongside their brothers in religion. Theirs was a natural decision. The Crusaders were in Tripoli and at other points along the Mediterranean coast. They were also anti-Byzantine. And the Maronites were impressed by their military prowess. But the Maronites eventually rebelled against the Crusaders, who punished them for helping the Moslems. The Crusaders called these renegades "men of the blood," and they were probably mountaineers, then as now a law unto themselves and suspicious of authority. Yet the Maronite Church, which throughout Maronite history played a key role, dispatched its Patriarch to Rome. In 1180 the historian William of Tyre recorded the Maronites' "wonderful change of heart" in returning to the papal fold and thus becoming the first Uniate church in the Middle East. (Despite Maronite disclaimers, the Monothelete heresy was quietly abandoned.) But the Maronites nonetheless extracted a price indicative of their independent ways. The Christian liturgy in Lebanon remained in

Syriac, not the Latin of Rome, and does so to this day. Nor did the Vatican insist on ending the marriage of parish priests or the Maronite practice of housing monks and nuns in the same building. Rome was willing to accept such questionable usage and doubtful theology in return for the Maronites' recognition of its ultimate theological authority.

Eventually, the Crusades, which had set out to free Jerusalem and the Eastern Christians from Islam, ended up with all the native Christians under the control of more vindictive Moslems, who imposed restrictions on them. The local Christians' desperate belief that the Mongols would provide lasting freedom and the separate, independent political states that the Crusaders had promised was a tragic error of judgment, and it was to be repeated over the centuries, in different circumstances. Almost alone, the Maronites proved the exception to this rule. Their mountain fastness, their access to the Mediterranean, and their intelligence in maintaining links with the West stood them in good stead.

In recent centuries the Maronites' dominant philosophy has seen Lebanon as a Mediterranean country not on the western edge of the Arab and Moslem world but on the eastern edge of Christendom. Yet history records that even before the Crusaders were driven out, the Maronites had turned against them and indirectly ensured the victory of the Moslem Mamluks who captured Tripoli in 1289. Hardened by the Crusaders' own brutality and fanaticism, the Mamluks, who were Sunni Moslems, persecuted both the Orthodox Christians and the minority Shia sect of Islam. But no historical record of persecution of the Maronites at that time has come to light. Indeed, the Maronites quickly ingratiated themselves with the conquerors, entering into tax-farming arrangements and generally maintaining law and order in return for being allowed to keep their own ways. The first recorded persecution of the Maronites at Moslem hands took place after the Crusader sack of Alexandria, when they, along with other Christians, were punished. The Maronite Patriarch Gabriel was burned at the stake in Tripoli, apparently after being falsely accused of adultery by fellow Maronite clergymen.

For the next several hundred years the Maronite community remained weak, disorganized, and torn by factionalism. Contact with Rome was at best occasional. Franciscans, charged by the papacy with keeping track of Eastern Christians, were intermittently active. Nonetheless, some Maronite historians have written that the amirs, rulers of Mount Lebanon, were Maronites from the very earliest times. Such claims in fact reflect yet another example of a latter-day desire to play down the Maronites' Arab origins and their subservience first to their Sunni and later their Druze masters. The record shows that the Maronites' emergence as a major factor in Lebanon was tied to their relationship with the Druzes, which evolved in the sixteenth century. The Druzes are a heretical Moslem sect founded in the late tenth century by the Caliph Hakim of the Shia dynasty of the Fatimids in Egypt. They were driven out of Egypt and attracted to Lebanon for the same reasons as the Maronites and the Shia: the Mountain provided a refuge for dissidents. The Shia and the Druzes, even more than the Maronites, had good reason to fear the Sunni rulers, who were more intolerant toward Moslem heretics than were Christians of any sect. For the Koran accepted Christians and Jews as "people of the book" and precursors of the Prophet, but it effectively brooked no successors to him. Hakim's followers believe he is not dead, but will reappear. In common with the Ismaelis, another Shia sect, the Druzes believe in emanations of the Deity and transmigration of the soul. Highly disciplined and renowned for their military prowess, the Druzes do not proselytize and only a minority are initiated into the mysteries of their beliefs. Throughout most of their history, especially in their early dealings with their sometimes zealous Maronite vassals, the Druzes have displayed a tolerance toward other religions that is scarcely characteristic of the cradle of revealed religion and fanaticism that is the Middle East. Along with some other minority Moslem sects, they practice *taqiyya*, which authorizes concealment of their beliefs to outsiders. "Bow down to every nation which passes over you," enjoined one of the sect's founders, "but remember me in your heart." That was a lesson not lost on others.

Maronite relations with Rome were resumed in 1439. By 1515 Pope Leo X in a bull praised the Maronites, who, despite persecution and other difficulties, and "placed among infidels, as in a field of error, the Almighty has deigned to keep the faithful servants as a rose among thorns." The Pope also commended the Maronites for opposing not just the Moslems but also "schismatics" (as the Orthodox were called) and "heretics" (in the form of the Jacobites, who were trying to nibble away at the Mount Lebanon faithful). Within a generation of the Ottoman conquest of Lebanon, François I of France and Suleiman the Magnificent of the Sublime Porte in 1536 signed the first "capitulation," providing French protection in the Ottoman Empire for both European and Asian Christians. Maronite historians make much of this first connection, made directly with the French crown rather than through the Vatican. But the realities of geography and travel in fact provided little succor. Both Paris and Constantinople were very far away from Lebanon. Half a century later, in 1584, a Maronite college opened in Rome to educate clergymen. Still, the Maronites lived in a state of isolation, without social or political influence in the life of Mount Lebanon. The patriarchs were so hounded—at times by their fellow Maronites—that they were forced to flee their see at Qannoubin, in the Qadisha valley, and hide in caves. Indeed, two patriarchs sought refuge from Maronite adversaries with Druze amirs in south Lebanon.

A century later, the Maronites launched an extraordinary expansionary drive with the blessing of the Druze Amir Fakhreddine. Impressed by the hardworking, docile sense of organization inculcated by the Church, the Amir encouraged the Maronites to leave their mountain fastness in the north. He counted on their activities to swell his tax coffers. The Maronites moved south into the Kesrawan, previously held by Shia Moslems, who were expelled eventually and pushed into the Beqaa valley. The Maronites also moved in large numbers into Druze districts farther south. Under the leadership of their priests and monks, the Maronites founded monasteries, cleared the valleys of stones, and terraced the land. It was during this period that the Maronite Church began to acquire land. Great tracts were offered as an enticement to move south, and ownership was promised in return for developing land for ten years. By the early eighteenth century, the Kesrawan was virtually all Maronite, and the Maronite Church had become the largest, most organized, and wealthiest institution in Mount Lebanon. By the mid-nineteenth century, the Church and the monastic orders were credited with owning a quarter or even a third of the land in Mount Lebanon, depending on the estimate. The drive south provided an outlet for the landless peasantry. Without the Church—and especially the monks, who did much of the pioneering—they might not have mustered the capital and techniques required by such homesteading. It was a method that Zionists applied in their own quasi-military expansion in the late nineteenth and early twentieth centuries in Palestine.

The secret of the Maronite Church's success was a hierarchical system leading from the humblest monk to the Pope in Rome. Syriac ceased to be the church language—except in the liturgy—as monks found Arabic an easier vehicle for communication with their illiterate peasant charges.

In the seventeenth and eighteenth centuries, the Maronites grew ever stronger—and were encouraged to push south along what is today the Beirut–Damascus road, in the center of the country, to the Shuf and then Djezzine and then even farther south along the present Lebanese-Israeli border. The belt of Maronite and other Christian villages effectively surrounded the Druze population concentrations massed in the Shuf and nearer Beirut in Baabda and Aley. Mount Lebanon, which the Maronites increasingly came to look upon as their national home, remained the impregnable fortress into which they felt they could retreat if threatened. As recently as the second half of the nineteenth century, Maronites discouraged construction of a paved highway between Beirut and Damascus for fear that Turkish troops could more easily penetrate their domain.

So influential did the Maronites become that the ruler of the Chehab dynasty, a nominal Druze, found it politic to convert to Christianity in 1756. But he kept his conversion secret in order to preserve domestic tranquillity, a practice increasingly resented by the Maronites. By the nineteenth century they were demanding that the Chehabs admit their Christianity in public as recognition of the Maronites' growing power. Finally, the Druze overlords awakened to the dangers represented by the Maronites, who, led by the clergy, were demanding political power commensurate with their greater numbers and wealth. A series of upheavals starting in 1820, and repeated in 1840 and 1860 with increasing ferocity, destroyed the balance of the two previous centuries between Druzes and Maronites. The new Maronite mood was once again underlined by their historians, who played down the Druze period in favor of the hazy myths of Phoenicia and anything pre-Islamic.

Whatever Lebanon's previous problems had been, the new ones were more terrible, and their legacy continues to bedevil the country today. Those two decades of mid-nineteenth-century civil war introduced religious strife and brought the country to almost total ruin. The Lebanese, who had enjoyed de facto autonomy from the Ottoman sultans, now proved incapable of settling their own political differences. In what was to prove a lasting pattern, with ever more damaging effects, the Lebanese were cast—and saw themselves—as impotent victims of international rivalry. Not for the last time were the Lebanese to use outside interference as a justification for their own unwillingness to come to grips with political problems before foreign meddling became inevitable. Thus did the Ottomans and various other foreign powers intervene in Lebanon's affairs, backing one or another religious community as a means of furthering national ambitions. The Turks hoped to end the Mountain's virtual autonomy by stirring up latent religious antagonisms. The Lebanese came to count on foreign consuls in Beirut for help, a tradition still very much alive today, as political parties and chieftains shamelessly seek armaments and financing from Arab and other outside powers. Starting in the 1840s, the French openly aided the Maronites, the British helped the Druzes, the Russians posed as protectors of the Orthodox, and the Austrians and Prussians disputed France's right to sponsor the Maronites and other Uniate Catholics. So disgusted was one Maronite nationalist that he scathingly suggested a cup of coffee spilled in Lebanon could cause trouble between Paris and London.

At stake for the Ottomans was their determination to reassert direct control over the Mountain, in which for centuries the taxes had been farmed out. The Europeans all had their own axes to grind. The Russians wanted to finish off the Ottomans by detaching their Asian possessions. Britain defended the status quo in protecting the Ottomans and preventing continental rivals from gaining advantage. France was often of two minds—torn between its traditional role as protector of the Eastern Christians, and more especially of the Maronites, and its desire to keep the Ottomans alive as a counterweight to Austria, Prussia, and Russia. A disabused Ottoman governor was reduced to denouncing the various French missionaries as "the Pope's light, irregular cavalry established in Lebanon who under the garb of priests were, in fact, political agents and disturbers of the public peace."

A long period of instability began with the downfall of Amir Bashir II, who ruled from 1788 to 1840. Reluctantly supported by Bashir and backed by France, Ibrahim Pasha of Egypt had occupied Syria and

Lebanon for eight years and threatened to overthrow the Ottomans. To avoid just such an eventuality, Britain landed arms and Turkish troops. Ibrahim Pasha retired to Egypt. But Bashir was forced to leave Lebanon. To this day (along with Fakhreddine, two centuries earlier) Bashir remains about the only Lebanese approaching the status of national hero, at least for the Christians. He was not above strangling, blinding, ruining, and otherwise disgracing those who stood in his way, whether they were Druze aristocrats or plebeian Maronite advisers. Violence in itself has never worried the Lebanese—if it has a point (which is not always the case). In the Orient, violence to prevent further violence was and is commonplace. What struck the European liberals of Bashir's day as subjugation to despotism was accepted as the price gladly paid for physical protection. A jaundiced British resident, David Urquhart, remarked in 1857 about the Lebanese penchant for violence, "If the work ceases for a time suddenly it recurs without apparent cause, as if springing from a periodical necessity giving to the annals of the country a harmonious march of atrocity: no season lacking its expelled prince, its stabbed rival, its ravished district." As the 1975–76 civil war proved, modern methods simply multiplied this basic phenomenon geometrically. Ruining a rival, helping oneself to the spoils, and gobbling up his political clientele belonged to methods as old as Oriental society. Bashir was only acting in keeping with the code of his society. His present-day, would-be apostolic successors have copied his technique without achieving his success.

Fueling the violence were tensions in Lebanese society caused by land and population pressures. Moreover, the Christians had waxed rich in Bashir's final years, encouraged by Ibrahim Pasha, who sought European support for his expansionism. As so often has been the fate of minorities throughout history, the Christians' sudden good fortune awakened envy and hatred. A mindlessly provocative penchant for lavish displays of riches and a refusal to understand the inequity and dangers inherent in an uneven distribution of wealth remain as true among them today as in the past. Colonel Charles Churchill, an Englishman who lived among the Druzes from 1842 to 1852, left a damning account of Maronite insouciance in the Shuf town of Deir el Qamar, where Bashir had driven the Druze aristocracy into exile. "Its merchants," Churchill noted, "built spacious houses with marble courts and fountains and furnished in a style of costly luxury. All the Druze landed property passed into their hands. They finally attained a position of wealth and cupidity of their feudal superiors ... Their leading men amassed riches, they kept studs, their wives and daughters were apparelled in silks and satins and blazed with jewellery, gold and pearls and diamonds ... The few Druzes who still inhabited the town were reduced to insignificance as hewers of wood and drawers of water." With Bashir's disgrace, the Druze feudal notables returned from exile and reclaimed their due.

Nor were the Druze-Maronite problems the only strain in Mount Lebanon. By 1858 Maronite peasants in the Kesrawan, egged on by ambitious clergymen, were in revolt against their Maronite tax-farming feudal lords. The Turks looked on without interfering. Better disciplined, the Druze peasantry did not follow their Maronite counterparts' example, and instead, together with their Druze masters, prepared for the inevitable armed showdown with the Maronites. The fighting began in May 1860. Druze discipline carried the day against the Maronites, whose squabbling dissipated their advantage in numbers and armament. Before the fighting was over, in little over a month more than twelve thousand Christians were killed in the Druze areas, four thousand more died in destitution, one hundred thousand were homeless in Lebanon. In Syria the Lebanese example prompted the slaughter of some fifty-five hundred Christians in Damascus. In both countries the Turkish garrisons did nothing to stop the massacres and in some cases actually encouraged them. Perhaps the greatest shock to the Maronites was the patent Sunni and Shia Moslem backing for the Druzes. Although the Maronites had themselves at least partly to blame for setting off the hostilities—and then complicating their plight by failing to come to one another's aid—that is not the lesson they remember from the events of 1860. Rather, those events have left them with a seemingly incurable trauma, as if they, who for so long had avoided major retribution, had chosen to concentrate in their collective conscience the memories of all Christian persecutions in the Middle East since the advent of Islam. Maronites, in fact, were not the only Christians to suffer in the massacres. Great numbers of Greek Catholics and Greek Orthodox were also slain. But only the Maronites had the organization, the sense of national purpose, the drive to make sure that 1860 would be remembered as a never-ending wrong.

Ironically, the Maronites emerged politically victorious from the conflict they so lamentably lost on the battlefield against the Druzes. With reluctant support from other European powers, France landed troops after the killing had stopped, and the Ottomans were obliged to accept a special autonomous province in Maronite-dominated Mount Lebanon, overseen by six European powers and run by a non-Lebanese Christian subject of the empire, aided by an elected administrative council. Never had the Maronites been closer to their goal of a state of their own.

Thus, inaugurated in the 1840s, was consecrated a scheme whereby political power was based on the millet system. Under the Ottomans, and even before, the various minorities, or millets, were run by their respective religious leaders, who were held accountable for their coreligionists' behavior. Politically, representation was decided as a function of the communities' relative numerical importance. In Lebanon that eventually came to mean representation for the country's sixteen officially recognized communities, although the exact weighting was increasingly disputed after the last census was conducted in 1932. Socially, every Lebanese was forced to adhere to one religion or faith whether believer, atheist, or agnostic. Civil marriage—or divorce—did not exist. Maronites forbidden divorce under their canon law were forced to convert to the Greek Orthodox rite if they wished to divorce and remarry. Civil-service appointments also came to be fixed "temporarily" in accordance with these religiously based quotas. The system proved a major irritant and a cause of Lebanon's final collapse, as key jobs were reserved for Maronites and, to a lesser degree, Sunnites. Since no one dared hold a new census, which doubtless would confirm Lebanon's growing Moslem majority, Moslems agitated more and more fiercely against the system's political implications while holding fast to its personal-status aspects in keeping with Islam.

If the millet system allowed Christians and Jews to maintain something of their communal life—and become a major factor in trade, finance, and various crafts—it also ensured that the communities never really mingled. Indeed, they looked upon each other with suspicion and contempt. Under the Ottomans, only the Sunnis displayed any self-confidence and self-respect—they identified with the universal nature and political power of the Sunni Sultan, himself the Caliph, or keeper of the faith. The other communities, deprived of power and responsibility, remained marginal. The rapacity and political myopia of Maronite-dominated Lebanon in the twentieth century have their roots, at least according to the Maronites' advocates, in a long-repressed desire to catch up and enjoy the fruits of power.

In any event, the five decades between 1860 and outbreak of World War I in 1914 have been sung by Lebanese and foreigners alike as Lebanon's golden age. Mount Lebanon, now shorn of Beirut, Tripoli, Sidon, as well as the Beqaa, prospered as never before. For the American missionary Henry H. Jessup, writing shortly after the turn of the century, Lebanon had become "the best governed, the most prosperous, peaceful and contented country in the Near East." Philip Hitti, a Lebanese-born American historian, insisted that "within the brief span of half a century it practically evolved from medievalism to modernism." Hitti was writing decades before the Lebanon he knew was swept away, in no small part because of differing appreciations of "modernism." For him, and for many Christians even today, modernism was and is synonymous with Westernization, itself not yet the object of suspicion in the Middle East. Indeed, Westernization still remains identified in some Lebanese minds with a universal model to be applied without harm—and indeed with guaranteed beneficial results—whether in science and technology or in politics. In the late nineteenth century, Christians had no qualms about accepting the West, its secular knowledge and methods. Westerners were fellow Christians who championed and protected their Eastern brothers. But for Lebanese Moslems—even educated Moslems—Westernization meant questioning one's innermost beliefs, starting with the traditional Islamic system that allows no divorce between religion and government. Westernization thus was a source of conflict. So much of the Lebanese success story in this century was a Christian success story, or at any rate it turned on the innate assumption of Christian superiority, encouraged by the West's own scarcely hidden contempt for the Orient. Lebanese Christians delved into history, linguistics, and science, and, in what is known as the "Arab literary revival," helped to rescue the Arabic language from stagnation. Thanks to a head start in education, which began in the 1830s with the arrival of American Protestant and French Catholic missionaries, the Christians put to good practical use their close commercial, cultural, and politicial links with Europe and the Americas.

By the end of the nineteenth century, Lebanon had far outdistanced the rest of the Ottoman Empire in popular education, almost all of which was run by local churches or foreign missionaries. Protestants founded the Syrian Protestant College—now called the American University of Beirut—in 1866. Nine years later, French Jesuits started the Université Saint Joseph, in a crosstown rivalry that eventually caused both institutions to stand accused by Arab nationalists of cultural alienation. (At least the Catholic-Protestant rivalry subsided after the late 1820s, when American missionaries briefly abandoned Lebanon after the Maronite Patriarch declared contact with the Protestants anathema and allowed a Lebanese convert to die in one of his prison cells to prove his point.) So widespread was printing that in the final quarter of the last century Beirut boasted forty periodicals—including fifteen newspapers. At the same time, Christians started emigrating to the Americas, Egypt, and the Sudan to seek their fortune. From 1900 to 1914, one hundred thousand Lebanese, mostly Christians, left Mount Lebanon, abandoning entire villages as relatives joined trailblazing émigrés. In Egypt, educated Lebanese became journalists, doctors, and businessmen, or worked in the civil service, where the British preferred them to native Egyptians. Remittances, which the émigrés sent back to their families, are estimated to have represented 41 percent of the Mountain's total income on the eve of World War I.

Nor was this Arab awakening without political ramifications. Lebanese intellectuals—again, mostly Christians—toyed with various ways of achieving their goal of political independence. European nationalism provided two models. One was out-and-out independence for the Maronites, who more and more thought of themselves as a nation. The other took European nationalism—especially its anticlerical aspects—and transmogrified it into Arab nationalism. In such thinking, Arab nationalism was basically an anti-Turkish vehicle into which religion—that is, Islam—would be sufficiently submerged to allow Lebanon's Christians to join with their Moslem Arab brothers and find a way out of their perpetual predicament as a religious minority.

At the same time, however, the Turks, desperately trying to strengthen central control—or to "conquer their empire," as it was said—wanted to end the autonomy and protected status of Mount Lebanon. The Young Turk revolution of 1908, with its glorification of all things Turk, irritated the Arabs and heightened Moslem interest in Arab nationalism. But perversely, as has been true before and since, Moslem interest in any political scheme sufficed to reawaken Christian fears of being drowned in the Islamic sea.

Indeed, it was the Christian desire to square that particular circle and mitigate such fears that buttressed intellectually various twentieth-century political doctrines in the Middle East. Many Christians hold important positions in leftist parties in Lebanon and throughout the Arab world. The Lebanese Communist Party, oldest in the Arab world, apart from the Palestinian Party which grouped both Arabs and Jews, was founded in 1924 in Bikfaya (also the hometown of the Phalangist Gemayel clan, at the other end of the political spectrum). In 1934, Antun Saadé, a Greek Orthodox Lebanese born in South America, founded the Syrian People's Party (SPP), dedicated to reuniting Lebanon, Syria, Jordan, Iraq (and, curiously, Cyprus, but not Egypt) in a single Syrian nation. In the 1940s, Michel Aflak, a Christian educated in Paris, elaborated the doctrine of the Baath, or Renaissance, Party, whose rival wings today uneasily run the hostile regimes in Iraq and Syria and pay lip service to him as the fountainhead. Whatever separated these doctrines, they all shared a lay approach to politics. So, too, did the late Gamal Abdel Nasser's Egyptian brand of Arab nationalism, which fell from grace during Israel's 1967 blitzkrieg and gave way to the Islamic revival of the 1970s.

But at the turn of the century, the dominant theme of Maronite thinking was narrowly sectarian and put its faith in the ancient ties with France. It all seemed so natural. French and native Christian capitalists led the way in developing Mount Lebanon's greatest money-spinner, the ancient silk-making culture, which was now modernized with silk-reeling factories dotting the mountainside. The modernization of the rudimentary port of Beirut was entrusted to a French firm, and entrepôt trade with the Arab hinterland increased, thanks to a French-built road and a cog railway to Damascus. Beirut grew from a village of eight thousand in the 1820s to twenty-seven thousand in 1845, forty-six thousand in 1860, and one hundred thirty thousand in 1914. So Francophile were the Maronites that their children routinely recited, "*Inna faransa immana hanuna*" ("Truly, France is our benevolent mother"). Among the educated, French was spoken in preference to Arabic. France, the French language, and French culture were for the Maronites a form of identification, a way to demonstrate once again their divorce from the Arabs and from Islam. In theory a knowledge of Arabic was compulsory for secondary-school graduation in the official Lebanese curriculum. But only in the past generation has the curriculum been made compulsory for all schools, especially the private institutions catering to the Christians. I know many upper-class Maronite women who were allowed to skip the requirement. During the

1975–76 fighting, less-well-educated Maronites took to speaking French while the upper classes dusted off their often shaky notions of Arabic to show their solidarity with the young men from the mountains and working-class suburbs doing the actual shooting.

From the very start, Maronite Francophilia was of a very special kind, dictated totally by Maronite desires. Rarely were French policy problems taken into consideration. In their single-minded view, France's own policy in the Middle East should be aimed at securing them an independent national home. Rarely did it cross the Maronite mind that the French interest in propping up the Ottomans to offset growing German and Russian power in Europe scarcely justified the potentially fatal surgery implicit in bringing about the Maronites' dream. As early as 1863 a French naval officer named de Chaillé took the measure of the Maronites and their Patriarch. He wrote that they "have no desire other than to be governed as in the past: they have ancient privileges which they owe to the protection of France and it is the concern of France only to preserve these for them . . . of the new trends, of the needs of our age . . . he [the Patriarch] refuses to understand anything, appreciate anything or even hear anything." At about the same time, Daud Pasha, the Armenian Catholic who was the first Ottoman governor of the Mutassiriffaya, as the Mount Lebanon entity was called, worried about the Maronites' intransigent behavior. They were defying his authority. "I am an experiment," he wrote in justifying his refusal to use his troops to shoot disobedient Maronites; and were he to satisfy a longing for martyrdom, "it is the fate of six million Christians [in the empire] that I would jeopardize." By 1910 René Ristelhueber, French chargé d'affaires in Beirut, had become so annoyed with the Maronites' "growing pretensions" that he wrote to his Foreign Ministry that he would welcome anything that would "remind them of the respect due authority." On the eve of World War I, the French consul general complained that "the feeling of devotion to this little nation does not exist among Lebanese officials, and every one of them is always ready, according to a well-known expression, to set his country on fire to light his cigaret."

However exaggerated their behavior may have struck these foreigners (and laudatory testimony about the Maronites also abounded) the Lebanese Christians were guiltless in provoking the disaster that befell them in that global conflict—unless long-standing pro-French sympathies among the Maronites could be labeled culpable. Seizing on the war in Europe, which pitted Mount Lebanon's half-dozen guarantors against one another, the Turks abruptly ended its autonomous status and systematically starved its predominantly Maronite inhabitants, stationing troops in the Mountain and allowing no food or medicine in by land; the Allies blockaded Lebanon's ports to complete the hapless country's plight. No remittances from emigrants arrived to alleviate the suffering. Partly by design—to punish the Maronites for their Francophilia—and partly because of disorganization, a quarter of the Mountain's population (or an estimated one hundred thousand people) died of famine or attendant epidemics during the four war years. To this day, Maronite families can—and often do—trot out horror stories about starving children and old people reduced to eating roots and grass in the fields. For years after the famine, peasants planted wheat in among the vines to ensure that their families would have enough to eat. Deserted villages of that period are still visible in Kesrawan.

World War I ended in 1918 with the demise of the Ottoman Empire, and with General Allenby's British troops—aided by a symbolic French detachment—in charge of a Beirut briefly festooned with the Arab flags of the Hashemite rulers of the Hejaz. The confusion of authority was the direct result of Allied wartime double-dealing. To enlist the Hashemites' help against their nominal Turkish suzerains, Britain had promised them control of the Arab provinces of the Ottoman Empire. But France and Britain in the Sykes-Picot agreement had carved up the same provinces between themselves, eventually disguising their duplicity in the form of mandates approved by the League of Nations they in turn dominated. Lebanon and Syria—the Levant States, as they were then called—were assigned to France. And the French made it no secret that they had come primarily to protect their Maronite friends and uphold their interests. When Faisal, the self-proclaimed Hashemite King of Syria, refused to knuckle under, the French, under the militantly Christian General Henri Gouraud, defeated his Arab army at Maisaloun in the Anti-Lebanon Mountains in July 1920. With the recent famine partly in mind, Gouraud created Greater Lebanon by adding to the Mountain the port cities of Beirut, Sidon, and Tripoli, and the fertile lands of the Beqaa valley and the south and north. The idea was to make Lebanon self-sufficient, but the predominantly Moslem population of those added-on areas felt cheated—

especially the Sunnis, who never totally abandoned their pan-Arab yearnings to become part of Syria.

A more dangerous harbinger of future tension was that iron law of underdeveloped societies that, in Lebanon's case, dictated that the generally poorer, less educated Moslems were outbreeding the Christians. The Christians were also emigrating in large numbers, further eroding their only marginal population edge and the foundation of their demographic claims to national leadership in a system of parliamentary democracy. The underpinning of the Lebanese state under the French and since independence in 1943 reposed on accepting the Maronites as the largest single community, representing nearly 30 percent of the total population. That assumption—increasingly questionable in the absence of a new census sure to confirm the Moslem majority—in turn buttressed Maronite "ownership" of the presidency of the Republic, the armed forces command, and other key offices. That had been the Maronites' price in 1943 for agreeing to the unwritten National Covenant, whereby they abandoned formal Western (French) protection and agreed that Lebanon should have an "Arab side." The Sunnis, in turn, abandoned their dream of becoming part of Greater Syria or of including Lebanon in any other predominantly Moslem pan-Arab entity. To complete the modern form of the millet system, the National Covenant gave the Sunnis the Prime Minister's office, the Shia that of speaker of parliament, and distributed less-august offices to the smaller communities. All public offices, including seats in parliament, respected the rule that there should be six Christians to every five Moslems. The late Georges Naccache, an enlightened Maronite who for years published in Beirut the French-language newspaper *L'Orient,* had few illusions about the system incarnated by the National Covenant. "Two negations do not make a nation," he warned. As for Lebanon's parliament—considered by official publicists as something akin to the ninth wonder of the world, given the Arab penchant for military dictatorships—Naccache dismissively wrote it off as "an arrogant alliance of money and the feudal system." (Later he was sentenced to six months in jail for describing Christian-Moslem tensions as involving a game between "two fifth columns.")

From the very start of the French League of Nations mandate, Christians—and especially Maronites—had had trouble making up their minds what they were going to do. For the first time in more than a millennium, Eastern Christians were in charge of a state—and thanks to Western Christians. It was as if the Crusades had gone right instead of wrong. Yet the Maronites, so inventive and ingenious while campaigning tirelessly for the realization of their dreams, proved devoid of imagination once in power. They could never forget their trauma, never (except during the presidential term of General Fuad Chehab in 1958–64) understand the need to keep the other communities happy. Sheikh Pierre Gemayel at one point put his finger on the real problem. "The Christian psychosis of fear is internalized, visceral, and tenacious. We can do nothing about it," he argued. "It is the Moslems' task to reassure us."

French education over a century had helped lure the Maronites out of the Mountain, turning them from narrow villagers into city dwellers, especially in Beirut, which with its suburbs accounted for half of Lebanon's population. Yet education was so Church-dominated that it did little to encourage understanding or cooperation among communities. Literacy, urbanization, and exposure to other communities failed to secularize many of these transplanted Maronite mountaineers. Indeed, among their uprooted ranks there developed the inward-looking school of "Lebanese" thinking, which competed with the "Arab" branch that argued that salvation—and prosperity—lay not in the narrow confines of village ways but in an opening on the world, especially the Arab world, where trade, jobs, and political respectability could be found. As often as not, the two schools warred within the same person, or certainly within the same family. During the civil war of 1975–76, for example, in an upper-class Maronite family with whom I often lunched, among the children—all adults—opinions expressed at the dining-room table ranged from full support for the Palestinians and their leftist Lebanese allies to equally vehement backing for right-wing Maronite militias, with the parents trying to hold the family together. To me it was as if the debate that should have been resolved somewhere between 1920 and 1970 were taking place at last, but violence would now provide the answers so long delayed. What the Maronites seem never to have grasped is that in a land shot through with the accumulated paranoia of so many minorities, legitimacy requires sharing power and privilege. If the Sunnis or any other community felt shortchanged, then rationally it was up to the Maronites, who were running the show, to make it worthwhile to keep the doubters believing that Lebanon as a state could satisfy their demands.

Part of the answer lay in the wooden sculpture, and its lesson about dominating or being dominated. But how were the Maronites to proceed in a democracy with its implied "one-man, one-vote" system, when they refused a new census? Or when they argued that the Christians had to keep the reins of power because they paid 80 percent of the taxes? (Not that anyone of any persuasion did so when a way to cheat could be found.) Or that the emigrants, predominantly Christian, should be given political rights, since Christians were entitled to run at least one country in the Middle East? The Lebanese Christians alone enjoyed what seven million other Christians in the Middle East could only yearn for—security and geographical and political unity. So publicly the Maronites kept on pretending that Christians were still a majority in Lebanon, while in private they acted like the minority they had become.

The inward-looking "Lebanese" Maronites eventually won out against the "Arab" Maronites, thanks to the gradual decline of Arab nationalism. Its great standard-bearer, Nasser, died in 1970, his reputation never having recovered from the Israelis' blitzkrieg victory against the Arabs in 1967. The Palestinians came to the fore after the disaster, and were pushing Lebanese Moslems' demands for greater political power. Any threat, any questioning of Christian prerogatives—tax reform, more and better schools—any change in the established order was met with a conditioned reflex as predictable as that of Pavlov's dogs. Years before, during my first trip to Israel, Uri Avneri, the maverick politician and magazine publisher, explained to me the then–Prime Minister Golda Meir's secret of political success. "She's basically illiterate in half a dozen languages," Avneri said, "but she rarely has to conduct a reasoned defense of her policies. All she has to do to win is push the Holocaust button. One allusion to Auschwitz, and she retires the side." So, too, with the militant Maronites. Lebanon's latter-day millet system provided the Maronites with an easy way of deflecting criticism away from themselves and toward another religious group—"the others." The real problems—economic, social, political—never got discussed. Change was thwarted. And when the fighting started in 1975, one reason the violence was so unremitting was that the Maronites and all the others persuaded themselves that they were totally without sin, and transferred to the enemy *en bloc* responsibility for looting, mutilations, and other excesses they themselves had committed.

Even before the civil war any suggestion that all was not well with their stewardship was turned by Maronite leaders into an attack on the Maronites as a community, as Christians. The atavistic persecution mania automatically blocked consideration of any grievances. Although the phenomenon was part and parcel of all Maronites, their militant enemies—often led by left-wing Christians—displayed a criminal ignorance of the confessional mechanism. One of the greatest errors of the civil war was the Left's blind shelling of Christian East Beirut and its efforts to isolate the Phalange politically. Such terror tactics and political maneuvering only strengthened the Phalangists, who became the unquestioned symbol not just of Maronites but of all embattled Christendom as they picked up support from other quarters usually suspicious of their political outlook.

In between early rounds of fighting, in June 1975, I argued with Karim Pakradouni, a member of the Phalangist Politburo. Didn't he see the country was being destroyed? When would the Lebanese come to their senses?

"In September," he said.

Why wait? Every day was important, I insisted.

He laughed. "Violence," he explained, "is good for us and good for the Left. It polarizes public opinion. But with elections next spring, everyone needs six months of calm." (Needless to say, the elections never took place that spring or any subsequent spring.)

In any case, Maronite presidents displayed little trust in the existence of the state. Only Fuad Chehab, a former army commander who was President from 1958 to 1964, even conceived that the Maronites' best chance of staying in power lay in strengthening the state. Rather, it was as if most of the presidents failed to appreciate the jewels the French had entrusted to them in 1943. Suspicion of the state and all its works, an enduring aspect of Lebanese life that the "sons-of-Phoenicia" school do not stress, left power in the various communities—and thus in the hands of the communities' leaders. Ghassan Tueni, the wordsmith publisher of the newspaper *An Nahar*, once noted that in Lebanon "the government does not exist, and whatever part of it does exist has no authority, and whoever has authority is not in the government." Even the Maronite leader Raymond Eddé argued in favor of a United Nations–protected, neutral Lebanon, without recognizing that Switzerland and Sweden maintain costly defense establishments to have their neutrality respected. The Lebanese Army was kept deliberately small and underarmed. That way, the Lebanese saved money and saved themselves, they argued, from the Arab penchant for military takeovers. And kept the Israeli wolf from the door even at the price of agreeing to ground their half-dozen Mirage fighters when the Jewish state took umbrage. It was that kind of penny-wise, pound-foolish thinking that also encouraged Lebanon's much-vaunted economic liberalism, which at times looked more like robber-baron capitalism. Grievances accumulated. Tepid reforms were voted but rarely carried out.

In the civil war, the Christians found it convenient to blame the Palestinians for all of Lebanon's problems. No one argued the Palestinians were guiltless. They were the antithesis of the revolutionary fish that Mao Tse-tung enjoined his men to be, swimming in the mass of the people. The Palestinians tended to become arrogant and contemptuous of the Lebanese and of the country, which they treated as if they were simply passing through like so many marauders. Their failings were both great and small. They didn't pay for electricity or for telephone service. They had too much money and too many guns. They couldn't maintain law and order in the territory they were supposed to control. By the mid-1970s, many well-disposed Lebanese Christians had stopped sympathizing with the Palestinians, much less championing their cause. In time they were to be held responsible by their erstwhile Moslem allies in equally blanket terms. But the facts were that Lebanon itself was sick, quite sick enough to trap itself in war. Lebanon was sick from not paying taxes (a prewar estimate suggested that two-thirds went uncollected), sick from its corruption (the unfinished coastal expressway was a constant scandal). But Lebanon was especially sick because the system could no longer provide the faith required to keep people hoping, to keep them in line. At times, it seemed, the old bosses never did really think Lebanon could work and were hell-bent on making as much money as possible while the illusion lasted that it could. For when you got down to it, *was* Lebanon really ever a country, much less a parliamentary democracy? The odd thing was that the Lebanon born in 1943—or in 1920—had lasted so long.

The "family portrait" photograph of independent Lebanon's first government told the story. Many of its members were still active a generation later, when the civil war began. The youngest were in their seventies. Something was very wrong about a system that so steadfastly discouraged the best and the brightest—and God knows there's never been a dearth of smart Lebanese—from getting anywhere in politics. Except for the brief Chehab period, both the politicians and the upper-middle class discouraged their own children—and those in less-fortunate circumstances—from entering government service if they had done well in universities in Lebanon or overseas. Working for the government tended to be the lot of those who failed to become doctors, lawyers, businessmen. Ambitious fathers routinely told their civic-minded children, "I didn't scrimp to send you to university so that you could disgrace me." At times Lebanon seemed like a discarded interlude from García Márquez's epic description of Third World political underdevelopment, *The Autumn of the Patriarch*, in which a Central American dictator lives for hundreds of years.

Step by step, Lebanon was falling apart. No one wanted to notice. For some, the end began to become visible on December 28, 1968, when the Israelis destroyed thirteen airliners of Lebanon's Middle East Airlines at Beirut airport without any interference from the Lebanese Army. Others looked back to President Nasser's death in September 1970, when traffic in and out of West Beirut was paralyzed by gangs of young armed men in an extravaganza of bullets and burning tires that passed for official mourning on the Moslem side of the city. That kind of mindless violence came to be the rule five years later. If you didn't know the background, it was easy enough to sympathize with the Lebanese, who blamed the foreigners for both interfering and not interfering enough. For in each camp there were good foreigners and bad foreigners, those who helped and those who should have helped but didn't. Foreigners did their share of turning the country into a killing ground to work out differences that they didn't dare contest on one another's home turf. No one was innocent. The Christians were justified in their anger when they were stopped by Palestinian guerrillas checking identity papers outside their camps, even if the Palestinians had reasons for being nervous. But the Levant breeds a kind of self-defeating short-term tactical view of life, in which a week can seem a long time. In theory, all the Arab countries agreed in principle that Lebanon's best contribution to the overall cause was political. But they seemed to delight in having the Palestinians bog down the tiny Lebanese Army, something they were careful not to let *their* Palestinians do to *their* armies. Yet, in the final analysis, the Lebanese themselves were at fault. Their very unwillingness to admit any responsibility for what happened may someday allow them to piece back together something of the life they once had, but in the meantime, their attitude is at best cynical, at worst psychotic in its implications. In the fall of 1981 I took part in a French television discussion about war reporting and was happily surprised when, in a film made to illustrate the program, a Moslem militiaman, all of sixteen years old, said, "We screwed up Lebanon, us and the Phalangists." He probably got into trouble with his betters for being so candid.

I've yet to hear a Maronite warlord say anything so straightforward. During the civil war, and for years thereafter, the Maronite leaders seemed to be writing off the Greater Lebanon that the French had fashioned for them, and retreating back to Mount Lebanon. I recall one sunny day in early January 1976, when I watched the port of Beirut burn. I had a good view from the promontory on which the highest magistrate in the land had built a graceful house overlooking the Mediterranean. I'd just risked my neck coming across from West Beirut on a particularly nasty day, and I mashed few words about what I thought of all Lebanese, Christian and Moslem, and their shared fascination with destruction. Why couldn't they stop before it was too late, before the Syrians and the Israelis stepped in and took the decision out of their hands for a good long time? It needed no genius to see what was bound to happen.

"Let it burn, let it burn," the magistrate said.

I stared at him. Speaking, I presumed, was the Maronite, not the judge. Was he writing off everything not within the purely Christian turf of what was beginning to be called "Marounistan," the Christian ghetto? Was he saying, "We built it and we'll destroy it"? Or had the Maronites somehow fallen under the spell of the "Masada complex" the Israelis keep talking about, which threatens emulation of those ancient Jews in their surrounded fortress who committed suicide rather than surrender to the Romans? Were they the loose cannon on the always pitching deck of the Middle East? Could, or would, the Maronites try to frustrate any Middle East peace settlement sometime in the future if it did not take into account their demands?

Years later I was talking to Fuad Ephrem Boustany, a somewhat pixieish historian and Maronite ideologist well into his seventies, and asked him what he thought the Maronites might do in such an eventuality.

"You should know that terrorism is not the monopoly of the Palestinians," Boustany said, explaining that he and other Maronite leaders had been talking about terrorism for years. "When we decide to become terrorists you and the entire world will know it," he added. "You don't know what a mountain people with six thousand years of history behind it is capable of doing when faced with the choice of suicide or fighting against the enemy."

The talk, meant to be cold and detached, reminded me of the French settlers in Algeria with their slogan, *la valise ou le cercueil.* They finally preferred the suitcase to the coffin and left Algeria, but not before indulging in a Westernized, technological demonstration of professional terrorism that shamed the artisanal methods of their Algerian nationalist adversaries. But here, in Lebanon, who was the enemy Boustany kept hammering away about? Foreigners certainly, starting for this Francophile with perfidious Albion, but including more recently the Palestinians and Syrians. Yet despite his self-satisfied lecture filled with simplification, despite the brilliant insights into Islam, he was glossing over the Lebanese dimension, the gnawing but repressed knowledge that the Lebanese had done much to undermine their own society by truckling to foreigners, including the foreigners they now decried.

Chronicled by Lebanese and foreigners alike over more than a century, the worst aspects of national character now took on exaggerated dimensions: nepotism, bribery, opportunism, petty rivalries in which cousins, sometimes even brothers, fought each other the better to slaughter the fatted calf at public expense. Indeed, so corrupt had the system become that virtually every politician was on the take from some foreign power, if not several. A Gulf oil state kept former Lebanese prime ministers on a kind of private retainer amounting to thousands of dollars a month. They might come in handy if returned to office. Radical Arab states helped their leftist and Palestinian friends. Islamic fundamentalists such as the Saudi Arabian monarchy bankrolled the Palestine Liberation Organization. (They'd also helped the Christians, until the Maronite massacres of Moslem civilians proved too much to stomach.) The guiding principle of these conservative Arabs placed politics above religion and saw in the Christians the only force capable of thwarting radical Arabs bent on overthrowing their vulnerable regimes. A generation earlier, Michel Chiha, a Christian thinker who did much to shape the institutional framework for an independent Lebanon, wrote that the Lebanese were "by vocation and necessity the friends of the masters of the world." Almost in the same breath he insisted, "We are not disposed to resign ourselves to the decline of Europe," not realizing that the Arabs were the new masters of what they considered to be legitimately part of the Arab world. The West, beholden to the same Arabs for oil and tiring of latter-day Crusades, was in no mood to dispute that reading. The Arabs—and everyone else, for that matter—took the Lebanese for granted, or what was perhaps worse, as a public convenience to be used and misused. Long before the Lebanese Moslems and the Palestinians began cooperating to squeeze what they saw as the Maronite state—the Moslems so as to extract political concessions, the Palestinians so as to acquire powerful local allies—the Lebanese had proved incapable of managing their country. The Lebanese talked about corruption, reform, the need for change. But they did nothing meaningful. Newspapers, pretty girls, guns, politicians—the whole lot was for sale. So war came to Lebanon.

A Maronite banker who resolutely refuses to live in Marounistan one day recited for me all the errors the warlords had committed. I suppose it made him feel better, although so many years had gone by that talking out problems had long since lost its attraction, even as psychotherapy. It all came down to political immaturity, that dread disease of underdeveloped societies. "It is not easy these days to be a Chilean, a Lebanese, a Kenyan," he lamented. In Lebanon's case it was probably the poisoned heritage of four hundred years of Ottoman rule. "Now we are once again but simple subjects belonging body and soul to the Sultan. But now there is the Sultan of Marounistan, the Sultan of Druzistan, the Sultan of Shiastan, the Sultan of Palestinistan, the Sultan of Sunnistan—I could go on, except that it depresses me," he said. "The Sultan is dead. Long live the Sultans."

But inside Marounistan the Maronites did not see it that way. Once derided as individualistic, effete, money-mad sybarites, they now demonstrated their ability to organize and sustain a war effort even if they had failed to keep their political heritage intact in peacetime. Bluff, fanaticism, megalomania—call it what you wish. They were so surprised when they did not collapse within the first weeks of fighting in 1975–76, so pleased that they finally had fought for what they wanted after having received their independence on a virtual silver platter. As the years wore on without the kind of solution they kept demanding, they came to invent motives for their enemies that were unprovable. When the Syrians gave them a good licking in Zahle in 1981, for example, they claimed that no defeat was involved, since they had thwarted Damascus in its hypothetical intention to occupy all Marounistan. (Despite Christian fears, in fact the Syrians never sought to occupy Marounistan on the ground, and indeed withdrew whatever troops it had there.) For years I have toyed with the notion that the Maronites' biggest drawback may be their gift for organization. Too much organization may prove counterproductive, preventing the Maronites from accepting the accommodation that a society of minorities requires to work out a new modus vivendi. Zeine Zeine, a respected, now-retired professor of history at the American University of Beirut, years ago invented a verb—*laflaflate* (derived from the Arabic word meaning to add on layers)—to describe how Lebanon used to muddle through. The war ended all that. Indeed, although many Maronites and other Christians would like to forget it, during the war they took to calling dogs Mohammed and referring to Moslems as *les muzz* or *les musiciens*. In theory, minorities in the Arab world would be well advised to mute their own feelings toward the majority in the hope that the majority would adopt a similar attitude toward them. In theory, it also would help if the minority eschewed provocations. But such is the division among Lebanese—even when they deny it—that it's doubtful the Maronite leaders realize that their discourse sounds condescending, even when they are convinced they are doing their best to induce dialogue. It's part of the ghetto heritage. The Maronite leadership pats itself on the back for ridding Marounistan of Palestinians and Syrians (and does not mention driving out the Moslems who once lived there). The Moslems should rise up and do what Marounistan did. There seems little realization that the Maronites have helped complicate the Moslems' problems by dumping East Beirut's unwanted Moslems, Kurds, Palestinians on them.

Indeed, many Lebanese living outside Marounistan think the Maronites there still have a tin ear, no matter how much they envy the law and order the Phalangists have imposed, in contrast with the anarchy and lack of security elsewhere in the country. But for Christians further afield—the Copts in Egypt, the Orthodox in Jordan or Syria, the various remnants scattered hither and yon—the Maronite tough talk is a comfort. In a Middle East dominated by zealots as varied as Ayatollah Ruhollah Khomeini in Iran and Prime Minister Menachem Begin in Israel, it is not entirely without merit to have Christians convinced of their own deadly certainties, especially those communities sufficiently distant to avoid the potentially disastrous practical consequences of such militancy.

At home in their Westernized ghetto, cut off from the Moslem majority, the Christians of Marounistan have become ever more persuaded of the justice of their cause. Muscling aside the state they had sworn to defend, robbing it of its revenues and humiliating its army, instituting military training for high-school boys in their purview, the ghetto Christians struck heroic poses and talked with great determination of "liberating" the rest of the country. Never mind that they had done so much to bring tragedy to Lebanon, that they refused any responsibility and kept pointing their fingers at others. Memory and consistency are not Middle Eastern qualities.

More than three years after the civil war, a maverick Greek Catholic bishop in Lebanon named Gregoire Haddad catalogued the changing views of the fighting with an irreverence that earlier had led to his being sidetracked by his ecclesiastical superiors. "The battle was between Palestinians and Lebanese, no, it is between Christians and Moslems. No, it is between Left and Right. No, it is between Israel and Palestinians on Lebanese soil. No, it is between International Imperialism and Zionism on the one hand and the neighboring states on the other." I never dared go back to see Haddad for fear I would find his list had grown even longer and sadder. In any case, his exercise was ample demonstration of the limits of reason. For beneath the image of Maronite truculence lay the legacy of fear. Christians love to recount for the benefit of foreigners their favorite story of the rooster and the psychiatric patient.

The patient is convinced that he is a grain of wheat in the barnyard and will be eaten by the rooster. The psychiatrist works with the man for a year and finally says, "Now, dear sir, you realize you are not a grain of wheat."

"Yes, doctor, but. . ."

"But what?"

"But does the rooster know?"

3. Things Fall Apart

F rom the airplane coming in low over Beirut on its landing approach, the spectacle was magnificent. The downtown commercial district was ablaze, great flames tingeing the billowing smoke against the night sky and clearly reflecting on the calm Mediterranean. In the three days I'd been away in Jordan, the war abruptly had produced this nightscape worthy of a Brueghel, a Bosch. Banished, at least for the moment, were the deadly but penny-ante battering of working- and lower-middle-class suburbs, the cometlike tails of rockets, the thud of mortar and artillery, the overnight ration of dumped, trussed bodies. Now in mid-September 1975, after five months of fitful fighting, the Green Line separating the two warring parts of Beirut was being replaced by a visible wasteland.

By the next morning yet another cease-fire of sorts was in force, and I drove down to take a closer look at the smoldering ruins of the suqs that lay just west of Martyrs' Square, so named to commemorate the hanging of sixteen Arab nationalists by the Turks during World War I.

Just off this traditional center of Beirut life, explosives had collapsed a cheap hotel for Egyptian workers, and dozens of people were trapped in the rubble. Three mannequins, the dresses they had advertised stolen along with everything else in a looted store, lay sprawled in the mud. Syrian firemen who had been rushed from Damascus to help fight the fires worked alongside their Beirut colleagues, now that the snipers had stopped shooting at them to prevent their efforts. Merchants were scurrying around, poking through what remained of their shops, loading merchandise into cars and trucks to be driven to the safety of the mountains. In four days of fighting, the Phalangists had succeeded in destroying that belt of mostly Moslem-owned shops dividing their eastern part of the city from the predominantly Moslem western sector.

In fact, what the Phalangists had destroyed was a neutral shopping area open to all comers. In their perverse calculations, the Phalangists had hoped to force the intervention on their side of the Lebanese Army—"their" army—which the Moslems and allies rejected for the very reason that they, too, believed it was the creature of the militant Maronites. For most Lebanese, downtown Beirut was the only place where people of the sixteen officially recognized minorities—plus foreigners of all descriptions—met and got to know one another. Work done, back they would go to their various neighborhoods, where all but the rich lived with members of their own sect and community. Intentionally or not, the Maronite militiamen by their actions were frustrating that process of mixing as surely as a forest ranger carves out a firebreak to circumscribe the flames. "We built Lebanon and we will burn it" became the defiant Maronite justification for favoring destruction rather than yielding to leftist demands for timid economic reforms, Moslem requests for a fairer share of political power, or Palestinian encroachments on national sovereignty. If this wasn't national suicide, it was the next best thing. When I pleaded with my Phalangist friends, the leitmotiv of their argument was simply that the West, and especially the United States, should get on board. They knew best. The balance of terror between armed Palestinians and armed Lebanese had failed to deter war—as it was supposed to, according to a briefly popular theory that overlooked the lack of self-control of all major players.

Sometime that fall, Beirut, or at least the Beirut I knew, died. Its failings were easy enough to list: arrogant vulgarity, mindless self-satisfaction, and desperate aping of the tastelessness of the West. But this bighearted whore of a port city also stood for what was best in the Arab world. Its contribution to Arab nationalism, the Arab cultural renaissance, its intellectual influence—the work of a century—were being dynamited, shelled, but more often pecked to pieces like some of those downtown buildings that bore pockmarks of thousands of bullets on their scarred facades. I should have understood immediately what was going on: the innate rejection of Beirut's role as a conduit, Trojan horse, gateway for the West to the Arab hinterland. Scarcely thirty years after independence from France, Lebanon was shedding its adopted skin with the help of its own adversary fanatics—new fanatics, spouting revolution and Marxism, and of course the muscular Maronites—both only relatively recently come down from their villages and both reacting with the atavism of people who have lived for centuries under persecution. The clues were there, staring me in the face in the form of the names of ruined streets commemorating those Europeans—Allenby, Clemenceau, Foch, Gouraud, Weygand—who, fewer than sixty years earlier, had represented the British and French empires come, they thought, to stay for centuries.

The last of the great Levantine cities, which within living memory had stretched from Algiers to Istanbul, was expiring without benefit of mourners, much less the help required to keep it alive. Not since World War II had such a great city been stripped so thoroughly of its riches. The historically minded noted that the rape of Beirut—like the sack of Alexandria and the plundering of Constantinople by the Crusaders— also involved Christians. But the most grievous losses were not necessarily those caused by material destruction. "Alexandria Quartet North," someone once called Beirut, as if to suggest that Lawrence Durrell's characters had migrated to Lebanon. With every passing revolution in the Arab world, Beirut had benefited from the brains, talent, and know-how of those unwilling to live under often-intolerant new masters. Long gone, certainly, were the dragomans, those professional guides and interpreters in the Arab East who under the Ottoman Empire made the Westerner's life bearable and commerce prosperous. But every Lebanese was in part his own dragoman; the Lebanese were hardworking, multilingual fixers and doers to whom commerce and money-changing were second nature. The legendary bars of Port Said and Suez were part of history, but Beirut still offered that once-standard fare of semicolonial Mediterranean ports—booze, drugs, and women. Beirut abounded in Swedish blondes and English barmaids who worked the clubs catering to thirsty American oilmen straight off the rigs of Saudi Arabia or to Gulf princelings eager to indulge their senses in an atmosphere both Western and still just Arab enough to put them at their ease. Later, Lebanese self-examination would fix on their own whorish defects, their willingness to sacrifice all to money—as if confessing to the desecration of greenery in favor of high-rise buildings was a sufficient ritually murmured mea culpa to foreclose deeper questions about their own responsibility for the death of the country.

What I loved was the sheer exuberance, even the outlandish pleasure with themselves displayed by Lebanese great and small. Never ones to hide their light under a bushel, the Lebanese paraded in American cars along their narrow, winding mountain roads. The men wore Pierre Cardin suits, the women Dior dresses and see-through blouses. The West was getting used to jeans and Small Is Beautiful, but the Lebanese delighted in clothes and jewelry, the clankier the better. There was something vaguely Miami Beach about Beirut. West Beirut was far more swinging than the Christian sector, perhaps because the mountain Arabs, as the Maronites once were called, were less open, less cosmopolitan than the other Christians and Moslems, those people of the coast open to fads and foreign influences since the days of Phoenicia. The cinemas, the nightclubs, the offices, the fancy new apartment houses with the view of the Mediterranean were all in West Beirut. East Beirutis went to Hamra for fun and culture. At some point the Lebanese fell to believing their own tourist brochures—skiing in the morning, lunch in the ancient port of Byblos, dinner at the Casino du Liban, gambling and watching the girls from the Paris Lido. What was Lebanon, anyhow? Lobster and champagne for the rich Lebanese and the Beirut-based Westerners and the petrodollar barons like Saudi Oil Minister Zaki Yamani, who kept a house here? Or as nasty an example of rags and riches, conspicuous consumption, and neglected poor deprived of state education, roads, plumbing, or other accoutrements of urban life as anywhere in the Arab East? Yes, the hashish was the best in the Middle East, arguably in the world, but why was the state unable to crack down on its cultivation? A land of genuine refuge for the persecuted and unloved as well as for the professional politicians who'd lost out in a recent or perhaps not-so-recent coup or attempted coup in some nearby country. There was a time when each ideological faction had its own café on Hamra, the fancy shopping street, and a reasonably quick-witted adult could find out what was going on in the entire Arab world and not a few Western capitals for the price of a few cups of coffee. In the land of *yanni*, Arabic for "you know," conversations unaffectedly drifted in and out of three languages—French, English, and Arabic. "*Shu haida, chérie*, how's business?"

To be a Levantine, the Middle East historian Albert Hourani wrote, "is to live in two worlds or more at once, without belonging to either: to be able to go through the external forms which indicate the possession of a certain nationality, religion or culture, without actually possessing it. It is no longer to have a standard of values of one's own, not to be able to create, but only able to imitate, and not even to imitate correctly, since that also needs a certain originality. It is to belong to no community and to possess nothing of one's own. It reveals itself in lostness, pretentiousness, cynicism and despair." Hourani was writing in the present tense and in 1946, two years before the creation of the State of Israel. Arguably, it was Israel's example—both for other minorities such as the Christians and for the Moslem-dominated regimes—that doomed the Levant and the Levantines. The Levant expired in Beirut in 1975.

Onto the garbage heap of history went the various pretentious claims foreigners and Lebanese alike had staked out for Beirut and Lebanon: Paris of the Orient, Switzerland of the Middle East, Tangiers (or sometimes Hong Kong) of the Levant, Crossroads of Civilization, Land of Welcome and Tolerance, the most developed of underdeveloped countries. Suddenly, this land, supposedly wallowing in the docile pleasures of the consumer society, was giving anarchy a bad name. The last remnant of the Levantine tradition of humanism and openness to the outside world expired with nary a protest. The other Arabs, who came to Beirut for gambling or plotting, sex or alcohol, contemptuously financed its opposing warlords, just as previously they had bought the Beirut press to express what passed for their militant ideologies. Beirut became the killing ground for the Arabs, the place where they let off steam with paid assassins or private armies against their enemies of the moment. As Beirut lay dying, ritual tears were shed by other Arab regimes, and not a few tried to carry off the spoils to their own capitals. But banks, newspapers, universities, the entrepreneurial instinct do not necessarily prosper in the oil-washed sands of Araby, and not all transplantation efforts succeeded. By the fall of 1975, tens of thousands of Westerners were fleeing. So, too, were many of the upper-middle- and middle-class refugees from a previous generation of the Arab world's revolutions and upheavals. They had perched here savoring this last livable outpost of the Orient and gracing Lebanon with their varied talents and civilized presence.

All of this I could deduce, describe, deal with intellectually. I was a journalist, and watching societies under stress—especially Third World societies—was my job, after all. But in little more than a month I personally experienced the helplessness and fear that already had become the fate of many Lebanese and was soon to engulf almost all of them.

In part it was my fault. I'd preferred not to see danger approaching, inching in like so many mortar rounds "walked" toward their target. God knows the signs were there. The packers were doing a land-office business, especially in my neighborhood, favored by rich Lebanese and foreigners. Moving vans were an unavoidable reminder that the wise were leaving for less dicey shores, their "just until things blow over" assurances belied by the valuables they were shipping out air freight.

I suppose I was too happy. Not that I was a war lover. It was just that I was delighted, after years of living in Paris and trying to work out a messy divorce, to fill in for six months between permanent *Washington Post* correspondents in Beirut. The apartment-office was spacious and airy, just three minutes' walk from the Reuters office where I filed dispatches to Washington, just down the road from excellent shopping, and at worst a short dollar cab ride from those comfortable clearinghouses for correspondents that bore the titles of the Hotel St. Georges, Quo Vadis, Le Grenier, and a half-dozen other seaside restaurants clustered nearby. I'd been happy to leave Paris with a witty Lebanese girlfriend and was looking forward to seeing other Lebanese friends I'd met on earlier visits. In fact, I'd brought almost everything I owned, which was never that much. Behind lay my bad times in France, oddly present only in the form of fancy English clothes that an enterprising Savile Row tailor had confectioned for me during quarterly visits to Paris: a woman friend, feeling sorry for me and no doubt horrified by the state of my wardrobe, had suggested the new clothes might get my mind off my troubles. I'd hardly worn them, since I didn't much like dressing up. And, I thought to myself, I didn't really need them now, since the reason my friend had thought up the scheme no longer obtained.

Then, within four days in late October 1975, I was trapped in my apartment-office during a two-day battle, captured by suspicious guerrillas, saved by an influential old acquaintance, only to find myself almost immediately trapped again elsewhere for three more days. When I returned to my home, I found it ransacked and uninhabitable.

I awoke before dawn one Saturday to the sound of battle down in the tree-lined streets of my neighborhood, called Kantari. Suddenly, my no-man's-land neighborhood had become a combat zone. The Phalangists had been probing in nearby streets—less, I figured, to protect the upper-class Christian residents, who traditionally looked down their noses at the Gemayels' Boy Scout antics, than to seize the gold in the Central Bank vaults some eight hundred feet farther west, in Moslem territory. Heavy machine guns, rocket-propelled grenades, mortars, and small-arms fire, I judged, and very close by. I didn't dare go out on the wide terrace surrounding most of the penthouse to find out. My only visual notions of what was going on were provided from peering gingerly through wooden shutters I painstakingly displaced in fear of attracting fire from the combatants. From the kitchen at the back I could see flames engulfing Myrtom House, an Austrian-run restaurant and rooming house only a stone's throw away. I worried about the owner, Hans, an old friend. In the street I could see an Alfa Romeo sedan on fire. Friends telephoned encouragement and promised that soldiers from the army barracks nearby would intervene to rescue me. In fact, I could see an old, French-built Panhard armored car no more than a hundred yards away. But it never budged an inch in my direction, and even if it had, I was unsure if I'd risk climbing down to the street. By nightfall, the telephone had gone dead. Earlier I had been able to dictate a story to Washington, which had kept my mind off my troubles for a while. Now I realized that I was alone in the building and could expect no rescue until the next day. The Lebanese in the other apartments had been wise enough to expect trouble and had stayed in the mountains with the Persian carpets they prudently had removed over the weeks before.

The mind plays tricks on people in tight situations. I was absorbed in weighing the probabilities of whether the Central Bank actually had kept any gold in its vaults. Only when night fell did I debate the wisdom of turning on the lights and risk signaling my presence to the gunmen. I decided to keep the lights on and sought out the safest place in an apartment that was, given the disposition of glass windows and doors, virtually without protection. I fetched two mattresses from the bedroom and plumped them down in the hall.

I was awakened from a fitful sleep at 2:30 a.m. on Sunday to see flames engulfing a charming three-story building across the street, a jewel of Ottoman architecture. As each succeeding explosion shook my apartment, I sleepily wondered what I could do if the armed men I could hear but not see in the street below should set fire to my building. Exhausted by the noise of the fighting, I finally dozed off reading a Lebanese historian friend's account of the civil war that had pitted Lebanese Christians against the Druzes in 1860. I remember having to reread the key passages—such was the complexity and perversity of that conflict. Moslems and Christians were at it again. I remember vaguely hearing the ground-floor bell ring just after dawn and dismissing the sound; no one in his right mind would risk going down to find out if indeed the bell had gone haywire in the fighting or if someone improbably had come calling in a combat zone.

Minutes later, my apartment door burst open and a dozen armed men rushed in. Much to my relief, they were from a breakaway offshoot of the Communist Party run by bright young Christians and manned, like so many of the West Beirut militias, with poor Shia Moslems. Amid the chaos these intruders at least represented authority—and a human, if threatening, presence. And over the decades I'd had enough experience with this kind of thing to know—and keep telling myself—that if you weren't shot out of hand and could start a conversation, the chances of surviving were very good.

Still, there is always something slightly ridiculous about putting one's hands over one's head. My sense of the absurd was not diminished by the fact that I was barefoot and wearing only boxer shots and a black T-shirt with pink lettering advertising a friend's restaurant in New York. It was in this inoffensive garb—after all, what self-respecting adversary would get himself up that way?—that I handed my calling card (luckily printed in both English and Arabic) to a brown-shirted teenager who, like his mates, was armed with a Soviet-built AK-47 assault rifle.

"*Washington Boast*," he said, pronouncing the second word as many Arabic speakers do, which even in these circumstances amused me. "Like that, you, downstairs," he said nervously.

When he got me beyond the apartment door, he realized I would need shoes, since the stairway was littered with broken glass from the explosions that had shaken the building. I was thus allowed to return to my bedroom, which other armed men were turning upside down, and permitted to put on shoes, socks, a sports shirt, and blue jeans. I also managed to pick up some money, my wallet containing credit cards and my driver's license, and two small address books—but not my passport or $1,800 in traveler's checks. Various gunmen kept pushing me in an effort to hurry me along.

"*Sahafi*," I said, repeating the Arabic word for "journalist" as if to buttress my innocence. Then someone found my army fatigues, mementos of a previous assignment in Vietnam. I regretted having brought them from Paris. My captors now said they were sure I was a Phalangist sniper, although they doubtless wanted me out of the way principally to take full advantage of the top-floor apartment and its wide terraces, which provided excellent fields of fire.

For reasons never explained, one man forced me to carry a suitcase, another carried my portable typewriter—dropping it a couple of times—and a third man brought along the uniforms and a tape recorder he insisted was a walkie-talkie. Down in the street, I was pushed and told, "Now run, and fast" across to the other side. I needed no urging, although later I wondered why I hadn't feared lest they pull the classic "shot while trying to escape" trick. Led through an alley full of gunmen, roughed up a bit in the process, shoved across a broad avenue, I was eventually forced into the back seat of a Volkswagen parked in a back street. With AK-47s pointing out the windows, we drove through various Moslem neighborhoods, across the dangerously exposed ring road, and thence to their headquarters.

A most urbane, tall man in a modified bush jacket came out of the one-story building.

I asked him if I could get out of the car.

"Of course," he said, introducing himself as Abu Daoud after I had identified myself. I almost expected him to hand me a calling card in return for the one I gave him. But I didn't really need one from him, since I knew of him: the man the Israelis held responsible for having organized the Black September attack on their athletes at the 1972 Munich Olympic Games.

My next gambit was to inquire if he knew the Algerian ambassador, Mohamed Yazid, a good friend of both the foreign press and the revolution since the 1950s, when he'd been spokesman for the Algerian insurgents during their successful eight-year struggle for independence from France. These proved magic words.

In that case, perhaps, he might call Yazid to verify my credentials, I suggested, although 6:15 a.m. was perhaps a bit too early for his excellency.

"He's used to it," my host said.

Yazid vouched for me, and Abu Daoud apologized profusely. "Sorry to have met under such conditions," he insisted. "Don't worry, our men will touch nothing, but nothing, in your apartment."

I was given a two-car escort to Yazid's residence, a bunkerlike structure with several basements (which came in handy, since it was located next to a favorite Phalangist target—the Sabra Palestinian refugee camp). During the ride, my escorts turned talkative in both English and French of sorts. They were Communists. The young man next to me kept fingering the American uniforms. From Vietnam, I explained. They were his if he really wanted them, but I said a GI uniform on a Lebanese Communist might look a bit odd.

"For the war, for the war," he said.

Minutes after I was ushered into Yazid's living room, he appeared in maroon pajamas. I joked with him, recounting other scrapes. My escort stood at a semblance of attention until Yazid, the most informal of diplomats, insisted they sit down. I explained how happy I was they had gotten me out of harm's way. Apricot juice appeared and was drunk. My escort rose to leave while one young man said in most formal French, "We deeply regret what has happened." I let Yazid go back to bed. His chauffeur, a friend since the Algerian war, drove me down to the Palm Beach Hotel, a journalists' favorite ever since the neighboring Hotel St. Georges, the most prestigious in the Middle East, had become too expensive for the liking of newspaper accountants.

The St. Georges, still the great clearinghouse for fact and fancy, boasted the best food in town as well as the prettiest women and some of the Levant's more outrageous high rollers. The next day, I walked across the street to lunch there and to check on my mail. It was still warm enough to eat out on the terrace overlooking St. George's Bay. I was having coffee with Mac—as the American ambassador, G. McMurtrie Godley, liked to be known—when he was called away for a telephone call. He returned, quickly signed the check, and was gone in his armor-plated Chrysler. Only minutes later, the reason for his hurried departure became evident when two dozen masked members of Interior Minister Camille Chamoun's Tiger militia drove up in Range Rovers and started unloading weapons and ammunition boxes. The hotel staff began rolling up the carpets rather than allow the militiamen to soil them.

Beirut's "battle of the hotels" had begun, the logical consequence of what was called the "Kantari operation," in which Moslems and leftists, with Palestinian support, had thrown the Christian militias out of my neighborhood. Starting at the coast, the Christians now rushed troops to the Hotel St. Georges, the twin-towered Hotel Phoenicia, and the Holiday Inn, farther up a steep hill. No more than a quarter mile above them all, the Moslems held the unfinished hulk of the Murr Tower, thirty-four floors of what was to have been a forty-story building, put up with incredible speed according to some new breakthrough in construction technique. From that vantage point, gunners dominated the entire city with rockets, mortars, and light artillery. Already the warring militiamen were shooting at each other in the hotels farther up the hill, their missiles either bouncing off the walls in an explosion of sparks or setting off fires when they scored hits.

By dusk we realized it was too dangerous for a promised security force to come rescue us. Accountants be damned. I had no choice but to stay at the St. Georges. I nervously punched and transmitted my story by telex from the ground-floor communications room, which was all too vulnerable even to small-arms fire because of its great expanse of plate glass facing the street. That first night, the Dutch ambassador, Harman Joreisen, and his wife, the CBS correspondent, Bill McLaughlin, and his crew, an American businessman, an American confidence man on the lam, and I—the only remaining guests—still felt confident enough to sleep in our rooms. Tuesday, the shooting became louder. Windows kept shattering. We spent the day on the telephone pleading with what passed for the authorities, friends, anyone with any influence to get us out. To no avail.

On Wednesday, Ambassador Joreisen left after a frugal ham-and-cheese sandwich luncheon, not much by St. Georges standards, but enough for the ordeal ahead. Like most of the remaining guests and staff, he did not like the look of things. (Many of the hotel staff had started drifting off early in the morning, but not before serving coffee.) Nor did he appreciate the waffling from the Lebanese Foreign Ministry or the obvious fact that the promised security force had still not shown up during the morning to evacuate the hotel. The ambassador and his wife walked across the street, got into their BMW coupe, and drove off slowly west along the seafront. Fifteen minutes later, a call to the Hotel Riviera, less than a mile away, confirmed they had made it to safety, thanks to their diplomatic license plates, which eased their way through one Christian and two Moslem roadblocks.

Back at the St. Georges, armed men belonging to Chamoun lounged in the elegant lobby. Ambassador Godley told us by telephone that the St. Georges and the Excelsior Hotel, just up a side street (where the *Chicago Daily News* correspondent, Rob Warden, his wife, and two children were), were "a low priority." That was fair enough, since neither hotel was directly in the line of fire now raking the Holiday Inn and the Phoenicia. Mac didn't know when help would be coming and he made no promises. Quite realistically, he said, "We've got no assets," meaning that the Western diplomatic community was having trouble getting the rapidly crumbling Lebanese government to concentrate on much of anything.

Henri Ferras, the French hotel manager, crept off at some point for the airport, but not before making himself odious by obliging his clients to pay up their bills to the last nickel. Four p.m. came and went—the cutoff time for any reasonable hope of rescue. The head Tiger telephoned Chamoun for permission to use the Chamoun family speedboat, parked in a marina adjacent to the hotel. The reason he needed it soon became obvious, when an outside caller reported that Phalangists had been kicked out of Clemenceau Street, just three hundred yards up the hill. An hour later, our Tigers started running in and out of the hotel in no particular direction, as bursts of small-arms fire slammed into the outside walls. Within minutes they were gone. The hotel staff ran white sheets out of second-story windows to advertise the St.

Georges' newfound neutrality. We began telephoning leftist and Palestinian friends for help.

Then suddenly the Phalangists arrived, a tough, nasty bunch. They made us sleep on the dining-room floor. Our cold dinner that night, in the dark, was not improved by the disappearance of the bartender, who had gone off with the keys to the liquor closet and the wine cellar.

The next morning, Mac Godley sent us his driver, Zuhair Moghrabi, with the armor-plated limousine, and we all piled in for a drive through the roadblocks to the Hotel Riviera. From there I doubled back to Kantari. Everywhere I went, wild-eyed men and women with suitcases were rushing in and out of buildings and dumping the contents into trucks and private cars. They worked with a devout frenzy worthy of a better cause, hurrying as if fearful that the rightful owners would return with the police and catch them red-handed in the act of plunder. Those were early days in the fighting, and a residual respect for the law still lingered. (The police had given up months earlier, as their gunless holsters proved when, during lulls, individual cops returned to their beats.)

Pushing my way through the people blocking the entrance to my apartment building, I slowly walked up to the sixth floor. On the way, armed men were carrying out Persian carpets that the third-floor tenants hadn't had time to remove. I peeked into their apartment: the furniture had been smashed into small pieces. I kept climbing. I knew the two top floors had been set on fire, and indeed that peculiar stench of waterlogged ashes met me as I pushed open the now-lockless door of my apartment-office. A quick inspection confirmed my worst suspicions. My Communist liberators, or whoever had occupied the building after they'd moved on to mop up the Phalangists, had stolen everything of value I owned and then turned arsonist in a clumsy effort to hide their theft. I scavenged through the closets, salvaging a shirt here, underwear there, which somehow had escaped the flames and thieves. I laughed to myself about the vanity of having splurged on three Savile Row suits and a cashmere sports jacket and wondered how they'd fit on some teenage gunslinger's back. But I was further taken aback when I opened the door to the room housing the office. The room had been lined with bookshelves. These had collapsed in the fire and, together with the volumes they once held, had been transformed into six inches of ashes neatly ringing the scorched walls. For the first time in six days of tension I began shaking. I needed a drink, but my visitors had finished off my meager supply of liquor. I sat down on a charred chair. From that moment on, I ceased attaching any importance to possessions. I never had been much of a collector. But the sight of my books reduced to ashes disturbed me. Even the medieval Mongols, no mean destroyers of civilization, had spared books when they captured the mountain redoubt of the Assassins, those hashish-inspired adepts of political murder whose name has passed into common parlance.

There I was with a few wretched belongings in a cheap suitcase. Cheap suitcases had become Lebanon's national symbol, the anonymous all-purpose accessory good for making off with plunder or, more mundanely, for saving what could be easily transported. The cheaper the better, cardboard if possible, to arouse little suspicion—not from the powerless police, who no longer dared do more than direct traffic, but from the gangs of armed men. What magnificent confusion! Suitcases were everywhere, sold on the sidewalks of Hamra, where the owners of established stores watched impotently as suq merchants displaced by the fighting jostled with free-lance looters selling gold Cartier cigarette lighters for two dollars apiece.

I was alive, but without a place to live, a predicament that one Lebanese out of three was to share before long. And I was lucky. I moved to a hotel—unlike the other displaced persons, obliged to live in schools, convents, or the flimsy cabanas of Beirut's exclusive beach clubs, if they did not take over empty middle-class apartments as squatters.

I was starting to comprehend that what was happening in Lebanon was in its peculiar way more frightening than any of the wars—from Algeria to Cyprus, from the Congo to Vietnam—that I'd covered in the previous twenty years. If the destruction of the suqs was a warning to the Lebanese, the devastation of upper-class Kantari and the luxury hotels conveyed a similar message to foreigners and those Westernized Lebanese who lived like them.

In their desire to prove themselves alien to all things Arab, Christians who prided themselves on their European ways seemed bound and determined to carry out a great enterprise of destruction. That the Moslems joined them in their great wrecking job was less of a surprise, for their roots lay in the Arab world (except for the rich, who, along with their Christian counterparts, aped Western ways). Together, Christians and Moslems united in tearing off the thin skin of Beirut's copycat Western affectation. Their joint revenge against the West was carried out with all the primitive atavism of men and women finally doing what was natural. Enough of the Rome-dictated constraints of a Christianity grown flabby and forgetful of the Church's militant tradition! It was fitting that never—not even on the evil days when two hundred or more people were killed—did Beirut Radio, the last surviving symbol of state authority, stop playing pop Western music. Even the masks the Phalangists wore during the first part of the war were meant not just to instill horror and prevent identification of young men who, when the fighting died down, went back and forth between the two sides of the city. The masks also were an antic throwback to that sense of theater that has ever been part of warfare. So, too, as a local Communist military commander confessed many years later, the sheer joy that came in using a poker to destroy furniture, objets d'art, and other valuables in those upper-class Christian homes in Kantari. He swore he had spared foreigners' property and attacked only homes with known Phalangist ties, but I think he was just saying that for my benefit, once I'd told him of my misadventure. He spoke in tones of awe of the vandalism he had committed.

As perhaps befitted a society given over to the laws of commerce, Lebanon began by sacrificing what it held in least esteem: human life itself. Even before the war, the nation's very incomplete records placed it ahead of the United States in murder statistics. Now, workaday murder and mayhem soon gave way to full-scale massacres. Upper-class Christians living in the cool hills above Beirut would show off before their visitors by dropping rounds down mortar tubes that had previously zeroed in on Palestinian refugee camps. Mutilation and torture became commonplace. The Christians took to carving crosses on their victims' bodies. Both sides dragged prisoners behind vehicles until death ensued. Traditionally fascinated with weapons, Lebanese and Palestinians alike strove constantly to procure the latest in deadly arms. From the revolvers of the 1958 civil war, they soon graduated to Soviet-bloc Kalashnikovs and American-made M-16 rifles, to heavy machine guns and mortars, rocket-propelled grenades, 105-millimeter cannon, then 122- and 130- and even 155-millimeter artillery, before obtaining Katyusha multiple-rocket launchers and Grad surface-to-surface missiles.

The Lebanese, who boasted prominent arms merchants within their own ranks, knew where to go to find weapons. Bulgaria supplied the Christian militias before 1975, and even after the fighting broke out, until the Lebanese Communist Party complained. Every gun dealer worth his salt either came to Beirut or received Lebanese emissaries in Europe. The Lebanese proved inventive. A Paris publisher friend of mine was once approached by Lebanese Christians determined to have arms shipped in containers of books his firm regularly dispatched to Lebanese bookstores. Weapons sent halfway round the world ended up back in the Middle East, but in different hands. Soviet infantry weapons that had been captured by the Israelis in the 1967 conflict from the Syrians and Egyptians were first sold to the rebels of Biafra. When Nigeria crushed Biafra, the weapons were sold to Ghana, where Lebanese expatriate businessmen purchased them and sent them to Marounistan. Such arms odysseys were commonplace. In the early 1970s, the CIA and Israel provided captured Soviet arms to the Kurds then fighting the Iraqi government. And Israel has sold arms to Iran—including American aircraft spares—to help Ayatollah Khomeini's war against Iraq. The Lebanese Christians boasted that their first arms were bought from money-hungry Palestinians. Iraq, Libya, Syria, Jordan, and Saudi Arabia kept supplies coming—as did Israel at a later stage in the war. Never mind that such heavy weaponry was unnecessary for urban fighting or that much of it was fired blindly, with the predictable result that no more than 10 percent of the casualties involved combatants. Rarely did the soldiers ever see enemy militiamen, for theirs remained a long-range war waged with indirect-fire weapons. Dr. Amal Chamaa, a young Lebanese woman physician at West Beirut's Barbir Hospital, got used to obscene telephone calls from Christian gunners, who would end their conversations, "We're sending bonbons for you"—that meant mortars on the fourth floor.

The degree of military proficiency was lamentable, but it improved in the latter part of the war, when the Lebanese Army split in two, and each side could count on professional advice. In the early months, though, fighters in West Beirut were using out-of-date city maps to shell their Christian adversaries in the East, and the percentage of dud ordnance reflected the inexperience of gunners who often did not know how to arm their projectiles properly. The militiamen never tired of human quarry. Quiet periods, even formal truces, were the best times for kidnappings and snipings, because civilians once again stirred from the shelters and innocently walked the streets again. End-of-the-month truces allowed all concerned to go to the banks and cash paychecks. For the better part of a year, most private firms in Beirut kept paying staff in hopes that the fighting would end and business could resume as before. The government paid civil servants and the army and gendarmerie long after they ceased showing up for duty. One friend of mine in the Information Ministry had five secretaries, but complained he was lucky if one showed up for work on any given day.

But as Lebanon became undone, such relatively tame pursuits as looting suqs and vandalizing residential neighborhoods proved mundane for all but the professional pillagers who made off with Persian carpets, cash, or other valuables. As the months went by, armed men broke into the country's principal insane asylum to release inmates, prisons were attacked and razed. Then, in a spasm of destruction, Christian militiamen looted the port while the Palestinians, probably with European underworld technical assistance, conducted the biggest bank robbery—or robberies—in history. Thus were Lebanon's two main economic money-spinners desecrated in what the Lebanese came to call a crime of *lèse-économie*. To this day, the damages remain anyone's guess, but are thought to run to billions of dollars. Nor was the loss merely material. Lebanon's reputation for more than a hundred years was bound up with the port of Beirut, and its importance in the thriving entrepôt trade with the Arab hinterland was well established long before oil created petrodollar fortunes in the Gulf. And the banks, of more modern vintage, had turned Beirut into the Middle East's major financial center: it had as many banks as London, a bank secrecy law without rival, and a currency backed by 9.4 million ounces of gold, the most impressive gold cover in the world. Now the Merchants' Republic lay in ruins, thanks to rival but complementary efforts by those sworn to its defense and those dedicated to its damnation.

Random violence became an accepted part of life. Walking a dog, driving down a street, attending a movie literally could be worth your life. If it wasn't a mortar or artillery round, it was a sniper's bullet or kidnappers manning roadblocks. At the beginning, Beirutis telephoned their friends to discover which neighborhood was being shelled. Even Lebanese who'd fled abroad would call long distance, often informing their Beirut friends of damage sustained only blocks away. People talked about the war then. But gradually only car bombs seemed to elicit any sense of common horror and then only in one's own side of town. East Beirutis went about their business or even such frivolous pleasures as skiing or car rallies when West Beirut was the scene of almost daily violence. And West Beirutis paid no mind to the pounding East Beirut absorbed now and again.

Who started the kidnappings is lost in the mist of the civil war, but their widespread occurrence became the conflict's only major innovation. Some Moslems claim the Phalangists began by forcing two Moslems off a Beirut bus and gunning them down after ordering them to run for it. Some Christians insist that a Shia Moslem gang calling itself the Knights of Ali started the process as early as May 1975 by killing some fifty Christians—including members of supposedly allied leftist organizations. The bodies were left in a Moslem cemetery near the dividing line, their penises neatly severed and stuffed in their mouths. Both sides commited atrocities and mutilations. Documented cases exist of Moslems caught in Christian territory—and vice versa—who had their trigger fingers, or all fingers, or breasts, or ears chopped off. Bellies were slit open, and men and women were burned to death inside their cars. Journalists who visited the devastated downtown area during a cease-fire in the spring of 1976 swear they were stopped by uniformed young women behind a barricade on the Christian side who proudly showed them a sack of male genitalia. But nothing was quite so terrifying—not even the car bombs—as the flying roadblocks, manned by teams of gunmen who stopped cars and arrested their occupants, usually on the basis of their religion, which is mentioned on official Lebanese identity cards.

My friend Samir Saab, a Maronite, twice was stopped by such roadblocks. The first time, he was driving home from East Beirut in the middle of the night, when he was stopped on the expressway, known as the Ring, that links the two parts of the city. It was in September 1975 and he was in a car with two other young Maronite men. The others had their identity cards, but he did not have his. Because both Samir and Saab are names that could be either Christian or Moslem, he desperately sought to convince his captors that he, too, was Moslem.

"They were beating up my friends. They were going to kill us because the Phalangists had killed five Moslems. They beat us with rifle butts," Samir recalled. "I knew I was going to die. Then I unzipped my fly and took out my penis to show them that I was circumcised like a good Moslem. They stopped beating me and started asking questions. Rich or poor? Where had I been to school? Once the conversation started, they seemed to hesitate. Then they asked me to recite the first verse of the Koran."

"Did you know it?"

"I didn't then, but I do know—'In the name of God, the Merciful, the Compassionate, Praise be to God, the Lord of all Being, the Almighty, the All Compassionate, the Master of the Day of Doom . . .'"

"How did you save your neck, then?"

"I didn't. I'd begun to say a lot of stupid things—that my parents were poor, but that I'd studied in Europe. It didn't add up and they were suspicious. I and my friends owe our lives to sheer chance. The Phalangists had telephoned someone on the Moslem side to say three guys had been kidnapped and did anyone know where they were. A man came looking for three young men—he didn't even ask our names. He just asked our captors what time we had been caught. That coincided with the time the other three people had been kidnapped, and that saved us."

"And the second time?"

"Same place exactly, but in broad daylight. That time I had an identity card, which a Moslem client had left by mistake at our office. I found it in the lost-and-found and took it. We looked vaguely alike, judging by the photograph."

"Any trouble?"

"None at all. They let me right through, but they stopped the cars right behind me."

By early fall 1975, Moslems refused to go to the Christian sector of the city, and indeed most Moslem residents there sought refuge in West Beirut. Tens and tens of thousands of Christians lived in West Beirut. And for the some one hundred thousand Christians who commuted back and forth between the two sectors on the way to the airport or to work, friends and money provided them with falsified official identity cards saying they were Moslems or with documents printed by the various armed groups operating in West Beirut. I have another young Christian friend, named Jean-Paul Zebbouni, a Chaldean Christian whose family fled persecution in Iraq in the 1930s. Stopped by Moslem gunmen in West Beirut, he showed his identity card. "Jean, that is clear enough, but Paul in addition is pure provocation," his captors said before letting him go.

Not everyone stopped at a roadblock was lucky enough to find gunmen with a sense of humor. I saw Moslems force two Christians to stop, check their identity cards, pull them out of their car, and shoot them—all in less than a minute. And I know that Christian gunmen also killed in cold blood in similar circumstances. The murder witnessed took place in possibly the worst part of town—the half-mile stretch of highway between Barbir Hospital, in West Beirut, and the Museum crossing point into the Christian sector. During much of the 1975–76 war the Museum was the only crossing point between the two parts of the city. Starting on the Christian side, those who were determined to cross over would drive down a narrow street, protected by an overturned bus that prevented one's gathering speed, before braving sniper fire at the most exposed sector of the gauntlet; sand-filled oil barrels and a broken water main that spouted for months at a time further complicated the maneuver, as one emerged from the narrow street at an angle and slalomed across to the relative safety of a Lebanese Army post. Even today I shudder every time I go down that narrow street, although it long since has ceased being snipers' paradise. In May 1976, during the mortar and machine-gun attack, I froze so badly there that my friend Joe Alex Morris, Jr., of the *Los Angeles Times*, had to threaten to leave me at a gendarmerie barracks where we had taken shelter, before I would get back into his car to return to West Beirut. (Joe was killed in the February 1979 revolution in Tehran.) And two weeks after my case of nerves, Henry Tanner of *The New York Times* was making the Museum crossing when a sniper shot and killed Edouard Saab, *Le Monde*'s correspondent, who was driving Tanner back from the Christian side. Even once past the Lebanese Army sandbags, one had not run the gauntlet, for it was there that the most extreme Moslem militiamen maintained their roadblocks. That was where one American and one French ambassador were killed.

Such summary executions were far from the rule. Tariq Mitri, a plump, bearded Greek Orthodox employee of the World Christian Student Federation and an American University of Beirut graduate in physics, became an expert on kidnappings in the process of trying to obtain the release of more than a hundred victims in West Beirut. Mitri distinguished three categories. The first involved militiamen whose fanaticism exceeded their official organization's stated policy. They were known, in civil war jargon, as "uncontrolled elements," and in Mitri's book were all the more frightening and difficult to deal with because they never got beyond an "us"-and-"them" view of the war. A second category included creatures of the various armed organizations who were ordered to kidnap a given number of innocents to help negotiate the release of some of their own who had themselves been kidnapped. (In a variation on this type, such organized kidnappings were justified on the ground that the other side had committed crimes so heinous that "the masses require vengeance," which meant that "if we don't do it, it will be worse." That, in turn, suggested that the organization in question feared it would lose control if it failed to act. There was enough mass bestiality committed by both sides to invoke this kind of reasoning repeatedly.) The third form of kidnapping was carried out on an individual basis and always in the name of "suspicions." As often as not, these were set in train by third-party denunciations and for reasons as varied as a lovers' quarrel or a business conflict. Mitri found the Lebanese Communist Party easiest to deal with: "Many of the leaders were Christians, and you could appeal to their sense of ideology." At the other end of the scale were fanatical Moslem groups whose lack of political sophistication and divided loyalties—sometimes they were financed by several rival Arab regimes at the same time—made them impervious to Mitri's best efforts.

Mitri stumbled into the hostage-retrieval business because of his membership in the Patriotic Christians, a group in West Beirut that sought to offer an alternative to the brand of Christianity then in vogue on the other side of the city. Mitri recalled, "I had a lot of friends who knew I had good Palestinian connections," which counted more and more as the war went on. In West Beirut, over the months, the Palestinians, partly by design, partly by default, found themselves becoming the final court of appeal as the Lebanese police and gendarmerie disintegrated and local authority devolved upon the neighborhood gangs armed and backed by the Palestinian commandos. "I think the first time involved a neighbor who had been kidnapped and his family came to see me," Mitri said. Then, bishops from "the other side" started telephoning, asking if he could find parishioner X or Y. That was in May 1975, less than a month after the first hostilities. People dropped by to report cases. So-and-So had disappeared at such-and-such an hour on his way between one fixed point and another, usually on the way from home to workplace or vice versa.

"Then I tried to think what groups were there," Mitri said, "and I'd go down my list and go see them. Very important to go see them."

"Every time?"

"Yes. I'd go to one group with my list. They'd tell me they had no one. Then I'd go to a larger group, who might say, 'We don't have them, but it's better for you not to go alone to the people who might. We'll send someone with you.' Invariably, I was offered tea or coffee. Off we'd go. There were often hitches. 'Yes, we have the men you're looking for, but we have to ask them some questions. Come back at noon.' "

"You went back?"

"Usually I'd phone the kidnapped people's families in the afternoon, and if nothing had happened, in another twenty-four hours I'd start all over again."

"If that didn't work?"

"Then the trick was to get someone else into the act because by yourself you didn't have much weight. I'd go to Fatah, which, as the biggest Palestinian group, did have clout. But sometimes Fatah disclaimed responsibility, and then you'd get into wheels-within-wheels. Say, the kidnappers would tell you, 'We know this guy comes from village X and the member of parliament from there is Y.' I'd go find the MP and ask him to call to apply pressure."

Mitri and his team of no more than fifteen helpers as often as not found themselves begging. "You had to know the case, and the best tack was the ethical one," he recalled. About the only constant was that the prisons were usually at the various organizations' headquarters. The kidnappers at the roadblocks were invariably young, in their late teens or twenties. But the bosses who handled the transactions were never younger than their mid-thirties. Although Mitri knew people at the various parties and organizations, he never managed to work out a real system. In late 1975 and early 1976 there was a kind of security coordinating committee to handle kidnappings, among other problems, but eventually it fell apart like almost everything else in the country. Then Mitri was without a central clearinghouse, and he was never able to establish durable contacts at the roadblocks. "By the time you got to know X or Y, he was either dead or had left for other duty."

The strain made the normally placid Mitri nervous. He developed an ulcer. "There you were, trying to save some innocent Christian from the clutches of some little militiaman who was paid a couple hundred dollars a month by some Arab country," Mitri said. "We took incredible risks to persuade those ideologically ignorant and often immoral gunmen that the hapless fellow they were threatening to kill was not a Phalangist or an Israeli agent." Mitri even intervened on behalf of kidnapped Christian militiamen, occasionally succeeding in that all but impossible task. Those Christians he did manage to save often had been badly beaten. He never succeeded in retrieving the dead. Both sides preferred to dump cadavers in the city or suburbs. A favorite dumping ground for the Christians was a deep gorge under the coastal expressway north of Beirut, near the Casino du Liban. Motorists routinely stopped to stare at the cadavers far below, as if the spectacle were a fixture of some regularly established circuit of tourist attractions. The Moslems' choices were less spectacular, but they, too, favored bridges and highroads, particularly an overpass near Barbir Hospital.

Yet, with some notable exceptions, few women were kidnapped or raped—probably because of the widespread Third World view that relegates women to the status of virtual non-persons. But kidnappers did seize a close friend of Mitri's because of a distant family connection she had with the Gemayels. They hoped to force the release of two of their men, but freed her when they were persuaded that her immediate family did not share Sheikh Pierre Gemayel's politics.

Eventually, Mitri himself was kidnapped. It happened one evening near Barbir Hospital, when he emerged from a meeting to find his car had broken down. Arrested at a roadblock while waiting to hail a taxi, he was driven off in a Jeep on the basis of his identity card—he'd never thought to carry a false one.

Like so many other kidnapping victims, Mitri never did discover which group had held him. "They refused to say who they were. I knew at least one person per organization, and I spent the time going through all the people I knew with them. The curious thing is that when they went through my wallet and found an American Express card, they got all excited—'American, American, this one is an American spy.' I said to myself, 'This time you risk your neck.' It lasted two hours and finally I was released."

As a Beirut resident, I knew the feeling. Time and time again, I've been stopped, and despite my press card or a special pass, my captors have delighted in refusing to telephone any of the officials of their own organization whom I mention as friends or acquaintances. Apparently, refusing to do so is considered a sophisticated interrogation tool. For that matter, insisting that a credit card is evidence of espionage is just as pitiful a sign of underdevelopment as my Communist liberators' conviction that my tape recorder was a walkie-talkie.

The Moslems' lingering and blanket suspicions of Christians—even of such demonstrably well-disposed ones as Mitri—were also part of the civil war's bitter heritage. The Christian warlords had only themselves to blame. For on December 6, 1975, in what the Lebanese still call Black Saturday, their militiamen perpetrated a daylong pogrom against Moslems that set the tone for a chain reaction of atrocities in which Christians slaughtered Moslems and Moslems massacred Christians with ever-growing savagery. No longer did the warring sides limit themselves to piecemeal mayhem. Indeed, at their most bloodthirsty, Christian militiamen slaughtered more than two thousand Palestinians and poor Lebanese Moslems when they overran the Tal Zaatar refugee camp in August 1976 after a fifty-two-day siege. Perhaps the most telling detail of that day of mass murder is recorded in a film shot by a Christian militiaman that shows survivors climbing aboard trucks leased by the International Committee of the Red Cross. There are no men among them.

Black Saturday demonstrated, were any further proof needed, just how out of control Lebanon had gotten. Apologists said that the massacres were provoked by a brutal ax killing of four Phalangist militiamen who had been murdered in the middle of the previous night as they imprudently came back from a late-night party along a road near Tal Zaatar. The ensuing slaughter in the center of Beirut left more than two hundred Moslems dead and set the scene for further Christian setbacks in the war.

I was caught up in the panic that day without immediately understanding what had caused it. I was trying to get to Bank Street to check on my account, when a desperate stream of cars, horns blowing and even less respectful of traffic regulations than usual, forced its way toward West Beirut. First reports of the killings were met with disbelief. Sheikh Pierre Gemayel, the Phalangist leader, that very morning had traveled to Damascus. There were rumors that President Hafez Assad of Syria was considering changing sides. Early on, he had backed the Palestinian guerrillas and their leftist Lebanese allies. But they now posed a threat. It was one thing for Assad to glory in the rhetoric of the progressive Left in Syria, another to live next door to the reality of revolutionary destabilization if his nominal allies won out. Thus, he was tempted by an alliance with the Christian warlords, who had all but replaced the hollow shell of the Lebanese state.

Gemayel's visit and the Black Saturday massacre illustrated two contradictory strands of Christian Lebanese thinking: the desire to deny all things Arab and Islamic, and the temptation to forge links with the Arab world as embodied in that quintessentially Arab country, Syria. The excesses of Black Saturday cut off Phalangist access—at least temporarily—to such important sources of cash as Saudi Arabia and other Gulf oil states. To confront the Left, which Saudis automatically equated with Communism, was one thing, but to slaughter Moslems wholesale was quite another.

Technically, Phalangists blamed the outrage on a prominent Christian journalist who started shooting Moslems at random to avenge his son, one of the four Phalangists killed the previous night. (During the summer, another son had been killed in the Beqaa valley, when he imprudently insisted on driving through that Moslem territory as part of an automobile race.) But in fact, the war had reached that degree of fanaticism at which almost any incident would have served as detonator. Only three days before Black Saturday, a truck carrying Korans to Saudi Arabia had been stopped and burned in the notoriously fanatical Maronite town of Kahhalé, on the Beirut–Damascus road in the hills right above the capital. Moslems burned churches in reprisal.

Black Saturday morning, Fuad Bizri, president of the state-owned Lebanese Electricity Company, was looking out the window of his thirteenth-floor office in East Beirut when he saw armed men running after—and arresting—civilians. "People were pouring out of everywhere," said Bizri, a Sunni Moslem educated by Lazarist Brothers in Lebanon before studying engineering in France. "I did not immediately realize what was going on, but as usual in such uncertain circumstances, I ordered the ground-floor doors closed. I didn't want the

Moslem staff to get scared, leave by car, and risk getting caught in what was obviously something nasty. I asked them to come up to my floor." He telephoned the gendarmerie commander and asked for two armored cars to escort the Moslems back to West Beirut. They never came, at least not to the building. "They'd start down a street, but not dare continue. Even when reinforcements came, the gunmen would hide while the armored cars passed, then go back to arresting people."

A Christian engineer entered Bizri's office, pale and obviously upset. "Sir, can you leave the office? Militiamen in camouflage uniforms are downstairs. They are wearing masks. They want to see you."

"Tell them I am here. They can come up." Bizri wondered what would happen when the door opened. Would he be shot on the spot? Or would he be taken off? Militiamen had never entered the building before. He telephoned the Presidential Palace, where he had served as consultant to two presidents. He was lucky and got through immediately—no mean feat in a city whose telephone service was no great shakes and was suffering from lack of repairs—to President Franjieh's aide-de-camp, who immediately called Phalangist headquarters.

When the door did open, in came a delegation of embarrassed high-ranking Phalangists. What Bizri discovered only later was that eight Phalangist troopers and an officer had forced their way into the building, demanding to see him. The porter had said Bizri was out, but the militiamen had recognized his Jaguar, parked in front; the quick-witted porter then said Bizri had gone on an inspection tour in one of the company's distinctive yellow cars, and he sent the Phalangists to the eighth floor, where the Christian staff was meeting.

"The entire Christian staff blocked their passage, and someone said, 'It's very simple. We are all Christians, but you'll have to kill us all before we let you by,'" Bizri explained to me.

"The militiamen said, 'But Bizri himself has told us to come up.'"

"'We know what you want. As long as he remains in the building we are here, and you won't get by us,' the staff said."

For Bizri, "It was obvious: the Phalangists wanted revenge, and I was the only Moslem of any importance they could lay their hands on. Their other victims had been largely dockers."

The Phalangist bigwigs put the fifty or so Moslems in a fifteen-car convoy and took them to the dividing line. Phalangist militias were still arresting people in East Beirut as the Moslem employees drove west, so the Moslem gunmen manning their side of the line were suspicious when the convoy emerged from no-man's-land and reached West Beirut.

"We said, 'For pity's sake,' and explained what we'd been through, and everyone laughed," Bizri recalled.

When he got back to his elegant apartment in West Beirut, near a Palestinian refugee camp, Bizri poured himself a whiskey.

"Only one?" I asked.

"Yes, and I did not tell my wife."

Within a week, he was back in his East Beirut office—and demanding that his top aides, Christian and Moslem, show up as well. Autocratic, well-connected, patriotic, Bizri was one of the few bosses who docked workers' wages if they failed to show up when needed. "I bullied them because the Electricity Company was for everyone." It was this determination that persuaded Christian and Moslem warlords, Sheikh Pierre Gemayel and PLO chief Yasser Arafat, to help him keep his beloved power company operating despite their militiamen's best efforts to destroy his lines. When, in June 1976, combatants did knock out all thirteen lines feeding Beirut, it was Bizri's reputation for scrupulous fairness that led Gemayel and Arafat into one of their stranger deals. By that time, the situation had deteriorated too far for Bizri's usual tactics to work. Until then he would get his teams stationed in Christian and Moslem territory to arrive at the same time in no-man's-land waving white flags and coordinating their efforts through megaphones to ensure that repairmen of both faiths started climbing the damaged pylons at exactly the same moment. That way, the militiamen couldn't pick anyone off without risking killing one of their own.

Bizri's new stratagem involved convincing Arafat to send two small coastal tankers with heavy fuel to a 5,000-kilowatt power plant in Christian territory at Zouk, a few miles north of Beirut. At face value, Bizri's scheme was an obvious enough trade-off. But Lebanon had ceased to be rational more than a year earlier. Still, the Christians had the only functioning power plant and controlled the capital's water supply. But they had no fuel. The Palestinians and their allies, who by then controlled West Beirut, did. Bizri, logical engineer that he was, argued that if the Palestinians would provide fuel for the generator, the Zouk plant could provide an hour's worth of power daily for each of the capital's neighborhoods. That was just enough to bake bread in electric ovens and to provide water. "Abu Nur," or "Father Light," as Bizri was nicknamed, didn't know Arafat, but the PLO leader was curious about the Black Saturday survivor. And so they met in the summer of 1976. "Things cannot go on like this," Bizri argued to Arafat. "The country will perish. You must help me." Arafat agreed. And Bizri promised to suspend the tanker operation if the Christians used the fuel for their war effort. Eventually, the Zouk plant provided the entire metropolitan area with four hours a day of power. And the PLO helped import the wire, insulators, and other material Bizri required to bring in a 50,000-kilowatt line from the south. Bizri negotiated both deals during the siege of Tal Zaatar, which marked the low point of relations between the Christian warlords and the PLO.

Arguably, Bizri's success was due to the vestigial traces of establishment comity that from time to time prompted rival warlords to act in their own self-interest, or, rather, in that of the cowed populations whose lives they controlled. Trying to keep track of what was going on during the civil war was still considered a rational exercise. There were whole patches of events that seemed to make logical sense or that followed some form of odd reasoning, obeying rules of their own, but that qualified as reasoning all the same. But I was taken aback at each new grisly twist, by the relentless refusal (or was it a built-in inability?) of any of the belligerents ever to stop for long. The pauses between what the Lebanese still counted as rounds in the fighting grew ever shorter, sometimes limited to an end-of-the-month truce to allow gunmen and civilians to go to the bank and to draw salaries. For much of the war, the Christians were getting the worst of the fighting— which, more often than not, they kept initiating, no matter how hard they had just been hammered. I came to admire their dogged refusal to give in, even though I was often appalled at the cost they inflicted on friend and foe alike.

In their desire to rid their areas of Palestinians and Moslem Lebanese, in January 1976 the Christians captured two enemy strongholds that effectively threatened communications between East Beirut and the Maronite hinterland to the north and east. The more important was called Karantina, and included an old quarantine area near the port and Maslakh, the slaughterhouse. An overcrowded slum of thirty thousand residents—mostly poor Shia Moslems from the south, with a sprinkling of Kurds and Armenians—the area was owned by the Maronite monks, among others, and many of the men worked as day laborers on the docks. Palestinian guerrillas had winkled their way into Karantina, distributing arms and generally running things. I had been shot at enough while crossing two strategic bridges—especially a humpbacked bridge made more dangerous by the impossibility of seeing the onrushing, and inevitably full-throttled, traffic from the other direction until it was too late—to understand the Christians' reasons for attacking Karantina.

It wasn't much of a fight. The Palestinians, according to Lebanese survivors, prevented the noncombatants from fleeing. The Palestinians themselves held out for three days in a furniture factory, called Sleep Comfort, until killed to the last man. What was as extraordinary as the violence itself was the Phalangists' naiveté in letting the press work freely and their inability to understand why the dispatches, film, and still photographs of their activities were so devastating to their cause. Tasteless enough was the Phalangists' joy in popping champagne bottles or playing mandolins over a corpse as smoke poured out of a gutted house. Worse yet were the scenes of Moslem males of all ages lined up against a wall, their hands behind their backs, guarded by Phalangists wearing prominent wooden crosses around their necks. Or the tearful processions of women and children carrying white flags without any of their menfolk in sight.

But what I will always remember from Karantina is the young children, hands in the air, being pushed around by the Phalangists. I happened to be with a Phalangist friend, and said to him that I was reminded of the famous photograph of terrified Jewish children surrounded by German troops taken during the Nazi destruction of the Warsaw Ghetto. He nodded in agreement, but my remarks had not registered, or, if they had, they produced no reaction. Half an hour later, I noticed a very old and very lame woman dragging herself along a street littered with rubble. I again took my Phalangist aside. As calmly as I could manage, I told him the Phalangists were acting atrociously and doing their cause no good. Why didn't he at least arrange for the terrified and obviously ill old woman to be put in a car? It might just make a photograph to offset the horrors. My friend looked at me as if I were mad. I left him, went back to my car, and drove back across town to write my story. Already, women and children from Karantina were being dumped at the Museum crossing point by the Phalangists. They told of their menfolk being gunned down in cold blood and having to pay the Armenians, who lived just across the Beirut River from Karantina, to save their own necks. A thousand dead was the best guess. Karantina was bulldozed level, though some houses were left intact where fresh recruits could be trained in urban fighting.

(When the film and still photographs reached the outside world, the Phalangists became enraged at the press for having chronicled what happened at Karantina. Six years later, after Shatila, an influential Maronite cleric asked me accusingly, "Why did they let the television in?" It was as if the Israelis or whoever he was referring to should have been able to hide a massacre in the middle of a capital saturated with journalists.)

Two days later, the Palestinians and their Lebanese Left allies overran Damour, a Maronite town on the coast, twelve miles south of Beirut. For some observers, the attack seemed more like a sack than a slaughter, at least by Lebanese standards. I personally saw entire families lying dead outside their burned and dynamited homes. But the relatively small number of victims in a town of 20,000 inhabitants— reports varied from a low of 60 to a median estimate of 150 to a high of 500—suggested that slaughter was not the Palestinians' only goal. In subsequent days, swarms of looters stripped Damour of everything of value, down to the tiles on the roofs and the metal wiring and pipes. I went down there day after day, wondering what they would find left to plunder, wondering why the old Mercedes communal taxis and pickup trucks bothered to drive back to Beirut at full speed with such increasingly pitiful pickings. But the halfhearted Palestinian guards weren't about to stop anyone, especially not the Karantina refugees desperately scrounging for beds, chairs, mattresses to furnish the beach cabanas where they'd been dumped in West Beirut. Finally, the Palestinians moved their own people into Damour and added a sprinkling of Karantina refugees for the symbolism.

It was this kind of mirror-image fascination with symbolism that produced the savagery of Tal Zaatar half a year later. By then Tal Zaatar was the last remaining Palestinian stronghold in Christian territory, and the Christian militias were bound to win, since they enjoyed aid from both Israel and Syria. But the Christians wanted victory—military victory—after so many reverses. The Palestinians wanted martyrdom, kept hailing Tal Zaatar as another Stalingrad. Both got what they wanted. An orderly surrender could have been negotiated easily. The International Committee of the Red Cross did its best to do just that. Instead, thousands of the camp's Palestinian and Lebanese inmates died needlessly.

As in Karantina, the Lebanese complained that they were bossed around by the Palestinians, who had the arms and kept most of the food and water for themselves. And many Lebanese and Palestinians from the camp were gunned down after it fell, including a considerable number slaughtered just before they reached safety at the Museum crossing point. Bodies were dragged behind vehicles—the Christians were getting even for similar desecrations of their dead, earlier on.

In the final stage of the siege of Tal Zaatar, Christian rhetoric became ever shriller in order to spur the troops on. In a class by himself was a former police officer named Etienne Sakr. He styled himself "Abu Arz," or "Father Cedar," and commanded the small militia called Guardians of the Cedars. "If you feel compassion for the Palestinian women and children," said Abu Arz—whose detractors ascribed his extremism to his birth in Palestine—"remember they are Communists and will bear new Communists." A European teaching brother at the Mont Lasalle secondary school in the hills above Beirut recalled that the Phalangists dumped the corpse of an enemy militiaman one hundred yards from the school. "We didn't touch it for days," he said. "Finally, someone came and poured gasoline on the body. We did nothing. We are not courageous." The school grounds accommodated artillery emplacements to shell Tal Zaatar. "There's not a square inch of Europe not covered by martyrs' blood," he said, "but that, for the most part, was a long time ago."

As such madness spread through Lebanon, the country's only mental hospital functioned with exemplary smoothness—in one of those ironies for which wars seem to be famous. Situated in the hills overlooking Beirut, the Lebanon Hospital for Mental and Nervous Disorders was caught in a near-constant cross fire between the Moslems and Palestinians to the west and the Christians who maintained a tenuous hold on the neighborhood. Sixty percent of the staff stopped coming to work either because they found jobs elsewhere or were too frightened to leave home or were Moslems who feared the Christian militiamen.

Among the patients—including prisoners remanded by the courts and the army when such institutions were still functioning—no friction occurred between Moslems and Christians. Consumption of tranquillizers and more potent drugs diminished significantly. Antranik Manoogian, the hospital's director and a member of parliament representing Lebanon's Protestant minority, remarked, "Curiously, life continued as if nothing were happening"—this was in keeping with previously documented clinical evidence that in the midst of such conflicts mental patients often bear up better than in less stressful times. "The war was very good occupational therapy. The patients were truly aware of what was going on because everything was on the radio, on television, or in the newspapers," he said.

The biggest danger to the hospital was not the exploding ordnance but the raids by Christian militiamen. The hospital lost only one inmate by shellfire, but militiamen took to showing up, shooting the locks off doors, and freeing relatives or friends. "They were armed and nasty, always in a hurry to get someone out and leave," Manoogian said. "It was never the patients' wives or mothers or girlfriends who came, just the hoodlums. And they'd never listen when we tried to explain they were asking for trouble in making off with real psychotic cases. They'd arrive and take the people they wanted. The problem was, the inmates would take advantage and conduct mass breakouts. Twice, between fifteen and twenty inmates rushed through the gates, and on other occasions smaller numbers did the same. Many returned on their own; some were brought back by families who couldn't cope. But others were found dead because they were fair game for the rival militiamen in the region, who shot at anything that moved."

Pointing to a much-repaired section of a green door in the main building, Manoogian said, "We had to repair that lock three times. Finally, we worked out a system. The gunmen arrived, asked for the person they wanted, and we'd fetch him. It was more convenient to hand over some inmates to relatives than have the gunmen keep breaking in and have the other inmates escape and get shot for their trouble."

It was not long before the inmates began questioning the sanity of what was going on outside. "They'd say, 'We are supposed to be unbalanced, but look at what they are doing,' " Manoogian recalled. " 'Why are people killing each other? Why all the explosions? Why are they shelling us?' "

Keeping the hospital functioning was as much a challenge to Manoogian, an infinitely proper man in his seventies, as providing power was to Bizri. It seemed to me that the hospital director took unreasonable chances. He somehow had arranged for fuel oil from the Moslem side and flour from the Christian-held port. But for months at a time, the hospital had no water or electricity. The seventeen gendarmes assigned to keep the prison inmates in line had disappeared early on. And every month, Manoogian had to run the gauntlet to collect cash from his bank to pay salaries. People long since had stopped accepting checks. At a time when members of parliament were universally despised by all the various gunmen, he drove his Chevrolet with his special parliamentary license plate—number 104—on his monthly bank run. Why? I asked. "Only car I had," he replied.

On such occasions, he rose in the middle of the night and was on the road by 5:00 a.m. to take advantage of the de facto truce that usually, but not always, obtained for the ensuing hour or so. (It was called the "newspaper truce," for the war's folklore had decided that the belligerents would allow one another's newspapers through in an early-morning truck run.) Manoogian would go through Christian territory to pick up his bank manager—who lived near the dividing line—then double back to the Museum, cross into Moslem turf, drive to the bank on Hamra—where the banker would open the safe and extract the money—and then retrace his journey. He never took a bodyguard—"wouldn't stop a bullet, now, would he?" Nor, apparently, did the psychiatrist worry about being robbed on the way back to the hospital, since he simply put the payroll funds in his wallet without trying to hide the money. He swore he had never been shot at, perhaps because he made it his business to befriend snipers, who would tell him when they thought it safe for him to pass.

Why did he not send someone else on the payroll runs?

"In Lebanon," he replied, "things happen only by personal intervention—it's the people you know and who trust you."

In retrospect, would he have made those runs so blithely had he known the war would last so long?

"But nobody believed things would last more than a few weeks."

Many years later, were any new forms of psychiatric disturbance starting to show up?

He thought awhile, then said, "Not yet, really, except that people are beginning to lose hope."

At one point during the fighting, Manoogian reflected, the penal wing at his hospital was the country's only functioning prison. For in two great waves those state institutions which had managed to escape the maelstrom finally succumbed. The first wave coincided with the fighting in Karantina and Damour in January 1976. Splits in the eighteen-thousand-man Lebanese Army could no longer be denied: it had been immobilized by political bickering between Christians and Moslems, and subject to isolated mutinies for months. Backed by the Palestinians, a disgruntled Sunni Moslem named Lieutenant Ahmed Khatib, who had been consistently passed over for promotion by his Maronite superiors, now announced on January 21 the creation of the Lebanese Arab Army. Within days he had persuaded two thousand Moslem soldiers to rally round, and at the zenith of his power, claimed control of three quarters of all Lebanese Army barracks.

Beirut airport, the country's main escape hatch, shut down for the first time in the war and stayed closed for a week. In West Beirut a mob of men and women, some of them well-dressed middle-class Lebanese, stormed Spinneys' supermarket in broad daylight, making off with food, liquor, television sets, and anything else they could carry. More than one looter returned to the parking lot with his plunder to discover his car had been stolen while he'd been inside the supermarket. Other looters shot one another in their frenzy to plunder. Beiruti landlords who had not previously installed complicated grilles on building entrances now did so. The few residents brave enough to dine out discovered the folly of their ways when gunmen burst into a French restaurant called Le Relais de Normandie, robbed its guests of cash, watches, and jewelry, and kidnapped and later raped two young women.

I remember walking down a busy street near my hotel one morning, and being stopped by an unshaven young man who pulled a revolver out of his jacket. He grabbed at my coat, but I pretended not to have noticed and kept on walking. Something told me he wouldn't shoot me in cold blood in that crowded street and that I'd run a greater risk if I allowed him to detain me. The next day, my money changer, with whom I'd done business for years, called up to say my last check had bounced. He was not friendly, nor did he appear to believe my protestations of innocence. I feverishly telephoned my New York bank, which discovered a computer error, but not before I had visions of turning into yet another trussed cadaver. At the end of that week, the Israelis allowed Syria to dispatch to Beirut a brigade of the Damascus-controlled Palestine Liberation Army, whose mere presence restored a modicum of law and order for almost two months.

By that time, at least half the city's population had fled. Those who remained learned how to survive. If your telephone went out, you borrowed the absent neighbors'. When power went on the blink, a jerry-built connection could be made with the main line in the street. Water supplies were cut, but many Beirutis drilled artesian wells in their courtyards. Sniper areas were marked off with warning signs. Trucks dumped loads of sand to block off dangerous streets. Because of the snipers, one avoided balconies and exposed windows, and often put in cinder blocks for added protection. When mortars became popular, top-floor apartments were abandoned as too dangerous. The advent of heavy artillery was dealt with by putting two or three walls, often sandbagged, between you and the artillery. Even on the demarcation line, people often lived in the back apartments while militiamen slugged it out in the front-line rooms. Hospitals, schools, barracks, markets—anywhere people gathered in numbers—were favorite targets. Mortars, rockets, artillery were zeroed in on such fixed objectives. But that was the limit of military skill employed in most of the fighting. Aside from the Christian siege of Tal Zaatar and a leftist offensive against the luxury hotels, both sides were singularly innocent of the rudiments of warfare. The casualties were higher among Moslems than among Christians in Beirut, largely because the Moslems were more numerous and lived in crowded neighborhoods where shelling took a greater toll. In the war's early stages, many Moslems forswore even the most primitive of precautions, such as sandbagging, and continued to congregate in known meeting places. Even after years of fighting, neither Christians nor Moslems systematically taped their plate-glass windows, despite the appalling wounds incurred from shards. *Maktoub*, which means "that which is written"—or fatalism, as Westerners would say—still exists in the Orient.

The midwinter break ended on March 11, when Brigadier General Aziz Ahdab, commander of the vestigial Beirut garrison, drove to the television station and announced he was seizing power. He demanded that President Sleiman Franjieh resign within twenty-four hours and that new elections be held within a week to choose a successor.

Although "General Television"—as Ahdab was subsequently called—commanded fewer than a thousand troops, his farcical performance apparently struck a chord in all Lebanese except Franjieh himself. Moslems and Christians, civilians and militia leaders, jumped on the bandwagon: sixty-eight, or more than the required two thirds of the ninety-nine MPs, voted to impeach Franjieh. Only a last-minute decision by Sheikh Pierre Gemayel prevented the Phalangists' Politburo from going along.

The remaining facade of state institutions crumbled. In a whirlwind offensive, the Lebanese Left prevailed on its reluctant Palestinian allies and together they finally had the Christians on the run. The Palestinians dislodged Phalangists from the twenty-seven-story Holiday Inn and then helped roll them all the way back to Martyrs' Square within less than a week. Kamal Jumblatt, the Druze leader of the loosely affiliated, leftist-dominated National Movement, emerged from the shadows to proclaim the necessity of a military solution to the war. The Christian militias—thrown out of the seafront Hilton and Normandy hotels, powerless to stop a mountain offensive their foes unleashed, forced to take in Franjieh, who had been driven from the Presidential Palace by Khatib's artillery—by the end of March were on the brink of defeat.

But Syria, which had hoped the Lebanese and Palestinians had got the message in January, now decided to intervene more openly. It was the Special Forces of Rifaat Assad, the Syrian President's brother, which prevented Khatib's troops from pursuing Franjieh to his very palace. Ever more obviously (but not obviously enough for his erstwhile allies to understand), Syrian President Hafez Assad inched his troops into eastern Lebanon, hoping Jumblatt would stop. Arafat was caught between his Syrian and Lebanese allies. He tried to reason with Jumblatt, but to no avail; nonetheless, mindful of the great debt he owed Jumblatt for sponsoring the PLO after the Jordanian disaster in 1970, Arafat reluctantly threw in his lot with the Druze leader. With Arafat incapable of moderating Jumblatt, Syria formally switched alliances and wholeheartedly backed the Christian warlords.

But the Christians could not be sure the Syrians would really come to their rescue. The tocsin sounding in late March in churches in Beirut and the Christian hinterland did not hide the lawlessness in Maronite territory that coincided with their military defeats. The Maronite leadership long had toyed with the idea of partitioning Lebanon, and threatened to carry it out unless its enemies did its bidding. Now partition was being forced upon the warlords. In the confusion, Christian militiamen stormed Roumieh prison, in the Christian suburbs of Beirut, releasing 570 prisoners and setting in train the sack of West Beirut's infamous Sands prison the next day, March 17. Surrounded by Palestinian guerrillas and prisoners' chanting relatives, various buildings inside the Sands complex were set on fire by inmates burning mattresses. Prisoners overpowered unarmed gendarmes, took their keys, and opened the outside doors. A ten-man Fatah squad, sent to help the prison's authorities, disappeared in the face of some 100 other commandos firing off their weapons in the air and waving Palestinian flags. Out poured 710 prisoners. All the records were burned (although they were later pieced together, thanks to ration lists kept by the prison caterer). The prison, dating from Ottoman times, was bulldozed into oblivion in a joyful scene compared by its authors to the storming of the Bastille in 1789. (The prison grounds now serve as a parking lot for the engineering school of the Egyptian-backed Arab University.)

The next day, 66 prisoners, including some foreigners, were freed from the women's prison in West Beirut. Christian prisoners in Moslem turf and Moslem inmates in jails in Christian territory were soon exchanged at the Museum crossing point. So absent were the police, who had even given up appearing for duty with empty holsters, that Fatah commandos entered the largely abandoned Sûreté Générale building across from the Museum itself and made off with the archives. Foreigners, including a handful of Americans serving time for drug offenses, turned up at the U.S. embassy, which had gloried in the stiff Lebanese sentences of yore. Now all the embassy could do was to issue one-way passports, good only for a return trip to the United States.

For the Phalangist leadership, brought up to respect private property as much as Lebanese nationalism itself, the last half of March was a time of shame and humiliation. Bad enough that finally they had been dislodged from their defiant perch in the Holiday Inn after months of myth-making prestige, when their propagandists compared the events to the siege of the Alcázar during the Spanish Civil War. Morale crumbled, and they were unable to stop the looting of the banks (principally the work of their enemies), or even the plundering of the port (carried out by their own militia). To the limited extent that the facts can be pieced together, it appears that the center of the economy fell apart once the army split after the Ahdab coup. Since the previous September the army had been stationed inside the port and along Bank Street. Suddenly, the army was gone. Gendarmes sent in to replace the soldiers proved no more effective. The Phalangists' many critics explained that they lost the Holiday Inn because they wanted to take part in the looting of the port. "They were much more interested in theft than in fighting the war," ran a common complaint. But in fact, it was a special Palestinian commando unit using armored vehicles lent by the Lebanese Arab Army that dislodged the Phalangists on March 21. And they had to return and do the job over again the next day, after a leftist Lebanese militia to whom the hotel had been handed for propaganda purposes got so carried away by celebrating that Christian militiamen sneaked back in at dawn. So determined was the leftist and Palestinian offensive that the retreating Phalangists had little time for looting until they reached their main line of defense at Martyrs' Square. Gone were the days so dear to civil war folklore when rival militiamen arranged their own private truces. A favorite story had it that militiamen fighting each other in a downtown street had finished looting the stores behind them and concluded a truce to ransack those between their rival positions. They met, formed a committee, and delegated joint teams to loot the stores, the story insisted, and once they'd completed that mission, they went back to shooting at each other.

Such apocryphal tales paled in comparison with the biggest bank robbery—or, more accurately, the biggest unopposed robbery of banks—in modern history. For weeks bankers had been forced to rely for protection solely on their generous payoffs to the various militias, a practice begun earlier when the army kept pulling out whenever fighting increased in the neighborhood. Even after the robberies, the banks continued to pay protection money. That was obvious when the fighting finally stopped in November 1976: the wholesale destruction visible elsewhere downtown stopped in Bank Street, where hardly a windowpane appeared to be broken. But the previous spring "it was a unique situation—one of the world's richest banking districts suddenly passed out of government authority and under the control of warring gangs," a banker recalled to me bitterly. "Even Fort Knox can be robbed if there is no army to defend it." Of the eleven banks robbed, the worst hit were those with safe-deposit vaults—the British Bank of the Middle East, the Banco di Roma, and the Bank Misr-Liban. The *Guinness Book of Records* claims the BBME alone lost as "an absolute minimum" $20 million and probably $50 million by way of qualifying as history's biggest bank robbery victory. But bank officials have dismissed such suggestions as "totally nonsensical." Deduct the $2 million maximum the thieves stole in cash and traveler's checks, they say, and to arrive at the *Guinness* figures would require that each of the four hundred safe-deposit boxes—all but one of which were robbed—contained an average worth of $45,000 to $120,000.

In fact, it wasn't the banks that lost the money, at least not legally. And no one may ever know how much the thieves made off with. The victimized banks have so thoroughly discouraged any inquiries about the robberies that no overall estimate has ever been made public about the losses sustained. The very nature of a safe-deposit box—which rented for less than $70 a year in Beirut—is that the owner alone knows the precise contents of his deposit. There is no insurance sold on what, after all, is a form of insurance itself. And international law has yet to offer victimized box holders any redress. Some merchants of the gold suq had put their gold and jewelry in safe-deposit boxes when the September 1975 fighting destroyed their traditional quarters. Others, however, may have found it prudent to remove their valuables, given the unsettled security situation. Valuables may have been buried in Beirut, if needs be, if the risk of transporting them to the airport or by road to the mountains seemed too great. Yet the presence of the army in Bank Street, and the obvious government self-interest in protecting the banks, plus the banks' own bribing of the militias, may have seemed so reassuring that no safer place could have been imagined in Lebanon. Moreover, among the box holders were many Arabs from other Middle Eastern countries, or foreign nationals, who had their own sometimes unavowable reasons for leaving their valuables in the boxes. Even more than in other parts of the world, wealth in the Middle East tends to be acquired in less than totally aboveboard fashion.

Bank Street appears to have changed hands several times before the army collapsed. That was enough to encourage rumors that two Christian militias—the Phalangists and the Tigers—shot it out with one another for the honor of stealing the BBME's cash and traveler's checks. Such an operation would have required no great expertise or perseverance, and the Christian rivals were said to have split the booty. But the Christians were too obviously on the run to do more. They didn't have time. And time was required. The Palestinians had plenty of time, and persistent reports credit them with robbing the two banks with the fattest safe-deposit vaults. Saiqa, the Syrian wing of the PLO, was identified with the Banco di Roma thefts, and the BBME was reputedly the work of the Marxist Democratic Front for the Liberation of Palestine. (At the time, Saiqa was held responsible for both bank robberies, for there was growing anti-Syrian sentiment among Lebanese and an increasingly notorious reputation for the Saiqa leader, Zuhair Mohsen, nicknamed "the Persian" for the quantities of valuable carpets of that provenance his men were blamed for looting from Beirut homes. Local legend has it that Syrian Defense Minister Mustafa Tlass promised the Italian ambassador in Damascus to make good the bank's losses.) Early on, the Palestinians at the BBME tried to dynamite their way into the vaults, with self-defeating and macabre results. One DF guerrilla told a friend he'd found a severed hand in the bank, which apparently had belonged to a fellow Palestinian who'd badly misjudged the explosive charge he'd been handling. Other Palestinians showed off bundles of dollars, torn and charred by explosions, as well as diamonds and platinum. Many suddenly became interested in Zurich and London gold prices for the first time in their lives. Most of the loot went into their organizations' coffers, but not before a shoot-out. Saiqa manned the checkpoints on Bank Street and tried to prevent the DF from carrying off its loot. After a brief firefight, the DF brought up Jeep-mounted heavy machine guns and had no more trouble.

At some point, the looters realized they had effective control of Bank Street for sufficient time to bring in two or three professional safecrackers from Europe, possibly supplied by the Mafia. At least that is what one BBME official has theorized. After the fact, it was easy enough to understand how the thieves had gone about their work. A wall was pierced from the adjacent Catholic Church of the Capuchins, which allowed direct entry to the BBME. The final approach work on the safe-deposit vaults was done with great skill. With the din of battle drowning out the noise of the blasting, the professionals made short shrift of Chubb of London's three steel-bar security gates and then the two armor-plated vault doors, each forty-five centimeters thick. Just the right dose of explosives was employed, carefully tamped down around the door frames. Any miscalculation literally could have brought the roof down on the thieves' heads. Instead, the heavy steel doors were blown back from the jamb just enough to let the looters slip in. In the subbasement, the treasury doors were blasted in the same exacting fashion. Safe-deposit boxes were opened by pouring acid on the locks. The fail-safe alarm is said to have functioned, and bells rang in the nearest flying-squad office. But the police long since had fled, and combatants who may or may not have been in the office either were part of the gang or were not about to risk their lives by being curious. The premises were firebombed, apparently to destroy any telltale traces such as fingerprints. BBME officials theorized that the jewelry was probably melted down or fenced, the bearer bonds as easily disposed of as cash, and title deeds and other hard-to-negotiate instruments simply thrown away.

As professional as the safecracking was, the disposal of the traveler's checks struck BBME officials as oddly amateurish. Only a few of the stolen checks have surfaced in the more than seven years since the robbery. Despite recurring rumors, none of the valuable jewels or objets d'art from the boxes are known to have come to light in European or American outlets. Asked if the banks had been victims of the perfect crime, a banker scowled and said, "Normally, a complicated bank robbery can induce a kind of sneaking admiration for the finesse involved. This job obviously had some elements of finesse—but precious few." He assured me the BBME had replaced the destroyed Chubb equipment with even better material from the same firm—with the exception of the safe-deposit vaults and boxes. "Somehow," he said, "we didn't think boxes are a number-one selling service in Beirut."

Sarah Salem, a West Beirut Maronite friend of mine, was luckier than most safe-deposit-box holders. On May 15, more than a month after word had leaked out about the bank robberies, she received a telephone call from a man at the Banque Nationale de Paris Intercontinentale, the Beirut affiliate of one of France's biggest banks. He was glad to have found her because today was the last day—the absolute deadline—for withdrawing valuables from her box at the bank's premises in the Fattal building. She protested that the latest truce was shaky, that snipers were active—especially downtown, where the Fattal building was located. The banker merely repeated what he'd said before, adding that the man to see was a ranking Phalangist named Dib Anastase, at their headquarters near the port. She now remembered that the newspapers had been running advertisements asking box holders to get in touch with the bank, and she decided to go. A quick check with her mother confirmed that the box contained no cash or jewelry, just title deeds and shares. And she decided to go, driving through West Beirut, across the Museum crossing, and into Christian territory.

"There'd been a bit of sniper fire on the way over, which got me in the mood," Sarah recalled. "Dib Anastase at the Phalangists' explained he'd send a militiaman with me, that we'd travel in my car, and that since the lad would be risking his life on my account, he should expect a tip. So I said OK.

"A young blond militiaman with a headband appeared and explained that we'd cross Allenby Street as quickly as possible to avoid snipers. I wasn't too delighted at that, and even less so when he started off, driving like a madman in my car through the rubble, across the clearly exposed area, and then stopped in front of a building. 'But this isn't Fattal,' I told him.

" 'Wait,' he said. There was occasional shooting in the street, further up. Then we entered a building and went through three or four buildings from the inside. They'd blown passageways in the inside walls to allow resupply without exposing themselves to enemy fire. We passed only a few militiamen. There was an ocean of paper strewn around the floors, and the offices had been ripped apart, apparently by looters. The militiamen had built positions all over, some blackened from taking hits, and the rooms were stacked with soap, chocolate, God knows what else the Fattal company imported. Finally, we got to a door, and my man said, 'I'll wait for you outside.'

" 'What do I do now?' I asked. He just pointed.

"Suddenly, in the half darkness—there was no electricity, although it couldn't have been later than ten a.m.—I saw some other militiamen. One asked me for my name, then checked a list and he said, 'OK. I'll give you a man.' I looked at him, and his eyes were eloquent with greed. I kept telling myself I had nothing to worry about because the box contained no jewels, no cash, but I kept thinking he was already figuring his percentage of the take. We were going through the main marble-lined hall of the bank, and he said, 'Get down on the floor. They can see us.' We crawled."

"What were you wearing?" I asked.

"Pants, luckily enough, but by pure chance, since that's what I had on when the banker phoned.

"Finally, we got past the dangerous part, which was less than two hundred yards from the Banque de Syrie et du Liban, where Ahmad Jibril's Popular Front for the Liberation of Palestine–General Command was. Anyhow, down we went into the underground safe-deposit vault. What a sight—a long room with all the box doors sawn off, blackened, an incredible quantity of pieces of wood and steel they'd been using to try to pry the doors open.

" 'Sorry, but I don't have the key. It's with my brother, who lives in Kuwait,' I explained.

" 'Don't worry. We have ways of opening the boxes,' the militiaman said, and out of nowhere appears a wild-eyed man with a blowtorch and a welder's mask to protect his eyes. He went to work, but apparently all the drawers jammed when whoever it was blew the vault doors in the first place, because he finally abandoned his torch and came back with a long hooked rod. He pulled and pulled, and finally out came the long drawer.

"It was one of those crazy moments. He's holding a flashlight and discreetly moves away to let me open the box in private, but all the time he's watching out of the corner of his eye. So I opened the box and took out two envelopes full of papers, shares, and title deeds. And he said, 'Is that all?' He wanted to be sure, made me open the envelopes. I swear his eyes were bulging out of his head—what greed to possess jewels and money! All I had were lousy documents.

"So back we went, the same way, up the stairs, with the sound of explosions in my ears. At one point, while we were crawling through the main room of the bank, there was a whole lot of shooting very close, and he motioned me to stop. 'Jibril's people in the other bank. It's like that all day long,' he said. I gave him five hundred Lebanese pounds—about a hundred eighty dollars at the time—as a tip. Friends had told me that was the going rate for documents. They got a cut on jewels, and some friends paid as much as three thousand Lebanese pounds.

"So we get back to the guy with the list on his clipboard, and I signed and was given a slip of paper saying I'd emptied my box. My blond guide was waiting. You should have seen the look on his face—what disappointment. He must have been counting on seeing me emerge with my arms drooping under the weight of jewels and gold bars. So back we went through the three buildings to the car and back to his headquarters. I showed him the envelopes and gave him a tip of five hundred Lebanese pounds. He kept asking me, 'Is that all you got out of the bank?' as if I'd been crazy to risk my skin—and his—for so little. It was only then that I dared ask who had blown the vault doors to begin with. 'Uncontrolled elements,' he said.

"I drove back to West Beirut. Funny that during the ordeal I was fairly cool. But once I got back home I was tense, uneasy, and excited. I was furious with those grasping militiamen—and who were those 'uncontrolled elements,' anyhow?"

That was not a thought that particularly pleased Nazo, an important Phalangist militia leader and the kind of strong, sincere, and upright young man that armies the world over describe as "perfect officer material." His devotion to the cause was somewhat unusual. Nazir Najarian was Armenian, and the Armenian community, by and large, had done its best to stay out of the fighting. He'd been wounded badly enough to carry a limp for the rest of his days, and his younger brother had been killed on another front. At eighteen, Nazo had commanded half the Phalangist troops in the downtown area of Beirut. I asked him once to show me his old positions, and, as Sarah Salem had done, we walked through holes blasted in the inside walls of buildings, through abandoned offices littered with papers, through an empty movie house and a department store, to arrive at a vantage point overlooking Martyrs' Square. Here had been the heart of old Lebanon. Now it was an empty shooting gallery whose daily—or, more accurately, nightly—exchanges of fire were taken for granted and routinely noted in the press. Behind those front-line walls lived the poor and displaced who had found accommodation within their limited means. There, too, were the eternal optimists like the militiaman who tended a vegetable garden or the movie operator who waxed eloquent over the heroes and heroines of old American movies he had shown in the square's shabby theaters. Upended containers stolen from the nearby port provided some protection from snipers for the more exposed Phalangist positions, and the square itself was all but obscured by an almost tropical growth of grass and small bushes that neither the Phalangists nor the Syrian-commanded Palestine Liberation Army troops on the other side were about to risk their lives to cut down. For some reason I kept thinking of William Jennings Bryan's Cross of Gold speech and his warning that "grass will grow in the streets"—and for good reason. Some of the best mining and sapper work in modern history was to be found here. On the West Beirut side, Russian advisers were reputed to have outdone themselves.

I took Nazo aback by asking him how he had felt in March 1976 after months of having his comrades—average age seventeen—killed as he watched other Phalangists loot the port. Estimates vary, but the losses were estimated by the Port Authority at $715 million—60 percent in the free zone, with the lion's share destined for transshipment to Iraq—to more than seven times that figure.

"Napoleon said there were two kinds of people in revolutions," Nazo said, "those who make them and those who profit from them."

"What's happened in Lebanon is a revolution?"

Nazo went back to my first question. "When it started I went around all our positions and talked it over. For me, looting was not normal. There was the port, a hundred yards away, no farther, and other militiamen, civilians—our militiamen, our civilians—were sometimes coming to blows, shooting each other in their greed to cart off the merchandise in their cars and trucks. I kept saying to myself and my buddies, 'We must keep our heads, that is the most important thing, resist material temptation, because material things will corrupt us. And if we become corrupt, we can't carry on the war, we'll be submerged, liquidated, and not just here in Lebanon, but as Christians throughout the Near East.' "

Nazo's Armenian background made him determined to fight to keep a strong Christian presence in Lebanon. That's part of a larger credo that stipulates that re-creating an independent Armenia in present-day Turkey depends on Armenians' staying in this part of the world, rather than emigrating to the United States, another favored refuge. Nazo didn't much appreciate it when I said that looting was often the work of armies in retreat and certainly the Phalangists were in retreat when the plundering of the port began.

"We all agreed not to have anything to do with the looting," Nazo said, "but it was Topic A for the duration of the looting, and that was for weeks. We said, 'If you want to stay with us, you have to remain pure.' "

"Did some leave?"

"Yes, but that's the way it was during the war. There was no real discipline. If a militiaman wanted to leave my troops and go somewhere else, he did, and nothing happened, because we needed fighters so badly at the time."

"But for you the looting of the port must have been absurd after all those months of defending the downtown front."

"It was one of the hardest problems I faced. I'm neither rich nor poor, but I know that what I've accomplished has been on my own. Plenty of militiamen looted during the war. 'So-and-So didn't have a bicycle and now he's driving a big American car,' my men used to tell me. Looting—that was human nature at its most animallike, its most instinctive. But the guys who made easy money blew it—gambling, drugs, they spent it stupidly."

"How about all the Mr. Bigs, the merchants who got even fatter by trafficking and looting while you were risking your necks, the guys who were selling the boys hashish, heroin, and cocaine? It was the first time soldiers used that rich man's drug."

"Not easy times. We wanted to live a pure life, and I decided to walk that path. I stayed in the Phalange or the Lebanese Forces, as it's called now. Others left—they had a taste for profit, money, they went into business. Everyone is free. We're still here, and the funny thing is that I was trained as an accountant."

I couldn't but think of a banker friend's less indulgent view of the plundering of the port. "You'd pay some Phalangist a fee, sometimes as much as six thousand dollars, and you could fill your truck up with anything you wanted. Then the Phalangists got smart and started centralizing the really valuable items—the carpets, the objets d'art, the cars, the precision steel, the booze, the color television sets, God only knows what. They held a public auction at the Christian Brothers College in Gemmayzé—you know, right near the port. It was the Christie's of Gemmayzé."

I've wondered since then if Nazo was reading my mind about the Christian Brothers auction, because uncannily he volunteered he had done his high-school studies at the Christian Brothers College, an institution for lower-middle- and working-class boys. The school was only about three hundred yards due east, at the end of an area all but abandoned by its original owners as too dangerous, and now inhabited largely by Christians displaced from their homes in the fighting.

"Sure, people stole merchandise from the port," Nazo said. "But what you've got to understand is that without all those goods Christian Lebanon would have been in terrible economic difficulty. Even those who didn't have a hand in the actual looting benefited, buying and selling what had been stolen."

Eternal Phoenicia. Eternal traders. I didn't say a thing. And I resisted the temptation to ask him whether he'd been educated not by the Christian Brothers but by the Jesuits. Even as dedicated and straightforward a Christian soldier as Nazo fell back on casuistry when faced with unpleasant facts. It was part of the Christian ghetto mentality, cleverly manipulated by the propaganda machine. Defeats were transformed into victories, cowardly horrors into acts of exemplary derring-do, optimism rekindled from the ashes of errors.

In fact, the only Lebanese I found without any illusions from the very start was Amir Maurice Chehab, a Maronite whose Ottoman title denotes kinship with a family that for two hundred fifty years, until the mid-nineteenth century, ran Mount Lebanon. Former head of Lebanese antiquities and director of the Beirut Museum, the distinguished septuagenarian shared none of his fellow citizens' long-undimmable optimism that the fighting would end as quickly as it had begun. "From the beginning I said these events"—as the French-speaking scholar euphemistically described Lebanon's endemic violence—"were going to last twenty-five years." As soon as the shooting began in April 1975, he'd emptied the Museum of its most valued possessions, starting with objects easiest to carry off. The sandbagged Museum, where he and his wife lived—despite an occasional rocket or mortar round in the apartment, the presence of a Syrian artillery battery on the adjacent racetrack, and Syrian troops outside the building itself—proved to be one of the most dangerous places in Beirut. (The site was heavily bombed by Israel in 1982.)

Where were the gold Phoenician riches, the early Egyptian collection that rivaled the Cairo Museum's, the jewelry from the Roman, Byzantine, and Arab periods, the much-admired mosaic collection, the sarcophagus collection? The Amir smiled, allowed that he had thought out the evacuation plan a long time in advance and been careful not to move everything out at once. How about the rumors that armed men from various armies had robbed the Museum? He smiled again. And reading my mind as I sought to frame a question tactfully noting both his advanced years and the patent danger of his remaining in the Museum apartment, he said, "Don't worry." About what? I felt obliged to ask. "The President of the Republic knows where everything is." In a way, that knowledge was as precious as the White House nuclear code, and his foresight as rare in Lebanon as the objects he sought to preserve.

At some point during those nineteen months of violence, I finally understood that my professional refusal to succumb to systematic pessimism was totally wrongheaded. Over the years, in many countries, I had seen many colleagues in maddeningly complicated situations simply give up and look at the confusion through a very special and simplifying pair of eyeglasses. It is always harder, much harder, to try to puzzle your way through the morass. As usual, it took a real resident, a native in the best sense of the word, to make me do this. My friend Lucien George cut through the miasma in November 1976, when the Arab League formally gave its blessing to the essentially Syrian presence in Lebanon, tarted up as a pan-Arab peacekeeping force. "This is not the end of our travail," he said, "but the beginning."

4. The Irresistible Ascension of Bashir Gemayel

"Longest coup d'état in modern annals," the Phalange politician said, smiling at his own insight, "or damn well looks that way, if a man didn't know better." In the final month of 1982, he was reflecting on nearly half a century of Lebanese history entangled with the meandering fortunes of his party and its founding dynasty, the Gemayels of Bikfaya. He knew that more than a half-dozen armies were stationed in Lebanon, that the future seemed uncertain, and that whatever dreams he and others had had for a quick solution to the country's problems had evaporated. Worse yet, Bashir was dead, assassinated before taking office. Still, what accomplishments the Phalange had to its credit! Under the tutelage of its founder, Pierre Gemayel, in forty-six years it had ceased fielding a militia of glorified Boy Scouts and now had a real army. It had ceased being just a party—indeed, was on its way to becoming a state. The old Lebanon Sheikh Pierre had professed to love was dead, had collapsed since 1975, but his own party and family ambitions had soared. Now he had seen two Gemayel sons elected President of the Lebanese Republic. (Within a week of Bashir's assassination, the older son, Amin, was President in his place.) And Sheikh Pierre—as he was always called, in keeping with the Lebanese fondness for Ottoman honorifics for their politicians—was the power broker between the Lebanese Forces, Bashir's strike force and state-within-a-state, and the Republic, headed by his son Amin. At seventy-seven, Sheikh Pierre had accomplished a life's dream. He had had to wait until 1960 to win election to parliament and, while minister often enough, never really came close to the presidency he so coveted. If anything, he was stronger now than in the past half-dozen years, when Bashir had overshadowed him.

Even as a young man—and he kept the physical attributes of youth well into middle age—there was something vaguely Iowa Gothic about Sheikh Pierre. Ramrod-straight, his white hair plastered close to the skull, he was punctilious and courtly in an Old World way. His detractors have long insisted that he was born not in Lebanon at all but in Egypt, as if to suggest that his radical Christian nationalism was due to being brought up on foreign soil, albeit of Lebanese parents. As a young graduate of Université Saint Joseph, run by French Jesuits in Beirut, Sheikh Pierre was really interested in sports. He boxed, wrestled, and played soccer; party hagiographers often reproduce a photograph of him in a university soccer uniform decorated with a large cross. Then he trained as a pharmacist and ran a drugstore in Martyrs' Square, whose proximity to Beirut's red-light district caused his enemies to dub him "Pierre the Condom." Those were still the days when the Lebanese felt they could joke about him and his Phalange Party.

Sheikh Pierre has freely acknowledged that it was his visit to the 1936 Berlin Olympics that inspired him to found the Phalange Party. In recent years he has come to prefer telling visitors that he was more impressed by the Sokol sporting clubs of Czechoslovakia than by his Nazi hosts, and it was *their* discipline that struck him, he would say. But in any case he returned to Beirut and fitted out his first followers with all the regulation 1930s accoutrements of right-wing Mediterranean nationalist politics—pith helmets, gaiters, dark shirts and ties (khaki in the Phalangist case), and stiff-armed salutes. Although in the 1940s the Phalange arrogated to itself the defense of Lebanon's small and dwindling Jewish community, Israelis looked on party members with distaste because of their outward similarities to the Nazis. Scholars attach less importance to European fascism's influence on the Phalange ideology than to its stress on paramilitary organization and on always having a single, all-important leader.

In the early days, Sheikh Pierre led his followers in pitched battles with baton-wielding French colonial troops. In the 1930s his main Lebanese adversary was a somewhat similarly organized group named the Najjad, which, like many Sunni Moslem political parties, demanded that France return Lebanon to what they felt were its rightful Syrian owners. As a Lebanese nationalist, Sheikh Pierre preferred speaking French, and indeed his Arabic is unimpressive to this day.

Throughout most of Phalange history, Sheikh Pierre looked on his armed forces as auxiliaries backing up the state—that is, Christian established power. The same nationalism that got him in trouble with the French colonial authorities made him a fervent believer in the National Covenant. Once British and Free French forces defeated the Vichy French administration of Lebanon in 1941, this unwritten agreement between Lebanese Moslems and Christians led to independence from a prostrate France—much to General de Gaulle's anger with the British and Americans, who acted as Lebanon's midwives. Sheikh Pierre never tired of singing the praises of the Covenant, which enshrined the first independent Christian political power in the Middle East since the Crusader kingdoms. Foreign visitors to Phalange headquarters invariably were treated to long exposés of past Moslem exactions. "My grandfather in Bikfaya was not allowed to wear silk or to ride a horse into Beirut, just a donkey," Sheikh Pierre would recall, as if the vexation had happened only yesterday. Such was Sheikh Pierre's deep-felt need to complain to everyone about the Christians' second-class-citizen status of yore that, one American ambassador recalled, "there was only a limited period during our conversation when I could register specific points." Over the years, Sheikh Pierre made thousands of daily pronouncements to the local press, ranging from denunciations of Palestinian excesses to those of the international terrorist Left and the fifth columnists determined to destroy the 1943 Covenant. Repeatedly he recalled that, unlike the Jews or Palestinians, the Maronites had never deserted their land and, he proclaimed, they would die fighting any efforts to push them out. This was the point that always struck a chord with the Maronites. Sheikh Pierre exerted a very real influence on two generations of Lebanese Christians, and especially, but by no means exclusively, on his fellow Maronites. His was a reassuring message that many Christians did not want to broadcast in public themselves, but were delighted to get across to the other, especially Moslem, Lebanese.

Though the party held little attraction for the established oligarchy that really ran Lebanon before 1975, or for intellectuals, the list of Phalange alumni reads like a Who's Who of successful Lebanese Christian politicians, even if many left the party after only a brief membership—particularly the better-educated, who bridled at Sheikh Pierre's often authoritarian ways. A standard Lebanese joke asks why there is no barbershop opposite Phalange headquarters. "Because they've all quit before they reach the age to shave" is the answer. Still, the Phalange, with its Politburo, Central Committee, and complicated structure of regional and professional organizations, allowed some political discussion, if not necessarily the democracy its defenders claimed. Its motto, "God, Family, and Nation," especially appealed to Maronites who had left their mountain villages to live in Beirut's burgeoning suburbs and to those who remained in the mountains but neither belonged nor were allied to the old influential Maronite families. For these uprooted, the Phalange as a party had *wasta*, or "influence," with the often recalcitrant bureaucracy. It was present at the village level in many, if not all, Christian areas.

Inside the Phalange, despite outward appearances of democratic practices, all final decisions were taken by Sheikh Pierre. But he was smart enough to advance the cause of the party itself and of its various organizations rather than to rely on a personal following, as his originally better-placed competitors did. The shrewdness of this tactic, his rivals—including former Presidents Camille Chamoun and Sleiman Franjieh, as well as Raymond Eddé, son of a President and himself a perennial presidential hopeful—learned to their sorrow.

The Phalange was lucky at the right time. Before the civil war, it looked as if it were running out of steam. Then, at the beginning of the fighting in April 1975, the Moslems, the Left, and the Palestinians made the major error of trying to excommunicate the Phalangists from the government, indeed from all political life in Lebanon. From then on, many Maronites, indeed many Christians of other sects who might have had nothing but amused contempt for the Phalange, rallied round. Now Christendom was deemed threatened, so to the barricades! In those early months the only barricades of importance were Phalangist ones. "Teenagers flocked to the barricades," a young Maronite recalled, "the way their older brothers had taken to pinball machines a few years earlier." By the rudimentary standards of the day, the Phalange Party was ready—thanks not just to its paramilitary training, provided in recent years by the army, but to its overall sense of organization. Fred Stokes, a British political scientist who had watched the Phalangists over the years, was astounded by their organization. He wondered if the Phalange weren't the strongest national liberation movement in the Middle East; he worried about what it would do with its muscle.

Once the fighting started, the Phalange's major allies were the Maronite monks, who had wrested real power in the important Maronite Church away from Patriarch Antonios Boulos Khoreiche, whom many considered a namby-pamby pro-Palestinian, born within spitting distance of the Israeli border, far from the Maronite heartland. As major landowners and teachers, the monks exerted great influence on the Maronites, especially in times of stress. They housed many Christian families driven out of their home districts by the fighting. And their Superior General, Father Charbel Kassis, shared that general Lebanese gift for making good investments. The Christians' enemies insisted that the monks raised the cash to buy arms. As the Druze leader Kamal Jumblatt put it, "The tonsured heads of Lebanese monks give off a golden halo."

The other Christian warriors never really caught up. The Phalangists' major rival was the Tiger militia of former President Camille Chamoun, who throughout most of the civil war served as Interior Minister, then also as Foreign Minister. Born with the century, Chamoun had stayed out of the early months of fighting, preferring instead to use his political influence inside his National Liberal Party (NLP). Within the NLP he shared power neither with his sons, Dory and Dany, nor with anyone else. He exercised only the loosest control over his often unruly fledgling militia. When eventually Chamoun committed these military forces to the war (they were commanded by his younger son, Dany), they deliberately initiated fighting—the siege of Tal Zaatar, for example—that the Phalange would have preferred in many cases to have avoided. Some Christians compared the Tigers to Begin's Irgun Zvi Leumi terrorists during the Palestine fighting in the 1940s, who prodded and challenged the mainstream Palmach for military and political supremacy. "We fought the battles, not the Phalange," Chamoun confided. "They were against our starting Tal Zaatar, but eventually they had to join us. If we'd had a regular supply of arms, we would have invaded West Beirut," he added, making it clear that he was sure they would have ended the civil war there and then.

Lebanon's President, Sleiman Franjieh, in 1975 approaching the end of his six-year term in office, certainly had been contested, but in the north of the country he and his clan still reigned supreme. Minorities under stress tend not to change leaders. Born in 1910, Franjieh was the youngest of the Christian politicians-turned-warlords.

Cooped up in Mount Lebanon, hemmed in by the Syrian peacekeeping troops who had come to rescue them from their tormentors, the Christian leaders fell to quarreling among themselves. The first of their number to lose out was Raymond Eddé, the urbane parliamentary gadfly who in his perennial quest for the presidency had neglected to secure the only essential ingredient for success: a militia. And his sometimes commonsensical, always cutting contempt for the other Christian leaders made him a favorite target for their wrath. I remember lunching with him in West Beirut in the spring of 1976 while a renegade Christian colonel, Antoine Barakat, shelled the neighborhood. The window glass was long since gone from the mansion Eddé had inherited from his father, who had served as President of Lebanon during the French mandate. Eddé was vastly amused when I dived under the table after several Barakat rounds landed on surrounding high-rise buildings. "Don't worry, in the Levant they only kill the horse, never the rider," Eddé said, by way of explaining that leaders were usually spared in the general carnage. But that was before Bashir Gemayel's gunmen ambushed and wounded him, forcing him into exile in France.

In retrospect, Bashir's humiliation of a leading Christian politician twice his age can be seen as the first concrete proof that he was becoming a power in his own right. Bashir's emergence became clearer in July 1976, when he became the Phalange's military commander: he succeeded William Hawi, who was killed inspecting his forces besieging Tal Zaatar on July 13. So providential was that death for Bashir that many Lebanese, including some members of Hawi's family, were convinced that Gemayel was responsible for it. (PLO officials, who had no reason to whitewash Bashir, insisted, however, that a teenage guerrilla who escaped from the siege had claimed credit for killing a man perfectly fitting Hawi's description.) Whatever the facts, Bashir never looked back. Despite his father's own reservations about entrusting such a powerful post to so impulsive a young man—indeed, both Sheikh Pierre and Hawi had opposed naming him even deputy commander—Bashir was in a position to call the shots from then on. His father and his brother never really challenged what one influential cleric approvingly called his "rapacity for power." With a real war on, the politicians lost face—and power—to the young men doing the fighting. In a world where political primogeniture was traditional, without the war the star of Bashir Gemayel would have had little chance to rise in the Lebanese firmament.

It was an odd destiny for a second son who had none of the physical grace, charm, and intellectual abilities his older brother, Amin, possessed. Those who knew Bashir well as an adolescent and young man found him an engaging but hardly striking person—except, that is, for a kind of freewheeling penchant he had for wild-eyed schemes, the more bloodthirsty the better, as one professor friend later said.

One day in the late 1960s, the teenaged Bashir opened his heart to that friend. Leafing through an album of photographs of Sheikh Pierre in the early days, Bashir started talking about his own future. He would become a lawyer, he would marry, but the political future seemed unpromising. His father was still active, Amin increasingly so. But the Phalange needed lots of new blood, the professor said encouragingly. Bashir said that his father had made his mark fighting the Moslems and the French colonial authorities. Sheikh Pierre had lifelong friendships with his comrades, the fruit of years of political activism. It was impossible to re-create such special circumstances, Bashir said dejectedly, for Lebanon was now experiencing its golden period, and no challenge suggested itself on the horizon.

The youngest of the six Gemayel children, Bashir was given a typical middle-class Maronite education—with the Jesuits at Jamhour for secondary school, and again with the Jesuits at Université Saint Joseph, where he studied law. Physically unprepossessing, troubled by pimples well beyond his teens, Bashir made up in application for whatever he lacked in natural brilliance. A woman who was a fellow grind recalled to me how hard he worked—with a diligence he used to good effect in later years. And despite his penchant for violence there was a charming side to his character, a kind of puppy-dog openness, a willingness to listen that one often finds among the callow and insecure, and a certain bewilderment about the world. And he was Sheikh Pierre's son, which helped in all kinds of ways. For example, in 1969 the Interior Minister, Kamal Jumblatt, used his influence with the PLO to gain Bashir's release. A group of Phalangist youths, including Bashir, had stationed themselves on the Beirut–Damascus road where it does a hairpin turn at Kahhalé and had opened fire on a Palestinian convoy returning to Syria with the bodies of slain guerrillas; the youths were on their way to East Beirut when they were seized by Palestinians who stopped Bashir's Morris 1100 at Tal Zaatar and found some bloodstained berets in the trunk (although not severed heads, as alleged in a civil war legend).

Back from a semester of postgraduate law studies at Southern Methodist University in Dallas and a short stay in a Washington law firm, Bashir began his formal political apprenticeship. Hitherto, starting when he was twelve, he had belonged to the Phalange's youth militia, and then was active in its important university student operations. Now, under the old Phalangist Jean Nader, Bashir learned the ropes in Ashrafieh, the most prestigious party branch in Beirut. Nader (who was killed in 1982 alongside Bashir in that Ashrafieh office) once told me that his protégé was something of a problem in the beginning. "He was not an easy student," Nader said. "He thought he could do everything with his fists, but with time he came to understand that it was not just through fighting that you accomplish something in politics. He fought with the police, gendarmes, in the street, with anyone; and I got him out of his scrapes. He was very impulsive. He made snap decisions, tended to believe his militiamen without checking. But he learned to accept criticism, and I assure you he never killed anyone with his own hands."

Sheikh Pierre had opposed the Ashrafieh apprenticeship, convinced that Bashir should start in the provinces and earn his way back to the capital. Bashir, always ambivalent about his power, insisted that he had paid his dues and worked his way up, but he was mindful that all his talk about the need for meritocracy in a new Lebanon, rid of its muscle-bound civil service based on quotas for the various religious communities, with himself running the show, stemmed from his being his father's son. Both Bashir and Amin suffered from parental obstruction, which was based in large part on Sheikh Pierre's concern that the Phalange not appear to be what indeed it was—an instrument for the Gemayel family's ambitions—and that his own stewardship not be questioned by his ambitious sons. Throughout his career Bashir was obliged to maneuver in the face of family rivalry—for Amin, too, often opposed his younger brother's brusque manner and abrupt methods. Indeed, family rivalry in some ways constituted a more serious challenge to Bashir's ambitions than that of his formal political adversaries among the Moslems, leftists, Palestinians, or, for that matter, among the other conservative Maronite politicians.

By his own admission, that part of his success not linked to his birth or to the war was due to sheer hard work. His faithful, jolly secretary, Isis, kept a box of Mars bars on her desk, knowing that Bashir liked to wolf them down rather than waste time at the copious luncheons that were so much a part of the Lebanese political tradition. The other Christian leaders played at politics, played at war, but Bashir worked and worked, often for fifteen hours a day. Aside from doing the traditional politician's chores of attendance at weddings, baptisms, funerals, and requiem masses, Bashir did make one decision of pure genius. Instead of trying to take over the Phalange—where his father, brother, and their friends were solidly ensconced—Bashir built his own organization.

The Lebanese Forces had been formed on paper in the spring of 1976 to coordinate the Christian war effort. It included the militias of the Phalange, the National Liberal Party (NLP), and two much smaller organizations (incorporated in 1980)—the Guardians of the Cedars, an ultranationalist, anti-Palestinian group close to the monks; and Tanzim, Arabic for "the Organization," made up of professional men—doctors, lawyers, engineers. But in fact it was Bashir who fashioned the Lebanese Forces, especially after the formal end of the civil war in November 1976, when a period of relative calm ensued thanks to the presence in Lebanon of pro-Christian Syrian peacekeeping troops. Within the Lebanese Forces Bashir promoted his own young men, often only in their early twenties, who had in some cases no formal Phalange connections.

Bashir never was more than an observer at Phalange Politburo deliberations, and he often skipped the once-sacrosanct Monday morning sessions, which began sharply at 11:00 a.m. Theoretically, some three quarters of his men were Phalangists, but they paid only lip service to the party. They were careful to leave the formal structure intact but effectively emptied it of its substance. As the Lebanese Forces took form, and as the often anarchical wartime militias cohered into an outwardly disciplined, regular military force, these were Bashir's men, not those of his father's and his brother's party. (In late 1981, Bashir took advantage of Amin's absence in Europe to disarm his brother's militia in the Metn.) Although Maronite mythology would have every Maronite fighter a stout mountaineer recruited from some remote village, in fact many of Bashir's troops were drawn from Beirut's working-class suburbs. Another sizable group were Christians either displaced by the fighting or choosing of their own volition to join the fortress of Marounistan and swearing to fight until they liberated their homes. Both groups were deracinated, the first cut off from their spiritual roots in the mountains, the second physically barred from returning to their homes.

By 1978 Bashir was ready to move totally on his own—in one of those risky spurts of violence that were his trademark.

Only a handful of the one hundred men he used in the operation were told the real target beforehand, but the three-pronged attack on the northern hill town of Ehdene began without technical hitch shortly after 4:00 a.m. that June 13, 1978. A diversionary force on the Bcharré road, to the east, drew defenders away from what served as the summer palace during President Sleiman Franjieh's term in office. On the road to Zghorta, which was the capital of the Franjiehs' fief, twelve miles down a winding mountain road to the northwest, raiders ambushed and killed the reinforcements alerted by the first sounds of battle. The main force attacked the palace itself. Within a quarter hour all resistance to Bashir's attack had ended. Within the substantial stone walls of the summer palace, they were all dead (scarcely surprising, given the firepower employed). Still sprawled in their nightclothes lay Tony Franjieh, thirty-six; his wife, Vera, thirty-two; their daughter, Jehane, just three; the maid; the chauffeur—and the family dog.

Like so much else in Lebanon, the attack had gone wrong. How *far* wrong remained moot, the subject of interminable and opaque speculation. Bashir swore later that he had no idea Tony was in Ehdene when he ordered the operation against the palace. It turned out that Tony's favorite Range Rover had broken down, thus preventing him from returning to Zghorta earlier that day, as he had planned. But was the breakdown an accident? Although Bashir and his operational commander said divergent things about the raid's objective, neither admitted planning to kill Tony, much less his family. In fact, the reasons Bashir and his men advanced to justify the Ehdene operation made little sense to the doubting Lebanese *unless* Bashir had hoped to eliminate his main rival among the younger generation of Christian warlords. (Years later, a member of the Ehdene commando operation confided to a friend that Bashir had told the strike force beforehand that killing Tony was the objective.)

Just thirty-nine months to the day after the outbreak of the 1975 war that pitted the Christian militias against the Palestinians, Moslems, and leftists, the Christian camp had now itself fallen prey to the violence and anarchy it so often and so contemptuously decried in its adversaries. That, at least, was clear.

For the Franjiehs, two things mattered mightily about the Ehdene massacre, which claimed thirty-four lives—half the number they had lost fighting all comers during the civil war. In the long-inaccessible mountains of northern Lebanon, the violent demise of underlings was of no great moment, and Zghorta women spent much of their existence wearing black for their feuding menfolk killed in vendettas. But in this instance, Tony was dead. That mattered greatly. But it was fine that he had died in the northern tradition, rushing instinctively to the kitchen, which afforded the best field of fire. Until grenade shrapnel killed him and the others, Tony bey fired back as he had been trained to do since his father first taught him to shoot at coins when he was a boy.

Sacrilege was how Lamia Daddah, eldest of Tony's three sisters, chose to describe the assassination to me more than two years later at lunch in her father's home in Zghorta. Sipping a Schlitz she poured from a can, she explained that it was sacrilege to lose the clan's heir apparent, a member of parliament, a former minister, the commander of the Zghorta Liberation Army, the oldest son of the family, who had been touted for the presidency itself. And sacrilege, too, to have the crime take place on the family's own turf, in summer quarters in the Qadisha valley, the Maronites' redoubt and refuge for more than a millennium, and the symbol of undaunted Christianity in what they perceived as a hostile Islamic sea.

"We believe sacrilege is punished," Lamia said, mouthing a Christian piety but betraying the self-assurance of those long steeped in vendetta traditions. And indeed it was the Ehdene massacre's promise of further violence that represented its most worrisome aspect to the Lebanese. Talleyrand's tart admonition, "worse than a crime, an error," sprang to mind among the many Lebanese imbued with French culture. The outbreak of this "first Maronite war" complicated the plight of *all* the country's Christians—and its Moslems, too. In Lebanese eyes, the most likely beneficiaries of the Ehdene massacre—and perhaps even its instigators—were Israel and Syria, each interested in keeping prostrate Lebanon in turmoil for its own purposes. This automatic assumption that outsiders were meddling in Lebanese affairs stemmed from centuries of foreign domination.

Even the normally outspoken Bashir Gemayel initially found it expedient to distance himself from the murder of his principal rival. Two days after it happened, he acknowledged that some of his own militiamen—"on their own hook" and in cooperation with unidentified "other parties"—were responsible for Ehdene. But his War Council had not ordered the "very regrettable" incident and it would be "investigated," Bashir assured the press; "disciplinary measures" would be taken against the culprits. These embarrassed words fooled no one among a people grown used to their leaders' fascination with high-sounding discourse to mask high-handed behavior. The Lebanese were without illusions about the efficacy of the various militias' promises to punish their own wrongdoers. The nation's courts, in any case, had long since stopped handling criminal cases. The half-truths in Bashir's statement were no more flagrant then those mouthed by a dozen other warlords—although some anticlerical Lebanese claimed that Bashir's showed the influence of a thorough Jesuit education. In fact, he was trying to placate his own disoriented followers as much as the general public. Not only had he failed to keep a foothold in the north, the traditional Maronite stronghold, but he had thrust his rivals into the arms of Syria, whose troops thereafter occupied a good portion of Christian territory in Lebanon. Thanks to what looked like his blunder, the Maronites, who were convinced they should run the *entire* country, were reduced to ruling over less than a tenth its area and fewer than half its Christian minority.

The real reason for the Ehdene affair went back to events during the civil war, when the still-feudal but fundamentally pro-Arab northerners in Lebanon had been obliged to call on the Phalangists for help against the Moslems. Previously, they had held Sheikh Pierre's party in contempt for its fascination with all things Western and its rejection of Arab culture, and before the war the Phalange had not been a major force in Zghorta. But after the war the Phalangists stayed on in the north, picking up recruits and muscling in on the rackets, notably in the cement and roofing businesses on the coast at Chekka. The local reaction to this was crude and traditional. By the late spring of 1978, the Phalangists were losing men every day, picked off by the Franjiehs' Marada, or "Giants Brigade." Commanded by Tony Franjieh, these armed forces in Zghorta were determined to keep the southern intruders out of their domain. Local Phalangists were denied service in Zghorta bakeries, gasoline stations, and drugstores, and the merchants who refused to respect Franjieh-supplied blacklists were lucky if they got off with having their premises dynamited.

A series of meetings between the protagonists, held under the auspices of the Maronite Patriarch at his seat at Bkerké, failed to bring about reconciliation. At the end of the last encounter, Bashir told Tony the days of feudalism in the north were over. "Put one foot north of Jounieh," the President's son replied, "and we'll break it for you." In early June, Joud Bayeh, branch manager of a Beirut bank and the Phalangist leader in Zghorta, was assassinated. Bashir Gemayel later claimed that President Franjieh refused to allow Bayeh to be buried in Zghorta with the sacraments of the church, and indeed the victim *was* denied a funeral service by the town priests and was interred by his father and his son. Bashir decided to strike back before the Franjiehs destroyed his remaining credibility in the north. Already the Franjiehs and the other northern Christian clan chieftains allied with them had mended fences with their wartime foes, the Moslems in the Mediterranean port of Tripoli, who in calmer times were kept in line by gunslinging enforcers from Zghorta. (In May, Sleiman Franjieh had stopped attending meetings of the Lebanese Front, a group of Maronite leaders who were determined to confront their erstwhile Syrian allies with Israeli aid and encouragement.) The Franjiehs were so bent on denying the Gemayels access that they were rumored about to arrange for greater Syrian military protection for the north.

Bashir's chosen instrument was twenty-six-year-old Samir Geagea, a policeman's son who was viscerally opposed to clan politics as symbolized by the Franjiehs and was, to boot, a native of Bcharré, Zghorta's rival in ancestral feuds. Well-read, thoughtful, and possessed of a revolutionary soul, he was plucked out of a final year's internship at Beirut's American University Hospital in early June. "The Doctor" asked for, and was given, carte blanche; according to his recollections, only Bashir and a few members of the War Council knew of his mission. (Many Lebanese discount this as a self-serving effort to avoid implicating the Phalange Party leadership in the operation.)

Bashir claimed that the Ehdene plan was simply to "arrest" Bayeh's killers, who, his intelligence had reported, were in the palace. The idea was to humiliate the Franjiehs by staging a daring raid on Ehdene just before they moved there for the summer. But Geagea has insisted that his plan was more ambitious. He was determined to seize Ehdene and hold it until the Franjiehs evacuated Chekka, site of the cement and roofing factories. The Franjiehs, convinced that Geagea's forces were earmarked for Chekka, had moved a considerable number of troops to the Mediterranean port, and all but two or three of Geagea's men were told that in fact Chekka *was* the target. (The Chekka rackets represented a lucrative source of revenue for whichever militia controlled the output, and in the preceding weeks, dozens of rival militiamen had died fighting for the privilege of monopolizing them. As so often was the case in Lebanon, men worshiped both God and Mammon—or, rather, Baal, as the god of wealth was known to the Phoenicians.) Geagea conceded that his wasn't much of a plan—he had too few men at his disposal—but "there was no other." Bashir was so hard pressed on other fronts that additional troops could not be spared.

Assembling his force at Qnat, a village on the Qadisha's southern rim, Geagea moved men down back roads and was in position at Ehdene just before 4:00 a.m. The main attack force naturally struck first at the palace, a symbol of Franjieh prestige as well as a communications center and arsenal. "Someone was shooting and we fired back. When we entered we saw Tony and the family—dead," Geagea recalled. "In any case, he was to be killed one day or another."

During the fighting, Geagea was seriously wounded in the shoulder and lost consciousness; his deputy aborted the mission. Withdrawal proved difficult. Syrian roadblocks abounded, and Syrian planes pursued and strafed the raiders. Franjieh militia was out in force. Many of the Gemayel commandos had to hide out until nightfall and then skulk back to their lines on foot. Largely because the raiders, mostly drawn from the Beirut suburbs, were accompanied by northern guides who knew the terrain, Geagea considered it lucky that only seven men were lost in the operation. When Geagea regained consciousness in the Hôtel-Dieu hospital in East Beirut late in the afternoon, Bashir had come to visit. "The situation is not bad, but the operation has not worked out as we expected," Bashir told him.

Bashir's uncharacteristic understatement betrayed his isolation. The stocky young man had legions of detractors. They ran from such traditional enemies as the Palestinians, the Left, and the Moslems to disaffected Maronites and other Christians who had fought under his banner during the civil war. Fighting among themselves was more than these Christians had bargained for, especially when it involved the murder of a rival leader's wife and child. Certainly, Lebanon's history contained other examples of rivalry and betrayal within the Maronite community. But the need for unity in the civil war had largely masked the differences among the major Maronite political and military families—the Chamouns, the Franjiehs, and the Gemayels. And now the Ehdene operation had compromised the power and effectiveness of that Maronite extremist temptation—and threat—to set up a purely Christian state without the bothersome Moslems and Palestinians.

Nor did the Ehdene massacre necessarily please Bashir's own family, despite the insistent Lebanese political folklore that the Gemayels operated according to an agreed division of labor: Sheikh Pierre, enshrined as the upright, principled, if unsophisticated, father and Phalange Party founder; Amin, the elder brother and member of parliament, a political moderate and astute businessman often opposed to his younger brother; Bashir, the charismatic, resolute, if impulsive, military commander. In their oversimplified view, the Lebanese tended to believe that these perceived differences in the family were contrived solely for public consumption and in fact did not exist. Yet Amin made no secret of his disapproval of the Ehdene raid—and of many of Bashir's other actions, for that matter. One party veteran of forty years' standing doubted that Bashir had consulted either his brother or his father about the operation. "Sheikh Pierre was livid, furious, touched to the quick by the Ehdene excess. As a father he tried to deflect criticism," he told me, "but Ehdene effectively marked the end of his struggle to reassert his authority under the increasing challenge from Bashir. Sheikh Pierre used to make scenes, denounce Bashir's violation of Phalangist principle. But he had serious arteriosclerosis and was resigned to Bashir's leadership, whatever his inner misgivings." Those who had heard Bashir dutifully defer to his father on matters great and small were less persuaded that Sheikh Pierre was totally left in the dark. But no one denied that Bashir's manipulation of the Lebanese Forces had effectively provided him with a separate power base.

To the outside world, the Ehdene affair appeared to consecrate Bashir's power within the suddenly shrunken Christian ghetto and within his own family. Perhaps closest to the reality was the analysis of a party adviser. "Bashir's intelligence was to act forcefully, guessing that his father would not want to know because if he knew he would feel obliged to scream and yell," he said to me. "In the end, Sheikh Pierre always covered for Bashir, always." But the Ehdene operation also revealed Bashir's vulnerability, the vulnerability of a born gambler who keeps raising the ante even when he knows the odds will eventually catch up with him. "I wouldn't sell life insurance on him," an American diplomat remarked the day after Ehdene. "He signed his own death warrant with that operation."

As always, Bashir struck a stoic attitude, arguing that even if he were to die, the party founded and organized by his father would carry on, whereas the Franjiehs were at the end of the line. He reasoned that the Franjiehs' forty-year struggle for hegemony, first in Zghorta, then in the nation, was already in decline during Sleiman's contested presidency. After all, many Lebanese blamed Franjieh for having exacerbated the civil war.

Yet the mood in Zghorta was not such to encourage Bashir's optimism. Driving north from Beirut, Lamia Daddah had relied on Zghorta tradition to help break the news of the massacre to Tony's son, thirteen-year-old Sleiman.

"Sleiman, you remember our dog at Ehdene? He was killed," she said.

"By whom?" the boy asked.

"The Phalangists."

"Did he manage to bite many of them before he died?" he asked.

"Maybe," replied his aunt. "Sleiman, you remember Fadwa, the maid at Ehdene?" she went on. "She, too, was killed."

"By whom?"

"The Phalangists," Lamia replied.

"She certainly was unable to defend herself, being a woman," the boy said.

"Yes," his aunt replied. "She was shot from behind."

As they neared Zghorta, she said, "Sleiman, you are grown up now, you are a man."

Guessing the truth, he interrupted her. "They killed my father, didn't they?"

"Yes."

"I'm sure he fought back," the boy said. "Did he kill many Phalangists?"

The boy's namesake, the former President, was credited with having dispensed with some seven hundred lives over the years, although "no one could prove anything," as an admiring relative put it. Known as "the Sphinx" because of his studied disdain for small talk, the elder Sleiman Franjieh had cultivated a mafioso style ever since the 1940s, when he became the enforcer and electoral agent for his more sophisticated older brother, Hamid. While Hamid was a suave member of parliament, a minister, and a presidential hopeful, Sleiman held a minor job with a Beirut ship chandler, commuting the fifty miles of winding, overcrowded coastal road between the city and his Tripoli home in an old Mercedes 170 because he was too strapped to pay for a hotel room in Beirut. In keeping with Zghorta custom, he saw to it that a gunslinger ostentatiously shot dead a Tripoli Moslem every month or so to remind the potentially forgetful who was running the show. Family legend had it that Hamid blamed Sleiman's antics for costing him the 1952 presidential election, won by Camille Chamoun.

Tempted to try for a constitutionally forbidden second consecutive term, Chamoun became determined to discredit his most serious rival in the 1958 presidential contest. The year before, he enlisted Father Semaan Douaihi, a pleasure-loving priest not immune to the charms of money or female company, who came from one of the five great Zghorta families; with Chamoun's encouragement he was promoted over the heads of less active but formally senior family members. In an incident that the Franjiehs to this day insist was provoked by Chamoun—and that Father Douaihi refuses to discuss at all—the two clans came first to fisticuffs, then a shoot-out.

The occasion was a requiem mass said for a pro-Franjieh parishioner in a church in the nearby town of Miziara. The Franjiehs insisted the Douaihis had no business there, although such religious occasions were traditional fixtures in the lives of electioneering politicians. No two versions of the mayhem agree in every detail. The shooting started when Sleiman Franjieh and his men arrived and became involved in a quarrel with the Douaihis. The Douaihis were more numerous outside the church; the Franjieh clan was more numerous inside. The Douaihis rushed into the church, but their eyes took crucial seconds to adjust to the obscurity. That gave the Franjiehs the edge. Some eyewitnesses claimed that both Sleiman and Father Douaihi fired. No one disputed that both were armed with revolvers. Sleiman's middle daughter, Sonia Racy, denied that her father actually fired and insisted he directed operations from behind a pillar, well protected by his liege men. "If something happens to us, it is not serious, but if something happens to you, we are all lost," Sonia remembered hearing someone say to him. In any case, the Franjiehs were credited with carrying the day. Father Douaihi, Sonia claimed, was caught in the sacristry and disarmed by a Franjieh supporter who wanted to kill him but was dissuaded by Sleiman. "Remember his cassock," Sleiman cautioned. More than twenty churchgoers lost their lives—mostly Douaihi partisans, but also a good sprinkling of Franjieh retainers and innocent faithful, including women and children. Hamid Franjieh, on the outskirts of Miziara, was alerted by gunfire and hustled back to Tripoli.

For Sonia Racy and all Zghorta, Chamoun's hand in provoking the incident was proven by the instantaneous issuing of forty-six arrest warrants for Sleiman Franjieh and his supporters (including a young man who for months had been in a distant seminary studying for the priesthood). Sleiman and his men fled across northern Lebanon into Syria, where they were put up at Syrian government expense at a hotel in the Mediterranean port of Latakia. (It is said that it was during his exile that Sleiman met two young officers, Hafez and Rifaat Assad, who later became President of Syria and commander of Syria's Praetorian Guard, respectively, as well as avid partners with the Franjiehs, father and son, in a number of lucrative black-market business deals.)

Within months of the incident at Miziara, Hamid Franjieh suffered a paralytic stroke, which ended his political career. That of Sleiman began in earnest. Pardoned eighteen months after the shoot-out, he returned to Zghorta, where he was universally respected for his doubly macho performance: normally, the *zaim*, or leader, either killed or—more usually—ordered his people to carry out killings; but at Miziara Sleiman had done both, or at least was so credited. He was elected to his brother's parliamentary seat and occasionally chosen as a lackluster minister in various governments.

Suddenly, less than a month before the 1970 presidential elections, Sleiman was seized upon by an unlikely combination of power brokers intent on defeating the outgoing regime's choice for the new term, Elias Sarkis. Two six-year presidential terms in which the government had made every effort to cut the traditional interest groups down to size had set off a last-minute search for a miracle candidate. In the ninth-floor offices of Ghassan Tueni, publisher of *An Nahar*, perhaps the most prestigious newspaper in the Arab world, the Franjieh ploy was carefully worked out, then sold to the Eddés, Gemayels, Chamouns, Jumblatts, Salams, and other political dynasties prominent since Lebanese independence. Sleiman Franjieh pledged to restore the great political families to preeminence, to banish the all-powerful military intelligence operation that had pulled Lebanon's most important strings for twelve years, to combat the Palestinians' growing influence, and to impose law and order on an increasingly undisciplined society. He was touted as the ideal candidate. His reputation as a northern clan leader and no-nonsense mountain "godfather" was trotted out as evidence of his qualities. Such arguments were reinforced by the presence of an estimated 4,000–6,000 armed pro-Franjieh partisans—mostly northern kinsmen—who descended on Beirut on August 17 to ensure the ninety-nine-man parliament did the right thing by their candidate. A gendarmerie captain favorable to the Franjieh cause slipped five Zghorta gunmen into parliament, where Speaker Sabri Hamadeh's own bodyguards eyed them uneasily.

The first two ballots failed to provide the required majority for either front-runner. Voting began on the third ballot. Before casting his vote, each member of parliament made flowery compliments to justify his choice of candidate—and the payoff that these elaborately coded messages (called "electoral keys") entitled him to. The count was fifty for Franjieh, forty-nine for Sarkis. The Speaker, a Sarkis supporter, announced that a fourth ballot was in order, since neither remaining candidate had won an outright majority, which he ruled was fifty-one votes. Franjieh's partisans began shooting outside in the streets, convinced their man had won. In the chamber, Franjieh, who was carrying a revolver, rushed forward and screamed at Hamadeh, "You can't pull that one on me!" The Speaker's sons were slugging it out with Father Douaihi (by now a Franjieh supporter whose differences with the clan had been forgiven, if not forgotten). Hamadeh's bodyguards moved in to protect him, their submachine guns at the ready. Franjieh's men had their revolvers out and pointed at them. Hamadeh retreated to his chambers, where he telephoned President Charles Helou for advice. "My information authorizes me to tell you that if you persist there will be no survivors among those present in parliament," Helou told the Speaker. "Do what it takes to avoid destroying the country."

There was no fourth ballot. Sleiman Franjieh was declared elected.

The Lebanon of the 1943 National Covenant survived for almost five more years. Some Lebanese, Christian but especially Moslem, argue that both before and during the 1975–76 war, Sleiman Franjieh hastened the process of disintegration by his narrow-minded, graft-ridden, and ineffective rule. Others blame those who decided he should be elected in the first place. But by general consent, Tony's assassination in 1978 brought out the classic northern clan leader in Sleiman.

Only once during the grueling ritual of his son's funeral did the sixty-eight-year-old leader show any emotion, briefly dabbing at tears as he sat, head in hands, in an armchair. Less than a month after being hospitalized with a heart attack, the frail, wispy-haired former President received his important guests, come to present their condolences. Black flags and blown-up photographs of Tony, wife, and child bedecked Zghorta's streets, swollen by tens of thousands of northerners despite the heat. Sleiman and his family were dressed in light colors: Zghorta tradition authorized black only after vengeance had been wreaked.

The Maronite Patriarch, Antonios Boulos Khoreiche, celebrated the requiem mass, attended by the papal nuncio, the French ambassador, Syrian President Assad's brother, various Greek Catholic and Orthodox dignitaries, General Victor Khoury, the army commander, Father Charbel Kassis, Superior General of the powerful Maronite Order of Monks, and other notables. Sitting next to Sleiman was his grandson, wearing, like a thousand other Zghorta boys and girls, a white T-shirt decorated with Tony's face. Women ululated inside and outside the five-hundred-year-old Church of the Virgin, a near-windowless edifice whose entrances were protected by blast-wall-like constructions originally designed to prevent Moslem cavalrymen from entering on horseback. Samir Franjieh, Hamid's youngest son and a family black sheep because of his left-wing opposition to Maronite Christianity, was welcomed back to the fold after three years of ostracism in Beirut. "Overnight, I was acceptable, even sought after," he recalled, "because I had always warned Sleiman that the Phalangists were bastards, and now I'd been proven right."

Neither at the funeral nor during the rest of the week, in receiving dozens of delegations, did Sleiman mention vengeance against the Gemayels. But as the French-language newspaper *L'Orient–Le Jour* reported, in Levantine understatement dictated by the lessons of three years of violence that had not spared the Lebanese press, "Given the traditions of the place, observers were sure that the tragedy they had just lived through would not end with this funeral service, celebrated on this torrid day." By the weekend, Sleiman had called in local Maronite priests and told them to get the word to parishioners: northern Phalangists should turn in party cards, weapons, and written undertakings of their resignations to a special office. Barring that, they should leave the region by the end of the month or be prepared "to be dealt with harshly." A stream of Phalangist delegations came to pay obeisance. The authorities in various northern towns asked to have their neutrality respected. The situation became so tense that the rector of the state-run Lebanese University allowed northern students to take their examinations in Tripoli rather than risk traveling south through Phalange territory to Beirut. Zghorta natives living in Phalangist-controlled areas fled back home or to West Beirut, then controlled by Palestinians and Syrians. Northerners opposed to the Franjiehs moved south, where many of their young men enrolled in Bashir's militia.

The Phalangists feigned shock that the Franjiehs had resorted to the Church to broadcast their warnings and scathingly denounced such behavior as typical of feudal northern lords long used to disposing of everything from a peasant's sheep to the virginity of their daughters. In riposte, the five main Zghorta families—given to feuding among themselves when not facing an outside danger—signed a long letter accusing the Phalange of trying to stamp out all other Christian movements, to partition Lebanon into Moslem and Christian zones, and to settle the hated Palestinians permanently. The letter charged that the Phalange ruled by "terror, money, and imported ideas"—a dig at its close ties with Israel—and accused it of taxing even "mothers and widows of martyrs" killed in the civil war, of extortion, and of holding fellow Christians for ransom. Did the Gemayels, it asked, intend to "become the rulers of Lebanon's cemeteries"? Refusing reconciliation, which was urged by a special Vatican envoy, other ecclesiastics, and lay leaders, the Zghorta families said, "We can never shake a hand that drips with innocent blood."

Camille Chamoun was caught uncomfortably in the middle. Unlike the Franjiehs in the north or the Phalange farther south in Mount Lebanon, his National Liberal Party and its Tiger militia had no geographically distinct and undisputed home turf. He had derived much of his considerable influence by playing his two rivals off against each other. It took Chamoun five days to decide to trek north to Zghorta. During a tearful, seventy-minute visit with Franjieh, he apologized for being unable to come earlier and denounced as a "precedent in our traditions" the murder of women and children "by assassins who ignore the moral values on which Lebanon was built." Such protestations of concern were received in the spirit in which they were given. Like everyone else in Lebanon, the Franjiehs were aware that Chamoun's Tigers had not spared women and children when they overran the Tal Zaatar refugee camp in August 1976. Yet the Zghorta ethic prided itself on fighting "clean" wars: no mutilations, no rapes, and (with one notable exception) no massacre of innocents. Northerners, proud of a military heritage from time immemorial, hinted that such practices among Christians in the south reflected their fear, a loss of identity due to being uprooted from their ancestral villages and becoming fascinated with foreign, Western ways.

"God is great," Sleiman Franjieh told Chamoun, "and will render justice. If what happened was a sacrifice required of us in Lebanon's interest, we would accept it."

Iris, Sleiman's wife, was blunter. "Watch out for your children. May God protect them for you."

On the first anniversary of Tony Franjieh's death, Sheikh Pierre Gemayel escaped with only slight injuries from an attempt on his life. A Renault 16 crammed with forty-four pounds of TNT, a 120-millimeter mortar round, and a jerrycan of gasoline was detonated by remote control on the express highway north of Beirut just as the Phalangist patriarch drove by in a white Buick. Two of his bodyguards were killed. That very day in Zghorta, Father Yussef Yamin said mass and laid down the Franjieh line: "All those who profaned Ehdene will be killed, particularly those of the Gemayel clan, those and their descendants for generations until not a single man or woman remains."

On February 23, 1980, a remote-control car bomb containing sixty-six pounds of explosives went off as Bashir Gemayel's green Mercedes 450-SEL was driving by the Foreign Ministry in East Beirut. Killed were Bashir's daughter, Maya, born on the eve of the Ehdene massacre, the chauffeur, two bodyguards, and four other people. The men were driving Maya to her grandparents' in Bashir's car: the assassins apparently thought Bashir was in the vehicle. Rescue workers were obliged to use blowtorches to extract the bodies. The chauffeur's corpse was found protecting the child's.

Bashir controlled himself and reiterated his insistence on the survival of the party and the unimportance of his person and his family. But from then on, Bashir, his brother, and his father constantly changed cars equipped with radio telephones. Bashir disdained bodyguards and escort vehicles.

When I talked to Sleiman Franjieh in 1980—we were in the vast Franjieh living room in Zghorta, its walls covered with daggers, swords, and nineteenth-century rifles with inlaid mother-of-pearl stocks—I got around to asking if Maya's death meant the time had come to end the vendetta.

"As long as we frighten them," Lamia said, "then it is not bad for us." Adopting a schoolteacherly attitude, as if dealing with the village idiot, she folded her hands on her lap and said, "If Bashir is first, then Amin, then Pierre. If Amin is first, then Pierre, followed by Bashir. If Pierre goes first—" She broke off her explanation. With a cold, self-satisfied smile she smoothed her light, striped skirt and said, "When I was in school, I was taught that when you had three variable elements there were nine possible combinations."

I was so taken aback that it was months before I realized—a friend had to point it out to me—that Lamia was wrong, at least in her arithmetic: there are only six combinations.

Zghorta purists also faulted Lamia, Sonia, and their younger brother, Robert, the heir presumptive, for talking too much. "Yes, they are virile, even the women, and that is a much-admired quality," a Zghorta connoisseur said, "but it was bad form to show pleasure about Bashir's daughter. Sleiman was right on the money—never showed any emotion at all, never said a word. If you are a *zaim*, you can allow yourself to be happy when you get even, but you don't have the right to show it." For years, Iris Franjieh visited the church every day and prayed over the coffins where Tony, his wife, and his daughter lay until a chapel could be completed for them in Ehdene. Iris's reaction when first informed of the massacre was, "This is the beginning of a hundred years' war."

Upon taking leave of Lamia and the family, I asked her how she would describe the state of play with the Gemayels.

"Act one, scene one," she said.

Sleiman bided his time. But within two months, helped by his Syrian allies, he began to wreak his vengeance. Scorekeepers counted 342 reprisal killings of Phalangist followers and their families—better than ten for every Ehdene victim. As Camille Chamoun commented in his published diary, "Cutting innocent throats to propagate terror is nothing new in the mentality of the Middle East." (He remained convinced that the Syrians, his pet peeve, had engineered the Ehdene incident to split the Christians, even providing Jeeps to facilitate the killers' way through Syrian roadblocks.)

Ehdene remained a blotch on Bashir's escutcheon, regretted by his supporters and denounced by his adversaries. His fortunes further faded that summer and fall. With Chamoun he provoked the Syrians, hoping for Israeli support that would drive Syrian troops out of Lebanon. The support did not materialize. Instead, with American and French acquiescence, the Syrians taught Chamoun and Bashir a lesson and shelled East Beirut; despite Christian propagandists' claims of genocide, it was largely empty of residents. Whatever honor was saved was thanks to Chamoun's spunky insistence on staying in his much-shelled apartment house.

Within the Phalange Party, Bashir's brother was now entrusted with wide-ranging, overall powers under the title of coordinator. Untainted as he was by any meaningful connection with Israel, on speaking terms with the Palestinians and Syrians, Amin had also succeeded in branding Bashir as a dangerous hothead. Brave (braver than Bashir, with two battle wounds to prove it), handsome, urbane, a parliamentary deputy and a member of the Phalange Politburo, now for the first time since 1975 Amin was in a position to sideline his brother and nail down his claim to primacy. But within six months Bashir bounced back, aided in no small way by Amin's apparent inability to take decisions and a rigidity that earned him the party nickname of *El Anid*, or "Mr. Stubborn." Amin kept control of the militia in his political fiefdom of Metn, and his many money-making enterprises, which ranged from a cooperative supermarket to an insurance firm employing former militiamen as watchmen and charging high premiums. Detractors found little difference between his Association des Services Urgents and a protection racket, but few found it politic not to pay up.

Then and there, Amin had lost out. His father had made his choice long before. As a Phalangist who knew both brothers well said, "The race was over, but the results hadn't been posted." Gradually, Bashir began to move away from Chamoun's political tutelage; he developed workmanlike relations with the Syrians to balance his strong Israeli ties. He was in a perfect position to wait for the volatile Middle East to provide an opportunity for him to strike. At precarious peace with his only neighbors, Bashir turned his attention to Marounistan and the real business of Lebanese politics. That had never had anything to do with the nebulous state but, rather, with exercising dominion within one's own community.

Contemptuous of President Sarkis, Bashir's Lebanese Forces in fact set about seriously undermining the Lebanese state. In the old days Sheikh Pierre used to declare that "our strength is our weakness," meaning that the Lebanese state gained security from being so unimpressive that it posed no threat to its neighbors, especially Israel. Now, so-called private ports shot up all along the Mediterranean coast—for the most part, mere stone jetties where small coastal vessels could tie up. The "fifth basin" at the official port of Beirut, capable of handling larger vessels, also came under Lebanese Forces' control. For a fraction of the official customs duties, whiskey, color television sets, cigarettes, food were landed in Lebanon. Moslem merchants preferred using these contraband ports in Marounistan to the official ports or similarly illegal jetties in the Palestinian or Syrian sectors, which were deemed less trustworthy. Deprived of its customs duties—the largest single source of official revenue—the Lebanese state was obliged to lower its cigarette and liquor taxes to compete.

Cement produced at Chekka was taxed by the Franjiehs, who controlled the turf, and also by the Lebanese Forces, who manned their own customs station at Barbara. Inside Marounistan, the Lebanese Forces levied additional taxes on gasoline, restaurant and nightclub bills, illicit gambling casinos, and real-estate transactions, and imposed a hearth tax depending on the size of the dwelling. As they grew stronger, they tried to extend their sway to all Marounistan residents. In both 1978 and 1979, Lebanon's hardworking Armenian community, descended from survivors of Turkey's massacres, came under attack from combined Phalangist and Chamounist militias. Although political allies of the Phalangists, the Armenians had learned their lesson: they had lost men and substance by fighting alongside the Christians in the 1958 civil war, and this time they stayed studiously neutral. Now they were accused of taking a free ride. Further infuriating the Christian warlords was the Armenians' refusal to pay taxes to the militias. With their backs to the sea and surrounded by militia territory, the Armenians stood their ground and gave as good as they got in the fighting. They succeeded in avoiding most of the militias' taxes, but at the cost of dozens of their own militiamen's lives.

Lebanese Forces financiers acknowledged that their income amounted to $100 million a year. Some private bankers put the take at three times that figure. This money was used to pay the estimated two thousand full-time militiamen, to cover the costs of training high-school graduates, and to cope with war matériel acquisitions, since Israel and other suppliers demanded cash. In return, the Lebanese Forces expanded the Phalangist social programs, instituting price controls on pharmaceuticals and starting cheap bus lines for people without cars and parking lots for those with them (a secondary purpose was to reduce curbside parking and the risk of car bombs). When car bombs exploded, the Lebanese Forces quickly cleaned up the broken glass and car carcasses, and made sure that the dead and injured were taken swiftly to the hospital. Bashir Gemayel made it a point to show up at the scenes of such outrages to show the cowed population that he was concerned. No such interest was shown by the warlords of West Beirut. On both sides of Beirut, people tended to go out as little as possible for ten days or so after a car-bomb explosion.

When Bashir wanted something, he usually—not always—got his way. Charles Rizk, director of state television, was arrested by two teenage militiamen one summer morning in 1980. He was shoved facedown on the back seat of a car, with the militiamen's boots ensuring he stayed that way, and driven to the port, where he was dumped into an airless, rat-infested container. A half hour later, Bashir and Pakradouni appeared, feigned surprise at his discomfort, and got down to hard tacks. They wanted a new television channel, both to get their political message across and to collect advertising revenues. Rizk had been refusing to give in, even failing to answer their telephone calls—which, they said, explained their present tactics. Now that he knew what was required, he could go. Rizk drove straight to President Sarkis and tendered his resignation, but Sarkis would not play ball. He remarked that government employment always carried risks but did not argue when Rizk later departed for extended leave in Europe. Bashir never started his rival television station, but he did gain access to the state-run channel. When Rizk returned four months later, Bashir noted contemptuously that his pay as director had not been docked during his long absence: civil servants who didn't earn the money the state nonetheless paid them were one of his pet peeves.

As the years went on, so, too, did Bashir's power struggle with Chamoun and the Tiger militia. As early as February 1976, the Phalangists and Tigers had clashed, but throughout the civil war the Christians managed to mask their disputes much more effectively than the Moslem and Druze militias in West Beirut, whose shoot-outs and bombings were a permanent and often dangerous part of life there. Christian flare-ups were usually described as the work of "hotheads," and the Chamouns and Gemayels were whitewashed of any direct responsibility in the violence.

Then, on Monday, July 7, 1980, Bashir's Lebanese Forces simultaneously attacked Chamounist barracks, NLP ports, offices, and other strongpoints. Bashir and his lieutenants had originally planned to attack at first light, at about 4:00 a.m., but, mindful of the Ehdene mess, they sacrificed the element of surprise and waited instead until 8:30 a.m., when Tiger militia commander Dany Chamoun had left his seaside home at Safra-Marine to go to work on a resort project in the mountains. The fighting went on all day and well into the night. I was stopped at the Barbara checkpoint, where one entered Phalangist territory, and was held until 10:00 p.m. There, vehicles coming from the Syrian-controlled north were checked by Bashir's men, and truck drivers paid duty on their cargoes. The rumble of heavy artillery and recoilless rifle fire was clearly audible as the Chamounist barracks at nearby Amchit was reduced. Despite the Phalangists' precautions, the Day of the Long Knives had its messy side. Because they delayed the attack to spare Dany, the militia killed a number of innocent civilians who were already out and about. The attackers seemed drugged and fired indiscriminately, eyewitnesses said, especially at the seaside marina and hotel complexes. At one resort, the Lebanese Forces stopped the elevators to prevent any escape, then climbed the stairways, shooting at anyone they saw, throwing people out of upper-story windows, shooting them as they plummeted to earth. One man, taking the day off, was in an Olympic-size pool when the militia arrived. He was shot, and bled to death in the pool. His family was allowed to fish the body out only two days later; several women and children killed in the same fashion were extracted at the same time.

Dany Chamoun said Bashir's men killed five hundred people, almost all of them innocent civilian bystanders. But Lebanese Forces officials finally owned up to only ninety-four fatalities, including eighteen of their own fighters, five civilians, and many luckless Pakistanis employed as stevedores in the NLP's ports and thus perfect cannon fodder or, rather, target-practice material. Months later, a Chamoun lieutenant figured the death toll was "one hundred fifty at the most," including thirty innocent bystanders, forty-five Pakistanis, and the remainder about equal numbers of rival militiamen.

Initially, the Christian community seemed genuinely upset by the bloodshed, but within a week, Bashir's gamble had paid off, largely because of his clever propaganda. The Tiger militia was accused of all manner of skullduggery—from running illegal gambling dens to smuggling hashish out of its five ports. (The Lebanese Forces always denied they kept up the hashish traffic thereafter. The Syrians controlled the areas where it was grown, and much of the crop was known to go across the Lebanon Mountains, through a pro-Phalangist Christian town called Deir al Ahmar, and then in large part through Franjieh territory and out by way of the Syrian-controlled port of Tripoli. That was the official Phalangist line. But Bashir's critics, without furnishing any hard proof, expressed doubts that the Lebanese Forces would pass up a cut of Lebanon's biggest, though illegal, export. As government writ disappeared over the years, hash-growing areas, once limited to the inaccessible northern stretch of the Beqaa known as the Hermel, gradually spread south, and by the early 1980s reached all the way to the Beirut–Damascus road, where its cultivation had replaced less lucrative crops such as wheat and potatoes. The crop was worth billions of dollars to the worldwide Lebanese underworld network, which shepherded the final product abroad to Egypt, the biggest traditional market, and also to black Africa, Europe, and the United States, where fine-grade Beqaa hashish was esteemed among the best in the world. The local growers, mostly poor Shia Moslems, also prospered, although to a lesser degree, as the new construction and stores bursting with expensive imported consumer goods in Baalbek bore witness.)

Bashir closed down the Tigers' five ports in an access of moral indignation (only to reopen them three weeks later, claiming they helped keep the cost of living down in inflationary times). An East Beirut friend of mine began a conversation by decrying the slaughter—Bashir jokingly called his attack on the Chamounists the "July seventh corrective movement," in keeping with the traditional Middle Eastern nomenclature for coups—but concluded by saying hopefully, "I've lost three apartments since 1975, and maybe now I can stay put." Bashir had brought order to Marounistan. Like the characters in Ionesco's play *Rhinoceros*, East Beirutis soon came to see only the good sides of a law-and-order society in which little, if any, deviation from official thinking was tolerated.

Telephones had been tapped before, but the indiscreet had always been able to appeal for protection to the other Christian militia. Now people became even more discreet and circumspect. Deprived of his muscle, Chamoun bent with the wind, ever true to his lifelong practice of using defeat as a stepping-stone to future victory. He participated in meetings with the Gemayels, singly or in pairs.

I once asked him why he did not retire from politics or join forces with Bashir's many enemies.

"You want me to be like Sleiman Franjieh, opening my arms to the Syrians? That's the only thing I could have done, and the result would have been civil war and a thousand dead. I didn't want even one hundred dead on my hands."

Was that the hardest choice he'd ever made?

"I don't give a damn," he growled.

His favorite son, Dany, flew north to see Franjieh, vowed vengeance, and went abroad, accusing Bashir of being a "fascist out to create a dictatorship." When the Lebanese Forces called off a press tour to the hotels where, Dany claimed, civilians had been killed, Dany said, "Of course, they haven't wiped the blood off the walls yet." (Bashir's contemptuous reply was "Dany is a good politician in his spare time.") Educated in English-speaking schools in Lebanon and England, son of a half-English mother, Dany now vented all his spleen against his erstwhile ally. "With the Israelis, who spoke English, Bashir would let me carry the conversation, then slyly slip off in private and see the same people. When you're in a situation of power, Bashir is the squirmiest, slimiest person. With my father, he bows down."

Bashir eventually won Camille Chamoun over. It took a good two months. Bashir desperately wanted him to come to the Lebanese Forces War Council, a sign that he recognized the younger man's authority. Chamoun accepted after Bashir agreed, through emissaries, to continue to allow him to take his old cut of the profits from the main port at Dbeyeh. A large sum—as much as $1 million—was said to have been paid to Chamoun. It was this kind of talk that accredited rumors that on July 7, once he was sure Dany was alive, Chamoun had telephoned Bashir and said, "No matter what happens, don't cancel the financial committee meeting," which divided up the take among the rival militias.

Bashir was King of Marounistan, but not King of the Christians, since probably half of them lived outside his fiefdom's narrow confines. "Bashir was the only serious, valid fellow in the whole thing," conceded a Lebanese Christian who had little use for him, "but he is a monster. So were Napoleon and Talleyrand. Bashir is the child of the myth that insists Lebanon needs fresh, young leadership." The geriatric ward of Lebanese politicians—the founding fathers of independence in 1943—certainly had little to recommend them. But Bashir's myth-making capacity allowed him to sweep away not only that generation but also the men in their forties and fifties who had suffered under the founding fathers and believed they, in turn, should have their place in the sun. Right after the civil war Sarkis consulted with Sheikh Pierre and Camille Chamoun, then in 1978 with Bashir and Chamoun, but after the "double seven," Bashir alone drove to the Baabda palace when Sarkis sought to line up support in Marounistan.

Never before had the Maronites been represented by a single man or a single organization. And never before had they been able to exercise their dominion over the other Christian sects, which, taken together, equaled their own numbers. Bashir's errors no longer counted. In retrospect, it would seem that the events separating July 7, 1980 and the Israeli invasion not two years later were all part of an inevitable scenario spelling liberation, triumph, and reestablished Maronite ascendancy. But even a casual analysis of the period belies such a reading. Yet Lebanese of all persuasions dismissively countered any objection to their tortuous thinking by noting, "This is not a rational place."

In October 1980, Bashir felt obliged to humiliate the Lebanese Army by brushing aside units that were protecting the rump Chamounist militia in Ain Remmaneh, the working-class suburb where the fighting all began in 1975, thereby undermining the Moslems' tenuous and recent faith in an army they had once viewed as part of the Maronites' repressive apparatus. Two months later, he maneuvered his forces in the hope of extending his influence to Zahle, a mainly Greek Catholic city never before in the Maronite—or, for that matter, Phalangist—orbit. The Syrian peacekeeping troops gave the Lebanese Forces a thorough drubbing.

Neither adventure improved Bashir's image, but both maintained his pressure on the ghetto Christians. Bashir's offensive tactics made the other parties suspicious, yet to his own people he argued that Marounistan—the only "liberated" part of Lebanon, to use his pet phrase—was under siege. Even as renowned a local psychiatrist as Mounir Chamoun insisted that the policy of "resistance"—as the ghetto Christians called their constantly shifting tactical approach, in language borrowed from the anti-Nazi undergrounds of German-occupied Europe in World War II—was necessary as "the point of departure for uplifting the Maronite self-image." Father Paul Kholy, pastor of the downtrodden Syrian Orthodox Christians, who had suffered Ottoman persecution in World War I alongside the Armenians, summed up the dominant Christian ethic. "We have a special hatred for Moslems," he said, articulating what even the most fanatic Lebanese Christians rarely said out loud in public. "During the civil war they thought we would last only two weeks. They thought we were combs and mirrors [his phrase for sissies] but we beat one hundred twenty million Moslems." His community provided cannon fodder for Chamoun's Tigers, the toughest, meanest fighters in the Christian camps. Used and abandoned by Chamoun, then picked up again by Bashir, they never got the papers, even the identity cards that would make them genuine Lebanese citizens. Yet they were totally committed to those who treated them so shabbily. They were simply more vocal than the other Christians.

Deep down, many other Lebanese Christians were delighted and amazed at their own strength. It was as if they had never really believed in the solidity of the Lebanese state the French had bequeathed them because they had not had to fight for their independence. With rare—almost personal—exceptions, the Marounistan Christians now fell into line behind their most militant, radical leader. It all made a kind of sense seen from within Marounistan, although Marounistan more and more seemed unreal to other Lebanese—including Christians—living outside its often suffocating confines. It was a place where in 1976 fighters spray-painted "Fuck Palestine" on walls in English rather than write the same insult in Arabic and have anything to do with the Arab world, where in 1977 professors at Université Saint Joseph worried about militiamen in a nearby outpost reading Nazi propaganda while hundreds of their fellow Christians traveled to Israel for military training.

Next to former Israeli Foreign Minister Abba Eban's memoirs on a shelf in Bashir's East Beirut apartment was a book entitled *Christ in Lebanon*. Its author, Rumanian-born Virghil Gheorghiu, was a right-wing Catholic writer, and had inscribed his Lebanese book to Bashir. The inscription read: "To Bashir Gemayel, great generalissimo and defender of the Maronite nation." Also providing Catholic backing was the Maronite Order of Monks, who, thanks to continued access to their churches and monasteries in Israel, guaranteed under the 1949 armistice agreement, were able to maintain overt links with the Israeli government. Church officials were the only Lebanese civilians allowed to travel freely across the border. Father Boulos Naaman, years before he became Superior General in 1980 and was entitled to wear the amethyst-studded gold pectoral cross of his office, made little secret of these ties, although he always good-naturedly wagged his finger at me and called me "naughty" for having described him as the "architect of the Israeli alliance."

He once boasted to me that he had told Syrian President Hafez Assad that Bashir was "not Pierre Gemayel's son, but the son of all the injustice that the Christians of the Middle East had suffered over the centuries."

Bashir, his cause, and his lieutenants were also being strengthened more directly by the Israelis. Their helping hand guided Bashir's American Lebanese League in the United States, headed by Alfred Madi, who soon wielded more influence in Washington than the official Lebanese embassy. Inspired by Israel, some Western media built Bashir into a paragon of Free World virtues. Geraldo Rivera, in April 1981 on ABC's *20/20*, depicted Bashir as a latter-day Crusader doing battle against the Soviet cat's-paw of the PLO in the name of common Western values shared, of course, by the United States and Israel. John Kifner, then Beirut correspondent for *The New York Times*, had to put his foot down with his New York editors when they got ready to commission a free-lance writer who wanted to be landed in Lebanon by Israeli submarine to interview Bashir, since, it was alleged, none of the foreign press resident in West Beirut "dared" to interview him. Even an initially hostile left-wing weekly such as France's *Nouvel Observateur* switched sides and found virtue in Bashir and his cause.

At home in Marounistan, Bashir basked in a sea of admiration. In East Beirut's often clogged, narrow streets, fathers would rush indoors to find their children and have them shake Bashir's hand as his car inched forward in traffic. His wife, Solange, the daughter of a Phalangist founding father and a militant herself from the age of fifteen, waited patiently at home and did her best to protect her husband. "I am not calm," she said, "Bashir is calm." She rarely complained about his late hours—he often returned well past midnight after an evening of party work—and disciplined herself never to call Bashir at the War Council (although she did check occasionally with his private secretary, Isis).

I spent a week in Bashir's company in the fall of 1980, tagging along to try to get to know him. The days slid into evenings, evenings into nights. He talked at length to party faithful, attended countless meetings and luncheons. He dispensed justice, telling a young swain not to run off with his teenage girlfriend, since "there's no divorce for Maronites and why ruin your life for a caprice?" Dinners were devoted to thanking his lieutenants for their good work and keeping their spirits up. On one such occasion a well-known poet drew prolonged applause when he proclaimed, "Our country is not Arabs, we will change the teaching of the Gospel and not turn the other cheek. We are willing to die for you, Bashir." As we crisscrossed Marounistan, I constantly tried to get him to talk about himself, his problems, his relations with the Israelis, the Americans, the Syrians. He rarely opened up. When pressed, he would retreat behind a noncommittal "You're free to interpret things as you like."

After one long Sunday of politicking, Bashir drove to a small stadium in the suburb of Jdeideh, where he arrived during the last quarter of a soccer game organized by his brother. Bashir had not mentioned the match beforehand, and now he displayed bristling displeasure at the idea of having a Christian team play a Moslem club for the first time since the civil war. But his father was in seventh heaven, both as a soccer fan and as a firm believer in the 1943 pluralist formula for running Lebanon. Almost all the players had fought on opposing sides in 1975–76. The West Beirut team, Ansar, was accompanied by three thousand Moslem fans, frantically waving green flags (the color of Islam) in a segregated section of the stands. Ansar won, 1–0, and its captain was awarded a cup by Sheikh Pierre. Carried away, the Moslem captain kissed the old Phalangist and his two sons.

Driving back home, Bashir fumed. "For forty years of false independence we always played soccer, never got to the heart of the matter. Yes, we did that for forty years and ended up with one hundred thousand cadavers."

Was it worthwhile, I asked?

"Yes, I suppose so, if you don't have any illusions. Games distract from the essential. Can they invite us to their side of town and provide security?"

Bashir could also rage against his own Maronites, although the bedrock of his appeal remained the Maronite ascendancy. Striking a revolutionary pose, he would rip into Maronite smugness. "The President of the Republic is a Maronite, the head of the army, the magistrates, the head of the Sûreté are all Maronites, and thanks to those posts Lebanon has been destroyed," he once told me. "Most Maronites think that a bad Maronite is better than a good Moslem in some top job, because he's our son of a bitch." But he always made it clear that despite this surface backing for meritocracy what he really wanted was a good Maronite in every top job.

By January 1982, Bashir had allowed himself to be talked into trying to put one particular Maronite into the very top job. At first the idea of running Bashir for the presidency was just the notion of his political inner circle. But when President Sarkis himself promised to help, that decided Bashir. Sarkis, of course, might still be angling for another term for himself, for an extraordinary extension of his mandate, which expired in September; if that was his plan, he would first have to brandish the threat of Bashir and scare everyone inside and outside Lebanon into backing him. But at other times Sarkis argued that only Bashir was strong enough to maintain the last remaining shreds of Lebanese sovereignty.

Bashir kept up the pressure in his own sector. He had already deftly isolated his brother by all but taking over Amin's militia in his fiefdom of the Metn, and by assuming control of the entire Beirut port operation, hitherto run by Amin and his friends. On the political front, Bashir kept insisting that the Syrian forces must first leave Beirut, then all Lebanon, before the start of the summer election campaign. Few Lebanese took him seriously: the Syrians still controlled enough of the country to block his election, and the Israelis had blown hot and cold so often that no one could be sure of their reiterated threats to invade. Yet the perspicacious sensed that Bashir's candidacy was serious. Michel Aboujaoudé, the liberal editor of *An Nahar* and a Maronite who refused to live in East Beirut, told Bashir somewhat wearily in March, "You are a little Mussolini, a little Franco, a little Hitler. You are determined to be President, and you've got seventy-five percent of the Lebanese for you. The others are sitting on the fence. At forty-eight, people like me, who disagree, are through. There is no room for us."

Bashir protested, but in fact the political pluralism that the editor represented, especially within the Maronite community, had no part in his plans. The Maronites—the Christians—must stick together in this critical hour. A diversity of views could come later, once the entire country was "liberated." That meant after Bashir was elected. One prominent Christian businessman marveled at Bashir's tactics. "They became masters of Beirut," he said of the Lebanese Forces, "latter-day James Bonds with a license to kill anyone they want, to keep the pressure up. This is no longer the stuff of movies; it is reality, or at least the reality we are living. They maintain tension and wait."

Bashir was telling businessmen what they already knew: 1982 risked being turbulent. Over the years they had taken their precautions and had transformed Marounistan into a self-contained, if far from self-sufficient, state. Some one hundred thousand Christians left every day to work in West Beirut but returned to East Beirut at night. No longer did they frequent the beaches, nightclubs, and cinemas that before 1975 had been located almost exclusively in the West. Speculators had raped the once uncluttered coastline of Marounistan, putting up marinas and high-rise luxury hotels along their own coast. Shopping malls, office buildings, and apartment houses replaced or dwarfed the graceful tile-roofed houses of yore.

Bashir's hat was already in the ring before the Israelis invaded Lebanon in June 1982. While much of the rest of Lebanon worried about sheer survival, Marounistan residents focused on Bashir's election campaign. Symptomatically, the official campaign manager was Michel Murr, the Telecommunications Minister who as a young man had made a fortune in Africa and knew how to get things done. Lebanese elections always cost money; and the members of parliament who chose the President were known to be among the most corrupt men in the Middle East. How much Bashir's election cost depends on whom you listen to. His enemies claimed that Speaker Kamal Aassad—a key figure, since he chose when to call parliament into session—received more than $10 million, and that recalcitrant deputies were selling their votes for close to a million apiece. Lebanese Forces aides insisted for the record that they spent far less than they had originally planned, although later in private they confessed their coffers were empty. In any case, they repeated with pride that all the money came from the organization—not, as in the past, from individual fat-cat donors in exchange for future favors. And, Bashir's aides charged, his enemies were taking even more money from the Saudis, the Libyans, and the PLO, among others, to block his election.

In retrospect, it is easy enough to see how Bashir won. He was, after all, the only candidate. No one else dared to run against him, although Chamoun waited until the last moment before withdrawing his half-hearted, eleventh-hour attempt, while warning against Israeli pressures. But until the very last moment before parliament forgathered for the vote at the Fayadieh barracks in the hills near the Presidential Palace on August 23, few people thought Bashir could do it. The Sunni Moslem leaders who traditionally choose Maronite presidents had their minds on saving West Beirut, still under Israeli siege. The first PLO guerrillas had left the port of Beirut for exile only two days before. Together with Nabbih Berri, the Shia leader of the Amal militia, the Sunnis wanted the election postponed until the Israelis at least withdrew from Baabda, West Beirut, and its immediate environs. Philip Habib, the U.S. special envoy, fully in Bashir's camp for more than a month, since he was convinced there was no other realistic alternative, desperately worked for a last-minute meeting between Bashir and Saeb Salam, and hoped the Sunni leader would drop his boycott plan. But Salam and his advisers were convinced they could dredge up thirty-one deputies to boycott the session and thus prevent a quorum. They reasoned that if Bashir did not carry the day immediately, he would be forced to give way in favor of a compromise candidate. Feverishly consulting their handwritten lists of deputies, Salam and his advisers added up their friends and predicted they would foil Bashir. But they were at a disadvantage. The Israelis and the Lebanese Forces had closed the roads leading out of West Beirut, telephone lines between the two sectors of the city had been cut, and the airport had been closed down since June 7. Deprived of mobility and communications, Salam was operating in the dark. So, too, were the Syrians and Saudis, who apparently remained convinced until a few days before the election that Bashir would be stopped. Karim Pakradouni, Bashir's close adviser, who visited Damascus a week before the election, did nothing to discourage Syrian overconfidence. Until the last minute, he feared a photo finish.

At Fayadieh that election Monday, the parliamentarians in their big cars—accompanied by swarms of bodyguards in Range Rovers—began arriving in dribs and drabs in midmorning. "They'll all be present—all sixty-two of them," Bashir's election specialists had confidently predicted earlier in the day, "unless they come down with diarrhea." They seemed to have left nothing to chance—Sarkis even had Lebanese Army helicopters fly to Cyprus to pick up three deputies recalled from their European holidays. The Speaker, wearing an overtight white colonial-style suit, had asked for an 11:00 a.m. quorum. But the appointed hour came and went at the military school, and fewer than fifty deputies had entered the low white building and walked down the stairs into the banked classroom-auditorium where the election was to take place. Even the sleekest among them looked worn. Because of the fighting, no parliamentary elections had taken place since 1972, and the parliament kept having its term extended from year to year. Few of the new, militia-backed forces had their people in parliament, which made these old men even less representative of the country than ever before. The neatly dressed young men of the Lebanese Forces, who were present in great numbers, became nervous and worked off their anguish by roughing up the press. Well past noon, only fifty-six deputies were present—six shy of the quorum. At some point, it seemed as if the Speaker would have to call off the proceedings and reschedule the election. Then Bashir's men announced triumphantly they had more votes. Two more deputies drove up in a screech of brakes—fifty-eight. Soon after 1:00 p.m., the last four deputies arrived all together in a dead heat at a side door. No one had wanted to be the last man. (Later, Pakradouni was to admit to me that, had they been unable to dredge up those last four deputies, "we couldn't have kept the rest there for more than thirty or forty more minutes.")

The first ballot was dispatched in twenty-four minutes. The celebratory shooting started right outside the auditorium after the forty-sixth deputy had cast his vote. Army troops and Bashir's men were letting loose with a vast array of weaponry: they had figured out that forty-six was the magic number to get Bashir elected by a simple majority on the second ballot. But four blank ballots and one for Raymond Eddé deprived Bashir of a first-ballot victory, since a two-thirds majority was needed for a first-round election. Yet the Speaker forgot the rules of the assembly over which he had reigned for more than a decade and declared Bashir elected there and then. An erect, patrician clerk pointed out the error, and the deputies shambled forward, as their names were called once again, to place their handwritten ballots in the glass box. Four deputies were so ill or unsteady—Parkinson's disease, cardiac problems, and great old age had taken their toll—that an usher carried the box to their seats. Outside, the noise grew even louder as the din spread across East Beirut and the Christian suburbs. Sheikh Pierre stood ramrod-stiff, acknowledging the congratulations of his peers. He and the other remnants of 1943 had just wittingly committed political hara-kiri.

Lebanese soldiers broke out color photographs of the new President. Israeli troops laughed and slapped one another on the back. Christian teenagers drove their cars through the streets blowing horns and shooting off submachine guns. Christians took out their weapons and shot in the air. A half-dozen civilians were killed by stray bullets. (The departing guerrillas' fusillades caused even more victims on the other side of the city.) Hundreds of cars drove up to Bikfaya, where an alert aide had already planted a sign describing the Gemayel family home as the "Residence of the President." U.S. Sixth Fleet ships rode at anchor, clearly visible from the mountain roads, where delirious Maronites stopped cars and forced their occupants to drink champagne. For once the church bells rang for joy. Among the well-wishers were the high and the mighty, the humble—and Brigadier General Amos Yaron, the Israeli commander of the Beirut area, who arrived in uniform. His presence was only fitting. Israel, after all, had done its share to get Bashir elected. And in any case, Israeli officials, from Mossad chief Yitzhak Hoffi on down, had been regular adornments of select East Beirut salons for months. The leftist Druze leader Walid Jumblatt glumly decried the victory of "the candidate of Israeli tanks," and the Sunni leaders denounced the first election of a Lebanese President chosen against their wishes, but stopped short of declaring the vote illegal. Saeb Salam said, "The very foundations on which Lebanon has always existed have been shaken." Even the Maronite taxidriver who took me back to Beirut from Fayadieh worried about the outcome. "Israel wanted it," he said.

With his War Council, Bashir watched the election on television, and broke out the champagne. "Remember," Father Naaman said teasingly as Bashir and a select group of friends laughed heartily, "remember, you've only got six years." As it turned out, Bashir had only twenty-three days to live.

Two Israeli planes flew over the funeral ceremony, Defense Minister Sharon paid a fleeting visit to the family mansion, and the new head of Mossad was one of the mourners at Bikfaya on September 15. "We really ate it," the Mossad boss told an Israeli reporter in Hebrew—meaning that the Israelis had blown their best Lebanese connection. Already, Lebanese of both faiths were blaming the Israelis for Bashir's death, despite Prime Minister Begin's statement that he was shocked to the depths of his soul. That Wednesday morning, the Lebanese Forces had met at the Gemayel house and decided to run Amin for the presidency. Amin spent the day receiving mourners, his puffy, tear-stained face half-hidden by dark glasses. Mourners, who were asked to check their guns before entering the residence, filed into the small garden, then mounted the stone steps. The women stopped at a room on the left, where Bashir's mother and wife and sister-in-law sat erect and red-eyed. The men walked around a delicate balcony into the large, timbered reception room. (This segregation of the sexes was quintessentially Maronite—and very Arab.) Chairs lined the walls of the reception room. Sheikh Pierre sat at the far end. From time to time, a visitor would get up and leave, making way for a newcomer who invariably was greeted by the patriarch, who stood up and shook hands. All Lebanon's leaders, religious and political, military and civilian, passed through that room over the next week. The unity that escaped the Lebanese in life was rediscovered at the time of a funeral.

Father Naaman, resplendent in his hooded cassock and gold pectoral cross, cried. He apologized to me.

"Mourning a friend is nothing to be ashamed of," I said, hoping to put him at ease, "it's not a crime."

"I am lost," he sobbed. "For me, it is the first time I have ever cried."

In Saint Abdo's Church, the militiamen broke down and pounded on Bashir's coffin until first Solange, then Amin, intervened. The militiamen hoisted Amin aloft to place him atop the coffin. His legs kicking in anger, he ordered them to desist. They obeyed instinctively. The Lebanese Forces had been Bashir's, but Lebanese politics are clan affairs. Whatever their misgivings, Amin was now the chief, although he had never hidden his contempt for Bashir's hirelings. That was how he thought of them. "We pledge to Bashir's followers that his march will go on for a better Lebanon," Amin was political enough to say in his funeral oration. "They did away with his body, but not with his spirit or his desire for liberation." The Maronite Patriarch, no admirer of the dead man, likened him to "a great star now vanished from the sky of Lebanon, a martyr to his ambition to rebuild the country, a dreamer, and, like so many dreamers, he met jealousy and hatred." The myth was born. Forty days later, in a requiem ceremony at the War Council that participants likened to the Nuremberg rallies of the 1930s, Father Naaman was to find the perfect pitch. "We knew him as tempest, cyclone, fire, and light," said the priest. "Sometimes a single person sums up an entire people and an entire nation with its aptitudes and its longings. The Lebanese Forces are the shield of Lebanon, its strength and its pride. He left us to become myth and example."

"Hard to elect, easy to govern" was Pakradouni's view of Bashir's victory. "Easy to elect, hard to govern" was his prediction for Amin's term of office. Along with Zahi Boustany and Joseph Abu Khalil, Pakradouni had overcome his sense of loss and gone about the business of electing a new President. "This time it was a cinch," Pakradouni recalled to me later. "The deputies came to us, we didn't have to go to them." Six days after Bashir's death, two days after the killing stopped in Shatila, the same deputies returned to Fayadieh and elected Amin on the first ballot, 77–3. His first act upon taking office on September 23 was to visit the War Council, to whom he pledged himself ready to follow in Bashir's footsteps, prepared even to "make the supreme sacrifice," as his brother had. The reception was lukewarm. Indeed, one story insisted that the military was so suspicious of Amin that Solange had to be called out in the wee hours of the day before his election to tell them, in effect, "Amin is Bashir and Bashir is Amin."

On the face of things, Amin had once again lucked out. Had he not been the handsome, clever son who married Joyce, daughter of Joseph "Zozo" Tyan, a man who had done nothing in his life except inherit fortunes? Had not Amin then been elected to parliament at the age of thirty, young for Lebanon, thanks to the death of his uncle Maurice Gemayel, whose seat he took? And at forty Amin, a leading compromise candidate in Moslem eyes, was finally President. Had he not entered the Fayadieh auditorium arm in arm with Saeb Salam, who waved a big Cuban cigar to delighted fellow deputies as if to say, The class of 1943 has risen from the grave? Innocent of ties with Israel, convinced of the need to get on with the Moslems, involved in business deals like any self-respecting Lebanese, Amin represented at first glance a return to the folkways of Lebanon's happier days.

The trouble was that initially Amin's writ ran only in Moslem West Beirut, not in his own Christian territory. The Lebanese Forces refused to disarm. After weeks of prodding, they finally trucked a considerable armory out of East Beirut and stashed it away in monasteries, churches, and other locations in the mountains. Sheikh Pierre kept talking a Lebanese Forces line with Amin and an Amin line with the War Council. The new President became so annoyed that at one point he told a foreign dignitary well acquainted with Lebanon to "go see my father and tell him I'm a grown-up."

Nothing so rankled Amin as the War Council's steadfast refusal to hand over Bashir's killer to the state for prosecution. Instead, they kept Habib Tanios Chartouny in their own jail, and this only underlined their lack of faith in Amin and his works. Others suggested that the reason they kept the twenty-six-year-old Chartouny was that he had implicated the Lebanese Forces in the assassination: that was the kind of twisted logic the Lebanese had learned never to discount totally. After all, how could the much-vaunted security of the Lebanese Forces so fail as to allow their leader to be killed in a major official party building? That was not the only question. Chartouny and his entire family were well known as members in good standing of the Syrian People's Party (SPP), the Phalange's ancient Christian rivals. And Chartouny and his sister and grandparents lived in the same building as the Phalange's Ashrafieh branch, in fact right on top of it. Jean Nader had kicked them out during the civil war, but the family had been allowed to move back in. (One version maintained that Nader in fact was blind to the security risks because of his liaison with Chartouny's attractive young sister.) The Lebanese Forces were so angry at their own stupidity for having them there that they sent troops up to the village of Chartoun in the Shuf, trashed the entire cemetery, and beat up men and women; they departed, however, without killing anyone.

They were lucky to catch Chartouny, who showed little intelligence in carrying out the assassination. He had installed the fancy Japanese long-range electronic detonator for the explosives before realizing that his sister as well as a friend and his family were still in the building. Chartouny telephoned his sister and told her to leave immediately for Place Sassine, a main intersection. She did, but was so unnerved to discover she had just escaped death that within minutes of the explosion she was hysterically telling people in the street about her good fortune. The others had no such luck. Chartouny had worked up a story to tell the parents: he would say their son was in the hospital and they must go to him immediately. Unfortunately, his friend answered the telephone. Chartouny feared his friend would recognize his voice, and so he hung up. The friend and his parents perished in the explosion.

Chartouny proved a tough nut to crack. Picked up thanks to his sister's indiscretion, he at first resisted his interrogators' ministrations. After four days' detention in Bikfaya, he succeeded in escaping but was picked up again in the coastal suburb of Jal al Dib. Then he started singing—and on videotape, at that, according to informants, who insisted that someday the Lebanese Forces would turn this evidence over to the state.

From what can be pieced together, Chartouny genuinely believed the explosive charge would only frighten Bashir, not kill him. As he told his interrogators, he wanted Bashir to realize that he was as vulnerable as anyone else in Lebanon. When it came to anything but the technical details, however, Chartouny insisted he had no real idea who was ultimately behind the assassination scheme. The SPP had recruited him when he was studying in Paris in 1979. A military commander of the SPP provided the explosives and detonator, and soon after the assassination disappeared to Syria. There were suggestions that the PLO or some element of it was involved, as was some part of one of the manifold intelligence outfits in Syria.

The Lebanese Forces also fingered the PLO, which had as many reasons as Syria (or Franjieh) to want Bashir dead. In the Palestinians' eyes he had been responsible for a string of massacres, and it was his alliance with Israel that furnished Begin and Sharon with the pretext for invading Lebanon and humiliating the PLO. What sweet revenge for the Palestinians, then, whom the Maronites had so often accused of being the sole source of all the country's troubles, to prove that the Lebanese themselves were ungovernable. For, whatever else Bashir's death meant, it was followed by renewed intercommunal strife that made that point without doubt. His death also underlined another standard PLO argument: that those Arabs who dealt with Israel ended up assassinated. The weakness of the Palestinian thesis, however, is that the PLO, by its own admission, never succeeded in penetrating the Lebanese Forces, and to have done so at the moment of the guerrillas' greatest disarray seemed to border on the miraculous. The Palestinians did not believe much in miracles. The most immediate effect of Bashir's death, after all, was the massacre at Shatila.

The operation had been professional, compartmentalized. There were so many possible string-pullers. Sleiman Franjieh, for example, told me—when I lied my way through Lebanese Forces, Syrian, and finally Marada lines to go see him the day after the funeral—that he had not done it or caused it to be done. "Unhappily, I was not responsible for this act of vengeance," he lamented, his face lit with a halo of ill-concealed joy. That was why, he explained, he was not wearing black, because in his eyes Tony and his family were still not avenged. Gazing out over the Qadisha valley from his mansion at Ehdene, Sleiman said, "We have tried since 1978, but have had no luck."

With Bashir dead would he call it quits and spare Amin and Sheikh Pierre?

"Absolutely not," he said, carefully explaining that vengeance had to be wreaked personally. Bashir's death simply didn't count in Sleiman's eyes.

"Allah is great," he intoned, "and that is all I have to say, since our tradition obliges us to respect the dead."

Could Tony and the family now be buried?

"Unhappily, no," he went on, because in their case, as he had explained already—in sufficient detail, he had thought—"you can bury someone only after vengeance has been wreaked."

Sleiman prided himself on the accuracy of his prophecy. "I said right after his election that Bashir would never live to take office."

How, I asked, had he known?

"Divine inspiration. I am close to the Good Lord." (In fact, a story had circulated which insisted that Syrians had given Sleiman that undertaking when he traveled to Damascus soon after Bashir's election.) So innocent was he, he said, that he had gone to bed early, muttering, "Too bad," when the radio first reported that Bashir had emerged unscathed from the wreckage. His daughter Lamia had brought him news of what he called the "agreeable surprise."

"I was awakened past midnight by shooting. It is a custom here to fire weapons as a sign of joy to mark great occasions, but it was only when Lamia planted a big, fat, warm kiss on my face that I realized Bashir was dead."

Even technically, the assassination bothered his purist standards. Playing with his worry beads as he stared over the green baize tabletop, Sleiman confided his distaste at the use of explosive. "I'm for face-to-face work, not this business of killing a man behind his back."

In fact, much of what Sleiman said was a facade. Lamia, Sonia and her husband, and Robert, it turned out, had attended a special mass for Tony and his family in the Ehdene chapel at 2:00 a.m., as soon as they heard of Bashir's death. Indeed, I recalled that Sonia had been wearing black when I called on the family the very next day. At least for the younger Franjieh clan, enough was enough. Their attitude was dictated, in part, by reality. They owed their safety to the presence of the Syrian Army, which had been badly mauled during the fighting and was likely to withdraw at some point, leaving them high and dry. Already, Sleiman's sway over the north of Lebanon was being contested. Despite his eve-of-ballot statement warning that he would consider anyone voting for Bashir as responsible for Tony's death, eleven of the eighteen northern parliamentary deputies, including Maronites from Zghorta, had dared to vote for Bashir. Sleiman leveled the graceful mansion of Fuad Ghosn, the deputy from Batroun, on the coast, but he did not dare punish, much less blow up the homes of two Zghorta deputies who had voted likewise.

Within days of Amin's election and his inauguration address, in which he offered to let bygones be bygones, Sleiman swallowed his pride and forgot his threats to exterminate the rest of the Gemayel family. At face value, he had little choice: the Syrians had sent a special emissary to him to make clear that they were determined to do business with Amin. However, some Zghorta residents kept insisting that Sleiman was accepting reconciliation only to lull the Gemayels into a false sense of security and get closer to his quarry. Lebanese delightedly recounted what was purported to be Sonia's telephoned condolences to Solange: "I'm delighted to hear Bashir is dead and only sorry it wasn't us. There'll be others wearing widows' weeds when we get there."

Such thinking jibed with persistent reports that a Lebanese Army officer from Zghorta, in coordination with SPP militiamen, had laid an ambush along the road from Beirut to Bikfaya the very day Bashir was killed. That would link the SPP, Chartouny, and Zghorta in an anti-Gemayel plot and, by extension, would link all three with their common Syrian protectors.

The Palestinians argued that the Israelis and their Christian friends were responsible for Bashir's death. Even some Christians agreed. "All Bashir's lieutenants were on the Israeli wavelength," reasoned one Christian businessman who was privy to their thinking. The motive was simple enough, if he was to be believed. The Israelis were angered at Bashir's newfound independence, his flirtation with the Americans, his temptation to become a national leader at the expense of an Israeli alliance. Rather than kill Bashir themselves, they simply let nature take its course—that meant encouraging his militiamen to kill him. He had sealed his own doom when he spoke of dissolving his militia and forming a national army of sixty thousand (even one hundred thousand) men. They struck to protect their power base.

The trouble with that argument was that no one had really ever believed Bashir would dissolve his militia. In one form or another, they would remain as his Praetorian Guard. And thus they had nothing to gain from killing him. Nor did the Israelis, by any logical accounting. Begin had been genuinely angry when he met Bashir at Nahariyya, but Sharon had visited Bashir later and all but formally apologized for the earlier blowup. On the face of things, the Israelis had an excellent investment in Bashir and every reason to believe that future relations between Israel and Lebanon could become pacific without a formal peace treaty. If indeed they decided to go the other route, to weaken and divide Lebanon, Bashir stood little chance of thwarting them, as they were certainly credited with the ability to kill him later if, once in office a few months, he turned out to be a danger. The poisons of Lebanese life were easy to activate. In any case, they had plenty of time to bend Bashir to their will. So why despair and eliminate him even before he took office, in favor of a brother who viewed them with deep-seated suspicion? For those convinced the Israelis had killed Bashir, lingering anti-Semitism and suspicions about Israel tended to replace hard analysis. The Palestinians were not the only ones to savor that famous saying, "I killed him and marched in his funeral."

What seemed more plausible even at the time was that the Israelis had little trouble in persuading their friends in the Lebanese Forces to take part in the operation at the Shatila camp. Israeli intelligence had been telling the Lebanese for most of a week that the Palestinians were planning to kill Bashir. And then he was dead. In their simplistic view of the world, the Palestinians had to be involved. Taunted by Israelis for not joining in the fighting, the militiamen fell into the trap. Without Bashir their commanders proved themselves inept, malleable fools. When a Phalangist political adviser active in getting Amin elected asked why he had not been informed about the Shatila operation, Fady

Frem, the commander of the Lebanese Forces, sheepishly said, "Oh, we knew you were working flat-out and we didn't want to disturb you."

Bashir's death and the massacre have gone unpunished for months. Chartouny very probably will pay with his life, but it is less certain that his interrogators will succeed in establishing who the real forces were behind Bashir's assassination. The massacre is likely to go unpunished, although the Lebanese Forces involved—the Joe Eddés, the Michel Zoueins, the Maroun Mashalanis, the Elie Hobeikas—are well known. Their real punishment lies in the latent dissension in their own ranks, due less to real strains and stresses among rivals than to the absence of a chief. For Bashir held his organization together despite that natural Lebanese proclivity for divisiveness and wrangling. Only after his death did it become apparent that the various groups making up the Lebanese Forces—the rival politicians, junior warlords, economic groups, monks—all thought that Bashir was "theirs." Without him, they still look strong and, indeed, are strong enough to challenge Amin and the state. Finally in February 1983 Amin went to the mat with the Lebanese Forces, which belatedly allowed the Lebanese Army to enter East Beirut and the Christian suburbs. No longer did his writ run only in West Beirut. But recent Maronite history suggests that further showdowns are inevitable. No more than Bashir in 1980 can they afford to shut down the private ports or stop levying taxes. Six years later, they are playing out the same role with Amin that Bashir played against Sarkis.

The same Phalange politician who mused about the Phalange's slow-motion coup d'état concluded his ruminations gloomily. "You know," he said, "if Bashir's killers really wanted to condemn this country for good, all they'd have to do is knock off Sheikh Pierre. He's the only thing holding this place together."

5. The Offhand Americans

"The dogs, the dogs," she said, her voice abruptly rising and choked with all the outrage, humiliation, and resentment now remembered with near-total recall. The former President of Lebanon's middle daughter, Sonia Racy, drew herself up.

"Do you realize? President Franjieh arrives at Kennedy airport in 1974 to speak on behalf of the Arab League, to introduce the Palestinian cause and Yasser Arafat to the United Nations. What happens?"

She bridled with anger. Innocently, I had asked her to delve into the past, to recall her father's relations with the United States. "What happens? The presidential party's luggage is sniffed at by dogs. Not once, not twice, but three times." The voice rose again. "When the President found out, he was fit to be tied, I tell you. Imagine! Accompanied by two former presidents, three former speakers of parliament, four former prime ministers—all of Lebanon's political elite representing the leadership of the nineteen members of the Arab League. The dogs, the dogs!" She did not have to explain, but Arabs consider dogs disgusting, and on this score, Lebanese Maronites feel themselves Arab.

There was no calming or stopping Sonia Racy as she recounted that November day in New York. Overzealous narcotics agents had used dogs to check the Franjieh party's bags for hashish, Lebanon's illicit but major export, estimated even then to be worth more than $300 million a year to the President's son Tony, among many, many others. Narcotics specialists at the American embassy in Beirut had been tipped off about a purported scheme to smuggle hashish aboard the presidential aircraft, and they had routinely informed the Bureau of Dangerous Drugs in Washington. Ambassador Godley had alerted Franjieh's personal secretary, Boutros Dib, who promised him that Lebanese security people would monitor the party's luggage before it was loaded aboard the presidential flight. In fact, U.S. embassy representatives were present to verify these proceedings, unbeknownst to Franjieh. The embassy thereafter sent the State Department a cease-and-desist cable, but the Lebanon desk officer in Washington was asleep at the switch and forgot to inform the BDD. "The narcs were not clever," an embassy staffer remarked years later, "for a greater insult could not have been imagined."

Franjieh refused President Ford's proffered excuses. He made Ambassador Godley's reappearance in Beirut conditional on a formal, written apology, and became more convinced than ever that the U.S. government was out to get him.

"Don't tell me it was fate or a mistake," Sonia intoned. "Why blame it on some little guy?" she demanded, peremptorily indicating her disdain for such evasion of responsibility.

Errors did occur, I protested. Only foreigners, I suggested brightly, were convinced that everything in the United States functioned like clockwork.

Her husband, Abdullah Racy, sought to come to my rescue. "Even if hashish had been aboard the plane," he said, "they shouldn't have done anything about it—*raison d'état*."

That set Sonia off, enumerating other American "errors." "Godley sent daily reports to Washington making believe that the Christians in Lebanon were a decadent lot, like Madame Nhu in Vietnam, that no one loved the President, that the family was getting rich, that Tony made millions as a minister," Sonia said, accurately reporting what many Lebanese, both Christian and Moslem, had said about her father's six years in office. "It was Godley who blackened the President, telling Washington how the Christian elite was getting rich and the people were dying of famine," she added.

But she then returned to what was really on her mind—the dogs. "It was a snub, an insult, not just for the President but for all the Arab League, inflicted not just by Godley but by the entire Ford administration."

More accurately, Sonia might have argued that the absurd airport affair was just one of the more bizarre misunderstandings strewn carelessly over a generation of bilateral American-Lebanese relations. Like two foreigners conversing in a language not their own—and claiming greater fluency than either possessed—the Lebanese Christian leaders and the Americans stumbled their way into tragedy. The Americans were sure at each stage that their message had been received loud and clear. The Christian leaders didn't like what they heard, refused to believe it, and preferred to reconstruct the conversation to suit their own purposes. Until it was too late, neither realized the extent of the gulf separating them. Humiliated and chastened by setbacks ranging from Vietnam to Watergate, the United States government in the 1970s was in no mood for the kind of adventure the Christians had in mind. But the Christian leaders in Lebanon automatically and steadfastly assumed that the United States once and for all had taken on responsibility for them—the newest in the long line of Western protectors stretching back to the Crusaders. Finally tiring of this dialogue of the deaf, the United States government washed its hands of Lebanon without even bothering to go through the formal motions. No one who counted in Washington paid attention, in any case, although pro forma statements pledged support for Lebanon's independence, sovereignty, and territorial integrity. By the time official Washington realized the stakes, it was too late. Itself powerless to act, the United States did nothing to stop those two deadly Middle East rivals, Israel and Syria, from carving up Lebanon. Suspicious Lebanese even insisted the United States had arranged the carve-up. It wasn't called that, of course; indeed, the operation was advertised as the only way to stablilize Lebanon. Perhaps no one in Washington realized the consequences. But a half-dozen years later, that remains the result.

No wonder that I had so much trouble seeing the Franjiehs. I first attempted to arrange a meeting in 1980, but was defeated by the antique telephone system after hours of effort. (That, too, was a theme in Lebanese history: the system's disrepair predated the civil war, and many Lebanese laid the responsibility at the door of Tony Franjieh, who was Telecommunications Minister during the early 1970s and was accused of pocketing huge sums as a fee for a major modernization scheme. Television transmission via satellite was delayed for a decade when potential customers, especially the American networks, refused to pay the swollen installation and user costs that Tony demanded as a hidden payoff.) That first time, I went so far as to go up and see the feudal leader without a formal invitation. He was in his fiefdom, at the summer residence at Ehdene. From miles away, there was no mistaking the summer palace—its low, limestone bulk was clearly indicated by freshly painted blue-and-white signposts, in considerably better repair than those pointing to the presidential residence near Beirut. Through streets festooned with color posters of the slain son, Tony, and his wife and daughter, I drove straight to the palace gate. There I was looked over by suspicious gunmen, who, after an interval that I felt lasted longer than was decent, deigned to act on my entreaties and took my calling card inside. But that time I made it no farther than the antechamber, where I explained my business, was heard out politely, but sent on my way with the contempt that the Franjieh household reserved for all things American.

Protracted negotiations through influential Lebanese intermediaries—and many hours on those excruciating telephone lines—were required before the family relented and I was granted access to "the President." Up in his mountains, Sleiman Franjieh was still President.

If effective access to Sleiman Franjieh proved difficult for me years after he had left office, it had been all but impossible for the United States government when he was in power during the 1975–76 fighting. Had relations been better between him and Mac Godley, I ventured to ask Sonia, might the United States have been able to help stop the violence? But I should have known better. "We are not the ones fighting the United States," she retorted. "It's American policy that wanted the situation in Lebanon to happen as it happened. That is the truth we believe, and we shall continue to believe until there is proof to the contrary."

In Lebanon, Sonia's somewhat cryptic message needed no decoding.

All jumbled up in that statement was the Maronites' paranoid heritage: chased out of Syria by other Christians (a fact they play down in favor of their mythic persecution at Moslem hands—thirteen hundred years of enduring Islam's powerful presence from their self-imposed isolation in the mountains), proud of their reputation for independence, the Maronites are adroit at playing all the angles with angelic surface sincerity. They also share a marked Lebanese penchant for fatalistic dependence on outsiders, especially Westerners across the seas. And Lebanese Moslems look to the Arab world for support to counterbalance the West's interest in the Christians. However clumsily, Sonia was trying to articulate the Maronite article of faith which insists that the United States was duty-bound to uphold the Christians, come what may.

In the local parlance, was pro-Western Lebanon supposed to be America's "economic aircraft carrier" in the eastern Mediterranean, just as surely as its neighbor Israel was Washington's "political aircraft carrier"? The United States, which before World War II had no vital interests in the Levant, found itself picking up the economic, political, and cultural mission abandoned by Britain and France as their influence waned, especially after the humiliating Suez adventure in 1956. What was more normal than to have the United States inherit the French and British mantle? Foreign powers now bought elections in Lebanon, as they had schemed and exerted influence in other ways for more than a century. Why all the fuss? Had not William Colby, when Director of the Central Intelligence Agency, testified before Congress in 1976 that the agency had provided arms and money to the Phalangists and the Armenian Tashnag Party in the 1950s? Those CIA activities were part of a Cold War policy of using pro-Western minorities in the anti-Communist struggle. The Lebanese Christians certainly considered themselves part of the Free World. Indeed, that was a locution they used without embarrassment long after it took on a slightly pejorative tone in an America reeling from the excesses of its own imperial presidencies.

So all-pervading were CIA activities in Lebanon in the 1950s that a former American ambassador years later remarked of that period, "We were buying people wholesale. I would not be surprised to discover that everyone important in Lebanon was on the CIA payroll, although I would need to see the proof." What purported to be just such proof was provided by Wilbur Crane Eveland, a former CIA operative in the

Middle East, in his book, *Ropes of Sand*, published in 1980 despite CIA efforts to delay its distribution. Eveland went well beyond the retired diplomat's confirmation of what in any event had long been Beirut schoolboy knowledge. In the name of fighting Communism and Arab nationalism, both suspect to John Foster Dulles, Secretary of State, and his brother, Allen, the CIA Director, the CIA financed the 1957 Lebanese legislative elections. Eveland wrote that U.S. Ambassador Donald Heath insisted on saturation financing to defeat seven powerful politicians who had resigned from parliament to protest President Chamoun's pro-American policies. Heath also demanded that Charles Malik, the extravagantly pro-American Foreign Minister, stand for election. That operation alone cost the CIA, according to Eveland, $25,000 for Malik's campaign expenses and a similar amount that Chamoun required to reimburse the minister's defeated opponent. In fact, the CIA slush funds were distributed by Chamoun himself. Throughout the election campaign, Eveland "traveled regularly to the presidential palace with a briefcase full of Lebanese pounds and then returned late at night to the embassy," where the CIA replenished the stock. "Soon my gold DeSoto with its stark white top was a common sight outside the palace and I proposed to Chamoun that he use an intermediary and a more remote spot," Eveland recalled. "When the president insisted he handle each transaction by himself I reconciled myself to the probability that anybody in Lebanon who really cared would have no trouble guessing precisely what I was doing."

Unsurprisingly, Chamoun's candidates won a landslide victory of such overkill proportions that wags suggested establishing a senate to mollify the President's defeated rivals who had been deprived of their normally safe seats in the legislature. Convinced that Chamoun now would ask parliament first to amend the constitution so he could succeed himself, then vote him a second term, Chamoun's opponents enlisted Egyptian and Syrian help. By March 1958, the crisis had turned into civil war. In July, the United States landed Marines—less to help Chamoun than to shore up other pro-Western Arab regimes in the Middle East, shocked by the army coup that had just toppled the British-protected monarchy in Iraq. Iraq meant oil, and the United States feared the Iraqi revolution would spread throughout the Arab world, thereby threatening Western oil interests everywhere in the region. Lebanon was a sideshow in American eyes.

The U.S. Marines' presence in Lebanon neatly froze the fighting and allowed Chamoun to serve out his six-year term. Much to his abiding chagrin, Chamoun was succeeded by General Fuad Chehab, the army commander whom he had accused of not using the troops to quell the rebels. With American blessing, Chehab patched up relations with Egypt, whose government continued to exercise proconsular influence in Beirut for years to come. He backed away from the more intransigent pro-Western attitudes of Chamoun's administration and adopted a neutralist foreign policy that, he believed, was more in keeping with Lebanon's status as a part-Christian, part-Moslem country in the Arab world.

By the end of the summer, the fourteen thousand Marines had packed up and gone back to their Sixth Fleet billets. The unofficial American after-battle report was one of dumb relief that the United States had been able to extricate itself so painlessly from a mess so largely of its own making. But those who studied the situation more profoundly did not particularly like what they saw. "Students of the Middle East—and they included the Dulles brothers—realized Chamoun had diddled us," recalled one American diplomat who was active in the Middle East then. "Nineteen fifty-eight really was a Lebanese revolution. By sending in the Marines, we blocked its natural development, which involved giving the Moslems a greater voice in politics." Washington was in no mood to foster revolution—or evolution, for that matter—in even so pro-Western a country as Lebanon. In the same way that, two decades later, it reacted against foreign entanglements after the Vietnam War, the United States abruptly ceased to be interested in what it decried as the sleazy Levantine complexities of internal Lebanese politics. "When you came down to it, very few people in the U.S. establishment were interested in Lebanon itself, except missionaries and perhaps a few oil men," a former CIA policymaker has said. "The United States had a policy for Israel, a policy on oil, a policy for radical Arabs, one for conservative Arabs, a policy for dealing regionally with the Soviets, but not a policy for Lebanon. Lebanon policy was what was left over."

The trouble was that the Lebanese did not get Washington's message. That cultural failing was to plague American-Lebanese relations for the next generation. Beirut had been an intelligence and commercial crossroads for so long that the Lebanese assumed truths that did not in fact exist. A case officer who was informative and sympathetic was misunderstood as supporting their cause. That's always been a problem in the Arab world, but it was constant and particularly acute with the Lebanese. "The Lebanese, especially the Maronites in power, believed that a lifted eyebrow at a lunch, an ambassadorial shrug, indicated some policy," an American specialist on the Middle East told me. "I do not believe there was ever any serious American side to what the Lebanese construed as a dialogue. Lebanese politicians were able to get access to medium- and high-level officials over the years—but only as a courtesy. They were received in Washington like so many other foreign politicians seeking official U.S. endorsement to impress the folks at home. They were treated courteously, but their questions were answered with universal obfuscation wrapped in banalities."

In the 1960s, the U.S. embassy in Beirut became a backwater. Then, after Israel's victory in the Six-Day War in June 1967, the major Arab countries broke diplomatic relations with Washington. It was their way of showing anger at America's support for Israel, but the gesture also reflected their humiliation and impotence. Lebanon did not follow suit, however, and the American embassy in Beirut took on regional responsibilities, trying to keep track of events throughout the Arab world. Once again, American foreign-policy makers were interested in Lebanon, but not in the Lebanese. Rather, Washington was fascinated by the Palestinians, who had grabbed the spotlight from the discredited Arab regimes so pitifully defeated by the Israeli blitzkrieg. The Americans' sudden interest in the Palestinians focused on their use of terrorism to gain attention for their long-neglected cause. The Palestinians had become a dynamic force in the Middle East, capable of disturbing the status quo, perhaps even of setting off a conflagration that would force a solution. Their hijacking of commercial airliners and their attacks on Israeli citizens inside and outside the Jewish state was the stuff of headlines.

The Cairo accords of November 1969, negotiated between the PLO and the Lebanese government and brokered by Nasser, marked the point of no return for Lebanese sovereignty, and effectively consecrated the PLO as a state-within-a-state. Lebanon's authority in its own territory was severely diminished. The PLO was authorized to police Palestinian refugee camps in Lebanon; its guerrillas were permitted to establish logistics bases and training camps in the Arqoub area bordering on Syria and Israel, near Mount Hermon; and a limited number of guerrillas were to be tolerated—under Lebanese Army control—in the so-called central sector, opposite Galilee. Within months the Palestinians had disregarded the limitations. Many Lebanese Christians were furious about this, but all but one parliamentary deputy (Raymond Eddé) had approved the supposedly secret text of the Cairo accords.

(As almost all American diplomats assigned to Arab capitals have lamented in private, official Washington's interest in the Palestinians was not political. Meaningful discussions with the Palestine Liberation Organization—as opposed to occasional dealings, dictated by security problems or other momentary necessity—was against government policy. That held true even before Israel extracted from Secretary of State Henry Kissinger a secret annex pledging that the United States would not negotiate with the PLO. That was the price Kissinger paid for Israel's acceptance of the major withdrawal of Israeli troops from the Sinai desert, a withdrawal worked out by the United States in September 1975. Known by its diplomatic code name Sinai II, the agreement implied far more than the mere return of Israeli-occupied territory to Egyptian sovereignty. It marked the first major split between Egypt, the most populous Arab country, and the rest of the Arab world; specifically, it consecrated the divorce between Egypt and Syria, which had been key allies against Israel in the 1973 Yom Kippur War. A long-standing, if only formal, dedication to global negotiations in the Middle East was abandoned. The U.S.-engineered "step-by-step" deal was roundly criticized by both radical and conservative Arabs, who accurately predicted that Egypt had taken the first step toward a separate peace with Israel, and that, they made clear, was only to Israel's advantage, since the Arabs would be deprived of the largest armed forces in the Arab world. Ahead lay the Camp David accords, which effectively took Egypt out of the regional military equation and provided Israel with the means to pick off its principal adversaries, Syria and the PLO, without major risk.)

The Christians in Lebanon had never wanted a real national army, for—good merchant descendants of the Phoenicians that they claimed to be—they did not want to pay for it. They did not want to provoke Israel, and they did not want to encourage the growth of an armed force that might then stage a coup d'état, as so often had been the case in other Arab countries. But they were to pay the price. In 1970, the Jordanian Army crushed the Palestinians in what became known as

Black September, and the thousands of Palestinian commandos who escaped the wrath of the Jordanian Army over the next year moved to Lebanon. Already, Lebanese officials were worried about the string of Palestinian camps surrounding Beirut, which were, as one man put it, "like a choker around our neck."

Especially after Palestinian commandos killed U.S. Ambassador Cleo Noel in the Sudan in 1973, Israel and the United States came to believe that both countries' fears, interests, and policies coincided when it came to the Palestinian guerrilla and terrorist threat. "We Americans were one hundred percent against the Palestinians," an American diplomat remembered. "We called them terrorists in our official documents and statements. We allowed ourselves to develop a mental block." But it was a policy the Israelis themselves came to regret. The official inquiry into the failure of Israeli intelligence to predict the Yom Kippur attack of October 1973 blamed Mossad's obsessive interest in countering the Palestinians worldwide, to the detriment of keeping track of its two major adversaries, Egypt and Syria. And Israeli officials now readily, if privately, concede that the only real military threat to the Jewish state is a conflict involving a conventional Arab army or armies, not the Palestinians.

As early as 1970, Joseph W. Sisco, then Assistant Secretary of State for Near Eastern and South Asian Affairs, stopped over in Lebanon with the Secretary, William Rogers. They were left with the impression that Lebanon was bereft of any real security force to enforce government fiat. And the Lebanese were already worried about the Palestinians' virtual state-within-a-state status. In succeeding years, Washington therefore encouraged President Franjieh's government to crack down on the Palestinians before it was too late, and the "Jordanization" of Lebanon became a catchword on the Beirut cocktail circuit; so, too, in the American embassy did the "Ammanization" of Lebanon—both labels a shorthand for the kind of armed showdown with Palestinians from which King Hussein had emerged victorious in 1970 and 1971.

The moment of truth came in May 1973. An Israeli raid in the heart of Beirut killed three leading Palestinian commando officials—without opposition from the Lebanese Army barracks located in the same neighborhood. Prime Minister Saeb Salam called for the army commander's resignation and then resigned himself when Franjieh refused his demand. The Lebanese Army's inaction reinforced Moslem suspicions that its Christian leadership tacitly approved of the Israeli strike. Finally, after four Lebanese soldiers were kidnapped by PLO commandos, Franjieh ordered the fifteen-thousand-man army into action. The army marshaled its forces at the Bir Hassan barracks near its objective, the heavily defended Sabra refugee camp in south Beirut. "It looked like a Fort Benning exercise—tanks galore," an American diplomat recalled to me. "It was the only time I ever saw the Lebanese military being really effective. There was fairly heavy fighting, and the air force's aged Hawker Hunters strafed the Palestinians at Burj al Barajneh, near Beirut airport, after the commandos had closed it down with a mortar barrage."

The trouble was that the army attack, scheduled for early morning, actually got under way only in midafternoon. The next day, there was a truce, and that was that, though skirmishing went on for days. In the American embassy's view, the last effective chance to crack down on the PLO commandos had gone out the window. So much for "Ammanization." Beirut gossips said Prime Minister Amin Hafez's pro-Palestinian wife had prevailed on him to go easy, and other Lebanese remained convinced that President Sleiman Franjieh never seriously wanted to destroy the guerrillas, only to scare them. Franjieh's real purpose, this argument ran, was to test the Moslems in the army. The only shelling of the PLO positions was done by a Moslem-commanded artillery battery, and the pilots were predominantly Moslems as well. Thus the allegedly Christian-dominated army had made its point that it could rely on its Moslems despite the growing assumption that they, like many Moslems in Lebanese civilian life, were increasingly pro-Palestinian.

Whatever the validity of these arguments, both sides drew strikingly similar conclusions. Franjieh, who had started raising his own Marada, or "Giants Brigade," as early as 1969 with the help of Lebanese Army officers, stepped up the training of his private militia. So did other Christian leaders, especially the Gemayels. Light arms were bought in Bulgaria. Soon, training was under way seriously throughout the Christian heartland and even in Jordan, whose King Hussein long had been a close friend of Camille Chamoun. Once-idyllic Sunday picnics in the mountains were now disturbed by machine-gun and mortar fire as young Christians underwent basic training. The Palestinians, too, beefed up their defenses. Politically, they moved closer to leftist and Moslem Lebanese allies, hoping their support would provide protection from what they claimed was a Christian-dominated government out to destroy their last refuge. Militarily, they established an armed presence opposite major Christian strongholds or potential communications choke points.

As a showdown approached, the Christians tried to enlist aid from their traditional friends, France and, especially, the United States, for what they viewed as the inevitable battle against the Palestinians, the Left, and the Moslems. Within a week of arriving as ambassador in February 1974, Godley was hearing extremist Christian talk about partitioning Lebanon. His very presence was the subject of controversy and provided a perfect illustration of what Western Arabists have condemned as the "wog factor." "Wog" is a derogatory British colonial description of a local as a "worthy Oriental gentleman," and the "wog factor" describes a Third World tendency to imagine ubiquitous conspiracy and to confuse fact and fancy. Godley's reputation while ambassador in Laos in the early 1970s as an unabashed proponent of American military muscle had preceded him: motions in Lebanon's parliament now demanded that the government withdraw its agreement to his nomination.

In fact, Godley had been told before leaving Washington "not to play field marshal or gauleiter," soubriquets he had earned at his Laos embassy. It was hardly surprising advice, given the times. The United States was mesmerized by the Watergate scandal. The final remission in Indochina was ending. The CIA was under Congressional investigation, its past excesses exposed to public scrutiny. Kissinger was no longer the miracle worker he had been in the early Nixon era—flitting off on secret missions to China, negotiating arms-reduction talks with the Russians, and arranging the "honorable" withdrawal of U.S. troops from Indochina. Kissinger, indeed, found himself at the very center of the web of strands that now unraveled, leaving intact little of the "Super-K" reputation he had so easily acquired barely a year before. No longer could he charm Congress and country with the derring-do of his high-wire shuttle diplomacy in the Middle East. Just ahead lay the humiliation of the botched CIA operations in Angola. Washington policymakers were so afraid to talk to Congress about a U.S. military presence in the Middle East that the Sinai Support Mission, the entirely American organization established to monitor the Israeli disengagement of forces under the Sinai II agreement, was entrusted to a private contractor rather than to the army. (For similar reasons, policymakers refrained from presenting long-mulled-over plans for a rapid deployment force in the Persian Gulf until late 1979.)

But the Maronite politicians in Lebanon paid no heed to this emerging American neo-isolationism—a surprising failing for a sect whose survival and prosperity over the centuries had depended so closely on an accurate reading of events abroad. In the summer of 1974, Turkey took advantage of the Greek military junta's collapse to invade Cyprus. Although that island lay scarcely more than a hundred miles off their shores, the Lebanese took little notice of the fact that the United States did not intervene to rescue the Christian Greek Cypriot majority from the Moslem Turks. Godley and many another diplomat preached moderation to the Christians, extolled the virtues of accommodation and compromise, and constantly discouraged Maronite hopes for another Marine landing. The Christians listened distractedly, then trotted out their arguments again and again and again. Years later, in 1980, when I asked him about this, Sleiman Franjieh brushed aside such considerations, and lambasted Godley and impugned his motives. "He came to us from Vietnam, the most dangerous of ambassadors," Franjieh said, "and you know better than I what an American ambassador can do."

He would have been more accurate had he reasoned otherwise, since, in fact, no one was listening to Godley, and ambassadors rarely make policy. Still, some Beirut optimists held out hopes that the worst could be avoided—thanks to the balance of terror between the Palestinians and their allies and the Christian militias. But, as I discovered myself during a week-long stopover in Beirut that September 1974, in private diplomats and politicians were scared stiff, convinced the explosion was only a question of time. When *The Washington Post* published my doomsday prophecy, I was roundly denounced as a mischief maker. I was banned by the Lebanese government from entering the country for six months. My little scandal caused neither the Lebanese, nor the United States, nor any other government to reflect or take remedial action. At most, friends told me, I was briefly the subject of cocktail conversation.

The Christian politicians simply could not—and would not—under-

stand that the United States wanted no part of their tiresome problems
and of their political system, more decadent than anything in the most
backward of Persian Gulf emirates. No amount of patient explanation,
replete with examples, did any good. They shut their minds to any
evidence that would contradict what they willed should be active
American support. Selective memory filtered out everything since their
romanticized impression of 1958. The United States was the leader of
the Free World, the mightiest power on the face of the earth, and a
Christian nation: thus, an unconditional ally. The Bay of Pigs, Martin
Luther King, the Kennedy assassinations, Vietnam, Cambodia, Laos,
Kent State, Watergate never registered on the Maronite leadership.
What mattered was that for years the United States had encouraged
the Lebanese government—that is, the Christians, the Maronites—to
crack down on the Palestinians. Now the Christian militias were ready
for a showdown, since the Lebanese Army in 1973 had proved incapable of doing the job. Another Marine landing would be fine, but not at
all necessary. This time they could do the job themselves if Washington
would provide the diplomatic support, arms, ammunition, even just
plain encouragement. As Godley recalled years later, "God knows we
gave the Maronites advice, but with a gracious smile they chose to
disregard it."

They always knew better. And they never took no for an answer.
Convinced that Godley personally was against the sacred Maronite
cause, they clung to the illusion that the State Department, the White
House, the Congress loved them. Personifying these unshakable certainties—and illusory claims to occult American support—was former
Foreign Minister Charles Malik, a Greek Orthodox more Maronite
than the Maronites when it came to obstinacy. His Harvard education,
his American friends gained over long years as ambassador in Washington and teaching at the American University of Beirut, his ties to
the Rockefeller family, his personal relationship with Richard Nixon—
all these gave him the prestige within the insular Maronite camp to
silence critics who came to question his strategic myopia. In Nixon's
days as President, Malik spent weekends at the White House. And he
was forceful enough as late as 1981 to use his American connections to
pull strings and arrange an interview with Secretary of State Alexander
M. Haig, Jr.

A Phalangist official recounted to me his unsuccessful efforts to demonstrate the error of this septuagenarian's ways to the Maronite leadership before more damage was done. "Early in the war, Malik claimed that Marines would land at his beck and call. As the months dragged on and no Marines came, he would admit, 'Yes, they are late, but they will come.' He caused me a lot of grief. I'd say, 'On the basis of talking to American diplomats and journalists, I conclude the United States will not help us.' But I was young, and he had Sheikh Pierre's ear. He and Chamoun were old confederates from the 1950s. Remember our mentality. Sure, the embassy said no Marines, but we were hoping for another *divine surprise*, another Iraqi revolution— anything, anything at all. Malik kept saying, 'Don't worry, I'll go to the United States, I'll do something on television, and it's public opinion that counts in America.' When we asked him where he got his information, why and how he was so sure all the time, he was evasive or tried to hint the White House was involved, but I think it was mostly just ex cathedra. We wanted to believe that any little nuance in the most mundane State Department statement was favorable to our cause."

During the year before and the year after the fighting began in April 1975, Kissinger by all accounts neither could nor would devote time to Lebanon. As much as anything else, it was his modus operandi that explained the neglect. He liked to act in a given situation when crisis point had been reached, then turn his total attention to it. Until it was too late, for both Lebanon and Kissinger, Lebanon never made it to the top of his list of priorities. For Kissinger the months of early 1975 were taken up by the initially unsuccessful effort to negotiate the Sinai II disengagement agreement. The Lebanese government at first did not oppose Sinai II, but it warned the American embassy "not to forget Lebanon," where, after all, rival Arab powers had long jockeyed for position and made their predilections known in the newspapers they subsidized in Beirut, and where now they were even more noticeable, since they were helping to subsidize their own private armies among the many militias that could be found all over Beirut. Then Indochina collapsed in April. Kissinger's increasing vulnerability over Angola further occupied his time in the fall of 1975. Yet Kissinger's lack of concern for Lebanon was surprising, given his detailed interest in Egypt, Syria, Jordan, the other Arab neighbors of Israel. Small, complicated, bothersome, Lebanon nonetheless bordered on Israel, and for that if for no other reason might have commanded more interest. Had not Lebanon been ready for years, in the words of that old saw, to be "the second Arab country to sign a peace treaty with Israel"? To be sure, that meant Lebanon did not want to be the first to do so. Now Egypt, the fairest catch of all, had set out to become the first.

Aside from positing the American mood against involving U.S. forces in shooting wars overseas, the kindest explanation for Kissinger's non-performance was that he was the victim of his own spotlight technique, which concentrated totally on any given problem that happened to be immediately at hand, and relegated everything else to the status of Ultima Thule, with no shading of concern. Despite his miracle-worker reputation, Kissinger could never deal with more than one crisis at a time.

Kissinger indeed forgot Lebanon. Nor did he instruct his ambassadors or listen to their information—even those who should have been directly involved in his projects. In Washington, the diplomatic cables from Beirut rarely got out of Sisco's in-basket. Younger staff members tried to dissuade Godley from cabling so much in the months leading up to the war, prompting Godley to note that he knew Kissinger wasn't reading him, but that others had to know the situation. He was expressing the professional diplomat's standard defense against being ignored back at the State Department. He had done his duty. But his staffers thought that he was, as one put it, "pissing into the wind." By their own accounts, official policymakers in Washington stumbled around without any feel for the unfolding Lebanese drama. In July 1975 the fighting eased off, only to start up seriously again just before Kissinger successfully concluded the resumed Sinai II negotiations on September 1. Perhaps inevitably, the renewed fighting in Lebanon prompted those Arab states opposed to the Sinai agreement to charge that the United States was behind the trouble in Lebanon. Did not the fighting conveniently distract attention from the disengagement deal? A diplomat intimately involved in the negotiations confided later, "I don't think Kissinger was particularly unhappy with the Lebanese trouble, but it was not part of any plan of his."

But in a part of the world where people are given to blaming the outsider—and also expect salvation to come from abroad—the American absence from a scene so long considered to be its own amounted to a plot. My friends sneered at what they considered my feigned innocence when I protested against such interpretations. For them the reason the fighting continued was that the two major foreign players in the 1958 crisis—the United States and Egypt—were now not directly involved.

In any case, as Lebanon skidded toward national suicide over the months, no American plan of any kind emerged. The Vatican clearly saw the dangers, however. In November 1975, the Pope dispatched Paolo Cardinal Bertoli, the first of a series of high-ranking emissaries, to talk moderation to the Maronites. Like the others who followed, his mission was of no avail. He left muttering, "These people are not Christians"—at least, so Beirut gossip had it. On his heels followed former French Foreign Minister Maurice Couve de Murville. General de Gaulle's long-time Foreign Minister, and Valéry Giscard d'Estaing's emissary, proved no more successful despite his personal prestige and the prestige France had enjoyed with the Maronites for centuries past.

In spite of daily evidence to the contrary, then, the conventional wisdom maintained that the Lebanese were reasonable folk and would come to their senses and stop. A prominent Lebanese banker friend of mine used to dismiss my catalogue of murder and mayhem, invoke the fact that the Moscow Narodny Bank building was under construction as proof the Russians still had faith, and argue that I should, too. Then, one fall day, construction on the building stopped. Soon thereafter, my friend left for Brazil, following hundreds of thousands of other foreign and Lebanese residents into exile.

Much to the surprise of Lebanese of all persuasions—and to many Palestinians—the United States still did nothing, at least nothing visible to the naked eye. "It was a Greek tragedy waiting for a deus ex machina, and it should have been us," a senior American diplomat said, years later. "But we were stuck in a classic limitation of power. Intervening was the only thing to do, and it would have been costly—a real donnybrook, not a walkover like 1958. Because of Vietnam, we couldn't do anything effective, and the Syrians were blocked from doing anything effective as well."

So confusing was American forbearance in any major crisis that many Middle Easterners became convinced that the CIA must have had a well-defined policy of its own—with or without the Ford administration's formal blessing. They assumed that the clandestine policy was to help the Christian militias remain in the game despite their own obstinacy, which kept them tottering on the brink of collapse; the purported goal was to weaken the PLO and please the Israeli intelligence agency, Mossad. Mossad, the argument ran, had to be mollified and its crucial cooperation guaranteed, especially since a series of highly publicized CIA scandals had shaken foreign confidence in the American agency's discretion and reliability. After all, Mossad's links with the CIA covered the Soviet bloc as well as the Middle East. Variations on this theme were developed by Eveland in *Ropes of Sand* and by a disaffected former Kissinger aide, Roger Morris, in his book entitled *Uncertain Greatness*. Both in their books and in conversations they suggested that the CIA station in Athens helped—as did Israel itself later, at American request—to supply surplus and captured Soviet weapons to the Christian militias in Lebanon. Eveland admitted he had "no positive proof," but insisted he had "talked to people who should know, and I believe them."

These suggestions were transformed into incontrovertible fact by the Lebanese. Senator James Abourezk of South Dakota, for example, was cited as an unimpeachable source who buttressed the charges made by Kamal Jumblatt, the leader of the Lebanese Left, and others that the CIA had given Israel $250 million to stir up the war in Lebanon and to channel arms and ammunition to the Christian militias. In fact, what Abourezk had said was that the State Department had told him the CIA had provided $70–$80 million to Israel to buy support in the United Nations among Black African delegates, and he had never heard whether Israel in fact actually spent the funds for that purpose. He was aware of rumors that some or all of that amount was used as Jumblatt and his friends suggested, but such assertions were virtually impossible to prove or disprove.

Pleading against their likelihood were a number of factors. One was the very disarray of the CIA, whose past covert operations were subject to minute Congressional scrutiny during 1975–76. Also difficult to credit was Morris's thesis that the CIA acted in Lebanon without Kissinger's knowledge—and much to his fury, when he was said to have discovered its antics later on. If the investigations of the CIA produced one central truth, it was that the agency does not operate on its own. Rather, it obeys orders from the executive branch. And during the Ford administration, Kissinger *was* the executive branch when it came to foreign policy and intelligence matters. True, the CIA had maintained links with the Phalange in the 1950s. And no less an erstwhile comrade-in-arms than Dany Chamoun, commander of his father's Tiger militia, insisted that the CIA gave the Gemayels' Phalange several million dollars through Lebanese Army channels in 1974 and 1975. (Admittedly, Dany made this accusation in July 1980, only a day after the Gemayels' militia liquidated the Tigers.) Even some American diplomats in Beirut during the 1975–76 fighting wondered whether the CIA was helping the Christians in late 1975. Yet during the civil war itself, the Christian militias constantly complained that the United States was doing nothing to help them.

It was just this kind of confusion—plus the CIA's own record—that prompted senior American diplomats active in Middle East affairs for the past generation to refuse to deny outright any possible involvement by the agency. And even those Middle East hands who had worked with Kissinger could never be totally sure what he was up to. All they could conclude was that there was no indication the CIA was involved in covert operations in Lebanon. Even CIA operatives in Lebanon itself, who readily admitted their numbers were increased during the civil war to provide in-depth reporting of events, doubt the covert-operations theory. "First of all, we would have had to have a policy," a CIA officer said, "and we sure as hell didn't have one." Both the embassy and the CIA station were so out of touch with Lebanon that when President Franjieh appointed a retired brigadier general to head a short-lived military government in May 1975, neither had any notion of who he was. But could the CIA have run a covert operation in Lebanon unbeknownst to the Beirut station chief? "It's just possible," a CIA man then in Beirut commented later, "that things were going on that we didn't know about."

By late autumn 1975, Western—and especially U.S.—paralysis was so patent that Syria and Israel, those two regional archenemies, decided, together and with American tolerance, to take Lebanese matters into their own hands. A Palestinian-dominated, radical Lebanese state as a mutual neighbor was an unpleasant prospect, now that the Christians were so clearly on the defensive in the Lebanese struggle. The Syrians dangled before the Christians a strategic alliance, and the Israelis saw a windfall: by tolerating a Syrian military presence in Lebanon, which by normal Zionist standards should have been anathema, Israel could bog down the only major Arab army that tactically was willing to use force to bring to heel that other prime foe, the PLO. The United States was ostensibly motivated by a desire to limit the war, to prevent total anarchy in Lebanon from taking hold and spreading to the rest of the Middle East. Whether Kissinger realized that such a policy would lead to a carve-up of Lebanon and the continuation—rather than the end—of violence is moot.

The Syrians were the first to be seen to act. In a deal with Israel brokered by the United States, on January 22, 1976, they moved Syrian-controlled regular troops of the Palestine Liberation Army (PLA) into Beirut to stop the wholesale looting and lawlessness. But Dany Chamoun, months before, had reactivated his father's long-standing relationship with Israel and had begun a series of visits to the Jewish state to arrange for arms shipments to the Tigers.

At American insistence the Syrian military entry into Lebanon in January was so delicately executed that two other more obvious and massive, but still partial, similar operations were required before the Palestinians and their Lebanese allies got the message. Early that month, Kissinger received a distinguished Israeli visitor in his seventh-floor State Department office. The Israeli said that Lebanon now represented a matter of crucial national interest to his government, which was determined to help the increasingly beleaguered Christians. The several accounts of the meeting differ on what Kissinger's reaction to this was. In one version he did not demur and indeed said nothing. In another he is supposed to have replied, "OK, but don't use American military equipment." "You watch," a witness to the meeting purportedly commented to a colleague, "Israel will take all this as American backing."

Ghassan Tueni, the newspaper editor and Lebanon's ambassador to the United Nations, tells this story. About the same time as the meeting in Kissinger's office, a Lebanese Christian leader was talking to a high State Department official who was justifying the Syrians' entry into Lebanon on the grounds that their armed presence would "check the Palestinians." "But," asked the Lebanese, "who will check the Syrians?" The answer was simple, candid, and very Kissingerian. "The Israelis, of course." Tueni adds that no one seems to have asked the logical follow-up question, "But who will check the Israelis?" That unanswered question was to cause increasing grief over the years to all parties involved in the Lebanese imbroglio. Even if it had been able to turn back the clock, Israel, despite its protestations of goodwill, had little interest in a stable Lebanon as long as its principal adversaries, Syria and the Palestinians, were bogged down there. Intervening at minimal cost, Israel could—and did—turn the pressure on and off the entire Arab world by raising the level of violence in Lebanon whenever it suited its purposes. It was the Middle East equivalent of the game the Russians played so assiduously with the Western Big Three in Berlin, until the status of the former German capital was settled in 1972.

Short of a real policy, in 1976, the Israeli-Syrian deal Kissinger brokered looked about the best that could be cobbled together. Syria was to send into Lebanon just enough troops to stop the anarchy. The United States encouraged Israel to supply the Christians with arms just sufficient to prevent them from going under, but not so many as to cause problems. The United States believed that it was in no position itself to provide weapons, and Israel was conveniently close enough to move fast.

With Israel and Syria thus oddly, if only temporarily, allied, they were now free to gang up on the Palestinian commandos, no matter what promises had been made. Throughout much of 1976, Israeli and Syrian naval vessels patrolled different sectors of the Lebanese coast to deprive the Palestinians of resupply. Both countries supplied arms and ammunition to the Christian militias during the long siege of the Palestinian refugee camp at Tal Zaatar. Given the Middle East's propensity for jumping to conclusions, these ad hoc arrangements doubtless smacked to local observers of a Kissinger plot. American intelligence analysts, who are convinced the CIA was technically "clean," are prepared to believe that the Israelis were not above hinting they were acting on behalf of a United States that could not afford to be seen so obviously involved because of its domestic political tribulations. A retired high-ranking CIA specialist on the Middle East remarked, "Oldest trick in the game."

Soon after the Syrians sent the PLA into Lebanon in January 1976, Godley left Beirut to undergo an operation for cancer of the larynx. He was never to return. Soon the Syrian peace team—Foreign Minister Abdel Halim Khaddam, Army Chief of Staff Hikmat Shehabi, and Air Force Commander Naji Jamil—were trapped in the endless luncheons that are a distinguishing and paralyzing characteristic of Lebanese politics. In its first outing as a regional superpower, Syria proved butter-fingered, and its representatives floundered unconvincingly between offstage Byzantine intrigue, public mediation, and crude displays of military force. Like its three dozen or so predecessors, the January cease-fire began to show familiar signs of collapsing. Backed by the Palestinians, a Moslem brigadier general named Aziz Ahdab seized Lebanon's state-run radio and television on March 11 and declared that Franjieh was through. But with virtually no troops backing him, "General Television," as he was dubbed, succeeded only in setting off the most destructive round of fighting to date. The army, which had begun to split apart in January, thanks largely to PLO backing for a Sunni lieutenant named Ahmed Khatib and his self-styled Lebanese Arab Army, now broke clearly along Christian and Moslem lines. Dissident Moslem artillerymen shelled the Presidential Palace and forced Franjieh to flee to the Christian heartland. The Christians were pushed out of their remaining West Beirut strongholds as Palestinians and Lebanese leftists unleashed a major offensive in the mountains above the capital. Once again, church bells sounded the tocsin. Like it or not, Lebanon once again had forced its way back into the headlines.

In Washington in March, Kissinger was going down an airport receiving line with his official guest, King Hussein of Jordan, when he noticed L. Dean Brown, a short, feisty man who once had been ambassador to Amman and had recently retired from the foreign service to head the Middle East Institute. Brown had a reputation for handling himself in tough situations: in 1970 he had driven in an armored car to deliver his credentials to the King of Jordan during the Black September fighting between the Jordanian Army and the Palestinians. Now Kissinger called him to the seventh-floor offices of the State Department; forty-eight hours later, Brown arrived in Beirut. It was March 31, 1976. His only instructions were to write his own. There were two provisos: the Christians were to be told yet again that landing the Marines was out; they were also to be told the United States wanted them to be "strong so that they could negotiate" an end to the fighting.

Brown's first order of business was to have a history of the war written, despite protests from George Lambrakis, the young chargé d'affaires in the embassy, who was clearly out of his depth, and who fruitlessly pointed out that the State Department had received two daily "sitreps"—detailed reports—since the fighting began almost a year earlier. Kissinger—and doubtless Brown as well—wanted to know who the players were, a tacit admission that the Secretary had failed during the past to follow the steadily worsening crisis with any assiduity. In the embassy itself, Brown's arrival prompted no great enthusiasm. There was a general feeling that after such neglect the United States could do little of use, even if it so chose. Nor was the staff convinced that the administration meant to grapple with the problem. From Washington came rumors suggesting that President Ford and Secretary Kissinger had dispatched Brown largely to deprive Ronald Reagan, Ford's serious challenger for the Republican presidential nomination that summer, of the argument that the administration had been derelict in attending to the festering Lebanese mess.

The Christians had no such doubts. With less than seventy-two hours' worth of ammunition left, they couldn't afford to. They were overjoyed. Finally, the Americans had understood! But these illusions were short-lived. The Christian warlords pressed Brown for a definition of what Kissinger meant by wanting them to be "strong." They quickly came away with the impression that the United States meant that they should get Israeli help. Chamoun, in the April 2 entry of his published diary, indirectly confirmed that he for one had never believed the Americans themselves would help. He had another string to his bow. "Exchange of views with important visitors who insist on remaining anonymous," he noted, in describing his meeting with Israeli Defense Minister Shimon Peres on an Israeli gunboat anchored off Jounieh harbor. "The conclusions are positive," he wrote. "They will bear fruit if the hostilities are protracted and if our forces continue to face a strong opponent."

Yet again, the Syrians in fact moved first and promised the Christians the help that the United States could broker with Israel but not itself deliver. The Syrians were clearly against the PLO. Ten days later, Zuhair Mohsen, Syria's man in the PLO, laid it squarely on the line. "Lebanon can only be saved by the U.S. Sixth Fleet or the Syrian Army," he said, waving his Cuban cigar at me, "there is no other solution. Two divisions would be needed at the very least, and more would cross the border if necessary. Three quarters of the people of Lebanon would welcome any force that can halt religious strife and theft in this country." As it turned out, his erstwhile allies in the PLO and their Lebanese friends did not get the message. Syrians disguised as members of the pro-Syrian Saiqa Palestinian commandos began lifting the siege of Zahle in the Beqaa valley. Syrian armor moved across the border and dug in—at first three miles, and then farther, inside Lebanon. When the Syrians invaded in earnest in June, exactly two divisions were used. With the Syrian Army involved to the hilt in Lebanon, Israel stepped up its aid to the Christians. A stalemate had begun that lasted until Israel invaded Lebanon in earnest in 1982.

Although the Christians had been saved by Syria—and then had taken out what they thought was an insurance policy with Israel—they were not happy. The West, especially the United States, had once again let them down, even though they had been so sure that this time Washington understood. Now they were to take their own peculiar revenge. Within days, they started circulating as gospel the news that Brown had allegedly offered to ship all Lebanon's Christians off to the United States and Canada. Never mind that the Sixth Fleet—like all good tales, this one's effect depended on a modicum of authentic-sounding detail—could scarcely handle more than a few thousand of the million or so would-be refugees conjured up in this dream, unless Brown had suggested an evacuation plan of Dunkirk proportions. Yet to find fault with the particulars was the first and fatal step toward accepting that the scheme in broad outline had some validity. Thereafter, American denials only served to reinforce the Christians' peculiar vision of their plight. If the Americans would not help, then the Americans would become the major villains. The Sixth Fleet story was the Christian leaders' defiant way of telling the United States that they would stay put. Never would the Christians become latter-day Palestinians and desert the land that they insisted (somewhat fancifully, in this constantly invaded part of the world) had been theirs for six thousand years. (In my 1980 interview at his luncheon table in Zghorta, over locally distilled arak and cigars, I asked Sleiman Franjieh point-blank about the story. Everyone else who was said to have been a witness either denied it or claimed to have heard it solely from him. Drawing on his ivory cigarette holder in vaguely Rooseveltian fashion, Franjieh grunted. Kissinger, he intoned, "is not an American—he's a Zionist." Perhaps, I said, but how about Brown and the Sixth Fleet? I pressed for elucidation. Franjieh disdainfully referred me to *Le Monde* of November 28, 1978, and to Carlos Khoury, the permanent secretary-general of the presidency. But that issue of France's newspaper of record shed no light on the problem, nor did Khoury. He refused to receive me, was noncommittal on the telephone, and never answered a formal, written request for confirmation of Franjieh's version. Yet, I found few Maronites who did not want to believe Franjieh's story.)

Like other interlocutors before him, Brown discovered how hard it was to place a word, much less a thought, with the traditional Christian leaders, whose average age was well over seventy. Brown was determined to talk about the Lebanon of today and tomorrow. They kept bringing him back to Lebanese history, and the more ancient it was, the happier they appeared. Brown thought he was getting one set of ideas across. The Christians were convinced they had heard another. Nor was the phenomenon limited to the Christian warlords. Brown visited Raymond Eddé, the only Maronite leader who was without a militia, on good terms with the Moslems, and opposed to the warlords of his own sect. He was greeted with congratulations for arriving just in time to foil a CIA ploy. Brown insisted that no such plot existed. Eddé remained unconvinced. The CIA, he said, wanted to prove that the Lebanese mode of a multisectarian state could not work. The CIA was working for Israel, Eddé explained, which had long resented that the Palestinians could cite the Lebanese example to buttress their belief in having a similar state in Palestine to replace the Zionist one.

Kamal Jumblatt, the Druze feudal patriarch who had emerged as leader of the coalition of Moslems, leftists, and Palestinians fighting the Christian warlords, talked to Brown about the need to kill twelve thousand Maronites to achieve reform and bring the Christians to their senses. Such talk was relatively mild stuff, for at the same period he was telling journalist friends in his Beirut home about his desire to "drink blood from Maronite skulls." Part the embodiment of revenge for 1860, part a campy imitation of the feudal leader he remained (his self-deprecating moments notwithstanding), Jumblatt was once described as a kind of Pablo Picasso of Lebanese politics. Feudal lord, ashram inmate during his contemplative days in India, Lenin Peace Prize winner, calculating capitalist, Kamal Jumblatt was out to settle old scores with the Maronites, especially with Camille Chamoun, with whom he entertained strained but prolonged relations as co-leader of the Shuf Mountains south of Beirut. Brown confided to Lebanese friends he thought Jumblatt a wildman, although on paper his formal demands for minimum political reforms hardly seemed radical to anyone cognizant with history since the French Revolution. Jumblatt chose to take Brown's careful remarks as full backing for *his* point of view, proof that *his* reform demands did not upset the United States, indeed that the Americans were giving him a flashing green light to resume his mountain offensive against the Christians, with a cautionary warning to the Syrians. Jumblatt was very wrong, and a year later was assassinated in the Shuf near Moukhtara, the Jumblatt feudal seat for centuries past. The killers were never identified officially, although Jumblatt's bullet-ridden car was overtaken and attacked near a Syrian Army checkpoint. That was proof enough for the Lebanese. They knew damn well that the Syrians were guilty, but didn't dare attack them. Instead, more than one hundred Christians were killed in retaliation, despite a plea by Jumblatt's son to eschew reprisals. In Lebanon you punish whom you can, not always whom you want.

Thus Brown came and went. His only visible accomplishment was the tragicomic election of a new President ahead of schedule. The American and Syrian plan was to force Franjieh out of office before his normal term expired on September 23, 1976. Under a mortar and artillery barrage, the deputies were taken—often under Syrian escort or at Syrian gunpoint—to a once-patrician villa that since the destruction of Beirut's downtown parliament building served as temporary premises. In fact, the deputies were made to undergo this ordeal twice—first in April to amend the constitution to allow the early election of the President, and again in early May to elect as Franjieh's successor the pudgy governor of the Central Bank, Elias Sarkis, a quintessential bureaucrat with no personal following. Local legend insists that Chamoun voted for Sarkis only after the Syrians paid him 4 million Lebanese pounds, then worth roughly $1.25 million. (Indeed, one variation claims Chamoun balked when the Syrians initially tried to pay the same amount in Syrian currency, worth considerably less. A further embellishment swears the Syrians paid with money that Syria's Saiqa Palestinian commandos had stolen from various banks they looted while they controlled the downtown financial district in March.) In any event, the effort ended in failure. Just as Chamoun had dug in his heels in similar circumstances in 1958, so now Franjieh handed over the very little that was left of presidential power only when his term legally expired in September. Reflecting on the sorry exercise, a CIA analyst lamented, "When you think of all the leverage we had with the Syrians then, it would have been useful to discuss with them what kind of leader we both wanted. Sarkis is a nice guy, but did we need a good referee or a more forceful man? To my knowledge, we never broached the question." Later, an American diplomat was to say that encouraging Sarkis to act was like "trying to push wet spaghetti through a keyhole."

In mid-May, Francis Meloy arrived to replace the ailing Godley as ambassador. He seemed a good choice—a bachelor with no family to worry about, cautious, and used to the constraints of ticklish situations. (When he was ambassador to the Dominican Republic, the security situation was so dicey he was not allowed to go out on his terrace.) On June 16, in the company of Robert O. Waring, the economics counselor, who was about to retire, Meloy set out toward the always dangerous Museum crossing, then the only passage from one side of the divided capital to the other. They had a date with President-elect Sarkis. They never made it. The bodies of the two diplomats and of veteran embassy chauffeur Zuhair Moghrabi were found that afternoon on a garbage dump near the beach in West Beirut.

Despite a six-month investigation, to this day the U.S. government says it does not know the killers' identities. But the most likely candidate was a purely Lebanese outfit called the Socialist Arab Labor Party; this was affiliated with the Marxist Popular Front for the Liberation of Palestine, founded by George Habash, and was one of several wild-eyed, long-haired Lebanese armed groups that controlled the stretch of road in West Beirut just before the Museum. They had little use for American journalists, much less for American diplomats. Inexplicably, the Lebanese security escort car had peeled off before the ambassador's armored limousine entered that dangerous stretch. And it is not clear why the chauffeur stopped instead of barreling through and past his assailants. The Lebanese are convinced that he had been "bent"—either blackmailed or paid to deliver the diplomats. Embassy staffers at the time disagreed vehemently. They were convinced they had a powerful hold over their chauffeur: Moghrabi and his entire family had been promised much-coveted immigration visas for the United States. Personally, I prefer the embassy version. The previous

October, when I had been the last paying guest at the Hotel St. Georges, Moghrabi had driven the same armor-plated black Chrysler limousine through the combat zone to rescue me and three other trapped colleagues.

Meloy and Waring were not the first or the last diplomats to be killed in Lebanon. French Ambassador Louis Delamare was shot and killed in the very same neighborhood as he drove home to lunch five years later. But the Americans' deaths embittered many embassy staffers. An impatient Kissinger had hounded Meloy to visit the Christians in East Beirut, despite the well-known dangers of the Museum crossing, according to diplomats who also hinted that all copies of the Secretary's order subsequently disappeared from the files. A more abiding bitterness was voiced by one junior diplomat I talked to. "They died victims of our inability to speak with the PLO," he recalled. "If we had had Palestinian interlocutors that day, they would still be alive."

The following December, Kissinger received Ghassan Tueni in his office. The visitor was on a special mission for Sarkis to discuss the postwar reconstruction aid vaguely promised by the United States, now that the civil war had formally ended the month before. Recalling they had both been students at Harvard soon after World War II, Kissinger sought to put Tueni at ease. He put his feet up on a low table and said, "Let's talk as one Harvard man to another," Tueni has recalled. "I want you to know that for the past six months the President and the Secretary of State have been the desk officers for Lebanon." What Kissinger did *not* say was that the war had been more than a year old before he took an active interest in Lebanon, and anyhow, what with Jimmy Carter's election, he was a very lame duck.

The bailing-wire-and-bluster approach for postponing disaster—an after-the-fact ersatz that passed for American policy—had demonstrated its limitations. That had been the ticket since 1975. Even in 1982, Israel and the viscosity of Lebanon got the better of a United States government momentarily determined to straighten out the mess in Beirut. "We tried to keep all the balls in the air to distract attention," an American diplomat said. "If we told the truth and said things were going to hell, they would only have gone to hell even faster." The truth of the matter was that Lebanon was still a sideshow. The United States wanted no major changes in the Middle East to take place without its blessing and was just powerful enough to prevent Lebanon from serving as the catalyst for yet another generalized Middle East war. But American policy, perhaps mindlessly, also condemned Lebanon. That was an unwritten but major clause both in the Sinai disengagement deal and then even more in the Camp David talks in 1978. Camp David encouraged Egypt and Israel into bilateral arrangements and piously provided the framework for a nebulous autonomy for the Israeli-occupied West Bank and Gaza Strip. But anyone acquainted with the Middle East knew that American efforts to reach an overall settlement were at a standstill. And it was just that absence of an overall agreement that kept Lebanon as a convenient killing ground where the major Middle East states could blow off steam without striking at one another's jugular. Carter, who began his term more committed than his predecessors had been to solving the Middle East problem, unwittingly ended up laying the groundwork for Begin's policy of piecemeal aggression. In 1982, as Israel's war in Lebanon unfolded, a young American diplomat, depressed at the Reagan administration's lack of reaction to it, confided to me, "I wonder how active an agent of evil the United States government really is."

Among American officials his was a minority view (and usually held by those who had retired from active government service). Americans, public and private, were so wedded to the pragmatic approach that they tended to forget the accreted errors of commission and omission that had characterized U.S. policy in the Middle East for a generation. When they came right down to it, there was something vaguely dismissive about their view of Lebanon. Did Lebanon really exist, after all? And, if so, why should it be protected from the buffeting such a strange territorial entity was bound to endure? Lebanon was a French creation, and traditionally Washington had as little enthusiasm for French colonial constructions as did the British in their heyday.

Lebanon, for the United States, ended up a disposable place of unknown loyalties and complicated workings, not to be entirely trusted. In its palmier days, Beirut was a useful place to take the pulse of the Arab world's more recondite recesses. When Beirut was useful to the United States, preventing others from using it as a listening post had its attractions. But the United States tended to retreat back into the carelessness of the rich. In any case, the real action had moved elsewhere. Beirut was no longer the banking center of the Middle East. The volume of Arab oil receipts had multiplied so rapidly that Beirut was too small: the oil billions went directly to the City of London and American banks. The Lebanese themselves were not middlemen in the Gulf oil sheikhdoms, giving advice and passing on orders to their American and other Western bosses: these Western firms discovered they had to station their own men in the Gulf if they wanted to keep the business. Beirut, the Western businessman's bedroom, was dead. It was not that the Lebanese weren't making money in the Gulf. They were making *more* money, but they were deciding less. It was the way of the world, and Americans have never been sentimental. Yet, the Americans acted like reluctant dragons. When they once again landed Marines in Lebanon in 1982, they bent over backward to ensure the soldiers would not get shot at, much less shoot anyone. Congress scrutinized the administration's every step. The Pentagon itself was wary lest politicians once again involve American troops in a messy foreign adventure and then leave the professional soldiers holding the bag.

"If the Romans want an empire," a Lebanese historian friend of mine argued, "they must pay the price." But if the latter-day Romans had no such desire, what was to be done? The most likely upshot was to submit to the whims and caprices of the regional superpower, Israel, which owed its status not just to American backing but also to its own willful ways. No wonder that Israel, despite its often bloody-minded policies, was respected and looked up to. The Israelis were acting out the part that the former imperial powers had played for so long. The Israelis at least looked as if they knew what they wanted.

6. The Israeli Connection

I can't remember the exact date, but it was still relatively early in Lebanon's civil war—say, late October 1975—because almost without exception the participants in the seminar were still wearing the peacetime business-suit uniform of the Lebanese elite. Lawyers, merchants, doctors, professors, they made it no mystery that their think-tank sessions were working on plans for the partition of Lebanon—that is, the setting-up of a separate Christian state if they couldn't run the whole country. Word of such radical planning is what had brought me to Kaslik and its high-sounding University of the Holy Ghost, just off the express highway leading north from Beirut and not far from the turnoff for Jounieh. The place looked like a glorified New England prep school, with its fake Gothic buildings, and its critics snipingly insisted that its intellectual level was scarcely inspiring. But the monks who ran Kaslik were rich, determined, and unreconstructedly single-minded. Their relatively unsophisticated students were of simpler stock than the middle-class Christian boys and girls who attended the French-supported Jesuit Université Saint Joseph or the Protestant

American University of Beirut. Kaslik dipped into its investments from vast landownings to buy many of the weapons used by the young Maronites who went into battle with outsize wooden crosses around their necks and Virgin Mary decals on their rifle stocks.

We argued about partition. Or, rather, I raised objections, and the other participants listened patiently. No one would recognize such a rump Christian state. Indeed, no one would even help it. The Christians would only further infuriate the Arab world, on which they depended to earn their livelihoods by providing services. The middle-aged seminar participants tarried briefly, then drifted off to their cars. A young man stayed behind. The Christians would never give up, he said to me. They would go back to their mountains and resist the way they always had. I objected that Lebanon's mountains no longer provided effective refuge in an era of jets, helicopters, roads, armored vehicles, and long-range artillery. "Then we will sup with the devil," he said, with evident pride. Indeed, he said, Kaslik officials were in touch already with the Israelis, thanks to the 1949 Israeli-Lebanese armistice agreement, which allowed Maronite clerics to cross the border to visit monasteries and other church property in Israel. "Simple," he said, "after Saturday, Sunday." That was a proverb meaning that the Moslems would dispose first of the Jews, whose Sabbath falls on Saturday, before doing in the Christians, who celebrate Sunday as their day of rest and worship.

I remember being taken aback: for the Christians to do business with the Israelis was supposed to be an original sin. I was more than vaguely aware that the Lebanese Christian warlords had been delighted in 1967 when Israel humiliated Egypt in the Six-Day War. In their eyes, Nasser had tried to take over Lebanon in 1958 and had got his comeuppance. Certainly in the ensuing decade the Lebanese Christians and Israelis had a common enemy in the Palestinians. But I could not imagine that the Christians would be foolish enough to seek aid from a source so suspect in Arab eyes. After all, the Maronite genius over the centuries had lain in contracting alliances with powers sufficiently strong *but distant* enough to leave them masters in their own houses, except in time of extreme danger. The Israelis were too close—and too powerful—and would call the tune. They, not the Maronites, would decide when enough was enough. Had I known my contemporary history better, I would have been less surprised.

To use the political code words of the Middle East, both nations were devotees of what was known as the theory of "mosaic states." "Only when Israel raises money from American Jews do we Israelis claim that the entire Arab world is a united juggernaut determined to drive poor little Israel into the sea," an Israeli Arabist of my acquaintance likes to explain. "In fact, the Middle East is a jigsaw puzzle of peoples and cultures. Minority regimes run Syria and Iraq. King Hussein and his Bedouin are a minority in Jordan, outnumbered by Palestinians. Sudan has a large animist and Christian minority. Algeria and Morocco have large Berber minorities. If Israel could succeed in contacting all these groups which oppose Arabism and Islam, then it could break the Islamic world into pieces" and live happily ever after. Even partial success along these lines would decrease the pressures on Israel and distract the attention of its sworn enemies. (There was nothing particularly new about such ideas. Israel had provided arms and ammunition—Soviet matériel captured in the 1967 war from Arab armies—to Kurds fighting the Iraqi regime in the early and middle 1970s, and earlier had funneled similar aid across Ethiopia to the southern Sudanese in revolt against the central government in Khartoum.) Christian radicals in Lebanon held similar views, and saw Israel as a determined, willful regional superpower and a potential ally, now that the West had let them down.

Better yet, Lebanon and Israel were neighbors. At the end of World War I, when Britain and France carved up the expired Ottoman Empire's Middle Eastern possessions, France at one point had divided its League of Nations mandate into five separate states, including a Greater Lebanon run by the Christians; it added to the Christian Mount Lebanon region such predominantly Moslem areas as Tyre and the south, Tripoli and the north, and the fertile Beqaa in the east, to make an economically viable state. In 1936, the Maronite Patriarch testified in favor of a Jewish state in Palestine before the Peel Commission established to end the violence there. The following year, David Ben-Gurion, then chairman of the Jewish Agency, told the Zionist World Workers Party meeting in Zurich that "Lebanon is the natural ally of the Jews of the land of Israel. . . . The proximity of Lebanon will furnish a loyal ally for the Jewish state as soon as it is created." Noting the common border, Ben-Gurion added this would "give us the possibility to expand with the agreement and benediction of our neighbors who need us." The major Christian population centers in Lebanon were well north of the border with Israel, but Christians controlled enough of the Mediterranean coastline to allow easy access by sea from Israeli ports. (Immediately after the Ottoman Empire's collapse in 1918, Zionists had tried unsuccessfully to persuade Britain to claim all of south Lebanon up to the precious waters of the Litani River for Palestine, but France carried the day and the border was established in 1920 where it stands today.) In what Israelis call the War of Independence, Israeli troops in 1948 occupied Lebanon up to the Litani River, withdrawing to the present border only in the following year.

Less than a decade later, then Israeli Prime Minister Moshe Sharett recorded other unfriendly designs on Lebanon in a series of entries in his *Personal Diary*. Sometimes described as the Israeli equivalent of the Pentagon Papers, the diary, covering events starting in the 1930s, appeared in Hebrew in 1979 and only after Sharett's son thwarted establishment efforts to prevent its publication. Long before the Palestinian guerrillas became a physical threat to Israel, Sharett recorded Israeli plans to destabilize, indeed dismember, Lebanon and install a puppet regime pliable to Israeli diktat. Various entries from the 1930s show Sharett discouraging Maronite extremist dreams of enlisting Zionist help to undo the Greater Lebanon created in 1920.

Sharett's February 27, 1954, entry deals with the then recently retired Prime Minister, David Ben-Gurion, Defense Minister Pinhas Lavon, and Chief of Staff Moshe Dayan, all of whom wanted to take advantage of a coup d'état in Syria to invade that country. Ben-Gurion insisted that if Iraq invaded Syria, as seemed possible, "this is the time to arouse Lebanon—that is to say the Maronites—to proclaim a Christian state." Sharett demurred:

> I said this is an empty dream. The Maronites are split. Those who favor Christian separatism are weak and will not dare do a thing. A Christian Lebanon would mean foregoing the Tyre district, Tripoli, the Beqaa. There is no force that will restore Lebanon to its pre–World War One dimensions, all the more so since it would then lose any economic viability. Ben-Gurion retorted furiously. He began putting forth historical justification for a small Lebanon. If a fact is created the Christian powers will not dare oppose it. I argued there is not a factor ready to create such a situation and that if we begin to agitate and push we will get entangled in an affair that will bring us

only disgrace. Here there erupted a torrent of abuse regarding my lack of daring and shortsightedness. We should send emissaries and spend money. I said there is no money. The considered reply was that this is nonsense. The money must be found, if not from the Treasury then from the Jewish Agency (!)—for such a goal $100,000, half a million dollars, a million could be risked, anything to get the thing established, and then would come a definitive reshuffling in the Middle East and a new era would begin. I tired of arguing with a whirlwind.

That very day, Ben-Gurion, from his Negev kibbutz retreat at Sde Boker, argued that Lebanon "is the weakest link in the chain of the [Arab] League" and that the Christians there

are the majority in the historical Lebanon and this majority has a totally different heritage and culture from the rest of the League. Even in the expanded border (and France's most serious mistake was to expand the borders of Lebanon) the Moslems are not free to do as they wish, even if they are a majority there (and I do not know whether they are a majority) for fear of the Christian schism. The establishment of a Christian state therefore is a natural step. It has historic roots and it will find support from large forces in the Christian world, Catholic and Protestant alike. In normal times this would be virtually impossible. First of all due to the Christians' lack of initiative and courage. But in a period of confusion, and to-do, and upheaval or civil war things change and the weak shall say: I am a hero. Maybe (of course nothing is certain in politics) now is the propitious moment to bring about the establishment of a Christian state as our neighbor. Without our initiative and our energetic help it will not come about. And it seems to me that this is now the CENTRAL TASK or at least ONE of the central tasks of our foreign policy, and we should invest means, time and energy and act in all ways likely to bring about a fundamental change in Lebanon. [Eliahu] Sassoon and the rest of our Arabists must be mobilized. If money is needed, the dollars should not be spared, even though the money may go down the drain. All our energies must be concentrated here. Perhaps Reuven [Shiloah, another Arabist] should be brought here immediately to this end. We will not be forgiven if we miss this historic opportunity. There is no provocation here of the world's powers. In fact we need not do anything "directly"—but everything should, I think, be done with alacrity and full steam.

Without a narrowing of Lebanon's borders, of course, the goal cannot be attained, but if there are persons in Lebanon or exiles outside who can be recruited for the establishment of a Maronite state—they will have no need for expanded borders or for a large Moslem population and such considerations need not count.

I do not know if we have people in Lebanon, but there are all kinds of ways if it is decided to make the suggested attempt.

Somewhat wearily, on March 18 Sharett wrote back to Ben-Gurion, arguing, "there is no point or purpose in trying to create from the outside a movement which is nonexistent inside. One can reinforce a spirit of life when it is already beating. One cannot inject life into a body which shows no signs of life. Now as far as I know, there is no movement today in Lebanon seeking to make that country a Christian state in which the final say would be in the hands of the Maronite community." Sharett basically thought the French had won their bet to make a Christian-Moslem state work. But in a prophetic passage he noted:

The transformation of Lebanon into a Christian state today is out of the question if an outside initiative were involved. I qualify this by saying "outside initiative" because I do not rule out the possibility of this coming to pass in the wake of some series of shock waves that will strike the Middle East, cause radical reshuffles and hurl the existing patterns into a crucible so that other formations will emerge.

Not only were all Christians no longer a majority in Lebanon, but the Greek Orthodox minority wanted no part of a Maronite-dominated Christian state, he argued. Even the major Maronite leaders had decided their best bet lay in partnership with the Moslems. Ben-Gurion's proposal would be

disastrous for it is liable to rend with one motion the fabric of Christian-Moslem cooperation within the framework of present Lebanon, which has been woven with stubborn labor and considerable sacrifices for a generation now, to throw Lebanon's Moslems into the arms of Syria, and at the end of the process to bring on Christian Lebanon the historic catastrophe of its annexation to Syria and the utter blurring of its personality within the greater Moslem state.

Brushing aside Ben-Gurion's possible objections to these arguments, Sharett asked what made anyone think the predominantly Moslem areas would want to be dissociated from the rest of the country, that the Arab League or the West would simply stand by, or "that the bloody war that must inevitably erupt after such an attempt will remain confined to Lebanon and will not immediately drag in Syria as well"? Christian Mount Lebanon had become viable only since its association with the Moslem areas in 1920. "To put things back the way they were," Sharett continued, "means not just a surgical operation, but a crushing of organs such as Lebanon would not survive." That said, Sharett made it plain he was no dove:

> I would welcome this agitation [in the Maronite community] in itself what with the destabilization it would entail, the trouble it would cause the Arab League, the diversion of attention from the Arab-Israeli conflict that would ensue, the very lighting of the spark of the desire for Christian independence which would come in its wake. But what to do: no such ferment exists. In this situation I fear that any attempt by us to raise the question would be taken as a sign of frivolousness and superficiality—or perhaps worse: as adventurist profiteering in the well-being and survival of others, and as readiness to sacrifice their fundamental welfare for the sake of Israeli temporary tactical advantage.
>
> Moreover, if the matter did not remain secret, but became public knowledge—a risk which cannot be ignored in the Mideast context—there is no calculating the damage this would cause us vis-à-vis the Arab states and the Western powers alike, damage for which the (eventual) success of the operation itself would provide no compensation.

Sharett's reasoned reply neither convinced Ben-Gurion nor persuaded him to drop his proposal to destabilize Lebanon. More than a year later, on May 16, 1955, during a meeting of senior officials of the Foreign and Defense Ministries, Ben-Gurion returned to what Sharett called "his old dream" of intervening in Lebanon. Ben-Gurion was back in government in the key Defense post. The occasion was renewed tension between Iraq and Syria, "and the possibility of an Iraqi invasion of Syria" prompted Ben-Gurion to suggest that the Druze and Shia Moslems might join in the destabilization venture. Sharett recorded that, for Moshe Dayan,

> all that is needed is to find an officer, even a captain. We should win his heart or buy him, to get him to agree to declare himself the savior of the Maronite population. Then the Israeli army would enter Lebanon, occupy the necessary territory and set up a Christian regime allied to Israel and everything would turn out just fine. If we were to listen to the Chief of Staff we would do this tomorrow, without waiting for a sign from Bagdad, but under the circumstances he is ready to be patient and wait until the Iraqi government does his will and conquers Syria. Ben-Gurion was indeed quick to stress that his own plan is intended to be put into effect only in the wake of Syria's conquest by Iraq.

A despairing Sharett wrote, "I saw no reason to get into a broad and trenchant argument with Ben-Gurion about his fantastic and reckless plans—whose crudeness and detachment from reality were surprising—in the presence of his staff officers." Instead, Sharett limited his remarks to warning that "the upshot would not be the strengthening of a Christian Lebanon, but a war between Israel and Syria." At Ben-Gurion's suggestion, a joint unit of the Foreign and Defense ministries was established to deal with Lebanon under Sharett's aegis, which in effect he hoped would pigeonhole the destabilization plans.

But Sharett nonetheless lamented the military's "simply appalling lack of seriousness" in its "whole approach to neighboring countries, especially to the more complex questions of Lebanon's internal and external situation." He wrote: "I saw clearly how those who had saved the country with their heroism and sacrifice in the War of Independence are capable of bringing catastrophe on it if they are allowed a free hand in normal times."

In yet another critique of Ben-Gurion, Sharett asserted:

> he still views Lebanon as it was during the days of the Ottoman Empire—an independent body whose population was overwhelming-

ly Maronite Christian. But in Greater Lebanon the Maronites have long since lost their numerical superiority, the Orthodox gravitate towards Syria, the Moslems constitute a growing majority by virtue of their higher birthrate, the Palestinian refugees have enlarged this majority even more and have dropped the Maronites to a one third minority, the Maronite community has lost all daring and momentum, most of its leaders collude with the Moslems and the Arab League, and any Israeli attempt to push the Maronites towards revolution is liable to cause their public stigmatization and make them sustain a crushing failure.

Two weeks later, in another entry, Sharett again complained that Dayan "favors hiring some [Lebanese] officer who would be ready to serve as a front man so that the Israeli army can appear to be responding to his call to 'liberate' Christian Lebanon from the burden of its Moslem oppressors." Although Sharett on June 17 dismissed the scheme as a "pipe-dream," he noted that "the truth is that we have ties with a certain group" inside Lebanon "and that we have made many attempts to sound out many others and in particular feelers should be put out to the [Lebanese] army."

That same month, Sharett reported Dayan's desire to reject a proffered U.S. security pact because "it would put handcuffs on our military freedom of action" and his developing a kind of war-is-peace doctrine along lines that George Orwell had prophesied in *1984*. The state "may, no—it *must* invent dangers and to do so, it must adopt the method of provocation-and-revenge . . . and above all—let us hope for a new war with the Arab countries—so that we may finally get rid of our troubles and acquire space," Sharett's entry read, before noting, "(such a slip of the tongue—Ben-Gurion himself said it would be worthwhile to pay an Arab a million pounds to start a war)."

These excerpts from Sharett's diary make uncanny reading in the light of what has happened in Lebanon since 1975. Civil war *did* envelop Lebanon. Israel *did* latch onto a renegade Christian army officer, Captain (later Major) Saad Haddad, who *did* do its bidding in the southern border area. The Western powers *did* go along with Lebanon's effective dismemberment, although less to save the threatened Christians—a theme of reproach constantly intoned by successive Israeli governments to justify their own more suspect motives—than out of lassitude. Lebanon *did* come under effective Syrian (and Israeli) military occupation. Israeli generals *did* end up calling so many of the shots in Lebanon that they risked compromising their country's international reputation and security. And entanglements with the Christians *did* contribute to causing a war between Israel and Syria that neither desired.

Within the single year 1976, Israel succeeded in setting the rules by which the game has been played in Lebanon ever since. The United States, beset by its own domestic and foreign tribulations, was happy enough to limit its role to honest brokering. That meant encouraging Syria to play a major regional role for the first time, and insisting that Israel see that its own best interests would also be served by allowing Syrian troops to pacify Lebanon. Israel extracted a high price for "giving in" to the United States on Syria's activities in Lebanon, while knowing full well that it maintained the decisive advantage at all major pressure points. It is not the slightest of Israel's strengths that it is able to convince world public opinion its security is being endangered at the very time when in fact it is being enhanced.

In geopolitical terms, Syria was allowed to invade and occupy Lebanon in order to stop the anarchy that threatened the entire Middle East but especially the always vulnerable Damascus regime, run by a much-hated Alawite minority sect of Islam considered heretical by mainstream Sunnis. In fact, there was a tacit division of Lebanon into Syrian and Israeli spheres of influence. Syria avoided de jure recognition of Israel, but did accept that Israeli vital strategic interests were involved in Lebanon south of the Litani River. Stripped to its essentials, the deal allowed Syria to maintain a police force in Lebanon but did not permit it to install ground-to-air missiles there, which would have endangered Israeli reconnaissance flights or air raids against Palestinian positions. That was the heart of the "Red Line" agreements brokered by the United States. Never published, very probably never written down, subject to differing interpretations and sudden, often unilateral geographical revisions (Yitzhak Rabin once told me, "Any interpretation of the tacit understanding is correct"), the Red Line or Lines were to plague the Lebanese from their inception until 1982, when Israel pushed the Syrian Army in Lebanon aside. While the agreement lasted, it banned the use of Syrian air power in ground operations and kept Syrian troops fifteen miles from the northernmost point of the Israeli-Lebanese border. That factor, later on, was to cause all parties considerable grief and in 1982 helped lead to war.

The troops that Syria maintained in Lebanon, sometimes as many as thirty thousand, were in modern military terms so many sitting ducks. For Israel they were that many fewer troops in the Golan Heights, which was the real locus of its confrontation with Syria and far too serious for the kinds of games Israelis and Syrians played in Lebanon. Yet for all its troops in Lebanon, Syria could have stationed twice as many and continued to fail to impose its will on such a basic issue as forming a government. Frustrated politically, Syria could do little to prevent its troops from succumbing to the many temptations of Lebanese life and license—ranging from gambling to drugs. With the Red Lines, Israel, which made no such major political and military investment in Lebanon, constituted a limiting factor. Syria, in fact, was trapped, unable to back out of Lebanon gracefully, if at all, without risking President Hafez Assad's own undoing in Damascus.

Only a prolonged period of quiet could rescue Syria from this dilemma, and Israel, to a large degree alone, could and did prevent that from happening. Thus, Israel held the whip hand, unable to dictate a solution for Lebanon, perhaps, but apt to use Lebanon to prevent Syria from doing so. Tactically, there were many advantages for Israel over the years: Lebanon distracted attention from Egypt's separate peace with Israel, bogged down Syrian troops no longer available for front-line duty, obliged Syria to stand by helplessly while Palestinian targets were hit indiscriminately, destroyed Syria's regional leadership pretensions, sowed doubts in American policymakers' minds about Syria's usefulness in the Middle East.

For the Lebanese, the most diabolical consequence of all was their across-the-board hatred of the Syrians. Brought in first to help the Christians against the Moslems and Palestinians, the Syrians succeeded in alienating almost everyone. Quite apart from their real or imagined abuses, the Syrians' main fault was just being there. Like many another occupying army before them, they outstayed their welcome. Israel helped bring about that situation as well. And Israel, too, was to learn that its troops in Lebanon would change from an army of liberation to one of occupation in a matter of months.

Yet, for all the history that is now part of the public record, no evidence has come to light to suggest that Israel did more at the beginning of the civil war than simply watch Lebanon fall apart. By any objective yardstick, the Lebanese themselves must bear the lion's share of the responsibility for the final, actual physical undoing of their country. Israeli politicians shed crocodile tears at the violence next door, but the death of the democratic Lebanon they had known was not an unmixed blessing for them. In years past, Israel had pointed to Lebanon as an economically flourishing, pro-Western democracy when lecturing other Arabs about the benefits of future coexistence in the Middle East. Now Israel stood accused by critics of having sapped Lebanon's foundations. Israel was now the only democracy in the Middle East—no mean talking point when impressing Americans with the prevalence of Arab military dictatorships. Palestinian involvement in the Lebanese civil war—and its Moslem-versus-Christian aspects—only helped to justify Israel's rejection of PLO proposals for replacing Israel with a "democratic, secular state" that grouped Christians, Moslems, and Jews together. As early as September 1975, Israeli Foreign Minister Yigal Allon said, "The Lebanese model is our best objection" to the PLO proposal and constitutes "proof of the impossibility of coexistence of groups of different nationalities and religions within a democratic state in the Middle East." In October 1976, he said that the Lebanese war showed the PLO plan was a "mirage." Israel defended its own interference in Lebanese affairs by claiming that it acted to preserve its neighbor's independence, sovereignty, and territorial integrity. No less a personage than Shlomo Avineri, Foreign Ministry Director-General (or highest civil servant), said in August 1976 that "without Israel, Syria would have annexed Lebanon."

Much of this talk was merely tactical sniping to score momentary advantage, a favorite Middle Eastern pursuit. But the public record does show a long Israeli tradition of violence toward Lebanon that contributed to the circumstances undermining the Beirut government. Sharett's diary, for example, as early as 1955 contains an entry recounting Chief of Staff Moshe Dayan's spirited if unsuccessful effort to win cabinet approval for a reprisal raid on a Lebanese village. Israelis traveling on a bus in Galilee had died in a terrorist attack, and Dayan wanted to retaliate even before investigators had established who was responsible for the outrage. Just this kind of retaliation against points in highly populated south Lebanon was to become a pattern in a few short years. But until the 1967 war the border area remained relatively calm. Then the defeat of Arab arms in less than a week brought the Palestinian guerrillas to the fore. The Lebanese state was no longer strong enough to keep the Palestinians in line. The cycle of raid, reprisal, new raid soon became familiar to the Lebanese.

Some Lebanese remain convinced that Israel spared Lebanon until the late 1960s out of consideration for France. France for many years had been Israel's principal arms supplier, and the symbol of the lightning Israel victory in 1967 was the French-made Mirage fighter-bomber. President Charles de Gaulle was personally interested in Lebanon, where he had served when it was a League of Nations mandate after World War I. But the United States was now becoming Israel's main source of weapons, while France tried to improve its relations with the Arab world after the Algerian war ended in 1962. De Gaulle had warned Israel not to start the 1967 conflict, and ever since, so went the theory, Lebanon was no longer safe. Although the PLO was active in Jordan and Syria as well, it was PLO offices in Lebanon that, more often than not, were targeted every time Israel retaliated for a Palestinian guerrilla attack, no matter where it had originated.

Even Israeli historians, for example, have criticized the scale and ferocity of Israel's December 28, 1968, retaliatory raid on Beirut airport, when Middle East Airlines, Lebanon's national flag carrier, lost thirteen airliners on the ground. But more damaging than the losses themselves was the humiliation that Rafael Eitan, the raid's leader, inflicted on the Lebanese in their holy of holies, the Middle East's busiest airport, a symbol of Lebanese prosperity, bought at the price of abandoning any effort at self-defense. It was a willful act, a message to the Lebanese that their golden age was coming to an end. Few Lebanese realized at the time that they had crossed a watershed. It was left for de Gaulle to draw the lesson: he embargoed further French military sales to Israel. And the less spectacular but cumulatively more physically telling Israeli raids, incursions, shellings, and kidnappings in south Lebanon went on. They were designed as much to turn the Lebanese public against the Palestinian guerrillas as to root out the commandos themselves.

In the early 1970s, tens of thousands of southern Lebanese, mostly poor Shia Moslems, fled the border area, which in any case had long been neglected by the Beirut government, unwilling as it was to provide basic education, health, or economic-development services. For the most part, they moved into poor suburbs of Beirut, where many Palestinians also lived in a poverty belt surrounding the capital. Leftist organizers succeeded in radicalizing the Shia in Beirut and in the south, scaring the right-wing Maronite leaders and prodding the Christians to take up arms.

When the civil war finally began in April 1975, south Lebanon paradoxically became a rare haven of peace in a country whose other regions almost without exception were ravaged by violence. The reason was simple enough: the Palestinian guerrillas had abandoned the border area and rushed to Beirut, where the main fighting was taking place. Indeed, it was well into 1976 before the Israelis succeeded in capitalizing on the plight of the southern Christians isolated in pockets along the border. Israel simply waited patiently while renegade Moslem units of the now-split Lebanese Army cut the Christians' water, power, and road links to Beirut, hoping to force them to submit. In desperation the Christians turned to Israel. According to apocryphal accounts, a note appealing for help was found stuck in the border fence by an Israeli frontier guard.

Suddenly, quite literally, the gate opened on what was dubbed the "good fence" between Israel and south Lebanon. The Zionists' dream became a reality. Under the guise of humanitarian aid to the beleaguered Christians in the border area, Israel moved in militarily and economically, provided jobs in Israel for Christian Lebanese, and smuggled Israeli goods north into the rest of Lebanon. Over the years, the Israelis succeeded in reducing once-troublesome Palestinian cross-border infiltration to practically nil. (By 1980, for example, cross-border infiltrations or attempted infiltrations accounted for only 8 of the 262 guerrilla attacks and bomb incidents recorded by Israeli officials.) On the ground a double fence, electronic sensors, constant patrolling, and increasingly frequent Israeli incursions to Lebanon did the trick. But northern Israeli towns and settlements remained well within PLO artillery and rocket range. Now the use of the isolated Christian enclaves provided Israel with the perfect tool to establish an embryonic presence on Lebanese soil that could be expanded as circumstances dictated. The Lebanese were not alone in suspecting that Israel had plans to annex the land up to the Litani River and divert its long-coveted water. Mindful of Maronite border villages that Israel had annexed in 1948, Western diplomats were convinced Israel would push its advantage anywhere it could.

A good half year before the "good fence" was built, northern Christians had been in touch with Israel, lining up arms and ammunition. Camille Chamoun's son Dany, commander of the Tiger militia, opened up the connection in the fall of 1975. It was a logical choice. The elder Chamoun had been part of the Middle East landscape for the better part of forty years. He was a statesman by regional standards, a former President, a known quantity. Sharett's diary, twenty years earlier, in February 1955, records receiving a Lebanese emissary "apparently on behalf of Lebanese President Camille Chamoun. Lebanon would be ready to sign a separate peace if we accept the following three conditions: guarantee Lebanon's border, come to Lebanon's aid if attacked by Syria, and buy Lebanon's agricultural surplus." Moreover, according to Chamoun's own associates, Israeli arms aid was nothing new. During the 1958 civil war, the embattled Lebanese President had received some five hundred Thompson, Beretta, and Bren submachine guns from Israel. Years later, Rabin, then commander of Israel's Northern Command in Nazareth, recalled cooperating with Chamoun in stopping infiltrators from Syria who were smuggling in arms to help unseat the Lebanese President. But the real Israeli aid—ranging from fuel, heavy artillery, and thirty-six World War II–surplus, U.S.-made Super Sherman tanks, to sophisticated electronic gear and uniforms— was forthcoming only after Syrian troops entered Lebanon in earnest in the spring of 1976.

Israel wanted to tie down two major foes—the Syrians and the Palestinians. The northern Maronite militias, saved from disaster by the Syrians, within days of that narrowest of escapes were delighted to recruit a countervailing force to offset their saviors. In proffering aid, the Israelis discovered they had to deal with two sets of warlords. For the Israelis, Chamoun was a happier initial choice than the Gemayels. The Phalangists smacked a bit too much of the Nazis, who indeed had inspired Sheikh Pierre when he attended the 1936 Berlin Olympics. (Yet the Gemayels had long maintained close relations with Lebanon's tiny Jewish community. The Phalangists were semiofficial protectors of Lebanon's Jews—and proved it during the Six-Day War in 1967, when their militia cordoned off the Jewish Wadi Abu Jamil neighborhood in

Beirut to keep away would-be molesters.) And Chamoun was resolutely anti-Syrian, whereas the more eclectic Phalange had a wing that had negotiated the eleventh-hour alliance between Syria and Lebanon.

At the beginning, Israel cleverly kept each of the two allied but rival Maronite warlords in the dark about the help it was providing the other. The first high-level meeting took place between Israeli Prime Minister Rabin and Camille Chamoun aboard an Israeli gunboat off the Christian port of Jounieh in early April 1976. Shimon Peres, then Israel's Defense Minister and architect of the scheme, recalled, "We were approached by the two factions separately." An Israeli close to the negotiations said that when it came Sheikh Pierre's turn to meet with the Israelis, he seemed ill at ease. "It was the first time he had met an Israeli Prime Minister," the Israeli said, "and obviously he was having to overcome a psychological barrier. He was sharp, shrewd, and had a lot of dignity despite the obvious stress of the situation."

The Israelis started out, at least, scrupulously splitting their arms and ammunition shipments fifty-fifty. This equal sharing allowed the Chamouns, whose militia was a fledgling operation compared to the Phalange's generations-old military organization, to recruit more troops—although they never matched the Phalangists in numbers or discipline. The Chamouns, moreover, added to their war chest by selling excess weapons they did not need to the Phalangists or to the smaller Christian militias. By July the flow of Israeli matériel had reached such proportions that an American diplomat in Beirut remarked, "The Christians are doing so well with Israeli help that we don't have to get involved even if we dared."

From the start, the Israelis made it clear that they were willing to help the northern Christians help themselves, but would not fight their battles for them—"the Nixon Doctrine," as Peres once described his version of the American policy of arming overseas allies but not fighting with them. Speaking of the northerners, Peres told me, "I had a lot of admiration for them. They fought bravely, although for us they were a bit poetic"—by which he apparently meant lacking in military organization. The Israelis openly helped the southern Christians and their Shia Moslem allies, running regular patrols inside the border strip and using it for their artillery on many occasions. As time went on, the Christians increasingly sought to involve the Israelis in their purely Lebanese schemes, and on several occasions they very nearly succeeded in bringing about a larger confrontation with Syria than Israel wished. Yet, in a series of conversations I had with Labor Party leaders in 1980, after they had fallen from power, they were at pains to stress they had been brutally honest with the Christians. "I never misled them," Rabin told me—with such fervor that he seemed to think I had suggested Israel had taken advantage of the warlords. Official Israelis and even Maronites such as Dany Chamoun all maintain that the Christians neither asked for nor were promised anything other than material aid except in case of genocide, that most-difficult-to-define threat. Still, Maronites love to suggest that they and the Israelis on several occasions came within an ace of launching major joint ground operations that were called off at the last minute.

Even under the Rabin government, official Israeli propagandists made much of Israel's protection of the Lebanese Christians, often to point up the alleged shameful Western abandonment of their coreligionists, sacrificed for the sake of Arab oil. This theme was amplified in 1977 with the arrival in power of Menachem Begin, who was genuinely convinced that the Lebanese Christians were threatened with a Middle Eastern version of the Holocaust, and who by all accounts gloried in the turnabout role of a Jewish strongman protecting persecuted Christians.

An Israeli Arabist told me that the Lebanese Christians had learned to manipulate Begin early on by invoking Israel's responsibility for protecting *all* the Middle East's minorities—from Egypt's Coptic Christians to the Kurds, who are mainly Sunni Moslems. "When Begin talks about the dangers of a Christian massacre," the Arabist told me, "you can believe every word." Other Israelis, however, were considerably more cynical about their country's relationship with the Lebanese Christians. They wanted to limit that relationship to the border strip, rather than extend it to Beirut and the Christian heartland farther north. Israelis cognizant of the realities know full well that the Christians in the border strip make up no more than 10 to 15 percent of the population, although the accepted convention is to describe the militia there as "Christian." As with the population, most of the militiamen are in fact Shia Moslems, and only its commander, the cashiered Lebanese Major Saad Haddad, and most of his officers are Christian.

"We don't really give a shit about them," explained an Israeli privy to the thinking of the armed forces. "We've always had a Druze brigade, and now we have a Christian brigade, or one that people think of as Christian. The whole arrangement with the Christians is like a modern marriage—a few good years together, and then who knows? Sure, the Lebanese Christians helped get Iraqi and Syrian Jews out to Israel right through the mid-1970s, but, face it, we even are tough on our own people. We use them until they get burned. When the Christians got involved with Israel in a big way, it was a sheer windfall for us. What did they get out of it? Enough weapons to dare the Syrians.

"And Israel's interest? Not so much intelligence—we already had that going with the Christians long before. Not just screwing up the Syrians and keeping the PLO on the balls of their feet. But also having a finger in future Lebanese governments. It's good to have friends in a hostile country. It was a perfect fit. Then Begin went public, and the whole operation became overt, not covert."

Israeli policy toward the northern Christians appeared designed to keep their heads just above water. Dany Chamoun, for example, complained to me that during the Christian siege of the Palestinian refugee camp at Tal Zaatar, which lasted fifty-two days in the summer of 1976, the Israelis doled out ammunition with an eyedropper. "They wanted the agony to go on for as long as possible," he said. One of his father's principal aides at the time insisted, "The Israelis never wanted us to win there. They didn't give us a single bullet more than we needed to defend ourselves."

Within weeks of the initial meeting between the Israelis and Chamoun off Jounieh, the first of more than a thousand Christian militiamen were sent via Cyprus to Israel for training. Seemingly overnight, Israeli military touches were visible in the Lebanese militiamen—from their army boots, weapons, and uniforms to the way they handled their assault rifles (hanging them on a sling around the neck rather than holding them in one hand). In south Lebanon, militiamen from Jounieh arrived in the Christian enclaves via the Israeli port of Haifa to beef up Christian ranks. Israelis close to Peres estimated that five hundred or so mainly Christian army regulars or veterans and fifteen hundred predominantly Shia Moslem militiamen were worth two brigades to the Israeli armed forces.

Right from the beginning in 1976, the whole border policy—and especially that governing the "good fence"—was awash in confusion. Prime Minister Rabin accepted the entry of Syrian troops into Lebanon, but he arbitrarily ruled they should not advance south of the so-called Red Line, which ran roughly from the Zahrani oil refinery on the Mediterranean coast south of Sidon to Kafr Mechki in the Beqaa valley. Originally, he was said to have toyed with letting the Syrians come right to the Israeli border, purportedly in order to bring the Palestinian guerrillas under control on their last autonomous turf and to use the Syrian Army to do the unpopular deed. (Palestinian officials readily admit that the PLO was powerless then to oppose such a Syrian takeover.) But Rabin's eternal Labor Party rival, Shimon Peres, objected. Peres's thinking was more conventional: how could Israel, after years of depicting the Syrian Army as the most bloodthirsty in the Arab world, accept its presence, even minus air defenses, within striking distance of Haifa and the main Galilee population centers?

Allowing the Palestinians free rein in south Lebanon was a policy that was to plague successive Israeli—and Lebanese—governments. This decision was an eloquent illustration of a shortsighted advantage masquerading as a long-term policy. Outside commentators wondered more and more often whether Israeli official thinking *required* a Palestinian adversary that was alert, well, and just enough of a threat to keep the Israeli electorate conscious of danger. Repeated American-backed efforts to persuade Israel to allow first Syrian, then Lebanese Army troops into south Lebanon in areas well north of the border were made in 1977, 1978, and 1979. Israel frustrated them all, which made diplomats suspect that it was rejecting a political settlement in favor of perpetual disarray in Lebanon. An American official closely involved in one such effort in 1977 with the Syrians recalled that the Israelis "went absolutely berserk." Whatever the Israelis' reasons at the time, it was a policy that was to cost them very dearly—which surprised the other regional players. They were used to Israel's being the winner.

At one point, the most obvious loser was Richard Parker, the American ambassador in Beirut. In the summer of 1978 he became a humiliated Lebanese government's scapegoat. Parker was caught in the middle when Israel at the last moment backed out of an American-brokered plan to move Lebanese troops into the south. The Israelis signaled their change of heart by firing American-supplied proximity-fuze rounds from American-built guns to wound a good number of these American-equipped Lebanese soldiers. The Lebanese government was furious, and a misunderstood remark by the foreign minister lead to a rumor that the ambassador was being asked to leave. In fact, Parker was ticketed to become Ambassador to Morocco, and the humiliated Lebanese did nothing to quell the rumors that he was leaving Beirut because of the fiasco in the South. The incident was illustrative of a willful Israeli attitude toward all comers, which led one key American policymaker to complain, "They can outlast us on almost any issue."

If Israeli policy at times seemed self-defeating, it was nonetheless admired by many American diplomats for at least having the merit of existing. Often the only visible American policy seemed to be enshrined in what the diplomatic community came to call "the war of the two embassies," pitting the Americans in the Beirut mission against their colleagues in Tel Aviv. (In fact, the Tel Aviv embassy was split, with Ambassador Samuel Lewis often forced to pull rank on members of his staff who violently disagreed with his unshakably pro-Israeli line.) The Beirut Americans wanted the "good fence" shut down in keeping with Washington's oft-repeated proclamations of concern for Lebanon's sovereignty, independence, and territorial integrity. Lewis and his backers in the Tel Aviv embassy echoed the official Israeli line: after a generation spent encouraging exchanges between Arabs and Israelis, how could Washington now oppose such an obviously humanitarian enterprise as the "good fence"? Lebanon was a hopeless basket case, they said, unworthy of the time its problems required and detrimental to the questions they deemed more important for U.S.-Israel relations. For one tough American there, Lebanon was a "situation not susceptible to solution under present conditions: diplomacy has no foundations on which to work. We see Lebanon, especially south Lebanon, as a moral problem, but one which cannot be solved until Lebanese sovereignty is restored. Israel sees Lebanon as a strategic reality."

The American diplomats in Beirut despaired of such defeatism. They questioned Israel's wisdom. "Israel does not worry about long-range implications. For them, south Lebanon is a chance to set up a *cordon sanitaire* cheap and get someone else to do the fighting," a senior American diplomat complained. "If eventually they succeed in annexing the south, that will be so much gravy. Israeli policy is made by the army's Northern Command, and they regularly repudiate the Defense Ministry. The Israelis keep telling the American government, 'We can live with south Lebanon, we don't care, let them kill each other off.' Here we feel the Israelis are shortsighted. Israel should have an interest in a stable Lebanon, and the best way is to allow the Syrians to help restore sovereignty throughout. Our Tel Aviv colleagues tell us the south is a sideshow for Israel, while we see it as vital for government stability." That was early on.

The Beirut embassy could not make its point when manifest U.S. policy interests were involved. Its diplomats, for example, proved unavailing in their efforts to shut down the Voice of Hope radio station—call letters WORD—which California evangelists of the Van Nuys–based High Adventure Ministries set up with Israeli encouragement in Major Haddad's border strip in September 1979. Nicknamed by critics "the Voice of Death"—since Haddad often used its microphone to announce his intention to shell civilian targets—the station's 30,000-watt medium-wave (AM) station dispenses country and western music, inspirational messages, and Old Testament passages as well as pro-Haddad news, much of which is provided by the state-owned Voice of Israel radio network. At one point, the U.S. government was troubled enough by the station's Israeli connections, its patent violation of Lebanon's state radio monopoly, and the whispered suggestions of official American support for it to threaten its American owners with an Internal Revenue Service suit alleging misuse of missionaries' tax-exempt status. Chuck Pollak, the station's born-again Christian manager, in February 1981 brushed aside suggestions that its American origin could be construed as giving official American backing for Haddad or for Israel. "The political implications of what we are doing, rightly or wrongly, are secondary to what God has told us to do," said Pollak, who lived in Israel and with six other Americans commuted to work with a border pass issued by Haddad. (The irony is that the Israelis would never have tolerated such Christian proselytizing in their own country.) The IRS suit petered out even before Ronald Reagan was elected President in November 1980, and since then the Voice of Hope has opened a $2 million shortwave station and started television broadcasts with equipment its owners valued at $4.5 million.

No other single issue better reflected the Tel Aviv embassy's victory over their Beirut colleagues in the 1970s than the tolerance shown in Washington for Israel's more and more open use of U.S.-supplied weapons in Lebanon. Eventually, American weapons were so routinely deployed as part of Israel's controversial preemptive-strike policy that I was laughed at as impossibly naive when in January 1981 I arrived in Jerusalem with the records of dozens of painfully researched and carefully documented violations of the American law under which

Israel has been prodigally provisioned with U.S. weaponry. The Mutual Defense Assistance Act of 1952 delimits the use of American-supplied weapons. Over the years Israel chose, among all its complicated clauses, to use only the "self-defense" exemption. Thus, in the Israeli view, for all intents and purposes no violations ever occurred.

On at least one occasion, an American officer serving as a United Nations military observer in south Lebanon confronted senior Israeli officers with photographs he had taken of civilian casualties caused by Israeli gunners firing American-supplied artillery. He threatened to publish the photographs unless the shelling in his sector stopped and despite the scandal in UN circles that his private initiative might cause. The Israelis relented. John Gunther Dean, then American ambassador in Beirut, took a similar, if more orthodox, view of Israeli depredations. Twice within a week in August 1980, he condemned particularly devastating Israeli attacks on south Lebanon, which, as was often the case, had killed many more Lebanese civilians than suspected Palestinian guerrillas, the advertised quarry. Although the terms he used were identical to those previously employed by the State Department itself, in Washington a State Department spokesman pointedly disavowed the ambassador. Cynics concluded that in the middle of an uphill—and eventually unsuccessful—reelection bid, President Carter wanted to avoid anything likely to discommode Israel and its influential friends in the United States. Cyrus Vance, who the previous year had backed a similar initiative on Ambassador Dean's part, which stopped Israeli free-fire-zone raids for nine months, was no longer Secretary of State.

Within a week of the State Department disavowal, gunmen in a Mercedes sprayed the ambassador's black armor-plated Chrysler with automatic-arms fire and landed a rocket-propelled grenade between it and one of the ambassador's two Lebanese security escort cars. He had been leaving an area near his residence above Beirut, which was within the six square miles administered by what was left of the Lebanese central government. His heavily armed, eleven-man bodyguard fired back, and the Mercedes was forced to stop. Three men, apparently the car's occupants, were held briefly, then released. Public rumor in Beirut credited the job to Lebanese Forces doing Israel's bidding. By Beirut's peculiar logic, the assailants were said to have meant only to scare the ambassador, since they fired only one grenade. Later, Dean went down the hill and attended a dinner party at the American

University of Beirut. After Reagan's election victory in November, the Israelis demanded Dean's removal from Beirut, and he left the following June. Through no major fault of his own, he had failed to stop the use of American arms in Lebanon, but he was still alive.

As a weary American diplomat in Tel Aviv once put it to me, "You accommodate to a lot of things in the Middle East." At one point in the spring of 1980, with some irritation, another American official in Tel Aviv estimated that 40 percent of the embassy's time was taken up with south Lebanon, and his tone of voice clearly indicated the effort had been largely wasted. It was as if the United States were still living in the 1960s, before the excesses of Indochina focused American public opinion on the effects of massive firepower. (Indeed, it was only in the post-Vietnam era that Americans questioned Israel's use of American weapons as prescribed by the law of 1952. In the 1969–70 war of attrition between Egypt and Israel, Israel had openly used American-supplied Skyhawks and Phantoms, and no one had complained—no one, that is, but the Egyptians and other Arabs.)

"The United States caved in on the weapons issue in south Lebanon," an American official closely involved with Middle East affairs conceded in 1980, "because the Washington bureaucracy is not ready to fight and die—they figure they have more important fish to fry with Israel." What about "end use" certificates, those solemn undertakings by the foreign beneficiaries of American weaponry that theoretically prevented its misuse or transfer without Washington's prior approval? Another foreign-policy insider shook his head. "No one has the heart to push it," he said. "The State Department will run in the opposite direction to ignore the law and its violations. No one pushes this kind of thing within the administration or on the Hill." He looked at me, searching for some way to make me understand how easy it was for Israel to bury the Americans in red tape. "The cable traffic between Washington and Israel," he said finally, "is second in volume only to that between us and the Soviets."

From time to time, the level of violence exceeded the previously tolerated level, and Washington would focus on Lebanon. Thus in March 1978, a Palestinian naval commando set out from the Lebanese shore, evaded Israeli detection owing to bad weather, landed on the Mediterranean coast of Israel, and slaughtered thirty-two Israelis. As was standard Israeli practice in such cases of Palestinian terrorism, reprisal was not a question of if, but rather of when and how much. As usual, the United States was consulted and raised no known objections in principle. When the weather cleared three days later, the Israelis struck. They invaded south Lebanon with an army of thirty thousand men backed by armor, self-propelled artillery, and massive air power. Code-named "Stone of Wisdom," this long-planned operation constituted the biggest Israeli military operation in peacetime. It was also a surprise for the United States.

The destruction was on a scale known well in Vietnam. Aping the prodigal use of American firepower in Indochina, the Israelis sought to keep their own casualties to a minimum—and succeeded. But they failed to wipe out the Palestinian commandos, who had plenty of time to scamper to safety north of the Litani River. Piling mattresses, clothes, and families in taxis and overloaded pickup trucks, more than two hundred thousand Lebanese also fled north out of harm's way. They became exiles in their own country, squatters seizing unoccupied apartments, the source of yet more tension in Beirut. The Israelis did succeed in massive killing: almost all the victims were Lebanese civilians—some one thousand, according to the International Committee of the Red Cross. More than six thousand homes were badly damaged or destroyed. Half a dozen villages were all but leveled in a frenzy of violence during which Israeli troops committed atrocities.

The destruction seemed more aimless than during most wars. Cowering in a Tyre hospital on the first day of hostilities, I watched Israeli planes screaming by at treetop level on their way to bomb Tyre harbor. They missed the ships but destroyed, among other buildings, a friend's Ottoman-era house nearby. Returning to the south a few days later, I ran into an Israeli string quartet playing Mozart in a field for the benefit of the troops. It was as if some Israeli Buñuel were trying to find the equivalent of those USO shows that so delighted American troops in the field in Vietnam. Yet the Israeli troops seemed ill at ease, almost ashamed of the destruction they had wrought.

To make matters worse, Stone of Wisdom was a military mess of such dimension that the Israeli government felt constrained to appoint an official commission to investigate its manifest shortcomings. The attackers had lost the element of surprise. They had failed to destroy the Litani bridges or to drop an airborne blocking force north of the river to trap the fleeing Palestinian guerrillas. Tactically, the invaders first stopped six miles inside Lebanon, then the next day moved north to the Litani River when the United States feverishly began putting together the United Nations Interim Force in Lebanon (UNIFIL) to police the south. Carter was furious, and determined to end the invasion, which went far beyond the scope of tolerated retaliation. The Israelis mistakenly assumed the American initiative would be vetoed in the UN by the Russians on behalf of the PLO. And, for fear of heavy casualties in their own ranks, they did not dislodge the Palestinians from the substantial pocket around Tyre.

About the only ones convinced the Israelis were on the right track were the northern Lebanese Christians—or, at least, some of them. They made plans to rush troops to Haifa to take part in the great pincer movement they were sure Israel would launch from the border as they moved south from their Mount Lebanon strongholds. Such were the powers of self-suggestion. In fact, the Israelis were obliged, under stout American pressure, to stop before they could hand the entire area over to Major Haddad's militia. At least, that is what the American government thought. In the end, the Israelis were obliged to pull their troops out of Lebanon, but only after President Carter sent a threatening letter to Begin. Unless Begin started withdrawing troops within twenty-four hours, Carter wrote, he would cut off American arms and aid and sponsor a United Nations resolution condemning the Israeli occupation. Begin complied. Even so, the Israelis had the last word of sorts. On June 12, the end of their third month of occupation and the day before they were to evacuate their troops from the last swath of Lebanese territory, they announced they were handing it over to Major Haddad. They thus defied UN resolutions ordering UNIFIL's six-thousand-man force to move up to the international border to help reassert Lebanese sovereignty over every inch of occupied land. At the same time, they so arranged their withdrawal as to leave a four-mile hole in UNIFIL lines. That was to prove a useful passageway for Israeli raiding parties, and in 1982 one of the Israeli invasion paths when Israel finally unleashed the major ground offensive the northern Christians all those years never quite got out of their minds.

Carter's administration had expended so much effort to get the Israelis out of Lebanon that no great American protest occurred when the Israelis carried out their transparent trick. A diplomat then in the

U.S. embassy in Tel Aviv recalled, "The UN raised hell with us and we raised hell with the Israelis, but we didn't sustain the effort. Haddad was considered relatively unimportant at the time." Armed, paid, aided by Israel, Haddad served as cover while the Israelis linked up three hitherto isolated Christian enclaves. Now, for the first time, Israel enjoyed a workable security strip under surrogate control and, thanks to UNIFIL's presence there, a second buffer zone along most of the east-west stretch of the Litani River. The Israelis' violations were so obvious that the United States at least fitfully complained about their growing habit of introducing American-supplied weaponry into "Haddadland." No longer could the violations be attributed to the heat of battle. During that invasion, the Israelis dropped cluster bomb units, a particularly devastating antipersonnel weapon widely used by the United States in Indochina. These bombs were still killing Lebanese and Palestinian civilians in 1982, when other such weapons were used on a much larger scale. But even in 1978 Israel could not dismiss these charges out of hand: their use of cluster bombs was brought up in Congress, and the State Department promised to investigate—publicity that deeply angered Begin. (The investigation led nowhere.) In 1982, the Israelis reacted with angered innocence when the 1978 Congressional investigation was recalled, and kept on using the CBUs even after the Americans ordered their supply stopped (the bureaucracy slipped up and the pipeline was never interrupted).

Later, a Washington policymaker recalled that the then Foreign Minister, Moshe Dayan, during one of his periodic American visits, had been taken to task by his U.S. interlocutors. American-built armored personnel carriers were in south Lebanon in violation of U.S. law. Dayan said the report was incorrect. But "a real-time photograph taken by satellite or U-2 was on President Carter's desk within an hour and pinpointed the vehicles in some village. Carter was furious, said he didn't like being lied to, that it was against our policy and our law and that he would be obliged to notify Congress and terminate all future military assistance if the APCs were not out of Lebanon within twenty-four hours. The APCs were removed, but the incident left great scars in our bilateral relations.

"Then Jimmy Carter stopped playing hardball. Even when he had, Lebanon's priority in those relations wasn't that high, maybe third or fourth place. It was the quintessential sideshow even in 1978 and 1979, when we were really after Begin—sometimes with three messages a day or a message from Vance or the President. Then things ran out of gas. It was sheer neglect, and there was no one in Washington who cared or carried water for Lebanon."

Even if Lebanon had found stouter supporters within the administration, that would not have meant Israeli forbearance. An Israeli official, musing over the problems of dealing with his Prime Minister, recalled reading the transcript of the Camp David talks: "At some point Carter said to Begin, 'I must insist on' something or other. Begin shot back, 'You will insist on nothing.' "

The United States indeed was to have other problems with the Israeli government, now determined to use Lebanon's northern Christians actively against Syria. President Sadat's visit to Jerusalem in November 1977 had been a revolution in static Arab world thinking, but as usual it was Lebanon that absorbed the first physical shock waves. Once Sadat made plain his desire that Egypt conclude a separate peace with Israel, Syria and the Palestinian guerrillas felt obliged to close ranks. Like it or not, they had to put aside the hatred that had grown between them during the open warfare they had indulged in the previous year, when PLO commandos fought the Syrian invaders in Lebanon. They had little choice in the face of an Israeli war machine that no longer had to worry about the Egyptian Army, the largest in the Arab world. Many months before Sadat's visit to Jerusalem, Bashir and his friends were cozying up to the Israelis, much to the genuinely injured innocence of the Syrians. They at first denied the increasing evidence of this collusion, produced by the Palestinians, then complained bitterly of Christian "ingratitude." Further encouraged by the Israelis, the Christians eventually sought to drive the Syrians out of Lebanon. Mossad operatives primed the Christians with tales of Israeli derring-do, the virtues of determination, drive—"creating facts," as the early Zionists had dubbed their policy. Starting in February 1978 with a shoot-out between Syrian troops and a Lebanese Army barracks in the hills near the Presidential Palace, a series of increasingly violent incidents pitted the Christian militias against the Syrians.

Ever since 1976, the Israelis had calculated that the honeymoon enjoyed by the Syrians and the Lebanese Christian warlords would end sooner or later. Even at its most idyllic, when Israelis, Christians, and Syrians were ganging up on the Palestinian guerrillas and their Lebanese allies, the odd alliance had grated. I once asked a high-ranking Israeli official, long associated with Peres, whether he wasn't bothered by the oddity of the strange-bedfellow arrangements. "That's life in the Middle East," he said. When I continued to express surprise, he retorted defensively, "Just because a girl flirts with my rival doesn't make her any less interesting. On the contrary. And anyhow, we didn't start the flirting." But the real point was that Israel feared the Syrians would withdraw their troops from near the Golan Heights, where the bulk of their forces were stationed. (In December 1981, taking advantage of the crisis in Poland that diverted world attention to Eastern Europe, Israel annexed those parts of the Golan occupied in the 1967 war.) Never mind that other Israelis were determined to drive the Syrian police-force army totally out of Lebanon. Consistency on such matters of tactics has never been an Israeli forte. They're the first ones to tell you.

Serious fighting broke out between the Syrians and the Lebanese Christians in July 1978. The warlords were getting the worst of it. East Beirut was largely deserted, the first time since the fighting began in 1975 that its Christian residents had refused to stay put. Then the Israelis sent two Kfir jets over the Lebanese capital to break the sound barrier—a common occurrence during times of tension. The Syrians stopped shelling. Despite that remission the United States was well aware of Israeli plans to alienate, and possibly destabilize, Syria.

Preparations were going ahead for the Camp David summit meeting, to be held that September in hopes of furthering Israeli-Egyptian peace negotiations. The Carter administration found itself odd man out on how to deal with Syria. Its Egyptian and Israeli partners had their reasons to be on bad terms with Syria. Yet President Carter strongly believed that President Hafez Assad was a reasonable ruler of a country that until his takeover in 1970 had resolutely refused to recognize Israel's right to exist, much less to negotiate. Assad was deemed an essential player in any serious Middle Eastern peacemaking, like him or not. The Syrian role in Lebanon was certainly open to various and often critical interpretations. But Washington still considered it vital, lest the Lebanese return to their self-destructive demons.

Throughout August 1978, France and the United States tried to talk the Lebanese Christians out of their headlong rush into Israel's arms. Camille Chamoun in his diary quoted French ambassador Hubert

Argod's warning that Israel is not "ready to make war for you," and added, "the defeatist spirit of 1940 continues to inspire French diplomatic circles." Ambassador Parker warned Chamoun he should avoid having to choose between Israel and the United States; Washington was more credible, he added, since Israel could not deliver on all its promises. That, at least, is what the political Lebanese thought was going on. The Israeli establishment was making ominously anti-Syrian and pro-Christian noises—Begin himself warning of genocide, Chief of Staff Rafael Eitan announcing that his army "was ready for any eventuality in Lebanon," and various members of the Knesset comparing the Lebanese Christians to the Jews of the Warsaw Ghetto in 1941 and denouncing American pressures that prevented Israel from helping the Christians. On August 23, Camille Chamoun went by sea to Israel, where he was received at Begin's home in the company of Eitan, Foreign Minister Dayan, and Defense Minister Ezer Weizman. "Defying American warnings and threats, Begin and his friends decided to give us their support without reservations to the limits of their means, without attaching any political or other conditions," Chamoun wrote in his diary. Although both Christians and Israelis stuck to their line that Israel had never *promised* help, Chamoun in private told intimates that indeed the Israeli leaders had done just that—if the Syrians intervened again. A Lebanese friend who cautioned Chamoun against believing the Israelis was told he knew as much about politics as he, Chamoun, knew about Chinese.

Some Israelis were convinced that Begin got carried away with his own words and did give Chamoun the impression that this time Israel would help the Lebanese Christians get rid of the Syrians. To the limited degree that logic plays a role in Middle Eastern politics, the evidence is against such an interpretation. The Camp David negotiations began on September 6 and ended on the 18th. Even those Israelis cynical enough to suggest Begin was forced into the agreement against his better judgment admit that in any showdown he had little choice but to sacrifice his Christian friends in Lebanon to the higher interests of preserving Israel's alliance with the United States. Within days of the Camp David agreement, fighting between the Christians and Syrians broke out again in Beirut. In separate but similar statements, Vice-President Walter Mondale and French Foreign Minister Louis de Guiringaud blamed the Christians for provoking the Syrians.

The Camp David accord, which started Israel and Egypt toward a separate peace, only deepened the sense of doom in Lebanon. The Lebanese had long since realized that any such disruption of the Arab world would be played out violently in their own country. There were those in the Lebanese Christian leadership who insisted the Camp David agreements gave the Syrians the perfect alibi for attacking, since Israel now had its hands tied. But in any case, all the Christian warlords were disappointed by Israel's lack of interest—not to mention military help. A high-ranking and well-informed Lebanese remains convinced that the Israelis welshed on them. "During the September and October shelling," he said, "there were innumerable nights when the guys went down to the shore with their chronometers, waiting for the Israelis to disembark." They never came. On one particularly bad day, Chamoun called his chief lieutenants together, hoping to find a way to knock out Syrian 240-millimeter mortars installed in the hills overlooking Beirut. The heavy mortars were causing enormous damage, their rounds going through the stoutest reinforced concrete and smashing entire apartment buildings. Told that a ground attack was impossible and counter-battery fire difficult, given the lay of the land, Chamoun scribbled on a piece of paper torn from a small notebook, rang for his secretary, and handed her the note. Some four hours later, the secretary brought him the answer. Chamoun peered at the typed reply through his thick glasses, shouted, "Fucking bastards!" in Arabic, and threw the message on the floor. When he wasn't looking, someone picked up the crumpled paper, which read, "Sorry not to be able to carry guns with you." There was no signature. But then, none was needed.

When the inevitable cease-fire was announced in October, the Christian leaders were still unrepentant, and at least some Israeli leaders were wondering how close they had come to having the tail wag the dog. From the bunker under his apartment house, where he had stayed courageously as Syrian artillery shelled his neighborhood, Camille Chamoun defiantly challenged Israel to live up to what he hinted had been a bargain. Asked if he thought the cease-fire would hold, he was quoted in the *Jerusalem Post* on October 9 as replying, "Frankly, that depends on how serious the Israeli assurances are about aid. If Israel keeps its promises, the militias will open fire to provoke the Syrians. Our leaders count on Israel to create a Christian state covering 10,000 square kilometers of Lebanese territory." That amounted to the entire 4,105 square miles of the Lebanese Republic. Chamoun had upped the ante from help for a rump Christian state to help in reestablishing Christian dominion over *all* Lebanon—quite another matter.

At about the same time, Begin said in public that he would examine the situation "a thousand times" before sending Israeli troops as far into Lebanon as helping the northern Christians would entail. For once, Begin appeared to have heeded the grave warnings that Washington gave to discourage the Israeli hawks. In any event, despite the stirring words of encouragement during the fall fighting between Christians and Syrians, Israel limited itself to a gunboat bombardment of Palestinian coastal positions well south of Christian East Beirut, which was taking the brunt of the Syrian punishment. That egotistical pursuit of Israeli objectives was not lost on the Christians, who became convinced they'd been left in the lurch. But they forgot the lesson later on, when once again they tried to involve Israel in a clash with Syria.

Indeed, the whole episode—the terrible Syrian bombardment of East Beirut, the failure to get Israel's help—was disastrous. Over the years, some Maronite militia leaders at Ashrafieh, the Phalangist headquarters in East Beirut, played down their own responsibilities there, and blamed the hammering on Sleiman Franjieh, their erstwhile ally, convincing themselves that he had prevailed on his Syrian friends to punish East Beirut in retaliation for his son Tony's assassination that June at Phalangist hands. But all this smacked of ex post facto justification, mixed with guilt and an acknowledgment of failure. The militias screamed that they were victims of genocide, but in fact the Christian death toll was no more than two hundred, as usual most of them civilians; the tales of having to burn cadavers in the streets were fabrications. The facts were that they were guilty of bad judgment. They had failed to note or properly evaluate Secretary Vance's visit to Damascus after Camp David, which had clearly signaled that the United States stood by Syria.

Eventually, the Syrians did evacuate East Beirut. But many Lebanese Christians were convinced the price paid for their departure—in destroyed property and economic and social dislocation—had been too high. In West Beirut, the most noticeable result of the hostilities was the reappearance in the streets of Moslem and leftist militias for the first time since the civil war had ended officially two years before. And to the Green Line dividing the Christian and Moslem sectors the Syrians dispatched Palestine Liberation Army troops under their command. These repercussions were scarcely welcomed by West Beirutis. The Christian warlords later harped on West Beirut's hatred of these Palestinian "occupation troops," and called on the Moslems to rise up and throw off their "foreign" yoke.

A month or so later, at the Maronite think-tank at Kaslik, I bumped into a monk I'd known for some time and asked him what the original game plan had been.

"We thought we could play like the Israelis—you know, the way the Israelis play with you Americans."

"What happened?"

"Nothing happened," he said. "We played the sorcerer's apprentice. We believed we were great magicians."

"Bit of a long shot, even by your standards, wasn't it?"

"Yes, I didn't have much faith myself, but like Saint Thomas, I wanted to see the proof, if proof there was. There wasn't. The Israelis didn't move."

It was not a lesson learned by the Christian warlords or by Israeli hawks. They shared a common, reinforcing inclination to force the odds, no matter how eventually perilous to their more obvious basic interests. Each new adventure at first appeared to prove that audacity alone paid off. Yet, often misled by easy, initial success, they found themselves caught in a maelstrom of unforeseen violence, brutality, and atrocity.

During their March 1978 invasion, the Israelis committed atrocities themselves and witnessed others carried out by their Lebanese allies, but did not intervene to stop them. Lieutenant Daniel Pinto, acting commander of an infantry company, was court-martialed for having tortured and killed by strangulation four Lebanese peasants. Their bodies, bound hand-and-foot, were found stuffed down a well. Pinto was sentenced to twelve years in prison. But General Eitan, the Israeli Chief of Staff, reduced the punishment to two years, then ordered the lieutenant's release. Eitan sought to hush up his handling of the case by imposing military censorship, but the *Los Angeles Times* published the facts. Eitan also intervened to whitewash Lieutenant Colonel Aryeh Sadeh, whose initial five-year sentence for the murder of a Lebanese civilian was halved and his commission restored. Older Israelis recalled uncomfortably similar whitewashes, starting in 1948 with Menachem Begin's responsibility in Irgun's mass murder of Palestinian villagers at Deir Yassin and continuing in the 1950s with the series of murders and assassinations involving Ariel Sharon and his special Unit 101 raiding commando. In 1976, the government first denied, then confirmed reports that an Israeli naval patrol handed over to Phalangist vessels Palestinians apprehended aboard a ship off Sidon. The Israelis were routinely patrolling Lebanese waters then, and normal procedure would have called for the Palestinians to be taken to Haifa for questioning. Handing them over to the Phalangists was tantamount to signing their death warrant.

But it was in south Lebanon that the Israelis allied themselves formally for the first time with men as coarsened to violence as were Haddad's militiamen. In three towns—overrun thanks to the Israelis during the Litani invasion—Haddad's forces massacred more than a hundred Shia Moslem men, women, and children. The worst outrage took place in Khiam, near the Israeli border, once the most prosperous and populated town of south Lebanon. The Shia victims were herded into a mosque. "We sank to Haddad's level," an Israeli military specialist said, ashamed. "I watched his men shoot seventy people in cold blood in Khiam."

I first heard about the Khiam killings while interviewing Lebanese refugees in south Lebanon who were fleeing north for safety. I was only a few miles from Khiam, but the Israelis refused to let correspondents in that sector move through their lines. I drove back to Beirut, and with *The Washington Post*'s blessing, flew to Athens and thence to Tel Aviv. That was then the only way to reach Israel in a single day—such are the ways of the Middle East, since even in normal times the Lebanese-Israeli border is shut to foreigners. Determined to get to Khiam to judge for myself, I spent a frustrating Easter Sunday in nearby Marjayoun arguing with obdurate Israeli officers, who had set up their headquarters in that Christian village. Despite promises from the army liaison headquarters in Tel Aviv, the local commanders kept refusing to let me go to Khiam, clearly visible on a neighboring hilltop. "Too dangerous," they said. I pointed out that the Israeli Army had made me sign a printed form waiving its responsibility for my person. They consulted, then said, "Too dangerous for your escort officer"— the obligatory watchdog the Israelis attached to all correspondents as their price of admission to sovereign Lebanese territory. Six hours passed. Only when I threatened to expose their lack of cooperation and report that they had prevented me from checking firsthand on the massacre allegations did they relent. Even then, Israeli troops in the badly damaged and deserted town blocked me from visiting the mosque where the murders had occurred. To its credit, the Israeli press exposed the massacre and asked the key question: What kinds of allies had Israel acquired?

Despite spirited Israeli public criticism of the Litani operation and of Haddad's excesses, the official Israeli sense of impunity grew steadily over the years as the rest of the world came, uneasily at first, then unblinkingly, to accept this "occupation by proxy." Lebanon complained to the United Nations Security Council that Israeli artillery fired white phosphorus at fields to destroy crops, in violation of the Geneva convention. UN observers' reports regularly noted such Israeli activities as laying new minefields, fencing in strips of land close to the border, and building access roads in Haddad's enclave. Also in violation of the Geneva convention, Khiam was used—and heavily damaged—by Israeli troops training for street fighting with live ammunition. In defiance of international law and Lebanese sovereignty, the Israelis routinely kidnapped from their homes Lebanese they suspected of sympathizing with the Palestinian commandos, and took them to Israel for interrogation, prosecution, and even imprisonment decided by military tribunals. These incidents were routinely reported in Lebanese newspapers. Their corrosive, cumulative effect on the fabric of the Israeli Army and of society in general was a matter of concern and conjecture for the many Israelis who questioned government policy. But the facts themselves were rarely disputed and were regularly described in antiseptic language in the reports of UN activities in south Lebanon published twice a year.

The most prominent Israeli opposed to the Litani operation—and the unfolding policy on Lebanon—was Moshe Dayan, then Foreign Minister. Despite his own provocative plans in the 1950s for seizing south Lebanon, he now feared Israel would be drawn into a trap the very way he had seen the United States ensnared when he visited Vietnam in the mid-1960s. Sharing his doubts was General Shlomo Gazit, former Chief of Military Intelligence and Governor of the West Bank and Gaza territories occupied in 1967. Concerned about his own authority, Defense Minister Ezer Weizman issued orders that put Israeli military incursions into Lebanon under close scrutiny, and often demanded supporting evidence of their necessity. But despite Weizman's soldierly bearing, American diplomats and UN officials who dealt with him came to realize that his orders were, often as not, repudiated by Eitan and the hawkish Northern Command of the Israeli Army with headquarters in Nazareth. Yet, Weizman was no dove on Lebanon. In January 1979, he officially announced a fateful change in Israeli policy. From then on, Israeli forces would strike not just in retaliation for Palestinian guerrilla attacks against Israel, but "at any time and at any place that Israel deemed desirable." Thus was born the controversial preemptive-strike policy that turned much of south Lebanon, and beyond, into a free-fire zone.

Weizman quit the government two months later. Israeli strikes against Lebanon became more daring and complicated, almost "art for art's sake," as one admiring UN military observer once remarked. As many as twelve hundred men were employed against Palestinian positions grouping no more than a dozen or so guerrillas. Israel's objectives were far from simple. In part they concerned seeking out and destroying a Palestinian equivalent of COSVN, the elusive Vietcong headquarters that obsessed the American military for a decade in Vietnam. A Northern Command general once boastfully assured me, "We can get rid of the terrorists in a matter of hours. We have enough equipment and tools, and we know exactly where they are, thanks to very, very good intelligence." Only political considerations and a desire to avoid inflicting casualties in the ranks of UN troops standing in the way prevented Israel from smashing the guerrillas, he argued. But the Israelis did not seem to share the total conviction that knocking out the enemy would somehow end the war that the Americans had had in Vietnam about COSVN and the French had felt in 1956, when they embarked on the Suez campaign, sure that overthrowing Nasser would somehow stop the revolution in Algeria.

South Lebanon was also a convenient faucet for Israel to turn on and off to raise or lower regional pressures. For the faucet to work in Lebanon, the Palestinians perforce had to be maintained as a viable adversary. The Begin government found them handy at election time: Israel could and did indulge in using the armed forces to bash Arabs. That was a sure-fire vote-getter among the majority of Israelis of

Oriental extraction—that is, those drawn from countries with Arab majorities. And Lebanon provided what one Israeli military specialist called a perfect terrain for "big maneuvers with live, human targets," in the only neighboring country where the Israeli armed forces had never fought a full-scale war. The Israeli military delighted in such operations, involving armor, artillery, air, and infantry. Soldiers in the elite Golani Brigade competed for the honor of participating in operations against Palestinian positions between the Litani and Zahrani rivers. Jumping off from Haddad's unofficial capital at Marjayoun, they infiltrated through the hole in the UN lines either on foot or by helicopter. American-built A-4 Skyhawks and F-4 Phantoms were the favorites for bombing missions, often with other U.S.-manufactured planes, the F-15 Eagles crammed with electronic gear and flying "skycap" missions to jam enemy ground-to-air missiles.

Normal Israeli government procedure required approval from civilian ministries for any military operation against Lebanon—or, for that matter, any foreign country. But once Weizman had quit, Begin took over as his own Defense Minister. He spent one day a week at the Defense Ministry, the only ministry in Tel Aviv, on the Mediterranean coast. But the rest of the week, the power of decision was in the hands of the armed forces. Even on his visits from Jerusalem, Begin rarely intervened. Such is his veneration of the military, a former aide said, that "all Begin has to do is see a general and he has an orgasm." With Eitan and his Northern Command acolyte, Brigadier General Avigdor Ben-Gal, in effective charge, the military was given its head. The excesses were such that, thanks to Ambassador Dean's intervention, Washington forced Israel to stop its preemptive strikes from August 1979 to April 1980. But after a Palestinian commando attack on the border kibbutz of Misgav Am in which two Israelis were killed, the Israelis resumed retaliatory and preemptive strikes with a vengeance.

Then, just before Christmas 1980, Israeli Deputy Defense Minister Mordechai Zippori apologized publicly to Syria. Israeli apologies of any sort are rare enough, and addressed to Syria they are virtually unheard of. Behind the apology lay the deaths of four Syrian soldiers inadvertently killed during a deep penetration raid against a suspected Palestinian base in Lebanon. The after-battle report had mentioned that the Israeli commandos had killed four men in a Jeep who did not behave like Palestinian guerrillas. In fact, the Israelis should have known that Syrian troops were in the target area, since the camp was north of the Red Line—in other words, on territory where the Syrians were entitled to station soldiers. Had the Israeli military listened to the civil servants they might have canceled the raid. Zippori's apology masked Israeli fears that the incident might prompt Syria to return two divisions from the Jordan-Syria border to near the Golan Heights, the major potential confrontation point with the Israeli Army. (Syria had removed the troops from the Golan area the previous month, during its threatened confrontation with Jordan.) For the time being, the troops stayed put, and Syria contented itself with firing three hundred heavy-artillery rounds at what it called "Israeli armor concentrations." In fact, all the rounds landed in Major Haddad's enclave, once again proving the usefulness of the buffer strip to the major players, if not to its residents.

Scarcely a month later, I was in Israel interviewing politicians and soldiers for a series of articles about south Lebanon. As on so many previous visits, I had misjudged the mood. No danger flags were flying. No mood of repentance or self-doubt was in the air. I had just come from a month's reporting in south Lebanon, as depressing an assignment as I'd embarked upon in my career. Day after dogged day, I'd set out by car from the relative comforts of Beirut into an atomized world without telephones, decent roads, electricity—a suspicious world where inevitably the person I wanted to interview had just left or refused to see me or imparted no significant information either in ignorance or in fear. I'd begun to feel as defeated as the people whose Hobbesian plight I was trying to describe. My Washington editor, to whom I'd foolishly promised the articles in no more than three weeks, was getting impatient.

In the Israeli interviews, which I conducted together with my colleague William Claiborne, the Jerusalem correspondent, I asked the "bad cop" questions so as to protect Claiborne, whose thorough reporting on Israeli policy in the occupied West Bank and Gaza Strip had often angered Israeli authorities. We needn't have taken the precautions. To my amazement and despair, at no point did the Israeli officials question the preemptive-strike policy, which to me seemed as shortsighted and eventually self-defeating as the search-and-destroy operations carried out by the American forces in Vietnam.

At Northern Command headquarters, an ebulliently self-satisfied general boasted, "The policy can go on forever. From our side there is no Red Line, nothing to hold us back. We can suffer to a point only."

"Any regrets?" I asked, almost sheepishly, so convinced was this abrupt soldier.

"Yes," he said, and for a tenth of a second I toyed with the possibility he might shed at least one crocodile tear for the desolation Israel so efficiently had shared in creating in Lebanon. "The mistake is that we do not do enough." As he expanded on his theme, my mind wandered back to Vietnam a dozen years earlier and to similar talk from vainglorious American generals.

Undaunted, I asked about Major Haddad's excesses and the tarnishing effect they must have on Israel's cherished reputation abroad.

Haddad was doing "just beautiful," the general insisted. I winced, recalling Haddad's wanton shelling of civilians in Sidon, Hasbaiya, and other Lebanese towns and cities; his responsibility in failing to prevent the murder in cold blood of Irish UN soldiers; his mad rantings and madder actions; the beating up of UN observers; and the shooting up—twice—of UNIFIL headquarters at Naqoura, his shelling designed to bring about the repair of a power plant put out of commission by his own artillery.

Claiborne and I must have registered incredulity, perhaps only for a fleeting second, for by now the general had sized us up for the doubting Thomases we were. So when I returned to Israel's responsibility for Major Haddad, the general was ready.

"We control Haddad," he said, much pleased with himself, "to the same degree that the United States controls us."

This cynical if accurate summation of American indulgence was not contradicted when, a few days later, I saw David Kimche, Director-General of the Foreign Ministry. I had asked to meet him because he had been one of Mossad's key men in charge of the Lebanese Christians, working directly under the agency's boss, Yitzhak Hoffi (known to the Lebanese as Mandy). Great was my surprise when we were introduced at the ministry, for I realized we had known each other nearly twenty years earlier in West Africa. The man I'd known then as David Sharon had been a friendly, reliable source about African developments whom I kept running into in odd places. Then one day he had disappeared abruptly—come to think of it, about the time the Israeli embassy in the Ivory Coast had been accused of some now-forgotten skulduggery. On my infrequent visits to Israel I'd inquired about Sharon, only to be told he had left government service. No one seemed to know his whereabouts.

With great self-assurance he defended the preemptive-strike policy, claiming that "no matter what government" would maintain it—elections were scheduled for June—because "no one could do otherwise." If Israel stopped helping Major Haddad in Lebanon, "there would be massacres," he said, and the UN troops "would never be able to prevent them." He brushed aside any suggestion that the then brand-new Reagan administration might crack down on Israel. He had seen Reagan's transition team after the election in November and was convinced the new administration would "understand, perhaps more than the previous one, our need to strike at terrorism." "We think," he added, "we will have more understanding."

That certainly was the universal impression that the new Secretary of State, Alexander M. Haig, Jr., left behind in Israel during his familiarization visit to the Middle East in late March and early April 1981. Obsessed by his "strategic consensus" plan to rally Egypt, Israel, and Saudi Arabia to an anti-Soviet alliance, Haig distinguished himself with remarks so imprecise, awkward, or naively provocative that his staff had to work overtime to correct the painful impression of willful ignorance.

By the time he reached Tel Aviv, serious fighting was in full swing between the Syrians and Bashir Gemayel's militia at Zahle. That Lebanese Christian city of 150,000, on the eastern flanks of the Lebanon mountain range overlooking the fertile Beqaa valley, was predominantly Greek Catholic, not Maronite, and the Gemayels' Phalangists had never been strong there. Yet since July of the year before, when they eliminated Camille Chamoun's Tigers in Marounistan, a certain logic had propelled the Gemayels to take over any Christian area they could. A victory at Zahle would swell Bashir's ranks by a good quarter and back up his claims to overall Christian—rather than just Maronite—leadership. Already just before Christmas his men and the Syrians had fought a brief, bloody battle at Zahle that quickly subsided. Several months later, according to Western intelligence, the Israelis had sent helicopters to move Bashir's men and matériel into the mountains close to the city. Somewhat tardily, the Syrians now realized that Zahle commanded the strategic Beirut–Damascus road; it also posed a potential threat if the Israelis were to punch through the UN lines and dash up the southern Beqaa to join Bashir's forces. The discovery of a road under construction linking Marounistan and Zahle across the mountains confirmed the Syrians' worst suspicions. And so on April 1, the Syrians moved, and did so in the only heavy-handed way they knew in their dealings with the Lebanese Christian militias.

The first day, the Christians in Zahle exulted: in trying to seize the high ground above the mountain-flanked city, the Syrians had lost three armored vehicles and more than twenty soldiers. The next day, the Syrians retaliated with an artillery barrage in East Beirut that caught residents there by surprise, inflicted heavy casualties, and effectively emptied the Christian side of the capital for the next six months. Also under way was a siege of Zahle, which was to be lifted only on June 30, the day of the Israeli elections, when it was calculated that the Israelis were too busy to disrupt the delicate disengagement operations. Before the Gemayels' militiamen were bused out of Zahle—and decorated and feted in a theatrical ceremony at Bashir's East Beirut headquarters—the United States was deeply enmeshed in a major international crisis. Without influence in Damascus because of its own ineptitude, the Reagan administration now had to call on its Saudi Arabian allies to buy off the belligerents. Sources claiming to be informed said the Syrians had held out for anything from $500 million to $1.2 billion. "Paying off," an Arab diplomat remarked, "is what the Saudis do easiest—and best."

Secretary Haig had no obvious interest in worsening the Zahle crisis (though he purposely had snubbed the Syrians by leaving Damascus out of his Middle East itinerary, thereby deepening Syrian suspicions about the Reagan administration). Even the PLO had bent over backward to stay out of the Zahle conflict, despite stepped-up Israeli attacks on its positions. Wise victims, the Palestinians knew better than to put their heads up during an Israeli election campaign. During his stopover in Israel, Haig had made a fateful, if technically accurate enough, description of the "brutality" of Syria's "army of occupation" in Lebanon. This played into the hands of those who wanted to profit from the crisis. Israeli hawks were not averse to stirring up trouble abroad, especially during a political campaign in which Begin hoped to hide the disastrous effects of his financial stewardship. The Lebanese Christians hoped to enlist Israel's support and provoke an international crisis to force the Syrians out. As it turned out, both groups were disappointed: the only clear-cut winner was Syria.

At the beginning of the crisis, the old familiar themes were trotted out. Even before the fighting actually began, Israeli intelligence was singing Bashir Gemayel's praises to foreign journalists, suggesting that interviews could be arranged with the promising young Christian leader; the gullible were told they would be landed directly on Christian territory without having to risk their lives by crossing from the Palestinian-controlled sectors of Beirut. To listen to the Israelis, the foreign press resident in Lebanon were under the thumb of Syrian and Palestinian killers and too scared to tell the truth. Such efforts proved unnecessary. In the first few days of the fighting, Christian militia propagandists appealed to the world, as they had in 1978, to rescue the beleaguered Christians facing genocide. Much to their amazement, their gambit worked. The press also helped unwittingly, by putting out the militia's bloodcurdling versions of events, which no reporters were allowed to cover at first hand. One American news agency kept referring inaccurately to Zahle's residents as Roman Catholics rather than Greek Catholics, an error calculated to arouse public concern in America. Few of the foreign correspondents in Beirut had been through the militia's propaganda blitz before, such is the turnover among them, and by the time the old hands arrived, the Christians had got in the first and telling licks. It was a much better show than in 1978. (But even then, Israelis and Lebanese Christians had collaborated on propaganda to telling effect. Chaim Herzog, then Israel's ambassador to the United Nations, gloatingly told me how he had embarrassed Arab delegates by waving in their faces telegrams from Lebanese Americans praising Israel for saving their countrymen from the PLO. Maronite churches in the United States had offered prayers for the ambassador, for Israel, and for Lebanon's Christians. "The Lebanese in America were hard, very hard to organize," Herzog told me, "but we managed to teach them the tricks of the trade.") Confronted with the Christians' claims of massacres at Zahle, Syrian Foreign Minister Abdel Halim Khaddam feigned disbelief. "A hundred dead, maybe," he is said to have protested. "What's all the shouting about? In Syria, we killed four hundred Moslem Brothers in a single night in Hama and nobody even chirped." (He was talking well before the massacre in the winter of 1982, when thousands of Syrians were killed.)

With the Israeli elections only three months away, Israeli hawks rushed to the verbal defense of their Christian Lebanese allies, hoping to bolster Begin's then far from sure reelection prospects. Begin himself repeatedly asserted that the United States had changed "and now agrees with us that the Syrians are not a stabilizing element, but a brutal occupying power wantonly killing men, women, children of the Christian minority." There was no formal denial from Washington. Moshe Arens, then chairman of the Knesset's Foreign Affairs and Defense Committee and later ambassador to Washington and Defense Minister, said that not since World War II had a city taken such punishment as Zahle. Agriculture Minister Ariel Sharon struck the jingoistic stance that had been his trademark for decades, denouncing the "thundering silence of the world in the face of the massacre in Lebanon," and inaccurately reported that Christians made up the majority of the war dead, which he exaggeratedly set at "120,000." Retired General Haim Bar-Lev, the opposition Labor Party's shadow Defense Minister, felt obliged to keep pace and said that Israeli aid to the Christians could lead to direct intervention, also in the north. For the first time since the Israeli connection with Lebanese Christians began, both Israeli political parties spoke publicly of possibly coming to the northern Christians' aid with more than the usual arms and ammunition.

Yet, it was Northern Command's Brigadier General Ben-Gal who, in his soldierly bluntness, came closest to understanding the Christian militia's psyche. He argued that Israeli and Christian interests coincided in their desire to force Syria out of Lebanon. He justified the Christians' "initiative," as he euphemistically described their provocative presence in Zahle, "if only for internal psychological and foreign policy reasons." He said, "If calm should reign for three years, the Christians' existence would be forgotten." In other words, Zahle was a now-or-never operation designed to force the issue. The general was pleading for his own cause as commander of Israel's only "live" front. If that front were quiet, any number of potential diplomatic possibilities with Syria and the Palestinians might open up, singly or together. Yet even Ben-Gal saw his Christian friends as a weak force facing the regular Syrian Army, and noted, "Beyond some point you are endangered by an explosion that will set off an avalanche."

The danger of provoking just such an avalanche set off an extraordinary debate between hawks and doves in the top echelons of Israel's elite. A close reading of its press revealed the depth of questioning that the Zahle crisis had aroused. Israel was at a crossroads. Its decisions would now affect not just the Lebanese Christians, or even the Syrians, but a maze of relationships around the globe, and especially in Washington. Begin and his generals were considering a course of action that risked bogging Israel down in the Middle East's most complicated and treacherous country—about which they knew next to nothing. Lebanon was not an "empty" Sinai with a scattered Bedouin population. It was not even the West Bank and Gaza Strip. Lebanon was the most densely populated nation in the Middle East, its people a crazy quilt of minorities. Only much later, after the Shatila massacre, did Labor opposition leader Shimon Peres ask, "What were Israeli soldiers doing in West Beirut—this city laden with hatred, devoured by resentment, weighted with mysteries we cannot penetrate?"

But eighteen months earlier, other Israelis had sensed the dangers involved in the Zahle operation. It is our moral duty to save the Christians, the hawks maintained, only to have the doves ask, Who would believe us? Now is the very time to strike, the hawks argued, because Syria is isolated in the Arab world, abandoned by Egypt, on the outs with Iraq and Egypt, estranged from Saudi Arabia. True enough, said the doves, but intervening to help the northern Christians is the best way to end Syria's isolation and possibly even give Iraq a pretext for stopping its ruinous war with Iran. Still, the hawks claimed, a war with Syria would test Egypt's intentions: if it helped Syria, Israel would have the perfect excuse not to return the last strip of the Sinai desert, due to be handed over in April 1982; and if Egypt didn't, the gap between it and the other Arab countries would deepen. The doves retorted that such tactics would scarcely win friends in Cairo or Washington, and these were needed in the long run. The hawks insisted that smashing the Syrian Army, the only major Arab fighting force since Egypt's had been neutralized, would provide ten years of peace. The Russians will only rebuild Syria's arsenal, the doves retorted, and probably even faster than they did after the 1967 and 1973 wars, since Moscow and Damascus have signed a treaty of friendship and cooperation. Back came the hawks, convinced that now was the chance to smash the Palestinian guerrillas in Beirut and elsewhere and sweep away their infrastructure. The doves yawningly asked how many times the army people had claimed to have eliminated those guerrillas.

Still, the hawks persisted, helping the Lebanese Christians, no matter what the reasons, would make them totally dependent and give Israel another ally to complement Egypt. Perhaps, argued the doves, but there was always the risk of having the United Nations forces all over Lebanon instead of just in the south, where the Israeli Army kept complaining about how they hampered Israeli maneuverability. The Reagan administration, the hawks countered, was not against ridding Lebanon of the Syrians and the Palestinian commandos. The doves replied that the Soviets might well feel obliged to get involved under the terms of their treaty with Syria. But a little war with Syria could boost Begin's reelection chances and help distract attention from three-digit inflation and the general economic crisis, the hawks whispered. Yes, responded the doves, but there is scarcely anything as unpopular as casualties in a country like Israel, which is still traumatized by its losses in the 1973 war.

The doves won that round. As General Yehoshua Saguy, chief of military intelligence, and an opponent of Mossad's alliance with the Lebanese Forces from the beginning, made plain at a nominally off-the-record news conference in which he scarcely bothered to mask his identity, "The term genocide used by the Christians is pure propaganda." Christian casualties were estimated at one hundred fifty, he said. (In fact, Christian dead throughout the siege did not exceed one hundred, and, as usual, most were civilians.) By mid-April, the Israeli press had also made it a matter of public record that much of the establishment felt the militia leadership was responsible for initiating the fighting—or at least blundering into it—with the hope of dragging Israel into a war with Syria that neither government necessarily wanted. Yigael Yadin, the moderate outgoing Deputy Prime Minister, publicly condemned those Israelis trying to enmesh the country in a larger conflict in the north. He also asked the government to control Major Haddad, "who shoots at the civilian population of Tyre and Sidon with Israeli-made shells." Three Israeli newspapers sounded similar alarms.

Three days after Haig left Jerusalem, and even before the doves' victory became apparent, David Kimche was dispatched on April 8 with the bad news for Bashir Gemayel. By now the two men called each other by their first names, but their two-hour meeting was stormy. Kimche formally read—but did not hand over—an Israeli government statement dating from August 28, 1978, pledging that it would "examine favorably" the use of Israeli airpower if Syrian planes attacked the Lebanese Christians. That was hardly the kind of support the Christians had hoped for. (Perhaps General Eitan had tipped the Israeli hand when he made a visit late in March to Marounistan, during which he confused his Christian hosts by asking to visit the quiet northern Phalangist defense lines rather than the tense Zahle sector. Some Christians later became convinced the Israelis had been hesitant all the time and invoked an American veto when none may have existed.)

In public, Bashir took his lumps stoically, but within weeks he was letting it be known that "the Israelis are no longer the Israelis of 1948, 1956, and 1967. They've gone soft, lost their self-confidence. We are like the Israelis used to be." Perhaps, but the situation on the ground hardly justified such tough talk. Militarily, his militia's positions in and around Zahle were untenable, with or without the still-unfinished "strategic highway" he was building across the Lebanon mountain range. In fact, the lay of the land made it impossible to defend Zahle from the Christian heartland. Deciding to teach Bashir a lesson, his erstwhile Syrian allies moved to take over the ridge line in the Mount Sannine sector of the range. The operation was basically psychological. The Syrians already controlled all but ten miles of the ridge line. The whole ridge was so exposed to the elements that at best troops could be maintained there comfortably only from May through late August, and Bashir's men and Syrian-backed Lebanese leftists had made an unusual spring ritual of racing to the summit. There was much talk of installing radar at Frenchmen's Refuge, at the very top, but it was just talk. Indeed, it was as much the manner of the Syrians' coming as their presence that was calculated to panic Marounistan, although Lebanese Army intelligence suggested that the Syrians planned to advance as far as the coast. That made little sense on the basis of past performance. Syrian artillery in Beirut and elsewhere in the mountains already covered the main Maronite population centers, including Jounieh. But on Saturday, April 25, the Syrians used helicopters to land special assault troops on the ridge line, where, thanks to rockets, they made short shrift of the surprised militiamen. The Christians lacked wire-guided and heat-seeking weapons to attack the helicopters. Within twenty-four hours the U.S. State Department publicly deplored what it termed this "major change in the status quo." The normally astute Ambassador Dean had been sold a bill of goods.

The State Department was to deny somewhat lamely that this statement was intended as a green light for Israeli intervention. But at the very least it was a throwback to the outspoken anti-Syrian language Haig had used when he was in Israel. The American ambassadors to Lebanon and Syria rushed to meet Haig, who was now in Jordan, and explain to him the subtleties and complexities of the Syrian position. And, in a message to President Assad, Reagan insisted that "Syria can play a central role in the construction of a just peace" in the Middle East.

In any event, on Tuesday, April 28, Israeli Air Force planes—American-built F-15s and F-16s—shot down two Syrian Army helicopters over the Beqaa valley, north of the Beirut–Damascus road. Israeli spokesmen kept insisting that the helicopters were gunships, despite reiterated and truthful Syrian assertions that they were transport craft on resupply missions. The helicopter incidents took place just as Syrian Foreign Minister Abdel Halim Khaddam was driving from the Syria-Lebanon border crossing at Masnaa to the Presidential Palace at Baabda to impose a "pax Syriana" on recalcitrant Christian militia leaders, until then left in the lurch by Israel. For many Lebanese, once again, as so often in the past, it seemed that Israel was intervening to prevent any movement toward a political solution inside Lebanon that it judged contrary to its interests: not the least advantage of the Israelis' alliance with the Christians was that Israel called the shots—determined when, where, and for how long events took place. Momentarily lost in the shuffle was a nice point: did the Red Line agreements between Damascus and Jerusalem rule out Syrian use of helicopters or just of ground-to-air missiles? Simcha Dinitz, Israel's ambassador to Washington at the time of the 1976 Red Line negotiations, claimed that no mention whatsoever had been made of helicopters.

Hafez Assad of Syria now moved quickly and decisively. At first light the next day, April 29, the Syrians drove across the nearby border in long tarpaulin-covered convoys and installed three batteries of Soviet-made ground-to-air missiles. Each battery consisted of a radar truck and three tracked vehicles on which were mounted a cluster of three missiles. There, glinting in the spring sun for everyone to see, alongside the Beirut–Damascus road, or nearby, were the slightly obsolescent missiles that had proved their worth in downing so many Israeli warplanes in 1973. By the second day, when three colleagues and I bumped down the side road to the Rayak airbase to look for other batteries, the radar was busily turning. The missiles were fully operational. Peasant women in brightly colored dresses, working in the freshly plowed fields, paid them no mind. They had become part of the landscape. Yet, I distinctly remember my feeling of fear. The road was crowded and so deeply rutted that our taxi could only creep along. We were as good as dead if the Israeli Air Force struck. I had been bombed enough by the Israelis to respect their skill, their ability to come out of nowhere, drop their bombs or fire their rockets, and be gone.

It was a cold, blustery day in the Beqaa, a good fifteen degrees colder than in Beirut, and I cursed myself for coming out without a jacket. I remember drinking more than my share of several bottles of local Ksara white with my excellent trout at Baalbek's Palmyra Hotel, a place much favored by hashish dealers now that more conventional tourism had stopped in Lebanon. It was my way of facing the return voyage down that same dangerous road. Much later, Prime Minister Begin himself justified my fears. Fending off parliamentary critics clamoring to know why he had not sent the Israeli Air Force into action that second day, he replied that only bad flying weather had prevented his warplanes from carrying out his thrice-repeated orders to destroy the missiles. Begin warned the Syrians to remove the missiles posthaste, on pain of having Israeli fighter-bombers do the job for them.

The Christians were delighted, less because the tardy Israeli gesture in itself reassured them than because Lebanon was now at the very center of an international crisis. Their elation was heightened when a visibly surprised and worried Reagan administration abruptly brought out of retirement Philip Habib, a former Undersecretary of State and a man of Lebanese extraction, and dispatched him to the Middle East as troubleshooter. Creatures of habit, the Lebanese Christians recalled that in the 1958 crisis another prestigious special envoy, Robert Murphy, had been sent to Beirut.

Tough, driven, dedicated, at sixty-one Habib combined all the old WASP diplomatic virtues of discretion and tact with a Levantine gift for putting Arabs and Israelis at ease. There was something about this short, balding man, his health ruined by decades of compulsive over-work, of a Le Carré veteran called back to untangle yet another mess at the Circus. It was a damage-control operation for a fledgling adminis-tration trying to prevent serious Soviet inroads in the Middle East. Habib's first order of business was to reestablish American influence in Syria, which had been reduced to virtually zero by a series of Washing-ton-directed snubs (including those administered to U.S. Ambassador Talcott Seelye, whose cables to the State Department from Damascus went virtually unanswered for months before his retirement from the foreign service in September). Habib's imaginative, unconventional approach was a far cry from the blunt method that, according to the Middle East grapevine, had been favored by an important and rabidly anti-Soviet young foreign-policy maker in the new administration who had suggested, so the tale went, that the United States destroy the missiles before the Israelis did so themselves. No wonder that State Department Arabists now began referring to the new crop of Reagan's political appointees in key policymaking posts as "the Huns and the Mongols."

Begin's threats played into Syria's hands. President Assad argued convincingly that Syrian troops were in Lebanon with official Arab League blessing. Without ever going into detail about the Red Line agreements, he seemed to be maintaining that the missiles' presence was justified because Israel itself had violated its end of the bargain by shooting down the helicopters. One Arab country after another felt constrained to rally round, and with the political support came mon-ey—lots of money—principally from Saudi Arabia. President Assad, hitherto isolated and strapped, was a clear winner. For Syria, a limited war, even if won by Israel, was better than knuckling under, losing face, and paying the probable price of having to put down more domestic opposition. And Assad's language, by Arab standards mea-sured and temperate, contrasted with Begin's increasingly shrill procla-mations.

Israeli military specialists increasingly blamed Begin for falling into a complicated trap. The Prime Minister should not have ordered the helicopters shot down and provided the Syrians with the very pretext they had long sought to get around the Red Line prohibition on deploying ground-to-air missiles inside Lebanon. SAMs north of the Beirut–Damascus road might not endanger Israel's security, but once

Israel had accepted the principle of their presence in Lebanon, what was to stop Syria from moving them farther south? Questions were raised suggesting Begin had misread the American "green light," especially from an administration so new and patently inexperienced in the subtleties of the Middle East. Begin's own advisers, it was said, had warned him the Syrians were likely to bring in the missiles if Israel shot down the helicopters, since their air force was no match for Israel's and they had no other obvious riposte.

Still, Begin's own hawks kept raising the ante. Foreign Minister Yitzhak Shamir argued that Israel "is fighting its own war on the soil of Lebanon—it is defending its own security from within the 'Land of the Cedars'!" And General Eitan now declared that not only would Israel not stop its preemptive raids and aerial reconnaissance over Lebanon, but henceforth it would ban all Syrian planes from Lebanese airspace.

But the pressure inside Israel was building up, and acting sweetly reasonable toward his only ally was not going to get Begin reelected. Prevented from striking at Syria, Begin turned on the Palestinians. As Habib shuttled discreetly around the Middle East, largely to prevent, by his very presence, Begin from destroying the Syrian missiles, Israel temporarily refrained from attacking the Palestinians. But fewer than twenty-four hours after Habib left Israel for Washington in late May to report on the first stage of his mission, as if to signal his displeasure, Begin ordered raids resumed on suspected guerrilla targets in Lebanon—only a dozen miles south of Beirut. No wonder Habib was mistrusted by even moderate Arabs as a fireman dashing to put out arson lit by America's Israeli clients.

There was little in all this to please the Lebanese warlords, who now began grumbling unconvincingly about switching sides, since "the Russians at least stand by their friends." Such talk expressed their frustration at seeing everyone but themselves profit from the crisis. The Syrians again were recognized as major Middle East players; Begin's popularity leapt ahead in the opinion polls as the June 30 election day approached. Especially hurtful to the Christian leaders was the exposure of their connections with successive Israeli governments—and in the Israeli parliament itself, of all places. Secretive to a fault, the warlords had always managed to brush aside the charge of collusion with Israel. But Shimon Peres and Menachem Begin were competing in the Knesset to reveal one compromising detail after another. Such were the folkways of Israeli electioneering. The two campaigning leaders could not have cared less about the embarrassment—indeed, trauma—such revelations caused their Lebanese Christian allies. Begin never acknowledged he had been fooled by the Christians—or had subsequently let them down. "I believe that through our actions we already saved them," he said of the Christians in an interview on American television in early June. "We are very proud the Jewish people in our time after the Holocaust can save another people." Peres, the architect of the alliance with the Lebanese Christians, seemed to think the Christians were getting too big for their breeches. Ever the pragmatist, he dismissively remarked, "You shouldn't start a war when you are not prepared." As Moshe Dayan's right-hand man for years and a former Defense Minister in his own right, Peres spoke with the authority of a man who had prepared more than one.

It was at this nadir in Bashir Gemayel's fortunes that the United States embraced him formally. Doubtless, the Reagan administration was better disposed ideologically than its predecessors toward the Christians, whose Cold War talk about the "Free World" was back in current usage among the Reaganites. The consecration took place in May at a meeting Habib granted Bashir all on his own, rather than as a member of a larger Christian delegation. It was an odd, but logical, decision. At face value, the United States was rewarding a headstrong young man who had done his best to frustrate American policy and complicate Lebanon's reconstruction. Bashir had thwarted American plans to reinforce the authority of Lebanon's government—specifically, he had crippled its efforts to reconstruct the Lebanese Army—and, together with his associates, was believed to have been responsible, despite formal denials, for the attempt on Ambassador Dean's life. But Habib's approach was pragmatic. Like him or not, Bashir Gemayel now was the strongest single force in Lebanon. The Syrians would no doubt ask if Bashir had been consulted, though the Moslems and the Left would scream that the United States was playing favorites and all but formally approving an alliance between its old Israeli ally and its new Christian friends. Habib was also well aware that the Reagan administration was under strong pressure from mainstream American Catholics and Protestants and not just the old Zionist lobby and their Bible Belt fundamentalist allies. But the most telling argument was that Bashir's asking price was next to nothing.

Almost immediately after his first meeting with Habib, and with admittedly little to show for it, Bashir was boasting that the new American understanding for his cause constituted "the greatest victory in our six years of struggle." Over the months he was to admit that in 1975 the United States, the Vatican, and Western Europe "were against us." This implicit acknowledgment of past errors of judgment was something of a novelty for a Lebanese Christian leader with strong claims to omniscience. In any case, Bashir's newfound American life buoy made it easier for him to acquiesce in the formal Syrian demand that the Lebanese Christian leadership—meaning Bashir himself—agree in writing to sever all ties with Israel. What Bashir trumpeted as U.S. endorsement also allowed him to move toward President Sarkis politically—a constant American concern and repayment for the crucial green light Sarkis had given Habib to consecrate the militia leader. Even after his return from a visit to the United States in August, where he was received by then Under Secretary of State William Clark and other officials, Bashir Gemayel conceded he had "nothing tangible so far" to show from the Americans. But the visit to America, although arranged by his own devotees in the Phalangist-controlled American Lebanese League, had helped him get over a very bad patch. Not for the first time, but for the first time with such insistence, questions were being asked in Marounistan. The American trip was yet another godsend that had friend and foe alike convinced that Bashir and his associates had more lives than a cat.

On the Israeli front, Begin in fact had accepted the U.S.-imposed freeze on operations in Lebanon. Now he turned his attention—and that of his electorate—to the much more spectacular Israeli Air Force raid that destroyed Iraq's Osirak nuclear reactor outside Baghdad on June 7. That one-shot operation was in the grand Israeli tradition, involved no troublesome Maronites, and surprised and embarrassed the Americans while gaining their sneaking admiration for its daring.

With his once-problematic reelection assured, Begin might have been expected to relax. But even before he began forming his new coalition government, on July 10 he ordered his air force to strike systematically at Palestinian guerrilla targets in Lebanon. Invoked to justify the aerial onslaught was the obvious buildup of conventional armaments in Palestinian hands, but that was itself the less advertised consequence of Israel's own increasingly ferocious preemptive-strike policy. To the familiar refugee-camp, crossroads, and port targets were added Lebanon's main oil refinery at Zahrani, and all but one of the nine bridges over the Litani and Zahrani rivers in Lebanon. Israeli generals were to argue that the objective was to create maximum havoc for Lebanese civilian traffic and turn the Lebanese against the Palestinians, that the destruction of the bridges was a necessary preparation for any major ground operation against the PLO between the Litani and the Zahrani designed to put northern Israel well beyond the eighteen-mile range of Soviet-provided 130-millimeter artillery and Katyusha rockets. (That the bridges had not been bombed during the 1978 Litani invasion was a major criticism of that operation.) Predictably, it was the Lebanese who suffered the most: many more Lebanese than Palestinians were killed, and the guerrillas long ago had stockpiled arms, ammunition, gasoline, and other supplies in anticipation of just such an Israeli attack. The Palestinians held their fire for three days, then began shelling and rocketing northern Israel with an efficiency that staggered the Israelis.

Begin's riposte came on July 17, when nine Israeli fighter-bombers of American manufacture attacked the crowded working-class Fakhani district in West Beirut that houses some, but by no means all, PLO offices. The Palestinians had long since dispersed their key men and offices. More than one hundred twenty Lebanese and Palestinians were killed, most of them civilians, in the thirty-minute raid. Ten buildings were hit, eight of them having nothing to do with the PLO—despite the Israeli Air Force's claims to pinpoint precision. In Beirut the attack was seen as a logical Israeli step in the ever-escalating war against the Palestinians—horrible, yes, but in fact not much more so than other violence committed against Lebanon since the Israelis first unleashed their retaliatory raids in the 1960s. Inured Lebanese watched the raiding aircraft from their apartment balconies and were genuinely surprised when the outside world reacted by universally condemning Begin for bombing Beirut. The outside world had soon forgotten other wanton Israeli acts of aggression in the past. Why should television footage of Fakhani move foreigners, especially Americans, to rage, when dozens of Israeli raids went virtually unnoticed in the West? Rabid anti-Palestinian Lebanese in Marounistan shrugged off the raid because they sensed that Israel would not have the nerve to unleash a full-scale offensive, which alone, in their eyes, would justify the bombing.

The spectacle was scarcely new. This was not the first time that Lebanese had seen civilian victims of Israeli bombings along the coastal road, their charred remains stuck to the cars where they had died without a warning buzzing. All too familiar, after six years of war, were the innards of apartments—a child's tricycle, or a twisted metal bed frame—dangling from shattered, paneless windows and broken balconies, the nervous teenagers firing their weapons impotently in the air as if to give themselves courage. To live in Beirut is to learn to die without reason.

No one could produce a rational explanation for the Israeli onslaught. Some Lebanese suggested Begin wanted to thwart efforts at a Christian-Syrian rapprochement, which had taken the form of a letter from Bashir Gemayel renouncing his ties with Israel. Others insisted Begin was out to bedevil American-Saudi relations: in its naiveté the Reagan administration, the theory went, thought its "regional damage control" had been successful when Habib's spring mission effectively put *Syria* off limits to Israel, but had failed to realize that the Israelis were convinced the White House had given them carte blanche to hit the Lebanese-based *Palestinians*; it apparently had not dawned on Reagan that the Saudis and other Gulf states bankrolled and supported the PLO, in return for the Palestinians' toleration of their vulnerable feudal political systems. Striking at the PLO—if done brazenly and in publicly announced concert with Israel—was potentially more damaging to American interests than Washington grasped. The Israelis, so the theory concluded, had found the foolproof way to make trouble for Washington while pretending to carry out its will by punishing terrorists.

But in Israel the Palestinians were administering the kind of lesson the Israelis had grown accustomed to meting out themselves. Instead of Lebanese fleeing, this time it was tens of thousands of panicky Israelis, their civil servants and elected officials in the van, who deserted the north—from Qiryat Shemona in the east, Metulla on the border itself, and Nahariyya on the Mediterranean coast. It was not just the Palestinians who savored this spectacle, as their gunners hit twenty-eight Israeli towns and settlements and damaged crops and orchards. Here, before a watching world, and despite the Israeli military censors' best efforts, was unfolding the negation of the Israeli rationale for preemptive strikes.

"Unless we retaliate when the north is attacked, word leaks out in five or six days, to Haifa, Tel Aviv, Jerusalem. And the predominantly underprivileged North African Jews who people the north will flee and spread panic as they go," an Israeli historian had told me the year before. Now the prophecy had come true. Israeli arms proved the catalyst of Israel's own embarrassment, and there was little for Begin to do but cut his losses. Philip Habib, who had returned to the Middle East, now had as his principal problem finding a formula to save face for Begin, who had sworn never to deal with the PLO. On July 24, for the first time in Israel's thirty-three-year history, an Israeli government agreed not to conduct military operations against the Palestinians anywhere, even temporarily. The vagueness of this cease-fire arrangement allowed Israel to deny direct or indirect dealings with the PLO, and the Palestinians to deny they had recognized Israel's legitimacy. Opposition leader Peres was not about to let Begin off so easily. "The cease-fire was made with the PLO," he said. "There's no point in concealing the truth, which must be spoken, even when you're in government." Begin's case was not improved by his threadbare insistence that he was negotiating not with the PLO but with the government of Lebanon, via the United States and the United Nations. After all, for years Israel, with Christian militia help, had done its best to frustrate efforts to reestablish Lebanon's central governmental authority. No less a personage than General Yaakov Even, the Israeli Army's chief spokesman, had boasted in April, "We are on the offensive, we are the aggressors who are penetrating the so-called border of the so-called sovereign state of Lebanon and we go after them wherever they hide." This view of Lebanese sovereignty was by no means unique in Israel.

In the United States, even as stalwart a friend of Israel as Senator Henry Jackson remarked that Begin had a "personality problem." As criticism poured in, the Israeli riposte seemed oddly discordant, lacking its usual true pitch. For example, cold-bloodedly summing up the previous two weeks' death toll—five in Israel as against more than five hundred in Lebanon—Rabin opined that Americans were overreacting because they "still remember the Vietnam War." Begin, he said, should have taken into account that "people there have an abhorrence of striking civilians indiscriminately." Rabin, the erstwhile hawk, was talking much like Moshe Sharett at his most dovish. In a 1961 diary entry, Sharett had ruminated on the 1955 Israeli massacre of Arab villagers and the fact that the political and military establishment had whitewashed those responsible. Sharett worried that "public opinion, the army, the police" had concluded "that Arab blood can be freely shed. . . . All this must bring about revulsion in the sense of justice and honesty in public opinion; it must make the state appear in the eyes of the world as a savage state that does not recognize the principles of justice as they have been established and accepted by contemporary society."

The United States was delighted that once again the worst had been averted. State Department spokesman Dean Fischer fatuously opined that the cease-fire would "evolve into a long-term solution to the problem of the region and enable the Lebanese government to maintain control over all areas of the country that are in dispute or where violence has flared." Taken literally, that would eliminate even the six square miles over which President Sarkis reigned precariously. Here was Israel going through the formal motions of desperately wanting to hold accountable a government that could not even enforce traffic regulations.

This four-month period of violence had shaken the foundations of Israeli geopolitical and military assumptions. Instead of an all-powerful, ever-wise Israel, such as was dear to the radical Lebanese Christians, the Jewish state had proved itself as bumbling, contradictory, and ineffective as any other Middle East player. The lesson that the rest of the Arab world had learned from its performance in the 1973 war finally had been brought home to the most thickheaded of Maronites. Now that the Palestinians had proved once again—and this time definitively—that their mobile rocket launchers and long-range artillery could hit northern Israeli settlements at will, even Major Haddad and his much-vaunted security belt had become less important to Israel. Israel, which in the past had disclaimed responsibility for Haddad as a way of continuing to use his territory and militia to harass the Lebanese and Palestinians, now insisted that his "Republic of Free Lebanon" be covered by the cease-fire provisions. For once, Israel was on the defensive. Air power wasn't capable of knocking out the Palestinians' firepower, especially the truck-mounted Katyusha multiple-rocket launchers. The long-rumored land operation was no assured cinch, either.

Within the establishment, officials were running to catch up. In the words of one well-placed professional observer, "Before they knew it, the Israelis were spending a lot of time looking at maps they had not looked at before." Masters of tactical intelligence, they found it a lot easier to know in whose garage the Palestinians had stashed a tank than to figure out what was going on in a Maronite leader's head. Bashir Gemayel seemed to have run the Zahle operation according to his own timetable, and now the Israelis were having serious second thoughts. Even if they were to believe the Christians when they claimed their presence in Zahle was never meant as a springboard for further expansion of "liberated" territory, the Israelis now had to realize that the Syrians had legitimate reasons to be doubtful. Soon the Israelis decided that they had become engaged in Lebanon beyond the horizon of their own best interests.

Even so normally hawkish a politician as Deputy Defense Minister Mordechai Zippori questioned Israel's relations with Bashir Gemayel, which "were likely to create situations not necessarily under our control." He warned, "The complex tangle of internal disputes in Lebanon poses a great danger," and then ticked off some home truths that the Israeli establishment had long played down. "The Christians no longer constitute a majority of the Lebanese population, and this minority is further broken up into small forces and groups sometimes hostile to one another," he said—as if dispensing some closely guarded secret. "Moreover, only one faction within the Christian population is willing to accept the aid we are offering, and this faction totals 35 percent of the Christians and has no chance of ever controlling Lebanon." Suddenly, the Israeli public was being told that their government had been backing a long shot, and that the old hope of creating a series of mosaic states was baseless. Such talk was the kind of brutal realpolitik scarcely likely to encourage Christian daydreaming about reestablishing their domination over Lebanon. No wonder the Syrians decided to risk a showdown, accusations of genocide notwithstanding.

So finally the realization dawned that Israeli priorities had been allowed to get out of whack. What are we Israelis doing up there in the north? asked some Israeli officials. Our guys shouldn't take needless risks for those Christian crazies, argued others. Suddenly, the clandestine relations with Lebanon's northern Christians—involving at times dozens of Israeli advisers in Marounistan—were out in the open and on the verge of being out of control. "Israelis at the very top were taking decisions about the employment of their armed forces," a senior diplomat recounted, "and talking to wild-haired guys in what passes for a political system in Beirut. Suddenly, this became a major part of Israeli policy. Then the Israelis took a deep breath and stepped back."

The July violence further cooled Israeli ardor for involvement in Lebanon. The Palestinians' new weapons had reached not only such old targets as Qiryat Shemona but also Nahariyya, where Soviet-built 130-millimeter guns guided by forward spotters had succeeded in walking in accurate barrages for the first time. "The Israelis had either forgotten or not understood the scale of violence, and their inability to stop it was a shock," a diplomat said. Begin, who had campaigned by promising an end to rocket attacks against northern settlements, visited Nahariyya, Metulla, and Qiryat Shemona and claimed he had never said that at all. "Everyone who knows the truth knows what I said was: 'Patience, the day will come when there will be no more Katyusha rockets on Qiryat Shemona,' and I repeat what I said then: 'patience, my friends.' "

To many Israelis, this sounded like the most transparent of justifications. A disaffected former Begin adviser expressed a much more widely held view when he denounced the Lebanese Christians to me as unreliable, vacillating, and dangerous. "They'll drop us at the first occasion," he complained. "We should stay well clear of them, at least of the northern Christians; Haddad still serves as a buffer. Let all the parties in Lebanon eat each other." Then he spat out, "Habib saved us, saved us from ourselves. We're lucky to be back at square one." He wandered off into an internal monologue about what Israel should do now that the Palestinians had accurate long-range weapons north of the Litani. "You cannot destroy every truck fifteen miles north of the border," he muttered. "We'll never have the strategic depth we need to confront modern weapons. There's no end of possibilities for transferring explosives from one point of the planet to another. But nothing compares with foot patrols entering a house, blowing it up, kidnapping people for interrogation—all done by hand."

7. All Fall Down

With the formation of Begin's new government in early August 1981, all the unresolved contradictions surrounding Israel's policy in Lebanon were swept aside in a riptide of willfulness and militarism. Chief architect of the new policy was Defense Minister Ariel Sharon, finally in possession of that most prized of portfolios because of his lifelong penchant for violence, recklessness, and power. During the 1956 Suez action, Sharon had disobeyed orders and committed his paratroop battalion against strong Egyptian forces in Sinai's Mitla pass; thirty-eight Israelis were killed, an enormous loss for the casualty-conscious Israeli Army. His career suffered from that incident, more even than from the series of provocative border raids that he had conducted in the 1950s, when he commanded the controversial Unit 101, raids involving high Arab civilian casualties—some critics called them atrocities. He had retired from the army—passed over for Chief of Staff, in large part because of the lingering scandal from 1956—only months before the 1973 Yom Kippur War with Egypt and

Syria. Then his fortunes changed, and he became the only Israeli hero of that war when he reversed a disastrous situation and in a daring, if close-run, operation, crossed the Suez Canal and trapped the Egyptian Third Army in the Sinai. After the war, he used that feat of arms to launch himself into right-wing politics. A great bear of a man with a shock of white hair and a substantial paunch, Sharon had the ambition, charisma, charm, and penchant for the unorthodox of a Middle East Napoleon. (That was not a comparison he discouraged.)

Within months of becoming Defense Minister, Sharon was insisting publicly that Israel's military sphere of influence in the 1980s spread far beyond the Arab world "to englobe Turkey, Iran, Pakistan, and up to Central and North Africa." Israel was "the world's fourth-largest military power," he boasted. Like many before him in similar situations, Sharon favored a forward policy, preferring to fight Israel's battles on the other man's territory. (Capacity often creates intention in the military mind.) His goals for an Israeli-dominated Middle East were clearly enunciated. He intended to crush the PLO as a military and political force in Lebanon; annex the Israeli-occupied West Bank and Gaza Strip; unseat King Hussein and give Jordan to the Palestinians, who already made up nearly two thirds of the population there. Syria and Iraq were to be destabilized, and the conservative pro-American oil kingdoms were to be cowed into grateful silence for being delivered from what Israel saw as PLO blackmail and for being protected against the encroachments of the Iranian revolution.

"Pax Hebraica" absorbed the old dream of crushing mainstream Sunni Moslem predominance in the Middle East, if not by out-and-out creation of friendly, dependent states run by religious minorities, then at least by encouragement of their aspirations. After all, the French and British had done just that during their League of Nations mandates in the area. Thus, the Christians were to be helped in Lebanon—and why not the Druze and Shia Moslems, for that matter, since they were located nearer to Israel's borders?

Interference in a neighbor's affairs verges on imperialism—which is a concept theoretically banished from the Israeli lexicon—and it presupposes a sound economic base, but Israel had a $25 billion foreign debt and quasi-total dependence on the United States for military, financial, and diplomatic support. However, a generation of American indulgence of willful Israeli policies—and, since 1975, massive infusions of money and arms to secure Israel's agreement to the Sinai disengagement and the Camp David peace process that ensued—had encouraged Israeli militarists to dream.

More than a decade earlier, Moshe Dayan liked to tell visitors that the "Americans give us money, matériel, and advice. We take the money, we take the matériel, but we don't take the advice." The Israelis, in any case, were always "a step and a half ahead of" the Americans, as an American diplomat with long Middle East experience noted. Now, despite increasing international criticism of Israel's willful ways, the United States government gave only advice. Thus did the Begin government prepare the fifth Arab-Israeli war. In Israeli eyes, it was to be the first of these conflicts in which the existence of the Israeli state was not threatened. What Begin and Sharon failed to appreciate—despite repeated warnings before and during the invasion from eminent Israeli Arabists—was that the war would involve Israel in the thickets of perhaps the most brutal and brutalizing society in the Middle East.

Israel telegraphed its invasion of Lebanon the way bad prizefighters telegraph punches. Yasser Arafat was so sure the invasion was coming that for months in 1982 he entertained foreign visitors late at night by drawing sketches explaining just how the Israelis would do it: a paratroop drop here, an amphibious landing there, smashing through UN lines in various places. "Don't be surprised," Bashir Gemayel confided to Lebanese newspaper editors in March, "if you stick your necks out of the office windows and see Israeli tanks in the streets." His brother Amin, during a visit to Washington the previous fall, had been asked by an American Arabist friend when—not if—the invasion was due. The Druze leader Walid Jumblatt was warned of the near-certain attack when he was received at the State Department during the winter.

Past masters at creating a sense of inevitability, the Israelis, virtually from the minute they agreed to the cease-fire in July 1981, began to make a case for the invasion of Lebanon by complaining vociferously that the Palestinians there were violating the cease-fire provisions. The United Nations, careful recorders of all violations in south Lebanon, failed to corroborate these charges. The world had become so accustomed to Israeli military operations in Lebanon that even the United States and other concerned governments took them for granted, and worried about other potential Israeli targets of opportunity. The Americans now offered Israel a security treaty designed as much to end the depredations as to protect Israel or to procure bases and facilities for the U.S. armed forces. But execution of the final arrangements was postponed when in December the Begin government annexed the Golan Heights seized from Syria in 1967. In the early months of 1982, Israel kept the world on tenterhooks before honoring its peace-treaty obligations to Egypt and evacuating the last settlement, Yamit, in the Sinai. Barely two weeks before the April 25, 1982, deadline for Israel to complete that evacuation, U.S. satellite photographs disclosed the massing of Israeli troops and matériel near the Lebanese border; this news was credited with thwarting the invasion now believed to be certain, a military offensive that would distract Israeli public opinion, which was divided over the withdrawal from the Sinai.

Thereafter, Israel again sought to justify an invasion to counter Palestinian cease-fire violations; the Israeli embassy in Washington produced a list of thirty-two alleged major ones. Close examination of the list revealed that these had all taken place inside Haddad's border strip, which was now known as "Free Lebanon." The first Israeli cease-fire violation—in which Israeli warplanes on April 21 killed twenty persons and wounded more than sixty—was carried out in reprisal for the death of an Israeli officer whose Jeep blew up on a mine in territory outside Haddad's lines and under nominal UN control. In theory, at least, no Israeli should have been in either place. The PLO did not respond. On May 9, the PLO and its Lebanese leftist allies did fire off thirty rounds from the Tyre pocket in the direction of Israel. But this was only after Israeli aircraft early in the afternoon heavily bombed Damour and Zahrani for no apparent reason. Israeli exaggerations were so well understood in Washington that the U.S. embassy in Beirut was not-so-gently told that its insistent cables reestablishing the facts need not be repeated.

The American government gave signs of exhaustion with Israel's reiterated feints. After all, Palestinian attacks had all but stopped, thanks to the UN buffer zone, the Haddad enclave, and sophisticated sensors along the electrified double fence at the border itself. Artillery and rocket fire directed against Israel was, almost without exception, in retaliation for Israeli provocations. In recent years the PLO guerrillas—and splinter groups at that—had been reduced to such stunts as hang gliding to maintain the myth of their ability to infiltrate men across the Israeli border. But Israel single-mindedly pursued its objective. In January, Sharon spent a night and two days in East Beirut with the Christian militia, planning the invasion. By mid-February, the entire operation was a notorious open secret in Beirut, and Israel had resumed its arms and ammunition deliveries to the Christians. Its favored delivery point was a cove at Tabarja, nicknamed "the Israeli embassy" because of the frequency of its after-hours operations. Foreign military specialists spoke authoritatively about the arrival by barge of American-built tank transporters and tractors for heavy artillery. These reports, true or not, produced delighted winks and nods among the Christians, who were desperate for any indication that the United States supported them. So, too, did the CIA, when it established links with the Lebanese Forces. This decision was dictated principally by a desire to give Bashir Gemayel an alternative to a renewed deal with Israel, and the Lebanese Forces provided intelligence on the PLO and Syria. No other Lebanese politician enjoyed such a prestigious arrangement with the CIA, which excluded, however, any active cooperation on the ground. What a change from the days when Americans held Bashir responsible for the attempt on Ambassador Dean's life!

With Sharon in the lead, the Begin government had worked itself into a situation so delicate that the slightest upset, the merest affront, was bound to set off the long-planned operation.

On May 20, Sharon flew to Washington, where he was closeted alone with Secretary Haig. For that reason, no official record of their conversation exists, and Haig, who has never made a mystery of his pro-Israeli proclivities, has steadfastly denied that he encouraged or condoned Sharon's invasion plans. Sharon explained he had traveled to the United States to tell Haig that Israel was going to invade willy-nilly, and that Washington should not be surprised, as he admitted it had been by the raid on the Iraqi nuclear reactor. In Lebanon "the situation is such," he said he told Haig, "we cannot hold ourselves back much longer." Former President Carter later claimed—and Haig vehemently denied—that the Secretary had given Israel the green light for the invasion, but in any case that view was almost universally accepted in the Middle East. In the Arabs' advanced state of political disintegration, blaming the United States had become a standard gesture to mask their own impotence. Years may elapse before the relevant documents fall into the public domain—if, indeed, any exist, since sensitive information is often not committed to paper for fear of photocopied leaks—and it may be impossible to establish the precise truth. But given the nature of Israel's dependence on the United States, it is fair to say that only Washington could have stopped Begin and Sharon once the invasion was under way. Past experience proved that passive reiteration of standing policy had no visible impact on Begin; active and forceful intervention was called for if the Reagan administration wanted to discourage the Lebanese war. No wonder that Bashir Gemayel listened politely when American diplomats told him that Washington opposed any invasion. He said the Israelis would invade anyhow.

The available evidence indicates that the Reagan administration did nothing to stop the invasion in its early stages—in contrast with Carter's initial forceful actions when Israel invaded south Lebanon in March 1978. In 1982, time and again, the United States refused to go along with UN Security Council draft resolutions demanding Israel's immediate withdrawal from Lebanon. Indeed, so consistently pro-Israel was the American voting pattern that Middle East Machiavellis were convinced that Haig was actively in cahoots with Israel.

The official Israeli justification for the invasion of Lebanon was provided on June 3, when Ambassador Shlomo Argov was shot and seriously wounded in London. Under its preemptive-strike doctrine, Israel held the PLO and Lebanon responsible for any violence done any Israeli anywhere. Within five days the ambassador's assailants were identified by British officials as members of Abu Nidal's discredited Palestinian terrorist group. Sometimes in the pay of Syria, sometimes in that of its archenemy Iraq, Abu Nidal was so much at odds with the PLO that Arafat had placed a price on his head years earlier. But both Arafat and Abu Nidal were Palestinian. The Israelis correctly gauged that the outside world had about as much time for the subtleties of Palestinian politics as the Americans had had in the Cold War of the 1950s for distinguishing "good" Yugoslav Communists from the orthodox Moscow variety.

After intensive Israeli bombing raids throughout south Lebanon on June 4 and 5, Israeli ground troops invaded the following day at 11:00 a.m. Within hours, Israel announced that the objective of "Operation Peace for Galilee" was a twenty-five-mile-deep demilitarized zone, comprising roughly a third of Lebanon, to protect Israel's northern border area from PLO rocket and artillery fire. By the next day the Israelis had seized Beaufort Castle, with its line-of-sight view of the

Galilee; the Tyre pocket they'd dared not take in 1978; and most of the PLO southern heartland between the Litani and Zahrani rivers. Begin had made good his election promise to Israelis of the Galilee.

But Sharon had other ideas. PLO resistance, at times spirited, was unable to blunt the drive of Israel's armed forces. They leapfrogged men and tanks around PLO positions by helicopter, staged amphibious landings, and, as always, dominated the skies. Within two days, Sharon had armored columns racing north along the narrow coastal strip to within sight of Beirut's southern suburbs. Other armored units sliced through the thinly defended Shuf Mountains, where few Palestinian or Syrian troops had been stationed, in deference to the Druze Moslems, whose turf it was. Israeli troops and aircraft pushed back Syrian troops, who were lulled into a false sense of security by promises to spare them if they refrained from helping the Palestinians. Israeli aircraft, mostly of American provenance and equipped with the latest U.S. weaponry, destroyed the Syrians' Soviet-supplied ground-to-air defense systems astraddle the Beirut–Damascus road in the narrow Beqaa valley of eastern Lebanon, and shot down more than eighty aircraft, roughly a quarter of the Syrian Air Force. Israeli drones, which confused Syrian radar, shared credit for the job with U.S.-provided Hawkeye aircraft, crammed with electronic gear that monitored the entire Syrian air-defense system. Beaten, but the only one of the Arab countries to fight, Syria agreed to a cease-fire with Israel on June 11. On June 13, Sharon led Israeli tanks into Baabda, seat of the Lebanese central government's unquestioned sovereignty over six square miles. Ostensibly, Sharon wanted to link up with his Christian allies. But his calculated act seemed also to be a defiant high sign to Bashir Gemayel to kick Elias Sarkis out of the Presidential Palace. That was perhaps the only surprise in a virtually unopposed early campaign. On the night of June 13, the PLO—and half a million Palestinian and mostly Moslem Lebanese civilians—were encircled in West Beirut, and within days Israeli officials began, under American pressure, vaguely promising not to enter West Beirut itself. The siege of Beirut, which was to last seventy days, had begun. As he was to do on other occasions, Sharon had forced his fellow cabinet ministers' hands. Begin was prompted to note wryly that he always knew what his Defense Minister was doing, "before or after."

In retrospect, it was easy enough to see what motivated Sharon. As critics of Israel's limited ground assault in 1981 so tellingly had argued, simply to seize the area between the two rivers meant perpetual occupation; if the Israeli Army were withdrawn, the PLO would come back in again, within rocket and artillery range of the Galilee. Every successive Palestinian target led farther north to yet another. So, from the very beginning, the only practical military solution was to destroy the PLO headquarters and infrastructure in Beirut. In Israeli military eyes, moreover, forcing the PLO leadership out of Lebanon seemed sure to weaken Arafat's political and diplomatic standing.

Arafat readily understood the danger Sharon represented. In any case, he was powerless. Before the invasion, he had chosen to rely on American diplomatic assurances that the Israelis would not be allowed to invade. If the PLO were now thrown out of Lebanon—or, better yet, reduced to mad-dog terrorism that would destroy its growing political and diplomatic legitimacy—then Israel stood a better chance of annexing the West Bank and Gaza Strip, still thoroughly loyal to Arafat's leadership despite his many errors.

Israel skillfully exploited those accumulated errors to justify its own war aims, and at first insisted it was acting solely to protect its northern citizens. But when Sharon ordered his men farther north toward Beirut, the argument changed. Israel insisted its armed forces were doing the civilized world a favor by ridding it of the "center of international terrorism" that was West Beirut. A decade *after* the height of Palestinian terrorism, years *after* the guerrillas officially eschewed airliner hijacking and other headline-grabbing spectaculars, Israel successfully recalled those past excesses to justify its expanded war. Furthermore, the Israelis argued that they were not invading Lebanon but, rather, liberating the country from the Palestinians and Syrians in a selfless act of generosity. Had not pretty Christian girls welcomed Israeli troops as "liberators" by throwing rice and flowers in their path?

The self-congratulatory Israeli mood at first knew few bounds. The Israelis had not invaded Lebanon, they said, but, rather, "liberated" it. The United States should see that it was as big a winner as Israel itself—and without the blood of a single American being spilled. The Syrians had been put in their place, their Soviet alliance and Soviet weaponry left in ruins; they, too, would fall into the American orbit, realizing at long last that their assassinated archenemy, Anwar Sadat, had been right when he preached that only Washington held the high cards. Syria's loss of influence should also count with the hectored pro-American oil-producing monarchies and sheikhdoms of the Gulf, beset as they were by Iran's threats of subversion: the Syria-Iran alliance now meant little. In any case, no one—except the Palestinians—even mentioned employing the oil weapon to bring about Western intercession. And all the other members of the so-called Steadfastness Front that had opposed Sadat's separate peace with Israel—Algeria, Libya, and South Yemen—were mute and ineffective. The peace treaty with Egypt was surviving its baptism of fire—and it was not a short conflict along classic Middle East lines, but a war that went on and on. More demonstrations against the war were staged in Israel and the Occupied Territories than in the Arab world. Did the notion of an Arab world, an Arab nation stretching from the Atlantic to the Persian Gulf, even exist? The once-proud Arab nationalist movement, that symbol of assertive mainstream Sunni Islam, had lost its voice as well as its muscle. "Thirty years behind, that's what we are," a Syrian officer gloomily confided to a Lebanese friend. "The Russians give us equipment which is ten years old; the equipment the Americans give Israel is ten years ahead of the Soviets' best today. That makes twenty years. And despite all the stress we've laid on education and technology, the Israelis are ten years ahead of us. So there's your thirty years."

Then, on June 25, as Sharon's forces for the second successive day unleashed intensive artillery, naval gunfire, and aerial bombardment against West Beirut, Haig resigned. He did so under pressure. Lebanon was only a part, most likely a fairly small part, of his undoing. But whatever deal Haig had cut with Sharon in Washington—and informed American diplomats concluded he had done just that—now came to an end.

His successor, George P. Shultz, did not assume full operating authority for the better part of two weeks, but up in the hills at Yarze, overlooking Beirut, at the residence of U.S. Ambassador Robert S. Dillon, Philip C. Habib was elated. He danced in jubilation. Had there been a bottle of champagne in the house (which had been transformed into a working embassy, since the downtown premises were closed for security reasons), he would have drunk it in celebration. Since arriving back in the Middle East on June 7, Habib had had an unenviable role to play. Hamstrung by Haig's obvious pro-Israeli bias, he nonetheless was supposed to be negotiating a series of cease-fires. Thanks to Israel's military prowess, Syria had accepted a cease-fire on June 11, but the

Israelis kept breaking it at their convenience. Habib had all but despaired of getting a handle on the situation. But now he had just talked the Israelis into their first meaningful cease-fire with the Palestinians. With Haig out of the way, Habib and the equally delighted embassy staff could get to work trying to salvage what he considered were vital American national interests. Those interests were vastly more complex and vulnerable than Sharon and Haig, two ambitious professional-soldiers-turned-ministers, could imagine.

For if by then the United States shared Israel's interest in forcing the PLO and the Syrian Army out of Beirut, any common interests ended there. Cutting the PLO down to size was fine with Reagan, who never progressed much beyond the view of considering all Palestinians as terrorists. Humiliating the Syrians, and especially their Soviet protectors, also paid dividends with the arch-conservatives in the White House inner circle. But the United States had no real Middle East policy—or, rather, had a theoretically impossible policy of having both Israel and the moderate Arab states as allies. At the best of times, this so-called policy depended on each ally's tolerating the other's existence and claims to American attention. But it risked coming apart when Israel inflicted such humiliation, embarrassment, and pain that the conservative Arabs felt obliged to denounce their would-be American protectors. Whatever misgivings the Saudi, Kuwaiti, and other oil sheikhs felt in their heart-of-hearts about the future existence of an independent Palestinian state, they could not afford to stand by as Americans acquiesced in Israel's blatant destruction of an Arab capital. American credibility was at stake. Never before had the Israelis dared go so far. Never before had the United States and the Arabs been so much at their mercy.

With every passing day, Sharon and his generals were proving they could and would use their awesome, often American-provided, firepower against their foes, without regard to mounting civilian casualties and destruction. For the first time in their long series of wars against the Arabs, the Israelis were using their unopposed air force to bomb an Arab capital systematically. Something was very wrong. The Sharon blitzkrieg had turned into siege warfare, the very antithesis of classic Israeli military doctrine, which favors fast, inexpensive wars. Like every other party to Lebanese violence since 1975, the Israelis were now resorting to heavy artillery, a sure local sign that they were unwilling to risk heavy casualties of their own (estimated at a likely six hundred) in storming West Beirut, and were trying instead to terrorize their foe into total surrender. But well provisioned, well armed, and left no choice but to fight, the Palestinians refused to buckle. Where were the triumphant Israeli troops of yore, winning their "clean" victories against professional Arab armies in the uninhabited sands of the Sinai or the sparsely settled Golan? Imperceptibly over the years, Israel had become part of its callous Middle East environment. Two myths were buried during the war: the myth that Lebanese Moslems loved the Palestinians; and the myth that Israelis whose families once lived in Arab countries empathized with the Arabs—if anything, they were tougher than their fellow Israelis of European stock. Why was the outside world so upset with this "non-invasion" of Lebanon, the Israelis asked, when the Syrians, only months before, had gotten away with butchering thousands and destroying whole neighborhoods in the city of Hama?

The very notion that Israel was a Westernized, if not Western, country had boomeranged and, with it, Israeli claims to a unique place in contemporary ethics. Here, for all to see, on color television the world over, was one Middle Eastern society dealing with another in keeping with locally acceptable norms. Israel's use of informers (hooded, at that), the arrest and detention of thousands of Palestinian and Lebanese men in the hot summer sun, the tales of torture and humiliation—all this smacked of "Arab-bashing." The Israeli government's reaction was predictable. These negative impressions could only be the work of Israel's enemies, it said, the invention of professional anti-Semites, the craven distortions of a foreign press corps in Beirut that was notoriously in thrall to the PLO, for fear of its collective life.

The Israeli government had had a whiff of the effect of television during its 1978 invasion of south Lebanon. The late Moshe Dayan, then Foreign Minister, had warned that TV coverage of that operation, with its "pictures of long, struggling lines of families with their old and young, leaving their homes and plodding to find a place of refuge, scarred our good name." Now, day in and day out, television was sending out, via satellite, film and tape showing the Israeli armed forces' handiwork. Efforts at censorship only caused further embarrassment, for here was a country that advertised itself as the only democracy in the region resorting to a subterfuge identified with dictatorships. In any case, the Israelis could not stop the film and tapes, the still photos and the dispatches, from getting abroad.

It was television that hurt the most. There's something strangely beautiful about the orange explosions, the slightly delayed sounds of impact, the billowing clouds of smoke and dust of massive artillery barrages and bombs, especially when filmed at the end of an afternoon, when the harsh light of a Levantine summer gives way to mauves and pastels. The effect is devastating when such scenes are juxtaposed with close-ups of men, women, and children, Palestinian and Lebanese, wounded by cluster bombs and high explosives and white phosphorous; with images of pathetic efforts made to dig survivors out from beneath the rubble of apartment houses. The disproportion between the quality and quantity of Israel's weaponry and that employed against them, especially in Beirut, did little to further its traditional image as David facing an Arab Goliath.

There is nothing quite so stomach-turning as the burns ward of a hospital; after Israeli gunners, once renowned for their precision, began landing rounds on Beirut institutions marked with enormous Red Cross flags, including the headquarters of the International Committee of the Red Cross itself, the makeshift clinics set up in Beirut's basements and garages were especially horrific. Surgeons began doing what they dubbed the "Begin amputation" of limbs shattered by cluster bombs and other advanced ammunition utilized by the Israelis. On three occasions—on August 1, 4, and 12—Sharon's men and machinery subjected West Beirut to punishment so intensive and indiscriminate that terror was the result, whatever the Israelis' objective may have been. No longer was the fire concentrated, as at the start of the siege, on the southern suburbs and the Palestinian refugee camps south of the Corniche Mazraa boulevard, which the Israelis had arbitrarily decided was the city limits. They had, after all, promised time and again not to enter West Beirut. Why, aside from blind vengeance, Sharon unleashed those three terrible August attacks remains unclear. He was certainly misrepresenting what was happening on the ground and was gratuitously using his heaviest weaponry against whole sections of the city proper, where few if any Palestinian guerrillas were stationed. The only rational explanation is that he was seeking to empty West Beirut of its Lebanese residents.

The United States was not pleased. Despite Sharon's claims that the punishment was required to force the PLO to leave Beirut, both U.S.

and Palestinian negotiators—as well as their Lebanese go-betweens—agreed that by the end of July Arafat wanted to go, and go fast. After a period of standing pat and proclaiming that West Beirut would be another Stalingrad and a new Hanoi, his spokesmen made it clear they felt no useful purpose could be served by prolonging the punishment of the capital. They had proved they could take the worst Israel could dish out. They had withstood the onslaught long enough to save face and salvage their honor from the ruins of military defeat. They had hoped against hope that a long-delayed Arab League delegation to Washington would win some form of recognition for them—perhaps only a willingness to talk to them face-to-face—from the Reagan administration. The mission had failed.

The Israeli blockade became serious in July, when water and electricity supplies were cut. Fresh fruit, vegetables, even bread became scarce, although the resourceful Lebanese made it a point of honor to defy the blockade with their knowledge of the terrain and with handsome bribes. West Beirutis hunkered down in their basements, candle-lit prisons both dark and airless. Cut off from what was happening outside, like hardened war addicts they listened to the news on a bewildering variety of radio stations—the official state station, two of the Christian militias', and two of the Left, as well as those broadcasting from Israel, France, Britain, and the United States. During lulls in the bombardment, children lugging large plastic bottles patiently waited their turn at the reactivated artesian wells dating from an earlier siege, six summers before, when the Syrian Army had briefly tried to reduce West Beirut. Mohamed Kasrawi, driver and office manager for more than a generation of *New York Times* correspondents, said West Beirut was "one hundred percent dangerous," a description no one argued with. He had lost his wife and two of his daughters when the apartment-cum-office of the *Times*, where they had been staying to discourage squatters, was blown up in still-mysterious circumstances early in the war. (That apartment was the third of various Beirut residences where I've lived or worked to be destroyed.)

In the four square miles of West Beirut, nothing was off limits. Detonation of booby-trapped cars by remote control alternated with around-the-clock artillery, naval gunfire, and aerial bombardment and periods of relative calm. For the first time since Beirut came under attack in 1975, the bombardment came from all points of the compass. Squatters who had fled from the Palestinian refugee camps or shantytown suburbs camped out for months at a time in empty apartments or in the once-elegant lobbies of upper-class buildings in and around the Hamra shopping district, where it seemed safer. The poor stayed put because they had nowhere to go. The middle class and the rich stayed put for fear of losing their apartments to squatters—who were the Israelis to tell them to get out of their homes, to lose their last possessions? After more than seven years of violence only the very rich had the money left to pay for accommodation elsewhere in Lebanon, much less in Syria, Jordan, or Europe. Even middle-class savings had been exhausted years before. There simply had been too many crises over the years for that kind of luxury or self-indulgence. First with leaflets, then with the pounding bombs, Israel told the West Beirutis to leave, but until that final Israeli spasm of violence in August, at least half the population of Beirut remained. With each new cease-fire—or, rather, if the new cease-fire held for more than a day—tens of thousands would brave the hours of waiting in their cars in the sticky Mediterranean summer to return to their homes. No wonder the Israelis misjudged these people. And no wonder the Israelis kept raising the threshold of pain, hoping to drain off the civilians and leave the city open to some final extravaganza of destruction.

The pursuit of safety was illusory. I recall watching entire families rush to the basement of a modern building opposite my hotel at 4:00 a.m. Sunday, August 1, when the first Israeli fighter-bombers roared low overhead in what was to be fourteen hours of uninterrupted bombardment. There was a pre-dawn haze when they went into the building and still a bit of daylight when they emerged, sensing that the cease-fire just announced would hold. Even the Hotel Commodore, the foreign press center, spared in all past conflicts, was shelled on August 4. I'd been sleeping on the sixth floor—after working all night updating my dispatch on the Israelis' largely unsuccessful post-midnight ground assault on West Beirut—when at midmorning my colleague William Branigin called on the house telephone to suggest in his quiet but persuasive way that I join the other journalists in the basement shelter. I grabbed my typewriter, my passport, and my address books and tumbled downstairs, still half-asleep despite the shells that were landing all around the neighborhood. The clouds of dust told the story. Less than a quarter hour later, an Israeli round slammed into a room only two doors down from mine. Luckily, it was empty. Two days later, I was near the Central Bank when two Israeli planes suddenly swept low after lazily circling for fifteen minutes. Just a hundred yards away, they dropped a bomb on a seven-story apartment house that Arafat had left only minutes before. (According to Western intelligence sources, an Israeli agent had tracked Arafat to the building and activated an electronic marking device to help pinpoint the bombing.) More than two hundred Palestinian refugees, mostly Christians, were killed or wounded there, many of them trapped in the basement, which also served as one of the PLO's many safe houses. Without cranes or other modern equipment, rescuers took weeks to dig out all the bodies from under the building, which collapsed in a pile no more than four feet high, leaving surrounding structures virtually intact. More than forty West Beirut buildings were destroyed by such Israeli bombs.

The Israelis very nearly succeeded in killing Arafat in a series of attempts that must have been the world's first manhunt by air. Fed intelligence by their own spies and by local informers, the Israelis on four different occasions bombed or rocketed targets less than an hour after Arafat's departure from them, and in four other cases the PLO leader had dropped by the bombed premises within the previous twenty-four hours. At one point in August, Arafat conducted much of his business in a car, driving through West Beirut's largely deserted streets with his various interlocutors.

How far and how fast had the Israelis come from their early, simple ideas about this complicated country! It had all been so simple, and simpleminded—like the Israeli blockade plan: with Beirut blockaded, the Lebanese could and would evacuate a besieged and shelled West Beirut, leaving only the Palestinians as "legitimate targets." But the trouble was that many West Beirutis refused to leave, and those who did insisted on coming back at the least sign of a return to normalcy. But at the beginning it served no useful purpose to argue with the conquerors. Those Lebanese who knew better were in no mood to argue. The Moslems either secretly rejoiced that the Israelis had cut through the Gordian knot of Lebanon's bewildering complexities or were too busy worrying about the death and destruction the Israeli armed forces had visited on nearly half the country. In any case, the Moslems had become realists. Someone in Lebanon had to be. They knew they had lost the war—not just the present one, but the one in

1975–76. They were candid enough to admit it. Perhaps the Christians would be easier to live with now that they really had won—albeit not through any of their own doing, but thanks to Israel.

Once the Israelis made clear in June that they were coming all the way to Beirut—and not stopping halfway—the Christians of Marounistan rejoiced. It was that simple—except to the more sophisticated, who had seen soldiers come and go since 1975 and remembered that the Christians had once prayed for the Syrians to come in 1976 and had lived to regret it. Still, upper-middle-class Christian hostesses competed with one another for the presence of Israeli captains, majors, and colonels at their dinner parties. "*Shalom*," said Christian motorists at Israeli roadblocks, and all too often heard rude rejoinders from Arabic-speaking Israeli soldiers. How clever of the Israelis to speak Arabic! the Christians remarked. Soon they came to realize that these Israeli soldiers were not the idealized blue-eyed, French- or English-speaking pioneers from the kibbutzim, but, as often as not, crinkly-haired, dark-skinned men who looked Arab for the excellent reason that they or their parents had come from Arab countries. Early on, the Lebanese forces forbade Christian girls from fraternizing with the invaders, and many Christians came to feel that in fact the invaders looked down on them as just another variety of Arab. That was a sore point with the Christians of Marounistan, especially the Lebanese Forces. And, in turn, they routinely called their allies Jews rather than Israelis (in contrast to the Palestinians, who rarely allowed even a suggestion of anti-Semitism to creep into their discourse). The Christians also looked down on the Israeli soldiers *as soldiers*: they seemed slovenly in contrast to their own smartly turned-out, closely shaven militiamen; timorous and unwilling to take risks, in contrast to the Lebanese (and the Palestinians, for that matter), who had a natural affinity for the dangerous rhythms of street fighting, as graceful and courageous as bullfighters in their long courtship with violence. The Israelis somehow lost points for preferring modern technology and proven firepower, F-16s, "smart" bombs, white-phosphorous rounds, tanks, cluster bombs, naval gunfire, to the artisanal methods of Lebanese warmaking.

On the other hand, the Israeli invaders were taken aback by the wealth of Lebanon. Their new Sparta—with the fourth most effective army in the world, as Sharon boasted—was mortgaged for military spending and short on consumer goods, its constantly devalued currency a joke; but the smallest Lebanese village had stores stocked with Scotch, imported foods, and even color television sets and videocassette machines. So many Lebanese had been forced to seek work abroad and leave their families at home that the Lebanese pound remained one of the miracles of the modern world, thanks to some $150 million a month in their remittances.

The Lebanese, whose economy at home had been destroyed by years of fighting, had emigrated abroad in ever-greater numbers. UN statistics indicated that the annual prewar emigration rate of ten thousand had quintupled since 1975. Lebanon's banks went international. Businesses expanded abroad, especially in the Persian Gulf states and Europe. Lebanese invested in French shipyards, American copper mines, and Spanish hotels; in insurance companies, advertising firms, and international construction groups. Lebanon supplied trained manpower everywhere, with men fleeing a country that since 1976 had witnessed the destruction or damage of sixty thousand housing units, a good percentage during the 1982 fighting. Yet, the Lebanese pound snapped back from an August 1982 low of 5.35 to the dollar, and by the fall was worth 3.8, thanks to the gold cover, remittances from abroad, Arab aid, and the tail end of war-chest financing that Arab countries had sent to pay for the left-wing militias and the PLO.

Now, with the Israeli invasion, it was the Lebanese version of the old Vietnam story: "We had to destroy the village in order to save it." Within weeks of the invasion, there were signs that the Israelis had begun to be "Lebanized": Israeli troops were arrested by Israeli customs officials when they tried to smuggle Lebanon's goodies—from hashish to American cigarettes—back home across the border.

The Lebanese Christians also had second thoughts—of a more practical nature. The war turned out to be bad for business. The Israelis flooded Lebanon with worthless shekels and cheap products— manufactured goods, fruits, and vegetables sold at what the Lebanese denounced as dumping prices. In July and August, Israel did more business with Lebanon at war than it had done during the entire previous year with Egypt despite the peace treaty. (By December the trade, almost all of it one-way from Israel, had leapt to $20 million for the month. The Israelis angered their Lebanese Forces friends by opening up Haifa as a free transit port, thereby competing with the main source of the militia's income from its "private" ports. The Israelis tolerated "private ports" in the south, however, to help defray the costs of the multitude of petty militias they armed and directed as part of their divide-and-rule tactics.) A leading Lebanese businessman said, "The Israelis are a hundred times smarter than we are. They make our elite look ridiculous and pretentious. They did their homework instead of talking through their hats."

This intimation that the self-styled descendants of the Phoenicians, the greatest traders of antiquity, might have got more than they bargained for was substantiated by the leaflets dropped from Israeli aircraft over Christian areas of Lebanon in the first days of the invasion. Aside from the usual greetings in Hebrew and Arabic, the leaflets also gave the Hebrew for "Merry Christmas!" Now, the Christians had supposed that the Israelis would be long gone by Christmas; their main concern was that the Israelis move fast to destroy the PLO before the war was halted by outside forces. Stopping halfway had always been the pattern, but now that the Israelis were in Lebanon, let them get on with it and finish the job. "Are we going to be put off by yet another destruction?" a cynical Lebanese Forces official asked, sighing, during the war's second week, when the Israelis appeared to be running out of breath. The punishment of West Beirut—indeed, its destruction—was worthwhile if the Lebanese Forces could triumph and enact their vision of the future of Lebanon. The first step was to root out the PLO. In the bunker at Lebanese Forces headquarters, a Lebanese Army map of Lebanon on the briefing-room wall had the mere mention of Palestine carefully inked over.

Yet the days dragged into weeks, and the Christians began worrying. Nothing was happening—that is, the Israelis had not yet stormed West Beirut, although they had not spared the shelling and bombing. In June, preceding Haig's disgrace, the illegal Christian radio stations, which often served as sounding boards for Israeli propaganda, had announced that the "battle for Beirut" was beginning—indeed, that it had. Still, nothing happened on the ground. Haig's sudden departure on June 25 was a terrible blow, for the Christians' worst fear was that without Haig the Israelis would be forced to stop. But the Israelis seemed to lack any long-range plan, much less a detailed scheme, for taking West Beirut. By some accounts, Sharon did not dare order such a plan for fear of its being vetoed; only by claiming that the invasion developed a logic of its own could he get away with encircling Beirut— no matter what he told the Christians or any other foreigners. Israeli officers who drew up the plans for invading West Beirut said they were assigned the task only in the third week of the war.

Naive or Machiavellian, the Israelis either didn't know or didn't care about Lebanon's twisted sociology. (Only in November 1982 did the Defense and Foreign ministries get around to establishing a joint experts' committee to help puzzle out its ethnic complexities.) Many Lebanese began to worry that Israel cared little whether it put a friendly man in the Presidential Palace or carved out a larger sector for itself—and for Syria—once the PLO was eliminated. The Israelis seemed powerful enough to afford errors, secure in their ability to bounce back and correct mistakes before adversaries—or allies—could take advantage. They had lots of friends in Lebanon, Israelis from Begin on down kept boasting somewhat mysteriously, lots of assets, and not just Mossad agents. Yet for every Mossad specialist, there were hundreds of Israeli troopers who couldn't tell a Shia from a Sunni, an Armenian from an Orthodox.

Still, the Israeli boasting seemed to substantiate reports that the Lebanese Forces helped the invaders capture the center of the port city of Sidon. They had collaborated so often before that the story sounded likely. (Just a month or so before the invasion, the Christians had interrogated a Syrian pilot shot down over Marounistan by an Israeli plane; they followed a detailed questionnaire provided by the Israelis, and Israeli helicopters picked up pieces of the downed MiG-23.)

Just as the Christians had feared, the Americans began to apply the brakes in July. Even before Haig resigned, the Reagan administration was trying to draw the line, if only to save its credibility in the conservative Arab world and turn the war to its own advantage. The United States had at first gone along with the war, but now opposed any extension of the conflict to the rest of Lebanon, much less to Syria. To the Christian warlords and their friends, that meant the job was only half done. It was as if Washington were saying that the Israelis must not threaten the regime in Syria itself, having so convincingly destroyed the Syrian air-defense system in Lebanon. So the Israeli Army stopped in the Beqaa valley a few miles south of the Beirut–Damascus road and along a fifteen-mile sector in the mountains leading east from Beirut. Christian hopes were dashed that the Israelis would push the Syrians all the way out of the Beqaa and set in motion the final stages of Bashir Gemayel's long-promised "liberation of all 10,452 square kilometers" of Lebanese soil. The Christian activists begged and begged—or, in the case of their militant clerical backers, prayed and prayed. But Israel refused to make good on what these Christians considered were previously firm promises to help push the Syrians out of the Metn valley—half Christian, half Druze—due east of Beirut. Without that parallel Israeli drive in the Beqaa, the Christians had to scrap dreams of conquering the Christian north, where Syrians were still protecting Sleiman Franjieh.

The Israelis themselves were angry with the Lebanese Forces for not joining the actual fighting, especially against the trapped PLO guerrillas in West Beirut. The Lebanese Forces steadfastly denied they had promised—or ever intended—to do any such thing, but on June 15 the Israeli cabinet had nonetheless decided that the Lebanese Army or the Christian militia should handle the Palestinians on the ground in West Beirut. Such was the Israelis' influence with the militiamen that the very next day a specially trained Christian commando unit wrested control from the PLO of the six-story Lebanese University Sciences Faculty building, which overlooked the airport and much of the suburban area to the south. A particularly indiscreet Israeli Army spokesman, watching the operation from the safety of his hill headquarters in Baabda, told reporters that the problem was not to egg the Christians on, but to prevent them from taking West Beirut all by themselves. The Lebanese Forces put out an embarrassed communiqué explaining that the operation had been in retaliation for a Palestinian provocation and by no means meant that the militia was joining the war in a general way. (In fact, this remained the militia's only major combat contribution in the immediate Beirut area during Bashir Gemayel's lifetime.) The Lebanese Forces did provide the Israelis with all kinds of intelligence—telephone numbers to tap, sewer maps, the locations of key installations and headquarters—and, of course, the Israelis used Marounistan as if it were theirs. They brought in supplies through Jounieh and installed tanks and artillery in East Beirut and the heavily populated hills dominating West Beirut—thus imitating the Palestinians, who, Israeli propaganda always remarked in horror, sited their heavy weaponry in among civilian buildings. Sharon himself poured scorn on his allies when he lunched at the Hotel Alexandre in East Beirut in July, contemptuously twitting those unwilling to fight for their own freedom. In fact, the Israelis wanted the Christians to do the fighting in West Beirut in order to save Israeli lives.

But Bashir Gemayel was in no mood to compromise his election chances, mightily improved by the Israeli invasion and the Syrians' loss of influence. "At each stage, the Israelis hoped we would come in," a ranking Lebanese Forces official said. "But we wanted to get Bashir elected. We could have carried out a coup d'état without Sharon and his histrionic show at Baabda." By late June, Bashir was privately cursing the Israelis for trying to drag him into the war and seeking to embarrass him with their heavy-handed public statements. Their continuous pounding of West Beirut had compromised the National Salvation Council Bashir had hoped would turn into a national unity government under his effective domination and further his presidential ambitions. From Prime Minister Shafik Wazzan on down, the Moslem members refused to attend committee sessions at the Presidential Palace, since Israeli artillery was firing only yards away. At one point, the Druze and leftist leader Walid Jumblatt suggested—between barrages from the nearby batteries—that the committee might simplify its task by inviting Sharon to attend. Sarkis smiled wanly. If Israel was determined to play the game its own way, the Lebanese Forces saw no reason to sustain casualties in West Beirut.

As far as it can be pieced together, this was the situation. Both Gemayel and Sharon had expected the Palestinians to panic and run away as the Israeli juggernaut approached Beirut. Instead, the Palestinians stood and fought—a predictable outcome for those who knew the PLO and Arafat. The Israelis and Christians certainly wanted to enter West Beirut thereafter, but each hoped the other would pay the price in casualties. The Lebanese Forces thought they had the Israelis committed to operations the Christians wanted; and the Israelis thought Bashir was willing to fight and accept a formal peace treaty with them when the war was over. But Christian officials still swear convincingly that until the invasion began, no political discussions had even taken place. Sharon was finally reduced to besieging West Beirut with four hundred tanks and more than one hundred heavy artillery pieces, plus offshore gunboats and Israel's unopposed air force.

Yet questions remain. If Sharon really wanted Arafat and his men to cut and run—and what a propaganda victory that would have been for Israel—why did he trap the Palestinians in Beirut with no exit? Sharon forced Arafat to make a stand. Why had Sharon chosen to lead his tanks in the linkup operation with his Christian allies at, of all places, Baabda—the seat of what little remained of Lebanese sovereignty? It was hard for Christians and Moslems to escape the conclusion that Sharon was inviting Bashir to stage a coup calculated to brand him as an out-and-out quisling in Christian and Moslem—and Arab—eyes.

Nor was the slow agony of West Beirut doing Bashir's presidential chances much good. Lebanese Moslems had been alienated from the PLO by years of guerrilla arrogance, indifference, and misbehavior— "It's not our country" and "Why should we pay the electricity and telephone bills?" they would say—and much of Bashir's appeal to the Moslems was based on the errors of the Palestinians and the Syrians. But the scale and determination of the Israeli bombing erased those differences during the siege of Beirut. And Bashir didn't dare speak out against Israeli excesses, a failing duly noted in the besieged sector of the city. His supporters argued awkwardly that the Israelis had needlessly complicated his presidential plans by not rushing right into West Beirut in mid-June and getting the job over quickly and painlessly. By late June, Arafat was boasting that with two thousand rocket-propelled grenade launchers he could reasonably hope to destroy two hundred Israeli tanks and their crews. The PLO guerrillas and their Lebanese allies began to lay mines on the main approaches and to block roads with sand barriers.

Frustrated in Beirut, Bashir made a fateful decision to send his militiamen to areas in the Lebanese provinces from which they had been expelled during the civil war, or, in some cases, to places where the Phalangist Party had never maintained offices. The Lebanese Forces, following in the Israeli Army's footsteps, almost without exception opened old wounds and produced a predictably bloody settling of accounts wherever they went. In Damour and Sidon, they harassed and sometimes murdered Palestinian civilians, in the hope of stampeding them out of the country. In other areas, they clashed with Major Haddad's rival militia, whom the Israelis had entrusted with large areas of south Lebanon all the way to the northern approaches to Sidon on the Awali River. In still others, such as the Metn, Aley, or the Shuf, Lebanese Forces fought with the Druze Moslems, who, thanks to Syrian protection, had held effective sway in these mixed Christian-Druze areas since 1976. The Israelis encouraged Haddad in some areas, Bashir's men in others, and gave arms to their enemies of the extreme Left on some occasions. By design or through ignorance, they were upsetting Lebanon's precarious balance among minorities seething with mutual hatred and revenge. And willy-nilly they were indulging in that classic imperial principle of divide and rule so familiar in Lebanese history: by either stirring up or tolerating trouble, the outside power could demonstrate its usefulness by sending in troops to separate the combatants. By the fall of 1982, Shuf mayors in neighboring Maronite and Druze villages were catching on when Israeli officers offered them arms and warned them of the other's evil intentions. A simple telephone call often got to the bottom of the skullduggery, but not often enough—as the steadily lengthening list of incidents, and casualties, bore witness. By the end of 1982, hundreds of Druze and Lebanese Christians had been killed.

The Lebanese Forces sheepishly admitted their errors in going into these areas, but did little to mend their ways. Their muscular tactics failed. They lost several hundred militiamen killed—their worst casualties in years—and instead of acting as a shield for dispossessed Christians to return to their former homes, the Lebanese Forces by their presence in fact ended up causing so much violence that many Christians who had stayed put since 1975 left the Shuf. The unpleasant reality was that Bashir was not in full control of his militia, especially the units farthest from his East Beirut headquarters. Made up in large part of young men whose families had been forced to flee their homes during the civil war and seek refuge in the Maronite heartland, these units were now sent back south to their home areas, which were occupied by the Israeli Army, and they had revenge in mind from the start. Indeed, the Lebanese Forces recruited these men as shock troops for that reason. The Israelis obligingly kicked out Druze soldiers from Lebanese Army garrisons in the Shuf and handed the barracks over to the Lebanese Forces. It was child's play for the Israelis to manipulate the situation. The Druze militiamen at times were no more obedient to their leaders than were the Christians to Bashir. "If we do send in our men, we are accused of causing trouble," a Lebanese Forces official fretted in June; "if we don't, then the Christians from the south who were driven out in 1975 and 1976 complain we are not sticking up for their right to return home." Ever since the fighting first started in 1975, the young men with the guns had frequently contested the authority of their political elders—as indeed Bashir knew full well, since his rise to power was a perfect illustration of that theme. The whole business was a drearily familiar rerun not just of the 1975–76 "events" but of the Druze-Maronite slaughter between 1840 and 1860—complete with an intergenerational struggle and interfering foreign powers.

By appearing to back the Christian militia against the Druze Moslems in the Shuf, the Israeli government created problems with its own vocal Druze minority. The fifty thousand Israeli Druzes had elected a member to the Knesset, and thirteen thousand more Druzes lived on the Golan, annexed by Israel the year before. Israeli Druzes served in the army, especially in the tough border police who helped maintain the Israeli occupation of the West Bank and Gaza Strip. Early in the invasion, the government had dangled the possibility of an autonomous Druze zone before Lebanon's Druze leaders—complete with a three-thousand-man Israeli-supplied army—and pointed to the area around Hasbaiya, where an Israeli Druze officer was military governor and the villagers had been encouraged to set up self-defense units with Israeli-provided arms. Still, there were no takers for the Druze statelet. Equally disturbing, in more than one of the on-again-off-again outbreaks of shooting in the Shuf, Israeli Druze soldiers had sided with their coreligionists despite army orders against such entanglements.

In short, the strife between Druze militiamen and the Lebanese Forces inevitably undermined the Israelis' power in Lebanon—where they were now the only organized force capable of maintaining law and order. But the Shuf disorders also pointed to further problems. Unlike the Syrians, never fazed by the loss of thousands of soldiers in Lebanon over the years, the Israelis realized that the occupation of Lebanon ran the risk of casualties, and casualties were highly unpopular at home. And even when the Israelis were not involved in the Shuf troubles, it pleased Lebanese of all factions to blame them.

In all this, the Israelis were only following in the footsteps of the Syrian peacekeeping force. The Syrians had been welcomed as peacekeepers in 1976, but had failed to keep the peace. They were blamed for keeping the country divided, and finally were regretted by virtually no one when driven back to the Beqaa and north by the Israeli invasion. The Israelis copied them in great things and small—all the way down to their efficiency in looting private homes. If anything, the Israelis went further. Quite apart from 520 tons of arms and matériel eventually hauled away from West Beirut, Israeli soldiers took private cars, telephones, telex machines, videocassette machines, even wooden school benches. All over Lebanon they left distinctive calling cards:

human excrement in drawers, on beds, in closets, in churches and mosques, and on the floors of hospitals. Israeli Arabists had warned the government of the dangers of the Lebanese quagmire and of the almost infinite potential for error and bloodshed. But Sharon and his group paid them no more mind than the U.S. government had the views of American specialists on Iran during and after the Iranian revolution.

So atomized had Lebanese society become over the years that the Christians—and many Moslems—outside West Beirut shed few tears over its fate. The Christians were aware that Israel had destroyed much of south Lebanon and had played an ambiguous political role there, but they believed this was a small and, they hoped, only a temporary price to pay for the invasion. They were, with rare exceptions, heedless of the siege of Beirut. Christian girls in bikinis water-skied in the bay of Jounieh, a bare twelve miles north of the capital. The Lebanese state radio's FM service advised about the dangers of traffic jams for those heading for the beaches. Many East Beirutis who left their homes did so not out of any sense of peril, but because they did not like the din from the Israeli bombardment, which was, curiously, more audible in their sector than in many parts of West Beirut. "Today is your turn, tomorrow mine" is an old French Foreign Legion song, and its message of doom had become quintessentially Lebanese. West Beirut, the Christians noted, had gone about its business, not worrying about the Christian sector when it was shelled by the Syrians in 1978 and 1981, so why should the Christians worry about West Beirut now? Alone of the Christian political elite, Joyce Gemayel, Amin's wife, spoke out against the Israeli destruction, and her husband paid one visit (much criticized in Phalangist and Lebanese Forces circles) to West Beirut to see PLO leaders. For many West Beirutis, the hardest burden was the knowledge that their friends across the city had even stopped telephoning them. It was as if they had been crossed off the map of the world.

On half a dozen occasions in late July and early August, I went to the Museum crossing (the main crossing point between the two parts of the city) on errands for Lebanese friends. Many Christians in the eastern sector of the city refused to come to West Beirut either because they saw no logical reason to risk their necks or because they didn't want to be harassed at the various checkpoints—Israelis and Lebanese Forces on the east side and left-wing Lebanese militia on the west side.

Foreigners, especially journalists, were useful, since both sides tolerated their movements; provided no food was involved, almost anything could be brought into West Beirut if carried a quarter mile through the no-man's-land between the two sectors. Each time I went to the crossing, the East Beirut friend who met me at the line made the same little speech. "Arafat and his lot never will leave, will they? The Israelis will have to blast them out. What are they waiting for?" I never quite figured out who the "they" were—the Palestinians who were supposed to surrender, or the Israelis who were supposed to invade. In those fleeting meetings—no one liked staying in the broiling sun of the exposed meeting area and risking a sniper's bullet—I always tried to tell my friend that the PLO were eager to negotiate their departure, sketching in details to buttress my argument as the trend in PLO thinking became more evident. In conversations with Palestinian officials, I had learned they were abandoning one previously tenaciously held condition after another to speed agreement, negotiate their departure, and avoid further destruction. (Later on, American diplomats told them that had Arafat held out a bit longer—after all, the guerrillas had held their ground and inflicted nineteen fatalities on the Israelis on August 4—he could have obtained stouter guarantees for the Palestinian civilians remaining in Beirut.) But my friend never believed me. He would make that most eloquent Levantine gesture of disbelief, a half-suppressed clucking of the tongue as the head is thrown back ever so slightly. After all my years in Lebanon, he was telling me that I obviously understood nothing, and never would.

On August 11, after a nasty day of shelling but nothing worse, I crossed over from West Beirut, leaving the Hotel Commodore in a taxi that was making the daily late-afternoon run to Damascus with videotapes for Western television networks. It was a later departure than usual. We drove slowly, partly because of the debris and shell holes gouging the streets, partly because we were scared. We didn't see a single human being for twenty minutes—until we cleared the crushed buildings, the burned-over pine forest, the empty expressway, and were outside Beirut proper and approaching a Lebanese Forces roadblock at the Galerie Semaan checkpoint. By nightfall I was in the garden of a house belonging to East Beirut friends, listening to their chatter, relaxing after my first warm bath in weeks, and recalling memories from the year before. Then, I had sat in the same garden, brooding over a city where I found myself shocked more by the Syrian artillery's recent destruction of the arching trees that once shut out the sky than by the daily ration of corpses and the black-bordered martyrs' photographs plastered on city walls. Now, Israeli tanks, less than half a mile away in the port, were shelling West Beirut. But the year before in the garden, outgoing Christian and incoming Syrian rounds had been much closer. I suddenly recalled a bit of my hostess's conversation then—"How nice the neighborhood is now! Everyone but a few old Greek Orthodox families has gone. It's just the way I remember things as a child—no Maronites." Now her husband said, "I hated the Syrians for shelling our side of town, but I hate the Israelis even more. Increase the caliber two hundred times, multiply the time element by thirty-six, that's what the Israelis have done. God knows we Christians schemed and dreamed to get the Israelis to intervene, but no one really thought an invasion would mean *this*." His was a minority view, but he has a reputation for sensitivity.

We drove into the mountains for dinner at an outdoor restaurant. On the way up, West Beirut was easy to discern, its blacked-out skyline (the Israeli power cut was still in force) lit up by Israeli flares and artillery rounds landing with their bright orange flames. Dozens of cars had pulled to the side of the road at various vantage points to watch the carnage below. My friends said the voyeurs had been out in force every night for weeks. At the restaurant, a nearby table was filled with Lebanese Forces and Israeli officers in earnest conversation. I concentrated on the food. For the first time in weeks I dug into lettuce, tomatoes, fruit—all the fresh produce missing in West Beirut. My friends looked at me indulgently. The owner complained that the war was bad for business. Would the Palestinians ever leave?

For years, East and West Beirut had formulated different answers to the same questions. Now even the questions differed. What West Beirutis asked was, simply, When would the United States wake up and stop the carnage? That was a question I discussed with two colleagues, one French, the other Lebanese, as we lunched in East Beirut the next day. Since dawn, Israeli planes had been bombing nonstop, paying special attention, or so it seemed, to the race course and Museum areas not half a mile distant. The noise was horrendous. The leaves fluttered from the explosions. The planes dived at a steep angle. The dust from the explosions filtered in through the windows, kept open to allow for the blast effect. No more than in other Beirut houses had there been any thought of crisscrossing these windows with

tape. It was not Beirut style to put the odds on your side. I was furious
with the Israelis, and even angrier with the U.S. government, which
knowingly allowed its Israeli clients to get away with large-scale
murder, all the more senseless since it was known that the PLO wanted
to leave. (In an earlier bout of massive Israeli destruction, with the
ambassadorial residence shaking with the outgoing rounds of nearby
tanks and 155-millimeter guns, Philip Habib had telephoned the State
Department to complain. Washington had called the American embassy in Tel Aviv—as usual, oddly willing to believe the Israeli line
without question—only to be told that its Israeli sources insisted,
"Nothing is happening." Habib stuck the telephone out the window
just as a barrage let loose, and added some of his characteristically
emphatic curses. Later, Sharon complained angrily, if indirectly, that
Ambassador Dillon had been guilty of misreporting the facts. That had
been that.) I was sick at heart, ashamed of being an American, as I
have been only rarely in more than a quarter century as a foreign
correspondent. Exhausted by a sleepless night, I took an after-lunch
nap. When I awoke I automatically turned on the radio, to learn that
for the first time President Reagan himself had expressed anger and
outrage at what the Israelis were doing. The shooting ended.

Nonetheless, it took another week for Habib to work out the final
details of the Palestinian withdrawal, largely because the Israelis
sought to impose new conditions. Then, suddenly, he had his deal. At
dawn on August 21, the French Foreign Legion arrived at the port of
Beirut, and in the early afternoon the first Palestinian guerrillas embarked and sailed away for the Palestinians' fourth exodus in thirty-
four years. As they left, they shot off weaponry of all calibers, in a
strange celebration mixing the obvious fact of their defeat and departure with all the trappings of victory. Along the departure route,
assault rifles and grenades were fired, men threw rice, and women
cried and ululated. From the Lebanese Army trucks taking them
slowly past the Holiday Inn, the Murr Tower, the Starco office building, the Hilton and Normandy hotels—all those burned-out hulks that
were once the pride of Beirut, where their comrades in arms had died
by the hundreds in 1975 and 1976—the PLO soldiers in fresh uniforms
had held aloft color photographs of Arafat and made V-for-victory
signs. Their Lebanese leftist militia allies had fired back. Then they had
inched their way through the iron gates of the port, where first the
French, later the U.S. Marines, waited to guide them to their ships. By

ship or by road, more than eight thousand guerrillas, thirty-five hundred members of the regular Palestine Liberation Army, and twenty-seven hundred Syrians of the 85th Brigade had left that day without a serious hitch.

Arafat himself was seen off on August 30, with Prime Minister Shafik Wazzan, former Prime Minister Saeb Salam, and other West Beirut leaders in attendance. "Tell the Arabs of your heroic resistance in Beirut," came the message over the loudspeaker truck, "and ask them where their MiGs and Mirages were, ask them why they abandoned us. Tell them you fought the Israeli Army with your Kalashnikovs and RPGs and dynamite sticks." An old Christian woman watched the departure from under an umbrella on a terrace overlooking the port. "Now I can die," she said, surprised and pleased to have seen the last of the PLO guerrillas—responsible in her mind for all Lebanon's woes.

On August 23, two days after that first departure, in one of those concentrated bursts of events that characterized the war of 1982, Bashir Gemayel was elected President of Lebanon. And the evacuation of the PLO, complete with its regular daily dose of wild shooting, was completed on September 1, two days ahead of schedule. Lebanese politicians suggested that Habib should be nominated for the Nobel Peace Prize. Even Prime Minister Wazzan, Walid Jumblatt, and other Lebanese who earlier had warned that the whole arrangement reposed on nothing more than Habib's proud promises that he represented the honor of the United States began to sound more optimistic. The Foreign Legionnaires began to demine the main approach roads. Rafic Hariri, a thirty-eight-year-old Sunni Moslem from Sidon who had made a fortune in construction in Saudi Arabia, donated $7.5 million to hire men, trucks, and bulldozers to haul away the wreckage and dismantle the sand barricades. The Prime Minister opened the Sodeco crossing point, closed for the better part of two years, and now yet another symbol of the reunification of the long-divided capital. Optimists predicted that Beirut airport, closed since June 7, would soon reopen. For the first time since 1975, the Lebanese Army was deployed in West Beirut. Stores and restaurants reopened. Civil servants trickled back to work. Electricity and telephone service was resumed. Life returned to its pre-invasion tempo. The President-elect was at his reassuring best. Gradually, he was winning over the Sunni Moslems, who had boycotted his election and professed their suspicions of his plans for Lebanon. Actively encouraged by the United States, Bashir Gemayel was preaching the virtues of reconciliation and a strong state, the very things the Lebanese had pined for all through the terrible years. In theory, such a goal was in keeping with Israeli policy, at least the publicly proclaimed version of it.

But for anyone acquainted with Lebanon, danger signals were flying. Within hours of the last PLO guerrilla's departure on September 1, President Reagan unveiled a plan for settling the Palestinian problem. This proposal contained nothing new, but, issued under the personal authority of the President, it was designed to show a doubting Arab world that Israel did not always lead the United States by the nose. The Palestinians, Reagan suggested, should be denied any dream of a rump, but still independent, state in the West Bank and Gaza Strip, and instead should work out their salvation with Jordan's King Hussein. Israel was to cease its creeping annexation and building of new settlements (or "thickening" of existing ones) in the Occupied Territories. (In itself, this last had been official U.S. policy for years, until Reagan during his presidential election campaign had been more tolerant of Begin's settlement policy.)

A furious Begin predictably rejected the plan out of hand, for he had hoped to cap the Lebanese war by annexing the West Bank and Gaza. In only two days, the first sign of his displeasure showed up in Lebanon. In clear violation of the accords Habib had negotiated, Israeli troops moved six hundred yards north under the pretext that they were demining roads. This put them for the first time on top of the Palestinians' Shatila refugee camp and the poor Lebanese and Palestinian neighborhood of Bir Hassan, just south of the main road running from the Mediterranean to the divided highway leading to Beirut airport. The Israelis were there to stay. No amount of American persuasion could make them budge, and soon the United States abandoned its demand that they move back to their original positions, accepting a smokescreen story that the Lebanese Army had perhaps agreed, as the Israelis claimed, to let the Israeli Army demine that politically and strategically sensitive stretch of road.

In fact, the Israelis resented what they saw as a developing American policy aimed at emboldening Bashir Gemayel to resist Israel's demands for a separate peace. The Israeli press during the first two weeks of September made that abundantly clear, for anyone used to officially inspired stories in Israel's newspapers. And, indeed, the Americans felt the Israelis were pushing the Lebanese leader too hard; he should, they thought, concentrate on national reconciliation. In any case, Bashir would be dependent on Arab largesse to underwrite the cost of repairing seven years of war damage, and if Begin got his way with a peace treaty, the Arab world was sure to boycott a vastly vulnerable Lebanon, as it had Egypt. The United States government, already laden with its two biggest foreign-aid programs—in Egypt and in Israel—was in no mood to take on a third such burden. Yet, Begin had set his heart on extracting just such a treaty from Lebanon. Those who talked to him during the summer insisted the treaty was every bit as important to him as destroying the PLO. He dreamed of extending Israel's realm and spoke glowingly of Israelis being welcomed from Beirut to Cairo.

The Americans now insisted on interfering seriously in Lebanon, after many years of indifference, but they soon learned that two could play the spoiler's game, especially in Lebanon. Israel could create problems for both Bashir and the Americans simply by postponing the withdrawal of its troops from Lebanon. That, in turn, would freeze Reagan's West Bank plans. State Department officials were quick to admit this, for there was nothing really new about the policy. It had for years been easy for Israel to cause trouble in Lebanon. Even if the Americans disagreed with what the Israelis were up to, what could they do about it? They lacked local assets on the ground and, if past experience was any yardstick, they also lacked the staying force to make Israel do their will. The last time the Americans had made a major decision that was not to Israel's liking and had made it stick was in 1957; then, President Dwight D. Eisenhower obliged the Israeli Army to evacuate the Sinai, which it had occupied with French and British connivance during the Suez campaign the previous fall. Successive U.S. administrations had armed Israel to the teeth, in the curious belief that once its armed forces were stronger than those of all its potential Arab adversaries put together, Israel, secure at last, would be more willing to seek accommodation with its neighbors. Whatever the intent, at least one major and ironic consequence of that policy was to limit American influence over Israeli military actions, which, predictably, became increasingly aggressive.

In any case, on past form, President Reagan was not inclined to seek a confrontation with Israel, for all his occasional criticism of the Israeli invasion. The Reagan administration was so intent on avoiding any military commitment in Lebanon that the twelve hundred Marines never left the port—there was concern they might suffer casualties—and they were gone on September 9. They were last in and first out, with a smiling Marine holding up a sign for the photographers that read "Mission Accomplished." In private, American officials tried to justify their departure by arguing that Bashir himself wanted the French and Italian contingents of the peacekeeping force out as well. He felt that the Lebanese Army, a demoralized, underarmed magma of twenty-three thousand men whose only function consisted in drawing their monthly pay, should shoulder the burden even at the price of foreseeable setbacks. He planned to double the army's size, and, in the meantime, his Praetorian Guard, the Lebanese Forces, could be used to stiffen the army's resolve if need be. President Sarkis had undermined his entire six years in office, right from the start, Bashir argued, by refusing to do anything about the army until it was deemed recovered from its disintegration in the civil war. Of course, if the Lebanese Army was in such piteous condition, it was thanks in no small part to Bashir's own intrigues. The United States knew this perfectly well, for it had run into his opposition when it had tried to help put the Lebanese Army back together again after 1976. But now the Americans argued that with a strong leader in Bashir, Lebanon could and should be encouraged to solve its own problems.

Bashir Gemayel was assassinated on September 14, and two days later his men were slaughtering Palestinian civilians in the Shatila camp. American hopes of tiptoeing out of Lebanon collapsed. Indeed, Bashir's death, Sharon's decision to invade West Beirut at first light the next day, and the massacres of Palestinians forced a greater degree of U.S. involvement in Lebanese affairs than at any time since the 1950s. American officials from the President on down were both contrite and outraged by Israeli duplicity in invading West Beirut, although some cynical Lebanese noted that the Israeli Army's disarming of the leftist militias was perhaps welcome in Washington. Initially, Reagan tried to excuse the Israeli violation of the Habib agreement by saying, "I'm sure what led them to move in was an attack by some leftist militia." But that would not wash. Reagan himself now realized the danger for American credibility of indulging the Israeli hawks. But at what a terrible price! American honor had been sullied. This combination of American disgrace and Lebanese weakness—now visible for all to see—forced Reagan to play the leading role that successive American governments had refused. Finally, the United States was having to take an active hand in the policy which it had set in motion after 1974 and which, whatever its intentions, had destabilized much of the Middle East, helped to destroy Lebanon, and contributed to the death of Anwar Sadat. In the process, the always latent conflictual nature of American relations with Israel burst into the open once again.

So back came the Marines—and the French and the Italians, later to be joined by a small British contingent—and with their return came a subtle change in the previous power relationship between Israel and the United States. A depressed American diplomat earlier in the summer had remarked, "The Israelis do not know what they are doing in Lebanon, and they are thrown up against an administration which knows perhaps even less." The invasion of West Beirut and the massacres certainly ended the PLO myth of its summer heroism, for the Israelis had arrested, searched, and robbed them with total impunity. The massacres succeeded in instilling such fear in the minds of remaining Palestinians that many would have welcomed leaving if any haven had been available. But these "positive" results were outweighed by the universal horror the massacres occasioned in the world. Sharon and Begin for the first time were on the defensive. Dissent within the army, an outraged Israeli public, a tarnished image —all encouraged the moribund Labor opposition, which from the beginning of the war had warned against the army's entry into Beirut.

In the most manifest fashion, the United States had proved incapable of making good on its own written promise to protect the Palestinians from the Israelis and the Christian militias, and now its Israeli ally had reneged on the agreement in the most obvious, insulting, and murderous fashion. The United States had done precious little to deserve its increased leverage, but now had to exercise a clear moral authority. "Anyone would have to be a fool to trust the United States again in the Middle East," a Palestinian professor at the American University of Beirut said to me when he learned of the extent of the massacre. It was that very thought that so depressed Morris Draper, in charge of the State Department's Middle East bureau, Habib's number-two man, and the highest-ranking American diplomat in Beirut at the time. When he heard a detailed account from a journalist of what had happened at Shatila, he was coldly furious. The compleat career diplomat, the State Department's institutional memory for the Middle East, said, "All I can tell you is that I feel professionally responsible." (The day before, he had told the Israelis on the telephone—this later transpired in testimony at the Israeli investigation—"You should be ashamed. Your troops are in control and thus responsible. You must stop the massacre. They [the Israeli troops] are obscene. I have an officer in the camp counting bodies. They are killing children.") He told the journalist the Israelis were tough people to deal with—always had been, right from the creation of their state in 1948—but once they gave their word, they had always kept it. This was by way of explaining why the United States had not seen fit to demand written guarantees from Israel about not entering West Beirut and, perforce, not harming Palestinian civilians. (But even a cursory look at the record disproved Draper's self-serving thesis. Israeli governments had been guilty of all kinds of skullduggery against the United States—not to mention their Arab neighbors. There seemed an excellent case for demanding guarantees in writing from the Israelis about things great and small. Where Israeli state interests were concerned, successive Israeli governments had few equals in ruthlessness. During the 1967 Arab-Israeli conflict, Israeli aircraft had killed 34—and wounded 164—crew members of the U.S.S. *Liberty* rather than tolerate the presence in the eastern Mediterranean of an electronic eavesdropping ship listening to Israeli military communications traffic. During the 1973 war, the Israelis had defied cease-fire arrangements so as to tighten the noose around Egypt's trapped Third Army. In 1978 Begin had left the Camp David summit and neglected to send President Carter a promised letter accepting a freeze on Israeli settlements until agreement could be reached on the future of the West Bank and Gaza.)

Throughout the summer, nothing had been quite so obvious as the threat to Palestinian civilians in West Beirut. Indeed, one major reason behind the PLO's reluctance to leave Beirut had been its fear for the physical safety of the Palestinians who would stay behind. Additionally, Arafat swore that the American guarantees worked out in August by Habib extended only to Palestinians inside the camps (or, more accurately, to those in Beirut). *The Washington Post* on July 7 had carried my front-page dispatch spelling out in detail the nature of the civilians' dilemma. I mention that dispatch not in self-congratulation, but to make the point that a major American newspaper was willing to stick its neck out and devote prime space to what the Israelis at the time condemned as speculative analysis, although my article reported the views of worried diplomats, international civil servants, and Lebanese political analysts. Infinitely more important, Habib had been warned time and again that the Israelis' oral promises, especially Begin's and Sharon's, were not to be trusted. As Prime Minister Wazzan said after the massacre, "I told Habib, in practice the validity of such a guarantee could not be assured. He put his hand on his heart and swore he personally guaranteed Israeli compliance." To other doubters, Habib had angrily replied that the "good word of the United States" was sufficient guarantee. Superpowers have a way of seeking to forget and overlook their errors, especially those involving the slaughter of innocents. Such indulgence is not extended to the smaller fry of this world. But it did apparently absolve Habib in his own mind of any responsibility for what had happened. His policy in ruins, his government discredited, his reputation as a "magician" of diplomacy exposed as so much hollow prestidigitation, Habib did not resign—or even express public regret—as might have been expected. Nor did he feel any need to lie low, for he continued to maintain an active role as an American super-diplomat in the Middle East.

Even before the United States, France, and Italy reluctantly sent troops back to Lebanon to prop up the government, Habib was on his way to Beirut. Flying back from the United States to attend the inauguration of Amin Gemayel as President, Habib told a fellow passenger that perhaps Wazzan might want to "hit" him. The special presidential envoy, who had made discretion and silence a hallmark of his diplomacy, at the inauguration affably exchanged notes and slaps on the back with members of the Lebanese parliament. Alone, Prime Minister Wazzan walked straight past him.

Habib was, in his own way, no more unfeeling than most Christians of Marounistan. So wound up in the death of Bashir were they that they quite genuinely took no interest in the massacres carried out by their own men. "A media event," a Lebanese Forces official confided to me on Sunday, September 19, the day after the massacres were discovered, "already filed and forgotten." Fresh from West Beirut and its bloated bodies, I tried to impress on him that this was not just another massacre, that by its scale, its Israeli involvement, its American dimension, Shatila was different. He listened politely enough, but changed the subject. It wasn't just that he was ashamed and wanted to avoid talking about the massacres—although that was part of it. Rather, he and other Christians were singularly given over to their grief: what counted was Bashir's death and assuring Amin's election. A West Beirut Christian who visited Amin's house in Bikfaya that same day patiently explained to him the importance of his denying responsibility for the massacre. Eventually he succeeded in persuading Amin to issue a carefully worded statement that tried to whitewash the high command of the Lebanese Forces. Increasingly, militant Maronites turned against Israel. Amin's wife, Joyce, said, "Bashir was not enough, now the Israelis are trying to stick us with this nasty business." A high Lebanese Forces official hissed at a Maronite priest well known for his pro-Israeli views, "You and your friends are the ones who got us into this damned Israeli alliance." Behind the bitterness of these remarks lay a dawning realization that the Israelis, if nothing else, had outmaneuvered them.

Some historically minded Lebanese fear that sooner or later the Christians will pay for the massacre, pay for all the violence in Lebanon since 1975 (even though by no stretch of the imagination is it all their doing). They argue that minorities challenge, much less slaughter, Sunni Moslems at their own risk. And whatever else they were, the massacred Palestinians were Sunni Moslems. This thesis has much in common with that lingering Palestinian view that Israel will disappear as the Crusaders did after their century of established power in Jerusalem, and once again the Sunnis will be left in control. But Christians draw radically different conclusions. Deprived of Bashir Gemayel's leadership, his Lebanese Forces argued in 1982 that more than ever they were needed to protect Lebanon's threatened Christian community, since he was no longer there to implement a renewed Christian domination of the state. "Christians in the Middle East haven't been this strong since 1258," a Lebanese Forces official remarked shortly after Bashir's assassination. "We'd be fools to disarm." Officially, the Lebanese Forces command made it clear that it had no intention of dissolving until the last armed Palestinian, Syrian, *and* Israeli had left Lebanese soil. In the fall of 1982, the new leadership maintained five thousand fully paid regulars under arms and doubled taxes to swell the Lebanese Forces' coffers from $100 million to $200 million a year.

The United States initially tried to speed these departures. The President demanded a daily National Security Council report on Israel's willingness to end its occupation of Lebanon. American officials took for granted the pull-out of Syrian and PLO forces once Israel was on board. But they were far from sure to accept the necessity of surrendering their arms, as the leftist and Moslem militias had at the hands of Israeli and Lebanese armies in West Beirut. But the Israelis went into winter quarters with no real sign of movement. Well before then, they had removed the standard signposts written in Arabic and Roman characters, and replaced them with signs in Hebrew. They seemed to be settling in, but the Lebanese Forces talked confidently about their right to deploy anywhere in Lebanon (an argument used to cover their increased presence in the Shuf).

It was all so transparent. Scratch an East Beirut Christian in early 1983, and you found that his real adversary was the same Moslem presence that had kept Maronite teeth on edge for centuries. The PLO had gone, and with it that threat to the old Maronite-run state, but Moslems were still in Lebanon. The ghetto mentality of Marounistan's citizens may change gradually with time, and the Christians of Lebanon may yet come to understand that the Moslems of Lebanon, too, have had their fill of the Arab world, its empty rhetoric and murderous actions on Lebanese soil. If anything, Lebanon's Moslems have paid a dearer price for Arab meddling over the years than the Christians have. Since April 1975, most of the dead in Lebanon have been Moslem, not Christian. And in 1982 no more than a handful of Christians died—and then by mistake—in the Israeli invasion, which claimed some nineteen thousand lives—most of them Lebanese and civilian—according to Lebanese estimates. As the Israelis knew well, Lebanese Moslems in West Beirut had been on the receiving end of most of the terrorism of their city. Without question, it was West Beirut, not the Christian sector, that had suffered most from disorder, lawlessness, and violence. The recompense had been West Beirut's greater freedom of expression, its less provincial and cloistered view of the world.

As for the Christians, a little imagination, a bit of flexibility, a small dose of humility, and a tiny gesture indicating acceptance of even a small part of the responsibility for what happened would go a long way toward furthering Lebanon's national reconciliation. It could even be argued that it would be in the militant Christians' best interests to emerge from their ghetto and get to know the rest of the country, which has changed tremendously since they first erected their fortress and raised the ladders and drawbridges. They might even discover they no longer have a monopoly on Lebanese nationalism.

In the winter of 1982–83, they showed no such disposition. A banker friend of mine who passes for something of a liberal in East Beirut confided that he had no reason to come to West Beirut except to eat at Ajami's, the best restaurant for Lebanese cuisine in the country. The year before, *Le Reveil*, East Beirut's French-language newspaper, published a series of articles for children that described the various neighborhoods outside the ghetto that they had never seen. Half a generation has grown up with Christians not knowing Moslems, Moslems not knowing Christians. Yet, in Martyrs' Square, once the heart of Beirut, entire families from both sectors started taking snapshots of one another once the French troops had demined the main streets in September. The French cut down the jungle growth. The vegetable gardens, cared for by the fighters, are now abandoned. The enormous bullet-ridden statues in the middle of the square serve as an heroic backdrop for photographs. Collapsed buildings and finely pockmarked facades stare out at each other across its broad expanse. At the Mediterranean end, the Rivoli movie theater still advertises its last feature attraction: *The Divorced*. As if to emphasize the title's applicability, the Lebanese Forces positions on the eastern side of the square were not dismantled immediately. The barrels and the sandbags and the upended containers remained in place to underline the Christian militia's siege mentality. My banker friend insists that Beirut will be reunified only when the square and its devastated streets—the old commercial district—are crawling with people again.

But perhaps the muscular Maronites were right, in a way, to live barricaded and armed. For in the past seven years the Moslems have grown tremendously in numbers, wealth, and education. More and more, Lebanon's big money is Moslem, according to bankers with branches on both sides of Beirut; it is money earned abroad by emigrants and brought home. Sooner or later even Lebanon must have a census, and its Moslem majority—owing especially to rapid population growth among the Shia—will have to be recognized. Bashir Gemayel, who intended to use force to reunify the country under Maronite leadership, was so well aware of the Moslems' demographic edge that he commissioned studies to encourage six hundred thousand Christians living abroad to return home to help redress the balance. Was he serious, or was the plan another wild scheme designed to put off the evil day? Either way, his repatriation scheme eloquently acknowledged the main problem facing Christian—especially Maronite—claims to political leadership in the years ahead.

Lebanese Moslems far outnumber the Christians and would do so even if the perhaps five hundred thousand remaining Palestinians were driven out of Lebanon—in keeping with the Gemayels' long-held view that they should be distributed among all twenty Arab League states until—and if—they succeed in achieving a homeland for themselves. Nor were Sunni leaders in Lebanon of a different opinion, although they never said so explicitly. Prime Minister Wazzan, who stood up for the PLO and the Palestinian civilians during the summer of 1982, by the fall was being quoted in print as suggesting that perhaps fifty thousand Palestinians were enough for Lebanon.

The slaughter, then, had a political goal, which was to rid Lebanon of the Palestinians. But that goal reposed on emotion, not fact. The facts were that the other Arab states were not willing to take in the Palestinians, who desperately wanted to leave after the massacres. The fact that Habib had enormous difficulty in finding Arab countries willing to take in the PLO guerrillas should have made that clear. The Palestinians did not need to be told what Lebanese Forces members who had carried out the Shatila operation were saying—that once the American, French, and Italian troops left, they would perpetrate further massacres. I remember asking Bashir Gemayel years ago where he thought Lebanon's Palestinians could go. Pounding the table in his office like a petulant child, he roared, "It's not my problem, not my problem, not my problem." There was no reason to think his successors in the Lebanese Forces were in a mood to listen to reason. The more extreme pinned their hopes on Sharon's scheme to overthrow King Hussein and dump all Lebanon's Palestinians on Jordan. My friends among the Maronite monks told me so, and I had no reason to doubt their determination to collaborate with Israel to bring that dream about. Whatever doubts I had about their seriousness vanished after the massacre, when I recalled a conversation a few weeks earlier at the monks' summer residence. A handsome Lebanese Army doctor, who volunteered that he was a member of the Guardians of the Cedars, said, "Soon there will not be a single Palestinian in Lebanon. They are a bacillus which must be exterminated." At the time, I dismissed his remarks as a broken-record repetition of old themes I had heard since the civil war, when the Cedars used to write graffiti on walls proclaiming, "Each Lebanese must kill a Palestinian."

With the new presidential term, various decades-old schemes for reforming Lebanon resurfaced, all eminently sensible. The civil service should be run on the basis of merit, not religious affiliation, said some. Next time, the President should be elected by universal suffrage and not by parliament, said others. Lebanon must become a modern country where army, trade unions, and political parties replaced the religious communities and their lowest common denominator, tribalism— the factor that was chiefly responsible for the destruction of the old Lebanon. But the old problems abounded. Perhaps Lebanon never had been and never should have been a nation, a state. The oldest cliché in Lebanon is that it is a place where everything can be found except the existence of the state. In mock despair, some Lebanese suggested, Bring back the Turks—for the Ottomans were interested in maintaining law, order, and taxes, although they bothered little with the other attributes of a modern state. And that is what the Lebanese really wanted, for they did best when allowed to live, work, and prosper without laws. Such thoughts sound cynical only to those who do not know Lebanon.

Nor were Lebanon's problems all Moslem-versus-Christian, by any means. Within the Moslem part of the country, the Shia majority wanted its numbers, power, and prestige recognized. But, as a former minister remarked, "No Sunni Prime Minister can accept the changes that no Shia politician can fail to demand." Fortified by a knowledge of these intractable Moslem issues, the Lebanese Forces believed that all they had to do was play on the theme of some new threat to the Christians to retain their hold on their constituency. *Their* state-within-a-state, built by Bashir Gemayel and now deprived of his leadership, had become a loose federation of regional fiefdoms and personal ambitions held together by a commonly perceived necessity to cooperate. They had a good thing going—but only if they stuck together.

The Lebanese Forces showed no disposition to abandon their special tax levies or the virtual control of Beirut's port revenues that both deprived the state of financing and guaranteed their own income and survival. It was easy enough to predict that the state, even one run by a

Phalangist President, would clash with the Lebanese Forces sooner or later. Once again, history provided a key: for more than a hundred years, opposition to central authority in Lebanon has come from the Maronites. No foreign government—whether Western or Arab—and no rational emigrant would be likely to sink money into Lebanon for reconstruction as long as the Lebanese Forces continued to siphon off state revenues. In the fall of 1982, UN experts estimated that Lebanon had sustained $12–$15 billion worth of damage since 1975. The once-prosperous transit trade to the Arab hinterland is dead, killed off not just by the war but by Beirut port's growing inefficiency and by competition from new ports built in the past decade in Syria, Turkey, Iraq, Saudi Arabia, and the Gulf. Israel seems determined to accelerate its economic penetration of its neighbor, as its unwillingness to close the frontier with Lebanon and its abolition of border formalities show.

In the long run, it is not at all certain that the Lebanese Forces and the Phalange Party will be able to maintain their near-total hold on the various Christian communities or even on the Maronites. If the past teaches us anything, any sustained sense of peace may encourage several, if not dozens, of Maronite political parties to reappear. "All Lebanese are not Christians, all Christians are not Maronites, and all Maronites are not Phalangists" is an old Lebanese political nostrum. The season of hallucination surrounding the Israeli invasion briefly allowed Bashir Gemayel to turn that saying on its head, and for a vital but brief moment he succeeded in making many, if not all, Lebanese believe that if they were not Phalangists, then at least they were "Bashirians." Such was the stuff of dreams, of myth, now crystallized in the Lebanese Forces' studied cult of Bashir's personality. Giant hand-painted portraits of the "martyr President" adorn the main thoroughfares of the Christian sector. Extracts from his speeches were blared out on loudspeakers on the occasion of what would have been his thirty-fifth birthday. On the fortieth day following his death—in a ritual followed by both Maronite and Islamic faiths—the Lebanese Forces staged a ceremony that foreign guests compared to the Nazi Party rallies Sheikh Pierre had been so impressed by in Berlin forty-six years earlier.

But these efforts to preserve the splinters of Bashir's true cross perforce deal with the past. Nothing in Lebanon's past suggests that he would have succeeded, and whatever his promise, Bashir and his followers had done their part—detractors, including not a few Christians, would claim more than their part—in bringing about one of the most curious examples of suicide in modern history.

I can only hope that in Lebanon's fury to get back to making money—the real Lebanese gift—the country will see fit to retain at least one of the sunken ships in the port. Or perhaps one of the finely pockmarked facades on Foch or Allenby street in Beirut's commercial district. Or perhaps that battered sign advertising a (possibly mythical?) company called Crisis Tourism: I never telephoned the number printed on the ruined wall advertising this agency, for fear I might learn something I did not want to know. Ruins should be allowed their mysteries. But any one of these choices would be a more fitting memorial to Lebanon's years of folly than the wretched monuments I fear the Lebanese will end up erecting in the worst possible taste. Had I a magic wand, I would restore the shabby cinemas, the bordellos, the office buildings, the churches, the mosques, the newspaper offices, the cabarets, the hardware stores, the sleazy bars, and especially the suqs that once constituted the delicious disorder of Beirut's commercial heart, in and around Martyrs' Square. And I would people them with schemers and dreamers, Egyptian whores and Maronite priests, Sunni street hawkers, sleek parliamentary politicians, bankers, Syrian construction workers—all those specimens from the ethnological zoo that is Lebanon.

It's not just that I would like to see the old Levant, "Alexandria Quartet North," come back to life so that I could spend the time required to savor one of the wonders of the world. Rather, if I could, I would will it back to life to save Lebanon's soul—that hodgepodge of twisting alleys, neon signs, layabouts, collective taxis bound for Tripoli, Amman, Aleppo, Hama, Homs, and beyond. That sounds pretentious, especially coming from a foreigner. But only in the commercial district (the French expression *centre ville* is more appropriate) did Lebanese and foreigners meet, argue, play, make love, and learn to live with each other. Turn the corner, cross from one sidewalk to the other, push a door, linger an hour in the suqs—and the world changed. Those were worlds that took centuries to piece together, and it will be a more difficult task than the workmen busy rebuilding the old parliament realize. For it was there, in the commercial district, and only there, that Lebanon's many worlds met, before the Lebanese retreated back into their communities, their prejudices, and their deadly certainties.

The pell-mell, mixed-up side of things never made Beirut a melting pot, but it did make it the most civilized of cities and validated its otherwise often bogus claims to pluralism, tolerance, democracy, and freedom. May Sheikh Pierre forgive me, but I prefer him as "Mister Condom," in the family drugstore on Martyrs' Square near the bordellos, than as the bereaved "Godfather" he became.

In the fall of 1982, Sheikh Mohamed Mehdi Chamseddine, of the Shia Higher Council, said, "We are all guilty one way or another of having created the atmosphere that maintained the crisis whose culmination was the Israeli invasion." It was the first time, at least to my imperfect knowledge, that any major Lebanese leader had admitted such collective responsiblity for Lebanon's travail. His confession struck me as ever so much more realistic than the new versions of that old, self-deluding Lebanese refrain, "neither victors nor vanquished." Had I heard anything vaguely similar coming from a Lebanese Christian of similar political displacement, I might be more sanguine about a country that I alternatively love and despair of. I was not the only doubting Thomas. "This has been going on in cycles for a century and a half," one Christian friend told me, "but what's worrying is that the cycles are now only ten years long. Do I really want to stay here for the next round?"

At least the Lebanese had a choice. It was their country, after all. But for the Israelis, Syrians, and Palestinians, and for the Americans, all seemed hopelessly mired for long months in the very considerable problems of troop withdrawal. They all had been burned in ways none of them could have imagined only short months before.

The Palestinians certainly had been deprived of their state-within-a-state autonomy and had lost hundreds of men—if only two field-grade officers—in the fighting. The PLO's fighting forces were scattered to the four corners of the Arab world and kept disarmed, almost under house arrest. The U.S. government showed no more willingness to talk to, much less negotiate with, Arafat than it had in the past. .

Yet, notwithstanding the PLO's infuriating habit of trying to portray every military defeat as a political victory, Arafat remained—for the time being, at least—politically active. Some analysts, perhaps over-quickly, thought the Israelis had done him a favor by doing for him what he could not do for himself—namely, nullifying the doctrine of armed struggle that had plunged the PLO into such hot water for so long. The doctrine of armed struggle against Israel had helped Arafat and his cohorts take over the PLO after the Arabs' humiliating defeat in the Six-Day War, and it had cemented support for the PLO in the Palestinian refugee camps. But armed struggle never physically threatened Israel. On the contrary, it gave Israel the pretext for destabilizing Lebanon and eventually smashing the PLO's military infrastructure. Perhaps its only justification was one never mentioned: to protect the Palestinian civilians in the Lebanese camps against the murderous instincts of the local Christians. But with foes like the Lebanese Forces and the Israelis, both of whom were willing to renege on their undertakings, the doctrine of armed struggle only justified the Shatila massacres; Sharon had insisted he was determined to destroy the "two thousand terrorists" in West Beirut's camps—who turned out not to be there. The PLO's determined resistance—and then the martyrdom of the massacred—did more to publicize the Palestinian cause than all the attacks it had made against Israel over the years. Even Senator Barry Goldwater, scarcely an admirer of the PLO, said that Begin's excesses had made Arafat "look like a Boy Scout."

Arafat's friends in the West had been telling him for years to abandon armed struggle and concentrate on diplomacy. Now Arafat and his error-strewn stewardship of the PLO were at a most critical crossroads. Perhaps it had never been realistic for the Palestinians to think they could obtain an independent Palestinian rump state in the West Bank and Gaza. Now the Reagan plan ruled it out. Perhaps in time the Americans may have done the PLO an inadvertent favor by forcing it to accept the notion that it must have some kind of future relationship with Jordan. The danger, of course, was that Arafat and his moderates could be overthrown and leadership of the PLO pass to younger, more radical men. Better to stop the Israelis from cementing over the rest of the West Bank, it could be argued, than to hold out for what looked increasingly impossible. (Sharon and Begin had anticipated such an outcome in invading Lebanon: that the defeated PLO would repeat its errors of the late 1960s and early 1970s and indulge in the sterile terrorism which discredited the Palestinian cause.) But at the Palestine National Council, or unofficial parliament-in-exile, held in Algiers in February, Arafat refused, in the name of sacrosanct PLO unity, to take the plunge. Rather than split his ranks, yet to recover from the loss of the Beirut stronghold, he allowed his radicals their say and just barely managed to stake out room for future maneuvering.

As for Syria, it was a humiliating end to a damaging six-year adventure in regional superpower politics. Tricked and sucked into an unwanted war by Israel, the Damascus regime was drained of military, economic, and political substance. Military dictatorships in the Middle East, especially those based on a minority, such as the Alawites in Syria under President Assad, do not easily admit error, much less initiate remedial action questioning the validity of its original policy. From that angle, Israel may have done Assad a backhanded favor by freeing his regime from the most visible part of its debilitating and humiliating Lebanese experience. All Syria's reasons for intervening in 1976 had backfired. Despite an occupation force of thirty thousand men, Syria had failed to bring the PLO to heel, as it was supposed to. Instead, it had foiled Arafat's diplomatic overtures to the West and helped the Israelis perpetuate the image of the PLO as an intransigent force. Syria had come to Lebanon to protect its flank from the danger of contagion from leftist Lebanese and Palestinians, who appeared to be on the brink of installing a radical government in Beirut. Outsmarted by Israel, and eventually abandoned by the United States, within eighteen months the Syrians were being subverted by their erstwhile allies, the Lebanese Christians. In time, they made themselves almost universally unpopular in Lebanon. Their army fell prey to very Lebanese vices and soon had a substantial finger in the hashish crop—Lebanon's biggest export earner—heroin laboratories, car theft, and other rackets. (A favorite story of mine has three Syrian soldiers waving down the driver of a new Fiat at gunpoint, getting into the car, inquiring about its performance, and then, having learned its make, asking to be dropped off well before their announced destination. What brought about the change of mind? the driver asks. "Oh," one soldier says, "our captain told us to go out and steal a BMW.") The Lebanese learned how to get their own back. Starting in 1980, arms smuggled through Marounistan to Sunni fundamentalists in the Moslem Brothers helped destabilize the Assad regime.

Syria, which never had recognized Lebanese independence on the grounds that the French had snatched away legitimate Syrian provinces in 1920, lost its traditional following among the Lebanese Sunni community, once fervent advocates of submerging Lebanon in greater

Syria. By 1980, the Syrians had openly opposed formation of a national unity government in Beirut. Rightly or wrongly, they stood accused of provoking car-bomb outrages and other acts of violence to justify their increasingly unpopular presence in Lebanon. The Israelis, either prevented by the Americans or on their own, had not forced the Syrian Army wholly out of the Beqaa valley, which, in Syrian military thinking, constitutes the soft underbelly for any attack on Damascus. Yielding to American pressure and evacuating the Beqaa would be justifiable as a price to be paid for making the Israelis go back inside their own borders. A carve-up of Lebanon, leaving the Israelis in the south and the Shuf, and the Syrians in the Beqaa and the north, could be blamed on Jerusalem. The Lebanese knew their history well enough to realize that Syria had been a major force in their country in the past—and would be in the future—with or without the presence of a single Syrian soldier on Lebanese soil. It was enough to look at a map.

For Israel, the war might well have been judged a success—on military grounds, at least—had its ambitions in Lebanon not been so high. The Israelis seemed sure to obtain a twenty-five-mile-wide demilitarized zone along their northern border from which artillery and other heavy weapons would be banned: that alone would have been unthinkable before Operation Peace for Galilee. But in the long run, did Israel achieve its other war aims? Backed by the United States, President Amin Gemayel (who, unlike Bashir, owed the Israelis nothing) had ruled out contracting a peace treaty. Was Israel's military success a Pyrrhic victory? Only the United States appeared to have benefited from the war, as Begin and his fellow ministers bitterly remarked. The PLO had been driven out of Beirut. But the Americans were in no mood to accept Begin's vision of the future for the West Bank and Gaza. Sharon's boast that he had "expelled" the PLO rang hollow, since it was Habib who had arranged for the guerrillas' evacuation—which had spared hundreds of Israeli lives, but for which a heavy price had been paid.

Moreover, the Palestinians were no longer in Lebanon as convenient whipping boys. The PLO, which had become increasingly cautious, was not even a player in the game, and the game itself was no longer being played. Why, in fact, did Israel need a twenty-five-mile-deep DMZ, now that the PLO was gone? The Israelis had proved adept at copying—indeed, surpassed—the Syrian example in Lebanon, in everything from pillage to the subtle techniques of divide-and-rule. But with every passing day the Israeli public, if public-opinion polls were any guide, were asking more vehemently whether the Lebanese adventure had not trapped their country in a swamp. The same Lebanese Christians—and Shia Moslems—who threw rice and rosewater on the invaders in June were now cursing them—and not always behind their backs. By November 1982, General Menachem Einat, serving in Lebanon, conceded on Israeli television that "the attitude of the Lebanese people, so warm only a few months ago, is cooling off fast." He added, "Our presence constitutes an undesirable occupation" in Lebanese eyes. He might have added that it was a costly one. Hardly a day went by without fresh Israeli casualties. A U.S. diplomat, mindful of America's Indochina quagmire, put it more succinctly: "The Israelis should call this place Lebanam."

The Kahan Report, published in early February 1983, further drove home Israel's responsibility for what had happened in Shatila. Cynics insisted that the report was designed principally to give the Israelis a good conscience: it dealt with the massacre, but not with the government's reneging on solemn undertakings to the United States not to enter West Beirut, much less the morality of having initiated the war. Israel's backers saw only that rarely had any other country dared hand down such an indictment of an incumbent government—certainly not Lebanon, where the investigation predictably was headed nowhere. But such moral self-congratulation was incomplete at best. The main culprit, Ariel Sharon, neatly dodged the spirit if not the letter of the 108-page report enjoining him to resign. Resign he did as Defense Minister, only to stay on as minister without portfolio and to join two key parliamentary commissions, on defense and Lebanese affairs. Sharon made clear this was his, and Begin's, way of rejecting the commission's verdict of Israel's "indirect responsibility" for the slaughter. That was a finding he indignantly likened to the "mark of Cain," which, he said, would besmirch Israel's reputation for generations. Truculent, assured, bullying, Sharon for the time being avoided the political limbo that Israeli and foreign—especially American government—critics had hoped would be his fate. He and Begin proved powerless to stop the polarization of Israeli society produced by the Lebanese war, the massacre, and their repercussions. Indeed, with the Labor Party opposition still unable to produce a charismatic leader to replace drab Shimon Peres, Begin seemed sure of winning reelection later in the year, when, he let it be known, he favored going to the polls. In the meantime, as if to underline his intransigence, he filled the Defense Ministry post with Moshe Arens, the ambassador in Washington, who, although diplomatic, was every bit as hawkish on many issues as Sharon.

Bashir Gemayel never tired of saying that Lebanon looked "easy to swallow, but was hard to digest." Israeli public opinion seemed schizoid, its majority pleased with Begin and Sharon, but nonetheless opposed to the casualties involved in staying on militarily in Lebanon. To that end, in late February the Israelis handed over to Saad Haddad all of south Lebanon up to the port city of Sidon. It was a rerun of Israeli tactics in 1978, which had frustrated Washington and the UN by setting up the renegade officer in his "Republic of Free Lebanon."

The United States kept sending Habib back to the Middle East in hopes of forcing Begin to agree to withdraw his troops. President Reagan's credibility was riding on it, American diplomats argued, insisting nothing could be done about the West Bank and Gaza Strip until the United States had reestablished its credentials with its moderate Arab friends by getting Israel out of Lebanon. But the American government scarcely improved its image with moderate Arabs when Congress voted Israel $225 million more in grant assistance than the President had requested. The Congress approved military and economic aid to Israel, which was defying Reagan, provided all the $785 million economic package as a grant, and increased the grant portion of the $1.7 billion in foreign military sales from $500 million to $700 million. By late February, a Gallup Poll showed that Americans had overcome their misgivings of the summer and held Israel in the same high esteem it had enjoyed before Sharon invaded Lebanon.

If Sharon continued to exert major influence and Israel in effect carved up Lebanon, Arafat would be proved only half right. In an order of the day sent to all troops and PLO offices in July, he had quoted the Bible—and the Old Testament, at that. "For the violence of Lebanon shall cover thee," read the quotation from Habakkuk 2:17, "and the spoil of beasts, which made them afraid, because of men's blood, and for the violence of the land, of the city, of all that dwell therein."

Epilogue: November 1983

A nd yet I was wrong, perhaps less about the Lebanese and their continuing inability to come to terms with themselves than about the other forces involved in their travail. Even by Middle East standards, rarely had power and influence changed sides so quickly, for by the fall of 1983 the Lebanese tar baby had mired two new victims—Israel and the United States (as well as France, Italy and Britain, which also contributed troops to the Multinational Force). Long gone were the heady dreams of *Pax Hebraica* and *Pax Americana*. In their place re-emerged the Syrians, so disgraced by the Israeli invasion of 1982, but now clearly in command under wily President Assad. With Soviet backing, especially in the form of hardware and the first modern air defense system, Assad wiped away that humiliation and re-established his claim as a regional superpower. In the process he further reduced Yasser Arafat's increasingly tenuous hold on the P.L.O. by fomenting and aiding the most serious split to date within the mainstream Fatah group. Indeed, in one of his typically astute gestures, Assad surrounded and disarmed the last pocket of Arafat supporters in the Beqaa just days before Syria agreed to a September 1983 ceasefire, ending month-long hostilities. The Syrians had so raised the ante that for the first time the United States was directly involved in the fighting, and voices in Congress had openly compared the Marine involvement in Lebanon to the Vietnam conflict. Yet, Assad was also signalling that he could prove accommodating to American, and more especially Israeli, interests by muzzling the Palestinians—if Washington would only recognize his own, long–ignored importance. Deprived of his gun and his olive branch, Arafat could be trussed up and delivered so long as the price was right. And indeed, he was.

In retrospect, the Reagan administration must bear much of the responsibility for the turn of events of the past year. As even superficial knowledge of the Middle East demonstrates, the only time that diplomacy can be made to work is in the immediate wake of fighting. Allow much more than a week, at most a month, and the protagonists will find dozens of good reasons to resist concessions. The window of diplomatic opportunity never stays open long. Throughout the crucial final months of 1982, that basic given somehow escaped Shultz at the State Department as it did Judge William P. Clark, the real, if inexperienced, power in foreign affairs, Reagan's close friend and the National Security Adviser. Had the United States acted forcefully by October 1982, all foreign forces would have been out of Lebanon and the rocky road open to reconciliation among the Lebanese. The P.L.O. had been evacuated from Beirut. The Syrians were determined to improve their relations with the United States. They made no secret of their anger at Brezhnev for his failure to heed their repeated entreaties for better air defense weapons, which they had argued since 1981 were needed to face the inevitable Israeli invasion. Haig's fall from grace allowed the Syrians to turn the page by attaching all blame to him for the Reagan administration's pro-Israeli tilt and consistent snubbing of Damascus. Diplomats and analysts in Damascus were convinced that Assad was so disillusioned with Brezhnev that he was ready to pay a high price for normalized relations with Washington. More important, the Israelis, who had every reason to perpetuate superpower tensions in the region by identifying the Syrians with Moscow, were in no position to thwart any such rapprochement. The Begin government's complicity in the Shatila massacres had set off such shock waves of revulsion abroad, and especially inside Israel, that Begin, Sharon and Eitan were by no means able to ignore sustained American pressure to evacuate not just West Beirut and Beirut airport, but all Lebanon. After all, in 1957 Eisenhower had forced Ben Gurion to evacuate the Sinai in far less dramatic circumstances.

The Reagan administration dithered, did nothing and thus squandered the last cards the United States held from the deck dealt in the wake of the 1973 Arab-Israeli conflict. At stake was the American-backed proposition that Israeli security could be assured by the return of occupied Arab land. The administration's own Reagan initiative was allowed to wither on the vine, apparently because Shultz was so convinced that it was a self-evident masterpiece that he never entertained the notion that its furtherance required hard work, lobbying, pressure and persuasion. Even then Clark was expanding his influence at Shultz's expense. And that meant—in his simple, homespun Californian way—rewarding Israel for its invasion of Lebanon by allowing not just security arrangements, but also political normalization, including a "liaison office" or disguised Israeli embassy, an end to the state of war and provisions for future negotiations calling for the free movement of goods and persons between Israel and Lebanon. It apparently never dawned on Shultz and Clark that opening one door with Israel meant slamming 22 others with the Arab world on which Lebanon depended for its economic survival. All that lay ahead. Indeed, the Israelis delayed the opening of the withdrawal negotiations until December 28, thus making fools of Habib and other American officials rash enough to have predicted the evacuation deal would by then be completed. Once again, the United States had been outmaneuvered by the Begin government, which was convinced that it had stalled its way out of the opprobrium of Shatila.

Yet if the Reagan administration could not get the Israelis out of Lebanon, then how could the United States be trusted to get them out of the West Bank? That constantly invoked question contributed mightily to the breakdown of the talks between King Hussein of Jordan and Arafat in April, designed to open negotiations with Israel under the Reagan plan. (So, too, according to Palestinian sources, did Kissinger's somewhat mischievous meeting with a P.L.O. emissary, which encouraged Arafat to think he could extract better terms from the United States.) At best Arafat and the king were involved in what the Arabs called "baking stones"—that is, going through the motions of an exercise they knew to be doomed. Israel, after all, had rejected the Reagan initiative right from the start. The protracted Arafat-Hussein discussions were designed principally to assure the United States, Israel and the world at large that they, the Arabs, had tried their best. That is not, however, how the world perceived what ensued. The Israelis were delighted that the greatest threat to their ambitions on the West Bank had receded. Suddenly, they stepped up the pace of their withdrawal talks with the United States and Lebanon. It was obvious to everyone—except, apparently, Shultz—that the Israelis were ready to bargain, especially since they realized that any such deal would provoke a Syrian veto. After two weeks of shuttling around the Middle East pushing through open doors, Shultz emerged with a deal on May 17, then professed astonishment at Syria's rejection.

Yet by their own lights the Syrians had valid reasons to reject the deal. The United States had not seen fit to keep Syria informed about the negotiations it was brokering with Israel and Lebanon. That fateful decision only served to increase the great suspicions, perhaps even paranoia, Syria nourished about the Reagan administration's motives. It was the political content of the deal—the normalization clauses that Shultz and Clark found only natural—that stuck in Assad's craw, not the military considerations. In Syrian eyes the United States was continuing its efforts to isolate Damascus that were begun back in the Sinai disengagement deal of 1975, then given further substance in the Camp David accords of 1978 that ended in the separate peace between Israel and Egypt. Assad was determined to prevent what his propagandists labelled a "Camp Shultz" that would lead Lebanon down the same garden path that Egypt had taken. As Kissinger once remarked, there could be no war without Egypt and no peace without Syria. As Israeli doves had so accurately predicted, Assad, careful player that he is, had taken the precaution in late 1982 of asking for—and receiving—an integrated air defense system capable of neutralizing Israel's traditional air supremacy. Yuri Andropov provided the weapons—SA 5s and Tu 124 AWACS-

like early warning aircraft and thousands of troops to man them—
and served notice that under his rule the Kremlin would be a reliable
ally. Andropov's was a minimum investment calculated to reap maximum gains. Still, as the late Soviet Premier Alexei Kosygin had
learned in June 1976, when Assad first intervened massively in Lebanon against the Kremlin's wishes, Syria was no mere puppet and
could prove a dangerous ally. Indeed, as dangerous an ally as Israel
on many occasions had been for the United States. The Reagan
administration nonetheless chose to ignore its own sins of omission
and commission in bringing about this state of affairs.

Once again the Syrians were cast as the spoilsports as Israel and
the United States cozied up to each other. The Reagan administration reversed itself and supported Congressional desires to increase
the giveaway portion of aid to Israel. The Defense Department
abruptly dropped its objections to providing Israel with high technology needed for its Lavie fighter-bomber. And in July the administration cast aside a policy in force since Israel conquered the West Bank
in 1967 by saying that dismantling Israeli settlements there was
"impractical" and "unrealistic" when "you look at the reality on the
ground." No wonder the Begin government beamed and declared
American-Israeli relations had not been sunnier since 1973. In practice the United States had abandoned a decade of efforts to return
conquered land to the Arabs in exchange for securing Israel's 1967
borders. What motivated the administration's thinking is hard to
fathom. Suggested reasons varied from the approaching 1984 American presidential elections, which traditionally freeze Middle East
diplomacy, to the declining price of oil in a still depressed world
economy and the concomitant ineffectiveness of once–powerful
OPEC. In other words, the Arabs' wild-card, oil, was deemed worthless. No one in official Washington dared say how that conclusion
might impinge on relations with moderate Arab oil states under
attack from radical regimes who long had accused them of selling out
to the pro-Israeli United States. Indeed, by late spring the administration was blaming the feckless Arabs for its troubles and putting
it about that a little benign neglect in the Middle East was not the
worst solution or, in the words of a *New York Times* editorial, "Let
the Middle East Simmer."

But those regional superpowers, Israel and Syria, had other plans,

plans basically calculated to perpetuate their *de facto* partition of Lebanon. Faced with Syrian refusal to evacuate its own troops, the Israelis announced that they would pull back from the Beirut-Damascus highway, the capital area and the Shuf to more easily defensible lines on the Awali River just north of Sidon. The Lebanese adventure was proving expensive for an economy already burdened by officially encouraged, runaway consumption, the ambitious West Bank Settlement scheme, 130 percent inflation and $21 billion worth of foreign debt (the highest per capita in the world). The star-spangled safety net—that automatic largesse ladled out by Congress in aid—barely covered Israel's foreign debt reimbursement. The war was proving unpopular and deadly now that more than 550 Israeli soldiers had been killed, a third of them since September 1982. Shorter lines would mean fewer casualties, a smaller garrison and reduced cost, the Begin government argued. (In fact, the casualties continued unabated.) That pullback would also create a major challenge for President Amin Gemayel, whom the Israelis basically abandoned to his fate—despite their earlier war-aim pledge to reinstate Christian political domination in Lebanon.

The stage was now set for the most obviously predictable round of fighting since the first shot was fired in April 1975. Nature abhores a vacuum. In the summer of 1983, Habib was finally put out to pasture at Syrian insistence. Robert C. McFarlane, Judge Clark's former aide at the NSC (who in October was to succeed him), shuttled ineffectively around the Middle East, trying to find a political settlement before the Israelis pulled back. Syria helped set up the National Salvation Front, grouping Druze leader Walid Jumblatt, Sunni former-Prime Minister Rashid Karame of Tripoli and former-President Franjieh. Jumblatt was receiving arms and ammunition from both Israel and Syria. Moshe Arens, who had replaced Sharon as Israeli Defense Minister after the publication of the Kahan report, argued that the Druze were more important to Israel than the Christians. There were 50,000 Druze first-class citizens in Israel and many Druze men served in the tough Border Police which helped maintain law and order in the West Bank and Gaza Strip for the Israelis. Anyhow, the Druzes were closer to the Israeli lines and Israel proper than the main body of the Christians located north of the Beirut-Damascus road.

As if to underline Israel's progressive abandonment of its 1982 dreams, on August 28 Begin resigned with his secretary, Yonah Klimavotsky, invoking "heartbreak." At the age of 70, the secretary said, Begin grieved over the casualties, the seemingly never-ending involvement in Lebanon—"he thought we'd be in and out of there in no time"—and the disappointed illusions which had led him to invade in the first place. As Ghassan Tueni, the gadfly Lebanese newspaper publisher-turned-presidential adviser, noted: "The Israelis are probably the people who knew the most about us as a state, but understood us least. Something must be wrong in Israel. There is a total misperception." For the first time Israeli society was split; at least a sizeable minority was convinced that Israel had fought its first unnecessary war. Even more than after the doubtful aftermath of the 1973 war, Israel was stricken by a crisis of self-confidence that paralyzed the political will to order the ground forces into battle.

Yet Begin could retire in the knowledge that his immediate successor was safe from American political pressures on the West Bank at least through the 1984 presidential elections. By then enough settlers would be resident to prevent any future Israeli government from abandoning the West Bank. Such is the nature of Israeli coalition cabinets that the settlers could not be forced out. Lebanon had proven a costly error but nonetheless had helped protect the strategic map that Begin had been drawing since he took office in 1977. Under Begin Israel had been stripped of its worldwide—if scarcely regional —image of innocence, even while signing a peace treaty with the major Arab military power, Egypt. Due to the disarray of the Arab world, that relationship had withstood the buffeting of the Lebanese invasion and of Israeli encroachments on the West Bank and the annexation of once–Syrian land on the Golan Heights. In the still considerable areas of Lebanon under Israeli control, Shin Beth (roughly the Israeli equivalent of the F.B.I.) took over from Mossad as the principal instrument of Israeli political and security penetration. That changing of the security guard justified occupied Lebanon's nickname—the North Bank—as the only other areas where Mossad had relinquished control to its rival were the West Bank and the Gaza Strip.

No sooner had the last Israeli military vehicles left the Shuf— shooting at both Christians and Druzes—than the fighting began. It raged through September. The Israelis had reached a major turning point. Even reports of anti-Arafat Palestinian guerrilla participation in the fighting could not tempt them back to the fray, especially when Syria was helping defeat Arafat's dwindling loyalists bottled up in the northern port of Tripoli. By the time the 179th Lebanese cease-fire took shaky hold on September 26, Jumblatt's Druze warriors had shattered Phalangist dreams of holding onto the Shuf, and the United States had fired its first shots against Arabs in this century to prevent the collapse of Gemayel's government. Thanks to the willful ways of Israel, the Reagan administration was caught up in the morass of Lebanese politics. To make things worse, the Druzes were doing the fighting, but the Syrians were pulling the strings and ensuring that just enough anti-Arafat Palestinians were involved to point up the bankruptcy of American policy. The message was un-quivocal.

The Reagan administration had snubbed the Syrians from the day it took office. Now McFarlane and Saudi Prince Bandar ibn Sultan were spending an inordinate amount of time trying to stop the shelling of 1,600 Marines and prevent the demise of the Gemayel government. All the anti-Soviet rhetoric emanating from Washington could not obscure the fact that the United States was being forced to deal with Syria as a major power, indeed on Assad's terms. If the mighty Israeli military establishment was evacuating 235 of the 1,330 square miles it occupied, how could the United States hope to command respect with so few assets on the ground? In Lebanon, as the United States should have learned from others' errors, the threat of military intervention is indirectly proportional to its actual use. The now-chastened Israelis, and for that matter the Syrians themselves, could have told the Americans that. The U.S. claimed that naval gunfire saved the Lebanese army garrison at Suk al Gharb, the mountain village south of Beirut that provides a direct field of fire on the capital. But gunboat diplomacy proved no substitute for diplomacy itself. The absence of a coherent policy ended up costing the lives of 239 American Marines and some 59 of their French colleagues—when, in two separate incidents on the morning of October 23, suicide-drivers drove their explosive-crammed trucks into the respective headquarters of the Multinational Force. For the truth of the matter was that the Marines were so many sitting ducks, and had been since their landing a year earlier. Judge Clark and Shultz somehow had overlooked that basic verity. The United States almost imperceptibly ceased acting as a mediator and became a protagonist. Over the past year, the Marines and the other Western contingents were sucked into the deadly maw of Lebanese politics. Originally, their post-Shatila mission was to protect the civilian population from further massacres, and also to prop up the sickly central government. Yet almost from the beginning the Multinational Force was obliged to stand by as the Lebanese Army—trained and equipped by the United States and France—sought to reassert state authority. Troops detained thousands of Palestinians and Lebanese, expelled Shia squatters and destroyed their makeshift lodgings. When Amin Gemayel filled many senior government posts with Phalangist officials the seeds were sown for growing Moslem alienation from the government.

Slowly, over a period of months, Amin dissipated the enormous capital of good will that had accompanied his election, especially among Lebanese who had been frightened by the prospect of his brother's rule. Gradually the Moslems, who had welcomed his election, came to look on him as the Phalangist president. For their part, the Phalangists never had much use for him. Amin himself felt too weak to break their hold right at the beginning of his term, when such a gamble, if successful, would have proved he really did intend to be President of all the Lebanese. Afterward it was too late. The West Beirut militias whom the Israelis boasted they had rooted out for good had by now reappeared on the streets. Thus the Syrians simply took advantage of the political rot. By the time the actual fighting began in September, the United States was helping the Lebanese army, which at least in some cases was back to its old 1975–1976 habit of saving Phalangist militiamen in tight situations. Given the Lebanese propensity for jumping to conclusions, it is no wonder that many considered the United States, the traditional ally of Israel, a backer of that other (if sometimes double-crossed and double-crossing) ally, the Christian militias. Balancing these negative considerations were two plusses: the Lebanese army, despite some notable Druze defections, had not split as it had during the civil war; and American muscle and resolve were largely to be thanked.

How far could the United States be trusted? Months earlier Amin

Gemayel answered a doubting Phalangist official who questioned this blind faith in Washington and asked where the guarantees were, by saying "behind you." The visitor turned around to see a framed photograph of the young Lebanese president shaking hands with Reagan. And what was Amin up to? In other words, the Americans could somehow be trusted to help him triumph over all the warlords who for years had carved out fiefs for themselves. Thanks to American support, Amin seemed to think he could succeed politically, where Bashir had been convinced that only muscle could do the job. In any case, Uri Lubrani, the Israeli "coordinator" in Lebanon, told Arens that Amin had refused to compromise with Jumblatt. "He's decided to bet on the Americans—Gemayel believes they'll deliver the whole of Lebanon to him on a silver platter with no price to be paid."

Of course, there was no reason to put total faith in such a partial source. Israel was playing its own game and not just with the Lebanese. Determined to cut their own losses by pulling out of the Shuf, the Israelis made sure their efficient lobby in the United States did its best to ensure that its friends voted in late September to keep the Marines in Lebanon for a further 18 months. Israel had succeeded in getting the United States to do its dirty work. Once again, Lebanon had become a side-show.

Even the Phalangists themselves questioned Amin's motives. A leading Phalangist assured me that Samir Geagea, the killer of Tony Franjieh and the Lebanese Forces' commander in the Shuf area, had begged Amin to send Army troops to Bhamdoun under cover of darkness to prevent the Druzes from taking over the key mountain section of the Beirut-Damascus road when the Israelis withdrew. Amin palmed Geagea off, the story went, hoping that a Lebanese Forces' setback in the sector would make them more pliant to his— and thus the central government's—desires in the future. That, of course, may simply be a Phalangist ploy to excuse their own short-comings. (In any case, the Phalangist heartland of Kesrawan was soon plastered with photographs of Amin with the simple caption "Pontius Pilate.") Indeed, the same Phalangists readily admitted that their strategy had not come undone just at Bhamdoun on September 6 when they lost more than 150 men—for them an enormous number in a single battle—and set in motion a rout which soon emptied the mountainous portions of the Shuf of Christians. Rather, he insisted, their comeuppance and the disappearance of Christians from more than 50 Shuf villages began a year earlier. Instead of uniting the Christians and dividing the Druzes, their tactics had done just the opposite. The pro-Phalangist Arslan faction of the Druzes had been forced to make common cause with the dominant Jumblatts. What revenge for Walid, whose fortunes had reached a low when his men failed to fire a shot against the Israeli invaders in 1982. And the Lebanese Forces had alienated the predominantly pro-Chamoun Maronites in a part of Lebanon where the Phalangists never had been strong before 1975. Once again, the Maronites had committed their old error of trying to settle their own scores rather than banding together against the outsiders. My Phalangist friend paid the setback no great mind. "Not our Christians anyhow," he said. That was his way of letting me know that the villagers who had been killed by avenging Druze militiamen or had fled to safety to Beirut or the beleaguered Maronite mountain town of Deir al Kamar were either Chamoun or Jumblatt partisans, or Greek Catholics and Orthodox, not Maronites at all. As such they were so much expendable fodder as, indeed, had been the Chamounist Maronites of nearby Damour, who were sacrificed by the Phalangists back in January 1976. For the Lebanese the spectacle of as many as 25,000 Christian refugees and more than 1,500 beaten Phalangist militiamen huddling in Deir al Kamar surrounded by Druze troops recalled the events of 1860, when the Druzes had besieged the same Maronite stronghold. The only major difference was that, in 1860, the Druze troops slaughtered as many as 10,000 Christians in the mountains before French soldiers disembarked to prevent further mayhem. This time, the latter day equivalent of those troops—the Multinational Force—did not budge. If it was any consolation, the number of slain Druze and Christian civilians this time probably did not exceed 1,000 once many of the missing turned up to be counted.

The Lebanese Forces never seemed to learn their lesson. They had nothing to show for their Shuf adventure; last year's allies had let them down. The Israelis had chosen the Druzes. The Americans, as usual, had backed the central government, meaning Amin, who in Phalangist eyes had betrayed them. The Christians of Marounistan finally cursed the Lebanese Forces. Yet even after the

Shuf debacle, the Lebanese Forces commander, Fady Frem, made a secret trip to Israel, where he begged Arens not to abandon them. Insiders reported that Arens told him it was time the Lebanese Christians grew up and started walking on their own like big boys. Frem insisted. What would change the Israelis' mind? "A peace treaty," Arens wearily replied, according to the insiders. Back in Beirut, Frem dispatched Father Naaman (Superior General of the Maronite Order of Monks) to plead with Amin to accept Arens' demands. Naaman even threatened Amin's life. Exasperated, Amin called the presidential guard to remove the monk, who had failed to understand the cruel irony in Arens' remark. For Arens had meant it was too late.

Indeed, for the first time since 1975, many Lebanese who had hoped against hope now became convinced that it was too late, and they left. Finally, the all-too-well-ordered mountains of corpses and destruction were familiar, so familiar that they lacked conviction. Nothing in Lebanon so resembles a corpse as another corpse, a massacre as another massacre. Also too familiar were the pious mouthings about reordering the Lebanese body politic, which this time would be brought forth by a National Reconciliation Committee. What had the first such group been called back in the fall of 1975, when the Lebanese still believed that salvation was at hand? It was all but impossible to believe that any workable reform could emerge while Syria and Israel still occupied large tracts of Lebanon, manipulating the citizenry. The United States, as usual, insisted on the need for "stability," that code word for papering over essential problems until the next inevitable explosion. Would the Reagan administration make it through the 1984 elections without such an eruption? The answer came within four weeks of the rickety cease-fire, with the kamikaze attacks on the American and French headquarters. Perhaps the next time, the much-vaunted battleship *New Jersey* and its 16-inch guns would be employed to create the illusion of policy just as the smaller guns of lesser Sixth Fleet ships had done in September 1983.

This band-aid approach to foreign policy had led successive American administrations from hands–off indifference in 1975 to tolerating an aggressive Israel to impotent involvement now that the Israelis had deserted part of the field. (In November, State Department efforts to revive Israeli ground operations in Lebanon proved to no avail.)

Were the Reagan administration not so ideologically anti-Soviet —and the 1984 elections so near—a rational solution might be found in an international conference, with European and Soviet participation, on the overall Mideast problem, not just Lebanon. For if the events of the past 18 months have proved anything, it was that there could be no separate peace for Lebanon without solving the central issue, which is that of the Palestinians, if not Palestine. That is the unsatisfactory epitaph of a decade of wholly American diplomacy in the Middle East that has accomplished little else than the destruction of a country still naively confident that the United States remained a superpower capable of solving problems.

Index

About the Author

JONATHAN C. RANDAL was born in 1933, in Buffalo, New York. After his graduation from Harvard College and a stint in the army, he went into journalism—working for the United Press, *The New York Herald Tribune*, *Time*, *The New York Times*, and, since 1969, *The Washington Post*, of which he is the senior foreign correspondent.

Mr. Randal has reported from virtually all the trouble spots of the globe —the Congo, Algiers, Vietnam, Poland, Eritrea, Tehran, and many others. He has reported from the Middle East for decades, and frequently from Beirut; he covered the civil war there in 1975–76. He returned often to Lebanon in the years 1977–81; in 1982, he was there during the Israeli invasion, at the siege and taking of Beirut, and for the events that followed in the autumn and winter.

When he is not at the front, Mr. Randal lives in Paris.